STUDENT EDITION
RESTATEMENT OF THE LAW
SECOND

CONTRACTS 2d

Pamphlet 3
§§ 316–End

With Reporter's Notes

Tables and Index

As Adopted and Promulgated

BY

THE AMERICAN LAW INSTITUTE
AT WASHINGTON, D.C.

May 17, 1979

ST. PAUL, MINN.

AMERICAN LAW INSTITUTE PUBLISHERS

1981

Reprinted from
RESTATEMENT OF THE LAW, SECOND
CONTRACTS 2d

Copyright © 1981
by
THE AMERICAN LAW INSTITUTE
All Rights Reserved
Library of Congress Catalog Card Number: 81-52209

3 Restate. of Contracts 2d Stud.Ed.
4th Reprint—1993

 PRINTED ON 10% POST CONSUMER RECYCLED PAPER

THE AMERICAN LAW INSTITUTE

The Executive Office
THE AMERICAN LAW INSTITUTE
4025 Chestnut Street
Philadelphia, Pennsylvania 19104

REPORTERS

ROBERT BRAUCHER, Associate Justice, Supreme Judicial Court of Massachusetts, formerly of Harvard University Law School, Cambridge, Massachusetts (Chapters 1-5, 9 [Topics 1-4], 13-15) [to 1971]

E. ALLAN FARNSWORTH, Columbia University School of Law, New York, New York (Chapters 6-8, 9 [Topic 5], 10-12, 16) [as of 1971]

CONSULTANT

ARTHUR L. CORBIN, Hamden, Connecticut [Deceased 1967]

EDITORIAL REVISER

PETER LINZER, University of Detroit School of Law, Detroit, Michigan

ADVISERS

ROBERT BRAUCHER [as of 1971]

CHARLES D. BREITEL, Chief Judge, New York Court of Appeals, [Retired], New York, New York

DANIEL ROBERT COQUILLETTE, Boston, Massachusetts, formerly of Boston University School of Law [as of 1977]

HAROLD C. HAVIGHURST, Alexandria, Virginia, formerly of Northwestern University School of Law, Chicago, Illinois

E. ALLAN FARNSWORTH [1970-1971]

CARLOS ISRAELS, New York, New York [Deceased 1969]

HARRY W. JONES, Columbia University School of Law, New York, New York

STEWART MACAULAY, University of Wisconsin Law School, Madison, Wisconsin

CARL McGOWAN, Circuit Judge, United States Court of Appeals for the District of Columbia Circuit, Washington, District of Columbia

ELLEN A. PETERS, Associate Justice, Connecticut Supreme Court, formerly of Yale Law School, New Haven, Connecticut

WALTER V. SCHAEFER, Justice, Supreme Court of Illinois [Retired], Chicago, Illinois

DAVID SCHWARTZ, Trial Judge, United States Court of Claims, Washington, District of Columbia [as of 1973]

ARTHUR T. VON MEHREN, Harvard University Law School, Cambridge, Massachusetts

CHARLES H. WILLARD, Guilford, Connecticut

ROBERT B. WILLIAMSON, formerly Chief Justice, Supreme Judicial Court of Maine, Augusta, Maine [Deceased 1976]

TABLE OF CONTENTS

Volume 1

TABLE OF CONTENTS

TABLE OF CONTENTS

Chapter 4

FORMATION OF CONTRACTS—CONSIDERATION

TOPIC 1. THE REQUIREMENT OF CONSIDERATION

TOPIC 2. CONTRACTS WITHOUT CONSIDERATION

TABLE OF CONTENTS

Chapter 5

THE STATUTE OF FRAUDS

TABLE OF CONTENTS

TOPIC 3. THE MARRIAGE PROVISION

Chapter 6

MISTAKE

TABLE OF CONTENTS

Chapter 7

MISREPRESENTATION, DURESS AND UNDUE INFLUENCE

Introductory Note

TOPIC 1. MISREPRESENTATION

TOPIC 2. DURESS AND UNDUE UNFLUENCE

Volume 2

Chapter 8

UNENFORCEABILITY ON GROUNDS OF PUBLIC POLICY

Introductory Note

TABLE OF CONTENTS

TOPIC 1. UNENFORCEABILITY IN GENERAL

TOPIC 2. RESTRAINT OF TRADE

TOPIC 3. IMPAIRMENT OF FAMILY RELATIONS

TOPIC 4. INTERFERENCE WITH OTHER PROTECTED INTERESTS

TOPIC 5. RESTITUTION

Chapter 9

THE SCOPE OF CONTRACTUAL OBLIGATIONS

Introductory Note

TABLE OF CONTENTS

TOPIC 1. THE MEANING OF AGREEMENTS

TOPIC 2. CONSIDERATIONS OF FAIRNESS AND THE PUBLIC INTEREST

TOPIC 3. EFFECT OF ADOPTION OF A WRITING

TOPIC 4. SCOPE AS AFFECTED BY USAGE

TOPIC 5. CONDITIONS AND SIMILAR EVENTS

TABLE OF CONTENTS

Chapter 10

PERFORMANCE AND NON-PERFORMANCE

Introductory Note

TABLE OF CONTENTS

TABLE OF CONTENTS

TOPIC 2. SUBSTITUTED PERFORMANCE, SUBSTITUTED CONTRACT, ACCORD AND ACCOUNT STATED

TOPIC 3. AGREEMENT OF RESCISSION, RELEASE AND CONTRACT NOT TO SUE

TOPIC 4. ALTERATION

Chapter 13

JOINT AND SEVERAL PROMISORS AND PROMISEES

TOPIC 1. JOINT AND SEVERAL PROMISORS

TOPIC 2. JOINT AND SEVERAL PROMISEES

TABLE OF CONTENTS

Chapter 14

CONTRACT BENEFICIARIES

Volume 3

Chapter 15

ASSIGNMENT AND DELEGATION

TABLE OF CONTENTS

TOPIC 3. EFFECT BETWEEN ASSIGNOR AND ASSIGNEE

TOPIC 4. EFFECT ON THE OBLIGOR'S DUTY

TOPIC 5. PRIORITIES BETWEEN ASSIGNEE AND ADVERSE CLAIMANTS

Chapter 16

REMEDIES

Introductory Note

TOPIC 1. IN GENERAL

TOPIC 2. ENFORCEMENT BY AWARD OF DAMAGES

TABLE OF CONTENTS

TOPIC 3. ENFORCEMENT BY SPECIFIC PERFORMANCE AND INJUNCTION

TOPIC 4. RESTITUTION

TOPIC 5. PRECLUSION BY ELECTION AND AFFIRMANCE

TABLE OF CONTENTS

Cite thus:

Restatement, Second, Contracts § ——

RESTATEMENT OF THE LAW

OF

CONTRACTS

Second

Chapter 15

ASSIGNMENT AND DELEGATION

Introductory Note: The subject matter of this Chapter is part of the larger subject of the transfer of intangible property. The historic rule in the common-rule courts of England was that a "chose in action" could not be assigned. The scope of that rule was progressively narrowed by the reception into the common law of doctrines developed in the law merchant and in the courts of equity and by statute. Little remains of it today, but modern rules, both decisional and statutory, must often be read in the light of the development.

The law merchant. The law merchant is a tradition with an international and maritime flavor. It was followed in special merchant tribunals in England; during the seventeenth century it became part of the common law of England. Under its influence mercantile instruments such as the bill of exchange were held transferable by delivery, or by indorsement and delivery, and similar rules have been extended in modern times, by decision and by statute, to documents of title and to investment securities. See Uniform Commercial Code Articles 3, 7, 8. The rules governing such instruments are beyond the scope of this Restatement. See § 6.

Law and equity. Also during the seventeenth century, it was established that an assignment could take effect in the common-law courts as a power of attorney enabling the assignee to sue in the assignor's name, and that courts of equity would protect the assignee in cases of death or bankruptcy of the assignor or revocation by him. During the eighteenth century the common-law courts began to give effect to the equitable rights of the assignee. In the United States statutes generally require actions to be brought in the name of the real party in interest, and the assignee of a contract right can sue in his own name without regard to the distinction between actions at law and suits in equity. That distinction is therefore not employed in the statement of rules in this Chapter, although references to the "equitable" character of an assignee's rights can be found in the modern literature on the subject.

Statutory Note: The extent to which remnants of common-law procedure survive in the United States is beyond the scope of the Restatement of this Subject. Statutes or rules of court in most States require an action to be prosecuted in the name of the real party in interest, as does Rule 17(a) of the Federal Rules of Civil Procedure. In addition most states have statutes providing for set-offs and other defenses against an assignee, and a number of States have statutes relating to other aspects of the assignment of contractual rights. Article 9 of the Uniform Commercial Code deals comprehensively with transactions intended to create security interests in personal property, including defined types of rights under contracts, and with sales of "accounts and chattel paper." The Code also provides a Statute of Frauds for the sale of personal property not otherwise covered and codifies part of the law governing assignments of contracts for the sale of goods. §§ 1–206, 2–210. Most states also have additional statutes regulating assignment of particular types of claims, such as claims for wages or claims against the Government.

Real-party-in-interest and related provisions. In most states an action by the assignee of a contractual right is required or permitted to be prosecuted in his own name. In many of these this is accomplished by a mandatory general real-party-in-interest statute or rule similar to Rule 17(a) of the Federal Rules of Civil Procedure. In Florida and New Jersey there are general real-party-in-interest provisions which are permissive. Connecticut, Hawaii, Illinois, Vermont and Virginia have statutes permitting the assignee of a non-negotiable chose in action to sue in his own name.

Additional statutes in some of these states, largely redundant, permit the assignment in writing or indorsement of particular types of contracts, such as bonds, promissory notes or non-negotiable written instruments for the payment of money, and provide that the rights of the assignor vest in the assignee and that the assignee may sue in his own name. Compare, as to negotiable instruments, Uniform Commercial Code §§ 3–201, 3–301.

In all the states listed below except Michigan and Delaware there are also statutes providing that an assignment is without prejudice to any set-off or defense existing before notice of the assignment. Some of these statutes refer to counterclaims as well; some refer only to defined classes of contracts such as non-negotiable written instruments for the payment of money.

Alaska	Rules Civ. Proc. 17 (1963), Stat. § 09.–65.060 (1962)
Arizona	Rules Civ. Proc. 17 (1956), Rev. Stat. Ann. § 44–144 (1956)
Arkansas	Stat. Ann. § 68–801 (1957)
California	Code Civ. Proc. §§ 367–68, 431.70 (1973)
Colorado	Rules Civ. Proc. 17, 13(j) (1973)
Connecticut	Gen. Stat. §§ 52–118, 52–140 (1958), § 52–139 (Supp. 1979)
Delaware	Chancery Court Rules 17, Superior Court Rules 17 (1974), Code Ann. tit. 10, § 3902 (1974)
Florida	Rules Civ. Proc. 1.210 (1967), Stat. § 68.06 (1969)
Hawaii	Rev. Laws § 634–1 (1976)
Idaho	Rules Civ. Proc. 17 (1957), Code § 5–302 (1947)
Illinois	Stat. Ann. ch. 110, § 22 (1968)
Indiana	Stat. Ann. §§ 2–201, 2–226 (1946), § 19–14–101 (1964)
Iowa	Rules Civ. Proc. 2, 7 (1951), Code Ann. §§ 593.1–.3 (1950)
Kansas	Code Civ. Proc. §§ 60–217, 60–213(d) (1976)
Kentucky	Rules Civ. Proc. 17.01 (1970)
Louisiana	Code Civ. Proc. arts. 681, 698 (1960), Civil Code arts. 2212, 2642–46 (1962)
Maine	Rules Civ. Proc. 17 (1959), Rev. Stat. Ann. tit. 14, §§ 2021, 5006 (1964)
Maryland	Rules Proc. 203A, 240A (1963)
Michigan	Gen. Court Rules 201.2 (1976), Stat. Ann. § 27A.2041 (1976)
Minnesota	Rules Civ. Proc. 17.01 (1968), Stat. Ann. § 540.03 (1947)
Missouri	Sup. Court Rules 52.01 (1969), Rev. Stat. §§ 509.480, 431.160, 431.170 (1969)

Montana	Rules Civ. Proc. 17 (1964), Rev. Code Ann. tit. 93, §§ 2802, 3403, 3409 (1964)
Nebraska	Rev. Stat. §§ 25–301, 25–303, 25–818 (1975)
Nevada	Rules Civ. Proc. 17 (1973), Rev. Stat. § 12.010 (1973)
New Jersey	Stat. Ann. § 2A:25–1 (1952)
New Mexico	Rules Civ. Proc. 17 (1953), Stat. Ann. § 21–4–12 (1953)
New York	Civ. Prac. Law & Rules 1004 (1976), Gen. Obligations Law §§ 5–1107, 13–101 (1978)
North Carolina	Gen. Stat. § 1–57 (1969)
North Dakota	Rules Civ. Proc. 17 (1974), Cent. Code § 9–11–02 (1975)
Oklahoma	Stat. Ann. tit. 12, §§ 221, 278 (1960), tit. 60, §§ 312–13 (1963)
Oregon	Rev. Stat. §§ 13.030, 80.010, 80.020 (1963)
Pennsylvania	Rules Civ. Proc. §§ 2002–03 (1975)
South Carolina	Code §§ 15–5–70, 15–15–60 (1976)
South Dakota	Code §§ 15–6–17(a), 43–42–2 to 43–42–5 (1967)
Utah	Rules Civ. Proc. 17(a), 13(i) (1977)
Virginia	Code §§ 8.01–13, 8.01–423 (1977)
Washington	Rules Pleading, Prac. & Proc. 17 (1961), Rev. Code § 4.08.080 (1962)
West Virginia	Rules Civ. Proc. 17 (1978), Code §§ 55–8–9, 55–8–10 (1966)
Wisconsin	Stat. Ann. §§ 260.13–.14 (1957), §§ 331.07, 331.13 (1963)
Wyoming	Rules Civ. Proc. 17 (1957), Stat. §§ 1–6, 1–536 (1957)

Most of the remaining jurisdictions have less comprehensive statutes, limited either to assignments in writing (e.g., Alabama, District of Columbia, Georgia, Mississippi, Rhode Island), or to the assignment of written instruments, contracts for the payment of money, or the like (e.g., Alabama, Mississippi, Tennessee). In Tennessee the assignee who sues in the assignor's name is treated as the real plaintiff of record. Each of these states has a related provision on defenses.

Alabama	Code §§ 8–5–20, 8–5–25, 8–5–26, 6–5–286, 6–8–82 (1975)
Dist. of Columbia	Code §§ 28–501 to 28–504 (1961), § 13–502 (Supp. 1964)
Georgia	Code Ann. § 85–1803 (1978), § 3–108 (1975)
Mississippi	Code Ann. §§ 11–7–3, 11–7–5 (1972)

Rhode Island   Gen. Laws § 9–2–8 (1969)
Tennessee   Code Ann. §§ 47–15–102, 47–12–104 (1979),
                      20–101 (1955)

A number of additional statutory provisions are included in the above tables. Four states provide for recovery from the assignor where the assignee is unable to recover from the obligor (Idaho, Maryland, Missouri, Tennessee). Two states permit such recovery subject to defenses the assignor had against any intermediate assignee (Virginia, West Virginia). In Vermont a defendant may set off a claim against the plaintiff acquired by assignment only if notice of the assignment was given to the plaintiff before suit. In New York an assignment in writing and signed by the assignor is not revocable because of the absence of consideration. In New Jersey the assignment of a sealed instrument by an unsealed writing is as valid as if under seal.

The Uniform Commercial Code. Article 9 of the Uniform Commercial Code establishes a comprehensive scheme for the regulation of security interests in personal property and fixtures, "including goods, documents, instruments, general intangibles, chattel paper or accounts." Because of difficulty in distinguishing between security transactions and outright sales, the scheme also applies "to any sale of accounts or chattel paper," and the interest of the buyer is treated as a "security interest." §§ 1–201(37), 9–102. Documents, instruments and chattel paper are beyond the scope of this Restatement, but accounts and general intangibles include many of the rights which are the subject of this Chapter.

Most contractual rights are covered by Article 9 of the Uniform Commercial Code unless excluded by § 9–104. Where the right is not evidenced by an instrument or chattel paper, " 'account' means any right to payment for goods sold or leased or for services rendered . . . whether or not it has been earned by performance," and "general intangibles" is a residual category including contractual rights to performance other than payment. Section 9–106.

Section 9–104 provides that Article 9 "does not apply" to listed types of transactions. Among the excluded types are transfer of a claim for wages, salary, or other compensation of an employee, of an interest or claim in or under any policy of insurance (other than proceeds), of an interest in or lien on real estate, including a lease or rents thereunder, or of any deposit account maintained with a bank, savings and loan association, credit union or like organization. Also excluded is "a sale of accounts or chattel paper as part of a sale of the business out of which they arose, or an assignment of accounts or chattel paper which is for the purpose of collection only, or a transfer of a right to payment under a contract to an assignee who is also to do the performance under the contract or a transfer of a single account to an assignee in whole or partial satisfaction of a preexisting indebtedness." Section 9–104(f).

As to transactions covered, § 9–201 provides generally that except as otherwise provided "a security agreement is effective according to its terms." Section 9–203 provides a Statute of Frauds. See Chapter 5 of this Restatement. Section 9–203 also states rules as to when a security interest "attaches" as between the parties, and § 9–204 provides for a security interest in after-acquired collateral and for security for future advances. Section 9–301 subordinates "unperfected" security interests to the rights of certain third persons; Section 9–302 provides generally for perfection by filing, but exempts "an assignment of accounts which does not alone or in conjunction with other assignments to the same assignee transfer a significant part of the outstanding accounts of the assignor." Section 9–303 provides that if filing occurs before the security interest attaches, it is perfected at the time when it attaches. Subsequent sections provide for priorities, for the mechanics of filing a financing statement in a public office, and for the enforcement of the secured party's rights. Of particular relevance to the subject matter of this Chapter is § 9–318 on the obligor's defenses against the assignee.

The provisions referred to above are far more than a restatement of the common law on assignment of contractual rights although in some respects they adhere to common-law rules. In view of their widespread enactment, statements in this Chapter are applicable primarily to sales of general intangibles which are contractual, to the residue of assignments excluded from Article 9 by § 9–104, and to questions not resolved by Article 9. Outside Article 9, § 1–206 provides a Statute of Frauds for kinds of personal property not otherwise covered, and § 2–210 covers the assignment of rights and delegation of duties under contracts for the sale of goods. Appropriate reference to the Code rules is made in the Comments to this Chapter, but no attempt is made to incorporate the provisions of the Code into the rules stated or to take account of variations in the Code as enacted in various states.

Wage assignments. Virtually every state has statutory restrictions on the assignment of wages. The most common type of provision applies only to assignments as security for loans under a stated amount, or to assignments for a consideration less than a stated amount. Other states, in addition to such statutes, have statutes relating to wage assignments generally, often without clear indication whether both statutes can apply to the same transaction. Still other states have statutory restrictions not limited to small loans.

Five states and the District of Columbia generally prohibit the assignment of future wages. In California and Connecticut separate prohibitions apply to lenders licensed under the small-loan laws.

Alabama	Code Ann. § 8–5–21 (1975)
California	Code Labor § 300 (Supp. 1979), Civ. Code § 1804.1(c) (1973), Fin. Code §§ 22471, 24472 (1968)
Connecticut	Gen. Stat. §§ 52–361(g); 36–236 (Supp. 1979)
Dist. of Columbia	Code § 28–2505 (1961)
Missouri	Rev. Stat. §§ 432.030, 408.210 (1959)
Ohio	Rev. Code § 1321.32 (1962), § 4113.16 (1973)

Five states have no small-loan provisions on wage assignments, but regulate wage assignments without regard to amount involved. The regulation in Indiana is limited to "wage brokers." Mississippi requires written consent of the employer for assignments for the purchase of goods. The other three states provide for written consent of the employer in all cases, and New Hampshire adds a provision for recording.

Indiana	Stat. Ann. § 22–2–7–2 (1974)
Mississippi	Code Ann. § 71–1–45 (1972)
New Hampshire	Rev. Stat. Ann. § 506:3 (1968), § 361–A:7 VIII 1 (1966)
North Carolina	Gen. Stat. § 95–31 (1975), § 1–55(1) (1969)
South Carolina	Code § 41–11–30 (1976)

Examples of states having both general regulation of wage assignments and wage-assignment provisions of the small-loan type are given below. The general statutes lay down a variety of formal requirements for assignment such as writing, signature, acknowledgment and witnessing. There are also requirements of consent of or notice to the employer, consent of the assignor's spouse, and recording. Assignments are limited to a percentage of the wages, or to the excess over a dollar amount, or to a period of time such as thirty days or two years.

Iowa	Code Ann. §§ 539.4, 539.5, 536.16 (1950)
Minnesota	Stat. Ann. §§ 181.04–.07 (1966), 56.16–.17 (1970)
Vermont	Stat. Ann. tit. 12, § 3022 (1973), tit. 21, § 344 (1978)
Wisconsin	Stat. § 241.09 (1963 & Supp. 1979)

The small-loan provisions in the various states show some variety.

A few prohibit the taking of wage assignments by licensed lenders, and many have one or more of the following provisions of the Uniform Small Loan Law: (1) the payment of money up to a stated amount as consideration for a sale or assignment of wages is treated as a loan; (2) the loan must be paid to the borrower when the assignment is executed; (3) the assignment must be in writing and signed in person by the borrower (4) and by his wife; (5) a maximum of ten percent of the assignor's compensation may be collected from his employer by the assignee from the time a verified copy of the assignment and a statement of the amount unpaid is served upon the employer. Some states allow such direct collection only after default by the assignor. Others make such requirements as consent of the employer or recording. Examples include:

Alaska	Stat. § 06.20.290 (1962)
Florida	Stat. Ann. §§ 516.02, 516.17 (1962 & Supp. 1979)
Montana	Code Ann. §§ 31–1–301 to 310 (1980)
Washington	Rev. Code Ann. § 31.08.190 (1961), § 49.48.090 (1962)

Retail installment sales. Uniform Commercial Code §§ 9–201 and 9–203 subordinate the provisions of Article 9 to statutes regulating retail installment sales, and many states have enacted one or more such statutes which contain provisions affecting assignment by the seller of his rights under a regulated contract. In some states only motor vehicle sales are covered; in others there are separate statutes for motor vehicles and for other goods.

Common provisions validate assignments to a financing agency on such terms as may be agreed upon by the seller and the financing agency. Many of these further provide that, as against creditors of or purchasers from the seller, no requirement of filing, notice to the buyer, or limitation of the seller's dominion over payments or over repossessed goods shall be necessary to the validity of a written assignment. By another common provision, unless the buyer has notice of the assignment, payment to the last known holder of the contract is binding on all subsequent assignees. A few states have further limitations on who may be an assignee and how much the seller may receive from the assignee.

Section 9–206(1) of the Uniform Commercial Code relates to "an agreement by a buyer or lessee that he will not assert against an assignee any claim or defense which he may have against the seller or lessor." Such an agreement is made enforceable by an assignee without notice, "[s]ubject to any statute or decision which establishes a different rule for buyers or lessees of consumer goods." Retail installment sales acts sometimes protect innocent assignees against particular hazards. In many states, for example, the buyer's written acknowledgment of delivery of a completed copy of the contract is conclusive or presumptive evidence in an action by or against an assignee that a requirement of such delivery has been met.

In 1975, the Federal Trade Commission promulgated a very important Trade Regulation Rule barring such agreements in transactions involving consumers. See 16 C.F.R. § 433.1–.3 (1975); Comment *f* to § 336.

In addition, in several states a statute establishes a "different rule" of the type referred to in Uniform Commercial Code § 9–206. Some of the statutes forbid the execution of negotiable instruments cutting off the buyer's defenses. Some forbid contractual waivers, and in some the buyer's defenses can be cut off unless within ten or fifteen days of receiving written notice of the assignment he or she gives notice of facts giving rise to a claim or defense. Examples of such statutes are:

Alaska	Stat. §§ 45.10.140, 45.10.150 (1962)
Dist. of Columbia	Code § 40–902(f) (1973)
Missouri	Rev. Stat. §§ 365.070(1), 365.110, 365.130(1), 365.160 (1968), 408.260(3), 408.260(9), 408.310, 408.350 (1979)
Ohio	Rev. Code § 1317.03 (1979)
Washington	Rev. Code Ann. §§ 63.14.020, 63.14.150 (1966 & Supp. 1978)

Government contracts. Federal statutes forbid the assignment of claims against the United States before the issuance of a warrant for payment, and the assignment of any public contract or order. Both statutes contain an exception, called the Assignment of Claims Act of 1940, permitting a single assignment to a financial institution where the contract does not forbid assignment and written notice is filed with appropriate Government officers and with any surety on a bond in connection with the contract. An assignment pursuant to the exception protects the assignee against liability to repay the United States, and in certain cases against setoff of a liability of the assignor to the United States.

Several jurisdictions also have limitations on the assignment of public contracts, or of particular types of public contracts. For example:

United States	31 U.S.C. § 203 (1976); 41 U.S.C § 15 (1976)
New York	State Finance § 138 (1974); General Municipal Law § 109 (1977)

North Carolina   Gen. Stat. § 147–62 (1978)

Wyoming   Stat. § 15–4–264 (1977)

REPORTER'S NOTE

See 3 Williston, Contracts §§ 405–10 (3d ed. 1960); 4 Corbin, Contracts §§ 856–60 (1951 & Supp. 1980); Ames, Lectures on Legal History 210–18 (1913); Holdsworth, The History of the Treatment of *Choses* in Action by the Common Law, 33 Harv. L. Rev. 997 (1920).

Earlier Statutory Survey. A considerably more comprehensive survey, prepared in 1965–66 for Tentative Draft No. 3 of the Restatement, is reprinted in Restatement, Second, Contracts, Tentative Drafts Nos. 1–7, Revised and Edited (1973).

The 1972 Amendments to the Uniform Commercial Code. Article 9 of the Uniform Commercial Code as originally promulgated used the term "contract right" to mean "any right to payment under a contract not yet earned by performance and not evidenced by an instrument or chattel paper." See Uniform Commercial Code § 9–106 (1962 Official Text). In 1972, Article 9 was amended to eliminate the term "contract right," and to modify "account" to include "any right to payment for goods sold or leased or for services rendered which is not evidenced by an instrument or chattel paper, whether or not it has been earned by performance."

Thus, "account" now includes what had formerly been called a "contract right." See Uniform Commercial Code, Appendix II, § 9–106 Reasons for 1972 Change (1978 Official Text). Conforming changes were made throughout Article 9 and in §§ 1–201 (37) and 5–116. Id., Appendix II General Comments E–8 to E–15.

Throughout this Chapter references will be to the 1978 Official Text unless otherwise specified.

Real party-in-interest and related provisions. See 3A Moore's Federal Practice ¶ 17.07–.11 (1979); Wright & Miller, Federal Practice and Procedure: Civil §§ 1545–53 (1971); Clark, Code Pleading §§ 23, 106 (2d ed. 1947); 3 Williston, Contracts §§ 430, 432, (3d ed. 1970); 4 Corbin, Contracts §§ 879, 896–97 (1951).

New York: According to the Advisory Committee notes, the Civil Practice Law and Rules omits as unnecessary the real-party-in-interest provision of former Civil Practice Act § 210. The General Obligations Law permits an assignee to sue in his own name.

District of Columbia: The statutes omit unliquidated obligations.

Georgia: An assignee must sue in the name of the assignor if the assignment is not in writing. Turk v. Cook, 63 Ga. 681 (1879); Lamon v. Perry, 33 Ga. App. 248, 125 S.E. 907 (1924).

New Hampshire: An assignee must sue in the name of assignor. Stavrelis v. Zacharias, 79 N.H. 146, 106 A. 306 (1919).

The Uniform Commercial Code. See Coogan & Gordon, The Effect of the Uniform Commercial Code upon Receivables Financing— Some Answers and Some Unsolved Problems, 76 Harv. L. Rev. 1529 (1963).

Wage assignments. See Havighurst, The Illinois Wage Assignment

Statute, 30 Ill. L. Rev. 759 (1936); Strasburger, The Wage Assignment Problem, 19 Minn. L. Rev. 536 (1935); Fortas, Wage Assignments in Chicago, 42 Yale L.J. 526 (1933); 1948 Rep. N.Y. Law Rev. Comm. 163.

California: Assignment of unearned wages is prohibited except to a person furnishing necessities of life.

Ohio: An exception is made for assignments for support of minor children in compliance with a court order. Rev. Code § 1321.31 (1962), regulating wage assignments, seems to be repealed by implication.

Indiana: Loan against or purchase of wages is regulated. Direction for payroll deduction is assignment and invalid unless for stated purposes.

Iowa: Requirement of writing and signature of spouse applies only to an assignment by the head of a family.

Montana: Code Ann. §§ 31–1–301 to 310 (1980) restricts assignments to secure loans, regardless of amount, to wages earned before assignment.

Pennsylvania: Stat. Ann. tit. 43, § 271 (1952) was held unconstitu-tional in Showalter v. Ehlan, 5 Pa. Super. Ct. 242 (1897). Stat. Ann. tit. 43, §§ 273, 274 (1952) were held unconstitutional in Foster's Application, 23 Pa. Dist. 558 (1914).

Retail installment sales. See Hogan, A Survey of State Retail Installment Sales Legislation, 44 Cornell L.Q. 38 (1958); Uniform Consumer Credit Code §§ 2.403–.404.

Indiana: Restrictions on assignments were held unconstitutional in Department of Fin. Insts. v. General Fin. Corp., 227 Ind. 373, 86 N.E.2d 444 (1949); Department of Fin. Insts. v. Holt, 231 Ind. 293, 108 N.E.2d 629 (1952); cf. Department of Fin. Insts. v. Universal C.I.T. Credit Corp., 237 Ind. 404, 146 N.E.2d 93 (1957).

Nebraska: Installment sales legislation was held unconstitutional in Elder v. Doerr, 175 Neb. 483, 122 N.W.2d 528 (1963); Stanton v. Mattson, 175 Neb. 767, 123 N.W.2d 844 (1963); Davis v. General Motors Acc. Corp., 176 Neb. 865, 127 N.W.2d 907 (1964).

Government contracts. See 2 McBride & Wachtel, Government Contracts Ch. 16 (1978).

§ 316. Scope of This Chapter

(1) In this Chapter, references to assignment of a right or delegation of a duty or condition, to the obligee or obligor of an assigned right or delegated duty, or to an assignor or assignee, are limited to rights, duties, and conditions arising under a contract or for breach of a contract.

(2) The statements in this Chapter are qualified in some respects by statutory and other rules governing negotiable instruments and documents, relating to

interests in land, and affecting other classes of contracts.

Comment:

a. Contractual right; chose in action. Statements in this Chapter are limited to contractual rights and duties. Such rights include debts, rights to non-monetary performance and rights to damages and other contractual remedies, whether or not a right to payment has been earned. On the other hand, "chose in action" is a much broader term. In its primary sense it includes debts of all kinds, tort claims, and rights to recover ownership or possession of real or personal property; it has been extended to instruments and documents embodying intangible property rights, to such intangible property as patents and copyrights, and even to equitable rights in tangible property. The rules stated here may have some application to non-contractual choses in action, but the transfer of non-contractual rights is beyond the scope of the Restatement of this Subject.

b. Negotiable instruments and documents; conveyances of land. The rules governing negotiable instruments and documents and the benefits and burdens attached to successive owners of real property by virtue of a contract in a prior conveyance or lease are to some extent different from the law governing contracts in general. The law governing negotiable instruments and documents derives from the law merchant and is now largely statutory. See Comment to § 6. The law relating to covenants in conveyances and leases of land grew up as part of the law of real property and is left to the Restatement, Second, of Property.

c. Assignment and delegation. In this Chapter rights are said to be "assigned"; duties are said to be "delegated." The phrase "assignment of the contract," which may refer to either or both, is avoided because "contract" is defined in § 1 in terms of the act or acts of promising. See § 328. "Assignment" is the transfer of a right by the owner (the obligee or assignor) to another person (the assignee). See § 317. A person subject to a duty (the obligor) does not ordinarily have such a power to substitute another in his place without the consent of the obligee; this is what is meant when it is said that duties cannot be assigned. "Delegation" of performance may be effective to empower a substitute to perform on behalf of the obligor, but the obligor remains subject to the duty until it has been discharged by performance or otherwise. Compare the usage of terms in Uniform Commercial Code § 2–210. Delegation of performance of a condition is similar in effect to delegation of performance of duty.

d. Involuntary transfer. In accordance with common usage, assignment and delegation in this Chapter include only transfers made or powers created by virtue of a manifestation of intention of the assignor or obligor. The manifestation may be made to the assignee or the person delegated or to another person on his behalf, but transfers made and powers created by operation of law are excluded. Such transfers and powers, including transfers to and powers of an executor, administrator, trustee in bankruptcy or receiver by virtue of his office, are in general beyond the scope of this Restatement. As to the equitable remedies of constructive trust, equitable lien, and subrogation, which sometimes operate much like an assignment, see Restatement of Restitution §§ 160–62; Restatement of Security § 141.

REPORTER'S NOTE

See 3 Williston, Contracts §§ 404, 407 (3d ed. 1960); 4 Corbin, Contracts §§ 859–64 (1951); Holdsworth, The History of the Treatment of *Choses* in Action by the Common Law, 33 Harv. L. Rev. 997 (1920); Corbin, Assignment of Contract Rights, 74 U. Pa. L. Rev. 207 (1926). 1 Gilmore, Security Interests in Personal Property Ch. 7 (1965), 2 id. Ch. 41 (1965).

Comment a. On the elimination, in the 1972 Amendments to the Uniform Commercial Code, of the term "contract right," and its inclusion within "account," see Uniform Commercial Code, Appendix II, § 9–106 Reasons for 1972 Change, and Reporter's Note to the Introductory Note to this Chapter.

Comment c. For some of the problems caused by unclear analysis (by both the parties and the court) of a transaction alleged to be an assignment, see University Caseworks Systems v. Bahre, 172 Ind. App. 624, 362 N.E.2d 155 (1977). For an analysis that would have been clearer and easier had "delegation" been used in the place of "assignment," see Smith v. Wrehe, 199 Neb. 753, 261 N.W.2d 620 (1978).

Comment d. For a distinction between the impermissible assignment of a personal injury claim (§ 317 Comment c and Illustration 8) and the permissible subrogation of an insurer advancing payment, see Western Cas. and Sur. Co. v. Bowling, 39 Colo. App. 357, 565 P.2d 970 (1977); Higgins v. Allied American Mut. Fire Ins. Co., 237 A.2d 471 (D.C. Ct. App. 1968); Annot., 19 A.L.R.3d 1054 (1968).

TOPIC 1. WHAT CAN BE ASSIGNED OR DELEGATED

§ 317. Assignment of a Right

(1) An assignment of a right is a manifestation of the assignor's intention to transfer it by virtue of which the assignor's right to performance by the obligor is

---

extinguished in whole or in part and the assignee acquires a right to such performance.

(2) A contractual right can be assigned unless

(a) the substitution of a right of the assignee for the right of the assignor would materially change the duty of the obligor, or materially increase the burden or risk imposed on him by his contract, or materially impair his chance of obtaining return performance, or materially reduce its value to him, or

(b) the assignment is forbidden by statute or is otherwise inoperative on grounds of public policy, or

(c) assignment is validly precluded by contract.

Comment:

a. *"Assignment."* The word "assignment" is sometimes used to refer to the act of the owner of a right (the obligee or assignor) purporting to transfer it, sometimes to the resulting change in legal relations, sometimes to a document evidencing the act or change. In this Chapter "assign" and "assignment" refer to an act which has the effect stated in Subsection (1). To avoid ambiguity, such an assignment is said to be "effective"; a similar act which does not have the stated effect is referred to as an "attempted" or "purported" assignment. In either case the actor is referred to as the "assignor" and the transferee or intended or purported transferee is referred to as the "assignee."

Illustrations:

1. A has a right to $100 against B. A assigns his right to C. A's right is thereby extinguished, and C acquires a right against B to receive $100.

2. A purports to assign to C a right to receive $100 from B. A has no such right. The assignment is ineffective, and C can recover damages from A under the rules stated in § 333.

b. *Assignment to obligor.* A purported assignment by a creditor to his debtor of the indebtedness owed by the debtor is not covered by this Chapter. Such an "assignment" may or may not be effective to extinguish the assignor's right and thus to discharge the debtor; it cannot create in the debtor a right to performance by himself. Compare § 9.

c. *Historical note.* As is indicated in the Introductory Note to this Chapter, the historic common-law rule that a chose in action could not be assigned has largely disappeared. It remains applicable to some non-contractual rights, particularly claims for damages for personal injury, and to certain claims against the Government. This Section is limited by § 316 to contractual rights, and the historic rule now has very limited application to such rights. Except as stated in this Section, they may be effectively assigned. Notwithstanding the historical background, recourse need no longer be had to the law merchant, to doctrines peculiar to courts of equity, or to the concept of a power of attorney irrevocable because coupled with an interest. The restrictions in paragraphs (2)(a) and (c) rest on the basic principle that rights based on agreement are limited by the agreement.

   d. Material variation. What is a material variation, an increase in burden or risk, or an impairment of the obligor's expectation of counter-performance under paragraph (2)(a) depends on the nature of the contract and on the circumstances. Both assignment of rights and delegation of performance are normal and permissible incidents of many types of contracts. See, for example, as to contracts for the sale of goods, Uniform Commercial Code § 2–210 Comment. When the obligor's duty is to pay money, a change in the person to whom the payment is to be made is not ordinarily material. Compare § 322; Uniform Commercial Code § 9–318. But if the duty is to depend on the personal discretion of one person, substitution of the personal discretion of another is likely to be a material change. The clause on material impairment of the chance of obtaining return performance operates primarily in cases where the assignment is accompanied by an improper delegation under § 318 or § 319: if the obligor is to perform in exchange for the promise of one person to render a return performance at a future time, substitution of the return promise of another impairs the obligor's expectation of counter-performance. But in cases of doubt, adequate assurance of due performance may prevent such an impairment. Compare § 251; Uniform Commercial Code § 2–609.

Illustrations:

   3. B contracts to support A for the remainder of A's life. A cannot by assignment confer on C a right to have B support C.

   4. B contracts to support A for the remainder of A's life. B commits a material breach of the contract, and A assigns his right of action to C. The assignment is effective.

   5. B contracts to sell to A for three years 250 tons of ice a week, and A contracts to pay on delivery a stated price per ton. A assigns his right under the contract to C. The assignment is

effective.   C's right to delivery is conditional on payment, but payment by C satisfies the condition.

6.   B sells his business to A and makes a valid contract not to compete.   A sells the business to C and assigns to C the right to have B refrain from competition.   The assignment is effective with respect to competition with the business derived from B. The good will of the business, with contractual protection against its impairment, is treated as an assignable asset.

e.   Public policy and statutory limitations.   The rules for promises and other terms of an agreement stated in Chapter 8 apply by analogy in determining whether an assignment is inoperative on grounds of public policy under paragraph (2)(b) of this Section.   Additional statutory restrictions are common.   Uniform Commercial Code § 5–116 prevents assignment of the right to draw under a letter of credit unless the credit is expressly designated as transferable or assignable, and renders ineffective an assignment of the beneficiary's right to proceeds until the letter of credit or advice of credit is delivered to the assignee.   As is stated in the Statutory Note preceding § 316, wage-assignment statutes often contain a variety of limitations, and there are statutes forbidding or limiting the assignment of rights under government contracts.

Illustrations:

7.   For value A, a public official, assigns to C salary or fees already earned and also his unearned salary for the ensuing month.   The assignment of the earned salary or fees is effective, in the absence of a contrary statute, but the assignment of unearned salary is against public policy.

8.   A contracts with B, a physician, for medical services, and later claims that B's negligence in performing the services caused personal injury to A in violation of B's contractual duty to use due care.   A assigns the claim to C.   The assignment is ineffective.

9.   A, a retired officer of the United States Army, borrows money from C and as security for the loan assigns to C whatever is due or shall become due to A as retired pay.   The assignment is ineffective except as permitted by statute under regulations prescribed by the Secretary of the Army.

f.   Contractual prohibition.   The effect of a term in a contract forbidding the assignment of rights arising under the contract is the subject of § 322.   Such a term may resolve doubts as to whether an assignment violates paragraph (2)(a) of this Section.   Where it seems to forbid an assignment clearly outside the scope of paragraph (2)(a), it may be read restrictively to permit the assignment, or to give the obligor a claim against the assignor rather than a defense against the assignee, or the term may be invalid by statute or decision. See Uniform Commercial Code §§ 2–210, 9–318. Even if the term gives the obligor a defense against the assignee, the assignment is usually partially effective as an assignment conditional on the assent of the obligor.

REPORTER'S NOTE

Subsection (1) is based on former §§ 149(1) and 150(1). The distinction in those sections between "assignment" and "effective assignment" is eliminated. Subsection (2) contains the substance of former § 151.

See 3 Williston, Contracts §§ 404, 412, 417–23 (3d ed. 1960); 4 Corbin, Contracts §§ 857, 861, 864–79 (1951 & Supp. 1971).

Comment a. Illustration 1 is a revision of Illustration 1 to former § 150. Illustration 2 is new; for discussions of what may be assigned, see Stathos v. Murphy, 26 A.D.2d 500, 276 N.Y.S.2d 727 (1966), aff'd, 19 N.Y.2d 883, 281 N.Y.S.2d 81, 227 N.E.2d 880 (1967); Factors Etc., Inc. v. Creative Card Co., 444 F. Supp. 279 (S.D.N.Y. 1977).

Comment d. Illustration 3 is new; compare duPont de Bie v. Vredenburgh, 490 F.2d 1057 (4th Cir. 1974) in which the right to accrued but unpaid support payments was held assignable. Illustrations 4 and 5 were substantially Illustrations 3 and 2 respectively to former § 151. As to Illustration 5, compare Crane Ice Cream Co. v. Terminal Freezing & Heating Co., 147 Md. 588, 128 A. 280 (1925); Comment 4 to Uniform Commercial Code § 2–210. For other discussions of when assignment may or may not be barred because it materially would vary the obligor's burden or risk, see, e.g., FinanceAmerica Private Brands v. Harvey E. Hall, Inc., 380 A.2d 1377 (Del. Super. Ct. 1977); Munchak Corp. v. Cunningham, 457 F.2d 721 (4th Cir. 1972); cf. Union Bond and Trust Co. v. M and M Wood Working Co., 256 Or. 384, 474 P.2d 339 (1970). Illustration 6 is substantially based on Illustration 4 to former § 151; see also T.E. Moor & Co. v. Hardcastle, 421 S.W.2d 126 (Tex. Civ. App. 1967), ref. n.r.e.

Comment e. Illustration 7 was substantially Illustration 7 to former § 151. Illustration 8 is new. Illustration 9 is based on Illustration 5 to former § 151; the applicable statute is 37 U.S.C. § 701 (1976). For a discussion of the interpretation of purported assignments to avoid statutory bars, see Stathos v. Murphy, 26 A.D.2d 500, 276 N.Y.S.2d 727 (1966), aff'd, 19 N.Y.2d 883, 281 N.Y.S.2d 81, 227 N.E.2d 880 (1967).

Comment f. See Annots., 75 A.L.R.3d 1184 (1977); 59 A.L.R.3d 244 (1974).

---

§ 318.   Delegation of Performance of Duty

(1) An obligor can properly delegate the performance of his duty to another unless the delegation is contrary to public policy or the terms of his promise.

(2) Unless otherwise agreed, a promise requires performance by a particular person only to the extent that the obligee has a substantial interest in having that person perform or control the acts promised.

(3) Unless the obligee agrees otherwise, neither delegation of performance nor a contract to assume the duty made with the obligor by the person delegated discharges any duty or liability of the delegating obligor.

Comment:

a. Duty and condition. A contractual performance may discharge the duty of a performing obligor, or it may satisfy a condition of the right of a performing obligee to a return performance. Where the same person is both obligor and obligee, the same performance may both discharge his duty and satisfy a condition of his right. The propriety of delegation is in general governed by the same standard whether the issue is performance of a duty or performance of a condition. In the interest of simplicity of statement, however, the rules are stated in two separate sections. This Section deals with delegation of performance of a duty; delegation of performance of a condition is the subject of § 319.

Illustrations:

1.   A owes B $100, and asks C to pay B. Payment or tender to B by C has the effect of payment or tender by A.

2.   A contracts to deliver to B coal of specified kind and quality. A delegates the performance of this duty to C, who tenders to B coal of the specified kind and quality. The tender has the effect of a tender by A.

3.   A contracts to build a building for B in accordance with specifications, and delegates the plumbing work to C. Performance by C has the effect of performance by A.

b. The duty of the person delegated. The rules stated in this Section apply without regard to whether the person delegated has a legal duty to render the performance in question or whether he acquires a legal right to render it or to receive a return performance. The person delegated may be an agent, gratuitous or otherwise, of the delegating obligor. For such cases this Section is a particular application of Restatement, Second, Agency § 17. Or the person delegated may be an assignee of a related right, entitled to enforce it for his own benefit. See Restatement, Second Agency §§ 14G, 14H. In either case he may or may not promise the obligor to render the performance. If he does so promise, the obligee may in some cases be an intended beneficiary of the promise, with the consequences stated in Chapter 14.

Illustration:

4. In Illustrations 1, 2 and 3, the stated consequences are not affected by the fact that C is an agent of A or an assignee of A's right to return performance or that C has or has not assumed A's duty.

c. *Non-delegable duties.* Delegation of performance is a normal and permissible incident of many types of contract. See Uniform Commercial Code § 2–210, Comment. The principal exceptions relate to contracts for personal services and to contracts for the exercise of personal skill or discretion. Compare § 317. Even where delegation is normal, a particular contract may call for personal performance. Or the contract may permit delegation where personal performance is normally required. In the absence of contrary agreement, Subsection (2) precludes delegation only where a substantial reason is shown why delegated performance is not as satisfactory as personal performance.

Illustrations:

5. A, a teacher employed in a public or private school, attempts to delegate the performance of his duties to B, a competent person. An offer by B to perform A's duties need not be accepted, and actual performance by B without the assent of the employer will create no right in either A or B to the salary stated in A's contract.

6. A contracts with B, a corporation, to sing three songs over the radio as part of an advertisement of B's product. A's performance is not delegable unless B assents.

7. A contracts with B that A will personally cut the grass on B's meadow. A cannot effectively delegate performance of the duty to C, however competent C may be.

8. A, a corporation, contracts with B to build a building. A delegates the entire performance to X and Y, the sole stockholders of A. Performance by X and Y in accordance with specifications discharges A's duty, since the supervision is not materially changed.

d. Delegation and novation. An obligor is discharged by the substitution of a new obligor only if the contract so provides or if the obligee makes a binding manifestation of assent, forming a novation. See §§ 280, 328 and 329. Otherwise, the obligee retains his original right against the obligor, even though the obligor manifests an intention to substitute another obligor in his place and the other purports to assume the duty. The obligee may, however, have rights against the other as an intended beneficiary of the promise to assume the duty. See Chapter 14.

Illustrations:

9. A borrows $50,000 from B and contracts to repay it. The contract provides that, if a corporation C is organized and assumes the debt under described conditions, A will be under no further obligation. C is organized and in good faith assumes the debt as provided. A is discharged.

10. A contracts with B to cut the grass on B's meadow. A delegates performance to C, who contracts with A to assume A's duty and perform the work. C begins performance with B's assent, but later breaks the contract. C is liable to B, but A is not discharged.

REPORTER'S NOTE

To reduce complexity of statement, Subsections (1) and (2) as they appeared in former § 160 are left to comment, and delegation of performance of a condition is made the subject of § 319. Both Sections employ the language of Restatement, Second, Agency § 17 and Uniform Commercial Code § 2-210, without change of substance from the former Restatement.

See 3 Williston, Contracts §§ 411–411A (3d ed. 1960); 4 Corbin, Contracts §§ 865–66 (1951 & Supp. 1980).

Comment a. Illustrations 1–3 are new.

Comment b. Illustration 4 is new.

Comment c. Illustrations 5, 7 and 8 are respectively based on Illustrations 2–4 to former § 160. As to Illustration 7, see also Union Bond and Trust Co. v. M and M Wood Working Co., 256 Or. 384, 474 P.2d 339 (1970). Illustrations 6 and 8 are new. As to Illustration 8, compare Macke Co. v. Pizza of Gaithersburg, 259 Md. 479, 270 A.2d 645 (1970) (containing a review of the authorities); Milton L. Ehrlich, Inc. v. Unit Frame & Floor

Corp., 5 N.Y.2d 275, 184 N.Y.S.2d 334, 157 N.E.2d 495 (1959).

Comment d. Illustration 9 is new; compare Ramey v. Koons, 230 F.2d 802 (5th Cir. 1956); J.R. Simplot Co. v. Chambers, 82 Idaho 104, 350 P.2d 211 (1960); Lee v. Ravanis, 349 Mass. 742, 212 N.E.2d 480 (1965). Contrast Smith v. Wrehe, 199 Neb. 753, 261 N.W.2d 620 (1978), in which the language of the agreement did not support a finding of novation. Illustration 10 is based on Illustration 4 to former § 160; compare United New York Sandy Hook Pilots Ass'n v. Rodermond Indus., 394 F.2d 65 (3d Cir. 1968); Brown v. Bowers Constr. Co., 236 N.C. 462, 73 S.E.2d 147 (1952).

§ 319. Delegation of Performance of Condition

(1) Where a performance by a person is made a condition of a duty, performance by a person delegated by him satisfies that requirement unless the delegation is contrary to public policy or the terms of the agreement.

(2) Unless otherwise agreed, an agreement requires performance of a condition by a particular person only to the extent that the obligor has a substantial interest in having that person perform or control the acts required.

Comment:

a. Types of conditions; related duties. A promissory duty may be subject to a condition either by virtue of a term of the promise or agreement or by virtue of a term of the contract supplied by a rule of law. See § 5; Comment c to § 226. This Section applies only to a particular type of condition, a performance by the obligee or some other person. When a promise is subject to such a condition, there may or may not be a return promise by the obligee or another that the performance will be rendered. If there is such a return promise, a breach of it often does not have the effect of the non-occurrence of a condition unless the failure of performance is material. See § 245. This Section deals with delegation as it affects performance of a condition; delegation affecting performance of a duty is the subject of § 318.

Illustration:

1. A contracts with B, a city, to clean the streets of B weekly for five years in return for monthly payments. A delegates performance to C, and C substantially performs until B can-

cels the contract. C's performance satisfies the condition of B's duty to pay, whether C is A's agent or an assignee from A.

b. *Non-delegable performance.* The propriety of delegation of performance that is made a condition is in general governed by the same standard as the propriety of delegation of performance of a duty. Indeed, the same delegation may involve both. See, e.g., Illustration 5 to § 318. Delegation is generally permissible unless otherwise agreed, but performance of personal services and the exercise of personal skill and discretion are not ordinarily delegable. Where the condition consists of the making of a promise, delegation substituting a different promisor is ordinarily not effective.

Illustrations:

2. Under an option contract A has a right to a conveyance of Blackacre on terms including execution of a promissory note secured by a mortgage on Blackacre. A assigns the contract to C, and C tenders a note executed by C but not by A. B is not bound to convey.

3. A, a corporation, contracts with B to convey Blackacre to B upon completion of installment payments B contracts to make. The deed is to include a covenant against incumbrances which gives rights only to the immediate grantee. A assigns the contract and conveys the land to C. B's duty is conditional on adequate assurance that he will receive a deed directly from A.

4. The facts being otherwise as stated in Illustration 3, B defaults and A becomes insolvent because land values are greatly reduced. The assignment and conveyance to C are made as a result of insolvency proceedings in which A is dissolved. In the absence of a showing that an incumbrance exists, C may obtain a decree of specific performance against B conditional on deposit by C of a deed containing a covenant against incumbrances by C only.

5. A, a corporation of State X, has a contract to act as B's exclusive sales agent for two years in a region including State X. A liquidates and assigns the contract and delegates the duties under it to C, a corporation of State Y, a state outside the region. B can properly treat the contract as terminated.

REPORTER'S NOTE

This Section is based on those portions of former § 160 dealing with the delegation of the performance of a condition. See Reporter's Note to § 318; 4 Corbin, Contracts § 865 (1951 & Supp. 1980).

Comment a. Illustration 1 is based on Devlin v. Mayor, 63 N.Y. 8 (1875).

Comment b. Illustration 2 is based on E.M. Loews, Inc. v. Deutschmann, 344 Mass. 765, 184 N.E.2d 55 (1962). Illustrations 3 and 4 are based on Coral Gables, Inc. v. Payne, 94 F.2d 593 (4th Cir. 1938). Illustration 5 is based on Wetherell Bros. v. United States Steel Co., 200 F.2d 761 (1st Cir. 1952). Compare Rosner v. Modern Maid Packers, Inc., 274 F. Supp. 685 (D. Conn. 1967), with Macke Co. v. Pizza of Gaithersburg, 259 Md. 479, 270 A.2d 645 (1970).

§ 320. Assignment of Conditional Rights

The fact that a right is created by an option contract or is conditional on the performance of a return promise or is otherwise conditional does not prevent its assignment before the condition occurs.

Comment:

a. Offers and option contracts. An offer can be accepted only by a person whom it invites to furnish the consideration, or by his agent. See §§ 29, 52. The power to accept can be exercised by a transferee only if the transferee is such a person. But an option contract, limiting the power to revoke an offer, is treated as creating a right which is assignable like other contractual rights. See § 25. Of course the assignment may be ineffective if it materially varies the obligor's duty, or if it is contrary to the terms of the option contract. See § 317.

Illustrations:

1. In return for $100 paid by A, B promises to convey Blackacre for $10,000 on receipt of that amount within thirty days. A assigns the option to C. On C's tender of $10,000 within thirty days, B is under a duty to convey Blackacre to C.

2. In return for $100 paid by A, B promises to convey Blackacre to A, if A gives notice of acceptance within thirty days, for $10,000 of which $2,000 is to be paid on conveyance and the balance in four annual installments represented by notes. A assigns the option to C. The assignment is effective, but C's right is conditional on tender of notes signed by A.

b. Conditional right and conditional assignment. Not every conditional right is capable of effective assignment. The fact that the right is conditional does not prevent effective assignment, but assignment is subject to the same restrictions as in cases of unconditional rights. See § 317. Either the assignment or the right assigned, or both, may be subject to a condition. See § 331. Thus there may be a conditional assignment of a conditional right.

Illustrations:

3. A holds an insurance policy in which the insurer promises to pay him $1000 at the end of twenty years if A makes specified payments of premiums. A can assign his conditional right.

4. A has a contract with B under which certain payments are to be made to A by B under a fixed schedule and other payments are to be made if B's earnings exceed stated amounts. As security for a loan to A by C, A assigns to C A's rights to payments by B, A to retain any payments falling due before default by A under the loan agreement. The assignment is effective according to its terms.

c. Return performance. The parties to an exchange of promises ordinarily contemplate an exchange of performances, and the right of each is often conditional on his own performance. See §§ 231–39. Or the right may be conditional on a performance by another, or on some other event. Such a condition does not prevent assignment by a promisee or beneficiary of his conditional right. Whether or not the return performance is delegable, and whether or not the assignor is under a duty to render it, the assignee's right is subject to the same conditions as was the assignor's.

Illustrations:

5. A, a builder, and B, an owner of land, enter into a building contract. A assigns to C payments due or to become due him under the contract. The assignment is effective.

6. In Illustration 5, B sells the land to D and assigns to D his right to performance by A. The assignment is effective.

7. A, a teacher employed in a public or private school, assigns to C the salary to be earned the following month. In the absence of statute, the assignment is effective.

d. Delegation and assumption. The question whether a return performance is delegable arises only if the assignor attempts to delegate it. Often an assignor delegates performance to the assignee, and the assignee assumes the assignor's duty to perform, promising the assignor that the delegated performance will be rendered. See §§ 318–19. If the performance is delegable, such an assignment does not of itself materially vary a condition of the right assigned. The assignor remains subject to the same duty as before, and the obligor of the assigned right acquires a new right as an intended beneficiary of the assignee's promise. In effect the assignor becomes a surety for the assignee.

Illustrations:

8. A contracts with B, a city, to clean the streets of B weekly for five years in return for monthly payments. A assigns his rights under the contract to C, and C promises A to perform A's duties under it. The assignment is effective. A is still bound to B, but as surety for C.

9. A, a builder, and B, an owner of land, enter into a building contract. A enters into a contract with C that C will take A's place in the building contract and that A will be freed from his obligation under it. B does not manifest assent or accept any performance from C. A is still bound to B.

10. A and B contract that B will sell and deliver goods to A in monthly installments for six months and A will pay for them on delivery. A assigns his rights under the contract to C, who assumes the duty of payment. C refuses to accept any goods from B. Both A and C are subject to liability to B, A as surety for C.

11. After the assignment in Illustration 10, C and B, without consulting A, agree to and do postpone deliveries for three months. A's duty is discharged.

e. Prospective failure of performance. An assignment is not effective if its effect is to impair materially the obligor's chance of obtaining return performance. See § 317. Thus an assignment accompanied by the assignor's repudiation of his duty to render a return performance may justify the obligor in suspending his own performance, in so changing his position that his duty is discharged, or even in bringing an immediate action for breach. See §§ 329 and 235–38. An attempt to delegate to an assignee a non-delegable performance may have a similar effect. Under Uniform Commercial Code § 2–210, the obligor may treat any assignment of rights under a contract for the sale of goods as creating reasonable grounds for insecurity if the assignor delegates performance. Under § 2–609 of the Code, the obligor may then demand adequate assurance of due performance, and failure of the assignor or assignee to furnish such assurance within a reasonable time has the effect of a repudiation. See also § 251.

Illustrations:

12. A and C, partners, contract with B to act as the exclusive distributor of B's product in a specified territory. The con-

tract is to last for one year, and they are to have an option to renew it from year to year. After six months A sells his interest in the contract to C and withdraws from the business. C gives notice of intention to renew, and B refuses to renew. B is not subject to liability to C for the refusal.

13. A, a corporation, leases railway cars to B by a contract providing that A will keep the cars in repair. A becomes insolvent, and as a result of insolvency proceedings A's rights under the lease contract and A's repair facilities and staff are transferred to C, a solvent corporation, which assumes the duty of repair and assures B of its readiness and willingness to carry out the terms of the lease. A remains in existence under court supervision. B remains obligated by the lease.

REPORTER'S NOTE

This Section consolidates former §§ 155 and 161. See 3 Williston, Contracts, §§ 412–21A (3d ed. 1960); 1A Corbin, Contracts § 271 (1963 & Supp. 1980), 4 id. §§ 865–69, 874–76 (1951 & Supps. 1971 & 1980).

Comment a. Illustration 1 is based on Illustration 2 to former § 155. Illustration 2 is based on Carluccio v. 607 Hudson St. Holding Co., 139 N.J. Eq. 481, 52 A.2d 56 (1947), aff'd 141 N.J. Eq. 449, 57 A.2d 452 (1948); cf. Phipps Land Co. v. Wilwat Props., 231 Ga. 305, 201 S.E.2d 408 (1973).

Comment b. Illustration 3 was Illustration 1 to former § 155. Illustration 4 is based on In re New York, N. H. & H.R.R., 25 F. Supp. 874 (D. Conn. 1938); cf. Rockmore v. Lehman, 129 F.2d 892 (2d Cir.), cert. denied, 317 U.S. 700 (1942); National City Bank v. Goess, 130 F.2d 376 (2d Cir. 1942); In re Allied Prods. Co., 134 F.2d 725 (6th Cir.), cert. denied, 320 U.S. 740 (1943); Miller v. Wells Fargo Bank Int'l Corp., 540 F.2d 548, 558–60 (2d Cir. 1976).

Comment c. Illustration 5 is based on Illustration 1 to former § 161. Illustrations 6 and 7 are new. As to Illustration 6, compare Prochemco, Inc. v. Clajon Gas Co., 555 S.W.2d 189 (Tex. Civ. App. 1977), ref. n.r.e., in which the rights under a contract were assignable but an option to renew was not. The court permitted the option holder to exercise the option on behalf of its assignee.

Comment d. Illustration 8 is based on Devlin v. Mayor, 63 N.Y. 8 (1875). Illustration 9 is based on Illustration 2 to former § 161. Illustration 10 is new; it is based on Imperial Ref. Co. v. Kanotex Ref. Co., 29 F.2d 193 (8th Cir. 1928). Illustration 11 is based on Illustration 3 to former § 161.

Comment e. Illustration 12 is based on Paige v. Faure, 229 N.Y. 114, 127 N.E. 898 (1920). Illustration 13 is based on British Waggon Co. v. Lea & Co., 5 Q.B. Div. 149 (1880).

§ 321. Assignment of Future Rights

(1) Except as otherwise provided by statute, an assignment of a right to payment expected to arise out of an existing employment or other continuing business relationship is effective in the same way as an assignment of an existing right.

(2) Except as otherwise provided by statute and as stated in Subsection (1), a purported assignment of a right expected to arise under a contract not in existence operates only as a promise to assign the right when it arises and as a power to enforce it.

Comment:

a. Rights under existing contracts. This Section does not apply to rights in existence at the time of assignment. Such rights are assignable under the rules stated in §§ 317 and 320 even though they are conditional or have not matured. For this purpose rights arising under a contract are treated as existing from the moment of its formation, even though the chance is slight that there will ever be a duty of immediate performance.

Illustration:

1. A contracts to build a house for B for a stated price. The contract provides that if A performs any work on the house beyond what the specifications require, he shall have compensation therefor, to be determined by the architect. Before any such work has been agreed upon, A, for value, assigns his right to compensation for extra work to C. Subsequently A becomes bankrupt, and still later extra work under the contract is agreed upon and performed. Immediately on completion of the work A assigns the right to compensation to D. The assignment to C is effective and is not defeated by A's bankruptcy or the assignment to D.

b. Rationale. The conceptual difficulty posed by transfer of a right which does not exist can be met by giving effect to the attempted transfer when the right later arises. Uniform Commercial Code § 9-204, for example, provides that with certain exceptions a security agreement may provide that all obligations covered by the security agreement are to be secured by after-acquired collateral; in an appropriate case, the security interest is said by § 9-203 to "attach" when it becomes enforceable against the debtor with respect to the collateral.

The effect given in such cases is limited, not because of any logical necessity, but by virtue of a public policy which seeks to protect the assignor and third parties against transfers which may be improvident or fraudulent. Similar limitations are placed on attempted transfers of future rights in property other than contractual rights. See Restatement of Property § 316; Restatement of Security § 10; Restatement, Second, Trusts § 86; Uniform Commercial Code §§ 2–401, 2–501, 9–203(4), 9–204(2).

   c. Continuing relationships. Subsection (1) gives effect to an assignment of a right to compensation for services expected to be rendered in the course of an existing employment, even though there is no contract to continue the employment, and states a similar rule for rights expected to arise out of other continuing business relationships. Even where there is no continuing relationship, a purported assignment of a right expected to arise out of a subsequent transaction may sometimes become a part of the subsequent transaction and take effect as such a part.

Illustrations:

   2. B employs A from week to week in his factory at a salary of $50 a week. A, in the first week of January, assigns to C any salary which he may earn during the last week in that month in his employment by B. The assignment is effective, and if A works for B during that week B will come under a duty to C to pay him $50.

   3. B employs A at a stated rate of pay from day to day. A assigns to C whatever A may become entitled to from work done for B during the ensuing month. During the ensuing month A not only earns his regular pay but acquires a right to extra compensation in the course of his employment. The assignment is effective both as to the right to regular pay and the right to extra compensation.

   4. In January A assigns to C as security for a loan the salary he expects to earn in March under his existing employment by B, though A has no contract with B to work during that month. A becomes bankrupt in February, and later receives a discharge in bankruptcy. He continues his employment during March. Even though the assignment is otherwise effective, A's debt to C is discharged, and A's March salary belongs to A free of C's claim.

   5. A receives from B an order for brick to be used by B in performing an existing contract with D to build a school, with an assurance that A "has been awarded the job of furnishing bricks

for the school." Before prices or specifications for the brick have
been determined, A assigns to C as security for a loan the money
to become due from B for material for the school. The brick is
later delivered as expected. The assignment is effective.

6. A is negotiating to sell to B property part of which is subject to a mortgage from A to C. In consideration of C's release of
the mortgage, A assigns to C a payment to be made by B. Later
the same day A and B sign a contract to sell the property which
provides for the payment expected. Notwithstanding the lack of
a continuing business relationship, the assignment to C is effective when the contract to sell is made.

d. *Other future rights.* In the absence of statute, a purported
assignment of a future right not within the rule stated in Subsection (1)
has only the effect stated in Subsection (2). That effect is that the
assignee has enforceable rights against the assignor only to the extent
that contractual remedies are available, as in the case of a promise to
make a future assignment. See § 330. As against third parties, the
purported assignment operates as a grant to the assignee of the
assignor's power to enforce the right. But unless specific enforcement against the assignor is appropriate, the grant of power is revocable and can be defeated by the assignor's creditors until it is exercised.

Illustrations:

7. A is employed as a teacher for the school year by X, a
municipality. A, in the expectation of employment by B, another
municipality, for the following school year, assigns to C the salary
for the first month of service which A may render for B. A is
subsequently employed by B as expected, and A's salary for the
first month becomes due. C makes demand upon B for payment
of the salary. B refuses and pays A. In the absence of statute, B
has violated no right of C.

8. The facts being otherwise as stated in Illustration 7, D, a
creditor of A, garnishes A's salary after it becomes due. C intervenes, claiming the funds as assignee. In the absence of statute,
D's claim is prior to C's.

e. *Statutory provisions.* The limitations imposed by this Section on the assignment of future rights are not the only possible mode
of safeguarding the interests of the assignor and third parties. Particularly when a method is provided for giving public notice of the transaction, statutes commonly relax the limitations stated here. For
transactions subject to Article 9 of the Uniform Commercial Code, the
Code provides a notice-filing system, and § 9–204 gives effect to a

security agreement (not involving consumer goods) providing that a security interest shall attach to after-acquired collateral. Such collateral may include contractual rights. Somewhat similar variations from the rules of this Section have been made in other statutes relating to the assignment of accounts receivable. Again, wage-assignment statutes sometimes limit amount and duration, but within the limits set may permit assignment of wages to be earned under future engagements. See Introductory Note to Chapter 15.

REPORTER'S NOTE

Subsection (1) of former § 154 is omitted as repetitive of § 317; former Subsection (2) is divided into two subsections. The provision for "other continuing business relationships" than employment is new. The last clause of the original Subsection (2) is omitted so as to leave to § 330 the consequences of an assignment operative as a promise to assign.

See 3 Williston, Contracts § 413 (3d ed. 1960); 4 Corbin, Contracts § 874 (1951 & Supp. 1971).

Comment a. For a discussion of the difference between the assignment of a future right and the assignment of a present right that is conditional upon a future event and may never mature, see Stathos v. Murphy, 26 A.D.2d 500, 276 N.Y.S.2d 727 (1966), aff'd, 19 N.Y.2d 883, 281 N.Y.S.2d 81, 227 N.E.2d 880 (1967). Glassman Constr. Co. v. Fidelity & Cas. Co., 356 F.2d 340 (D.C. Cir.), cert. denied, 384 U.S. 987 (1966). Illustration 1 is based on Illustration 1 to former § 154.

Comment c. Illustrations 2–3 are based on Illustrations 2–3 to former § 154. See also Valley Nat'l Bank v.

Flagstaff Dairy, 116 Ariz. 513, 570 P.2d 200 (Ct. App. 1977) (proceeds from future sales of milk to regular customer without contract; decided under pre-1972 text of Uniform Commercial Code § 9–204); du Pont de-Bie v. Vredenburg, 490 F.2d 1057 (4th Cir. 1974) (assignment of future support payments). Illustration 4 is based on Illustration 4 to former § 154, but is revised to reflect the decision in Local Loan Co. v. Hunt, 292 U.S. 234 (1934). Illustration 5 is based on Claycraft Co. v. John Bowen Co., 287 Mass. 255, 191 N.E. 403 (1934); cf. H.S. Mann Corp. v. Moody, 144 Cal. App.2d 310, 301 P.2d 28 (1956). Illustration 6 is based on Bergson v. H.P. Hood & Sons, 300 Mass. 340, 15 N.E.2d 196 (1938); see Annot., 116 A.L.R. 955 (1938). See also University Casework Systems v. Bahre, 172 Ind. App. 624, 362 N.E.2d 155 (1977). Illustration 7 is based on Illustration 5 to former § 154. See also Trak Microwave Corp. v. Medaris Mgt., Inc., 236 So.2d 189 (Fla. Dist. Ct. App. 1970). Illustration 8 is new and is suggested by Herbert v. Bronson, 125 Mass. 475 (1878).

§ 322. Contractual Prohibition of Assignment

(1) Unless the circumstances indicate the contrary, a contract term prohibiting assignment of "the con-

tract" bars only the delegation to an assignee of the performance by the assignor of a duty or condition.

(2) A contract term prohibiting assignment of rights under the contract, unless a different intention is manifested,

(a) does not forbid assignment of a right to damages for breach of the whole contract or a right arising out of the assignor's due performance of his entire obligation;

(b) gives the obligor a right to damages for breach of the terms forbidding assignment but does not render the assignment ineffective;

(c) is for the benefit of the obligor, and does not prevent the assignee from acquiring rights against the assignor or the obligor from discharging his duty as if there were no such prohibition.

Comment:

a. Rationale. In the absence of statute or other contrary public policy, the parties to a contract have power to limit the rights created by their agreement. The policy against restraints on the alienation of property has limited application to contractual rights. Compare Restatement of Property §§ 404–17. A term in a contract prohibiting assignment of the rights created may resolve doubts as to whether assignment would materially change the obligor's duty or whether he has a substantial interest in personal performance by the obligee (see §§ 317–19); or it may serve to protect the obligor against conflicting claims and the hazard of double liability (see §§ 338–43). But as assignment has become a common practice, the policy which limits the validity of restraints on alienation has been applied to the construction of contractual terms open to two or more possible constructions. Compare Restatement of Property §§ 418–23.

b. Ineffective terms. In some circumstances where contractual prohibitions of assignment are regularly limited by construction, explicit contractual provision would not change the result. Where a right to the payment of money is fully earned by performance, for example, a provision that an attempt to assign forfeits the right may be invalid as a contractual penalty. See § 356. If there is no forfeiture, and the obligee joins in demanding payment to the assignee, a contractual prohibition which serves no legitimate interest of the obligor is disregarded. Uniform Commercial Code §§ 2–210 and 9–318 render contractual prohibitions ineffective in additional circumstances, and in some situations a prohibition is invalid as a restraint on alienation aside from statute. See Uniform Commercial Code § 9–311.

Illustrations:

1. A holds a policy of industrial insurance issued to him by the B Insurance Company. After lapse for failure to pay premiums, B refuses to pay the "cash surrender value" provided for in the policy. A and others similarly situated assign their claims to C for collection. The assignment is effective without regard to any contractual prohibition of assignment.

2. A and B contract for the sale of land by B to A. A fully performs the contract, becomes entitled to specific performance on B's refusal to convey the land, and then assigns his rights to C. C is entitled to specific performance against B without regard to any contractual prohibition of assignment. See Restatement of Property § 416.

c. Construction. The rules stated in this Section do not exhaust the factors to be taken into account in construing and applying a prohibition against assignment. "Not transferable" has a clear meaning in a theatre ticket; in a certificate of deposit the same words may refer to negotiability rather than assignability. Where there is a promise not to assign but no provision that an assignment is ineffective, the question whether breach of the promise discharges the obligor's duty depends on all the circumstances. See §§ 237, 241.

d. Consent of the obligor. Ordinarily a contractual prohibition of assignment is for the benefit of the obligor. In such cases third parties cannot assert the invalidity of a prohibited assignment if the obligor makes no objection. Where, however, the prohibition is not solely for the benefit of the obligor, waiver by the obligor may not validate the assignment. The validity of restraints on alienation in such cases is governed by considerations similar to those governing the validity of spendthrift trusts. See Restatement, Second, Trusts §§ 153–57.

Illustrations:

3. B contracts to transfer land to A on payment of $5000. The contract provides that A shall not assign his right. A assigns his right to C. B, on receiving $5000 from C, conveys the land to him. B's duty under his contract with A is discharged.

4.   A Manufacturing Company contracts with B Insurance Company for group insurance on the lives of A's employees.   The policy and certificates issued under it to individual employees limit the class of permitted beneficiaries, permit the employee to change the beneficiary, forbid irrevocable designation of a beneficiary, and provide that the certificate is not assignable.   A certificate is issued to C, a widower, who designates his son D as beneficiary and delivers the certificate to D as a gift.   Later C remarries and designates his second wife E as beneficiary.   On C's death B interpleads D and E, paying the insurance money into court.   E is entitled to the fund.

REPORTER'S NOTE

This Section is new.   Subsection (1) is based on Uniform Commercial Code § 2–210(3), which applies to contracts for the sale of goods. Comment *d* changes former § 176 from a rule of law to a canon of construction.   See 3 Williston, Contracts § 422 (3d ed. 1960); 4 Corbin, Contracts §§ 872, 873 (1951); Annot., 37 A.L.R.2d 1251 (1954).   But see Gilmore, The Commercial Doctrine of Good Faith Purchase, 63 Yale L.J. 1057, 1118–20 (1954).

Comment b.   Reasoning from Uniform Commercial Code § 9–318, the Oklahoma Supreme Court found a legislative purpose to bar all anti-assignment clauses, even in situations not subject to Article Nine of the Code, American Bank of Commerce v. City of McAlester, 555 P.2d 581 (Okl. 1976).   Illustration 1 is based on National Life & Acc. Ins. Co. v. Magers, 319 S.W.2d 53 (Ct. App. 1958), aff'd, 329 S.W.2d 752 (Mo. 1959); see also International Rediscount Corp. v. Hartford Accident and Indem. Co., 425 F. Supp. 669 (D. Del. 1977); Annots., 56 A.L.R. 1391 (1928), 122 A.L.R. 144 (1939).   Illustration 2 is based on Gunsch v. Gunsch, 71 N.W.2d 623 (N.D. 1955); cf. Socony Mobil Oil Co.

v. Continental Oil Co., 335 F.2d 438 (10th Cir. 1964); see Annots., 138 A.L.R. 205 (1942), 148 A.L.R. 1361 (1944).

Comment c.   See Trubowitch v. Riverbank Canning Co., 30 Cal.2d 335, 182 P.2d 182 (1947); Union Bond and Trust Co. v. M and M Wood Working Co., 256 Or. 384, 474 P.2d 339 (1970); Detroit Greyhound Emp. Fed. Credit Union v. Aetna Life Ins. Co., 381 Mich. 683, 167 N.W.2d 274 (1969).   But see Rother-Gallagher v. Montana Power Co., 164 Mont. 360, 522 P.2d 1226 (1974).   As to franchise agreements, see Annot., 59 A.L.R.3d 244 (1974).   As to certificates of deposit, see Annot., 59 A.L.R. 1478 (1929).   As to assignment of wages, see Annot., 76 A.L.R. 1304 (1932).

Comment d.   That a waiver by the obligor must be clear and unequivocal, and that the assignee of an ineffective assignment retains rights against the assignor, see Paul v. Chromalytics Corp., 343 A.2d 622 (Del. Super. Ct. 1975).   Illustration 3 was Illustration 1 to former § 176. Illustration 4 is based on Bimestefer v. Bimestefer, 205 Md. 541, 109 A.2d 768 (1954); cf. Thomas v. Thomas, 192 Cal. App.2d 771, 13 Cal. Rptr. 872 (1961).

§ 323.   Obligor's Assent to Assignment or Delegation

(1) A term of a contract manifesting an obligor's assent to the future assignment of a right or an obligee's assent to the future delegation of the performance of a duty or condition is effective despite any subsequent objection.

(2) A manifestation of such assent after the formation of a contract is similarly effective if made for consideration or in circumstances in which a promise would be binding without consideration, or if a material change of position takes place in reliance on the manifestation.

Comment:

    a. Effect of assent. The assent of the obligor is not ordinarily necessary to make an assignment effective. But his assent may operate to preclude objection based on a change in his duty, burden or risk or in his chance of obtaining return performance. See § 317. It may permit a separate action by a partial assignee. See § 326. It may be an offer of a new contract by novation, or the acceptance of an offer of novation, and may thus terminate the assignor's power to revoke a gratuitous assignment (see § 332), or may discharge or modify a duty of the assignor or a condition of the right assigned (see §§ 318–19). Which of these effects is produced depends on the circumstances and the scope of the assent manifested.

    b. Promises to or by "assigns." Contracts often refer to the "assigns" of one or both parties. A purported promise by a promisor "and his assigns" does not mean that the promisor can terminate his duty by making an assignment, nor does it of itself show an assumption of duties by any assignee. It tends to indicate that the promised performance is not personal, just as a promise to a promisee "and his assigns" tends to indicate that the promisor is willing to render performance to an assignee. Whether there is a manifestation of assent to assignment or delegation, however, depends on the interpretation of the contract as a whole. Notwithstanding references to "assigns," other terms and the circumstances may show that the assent is limited or even that there is no assent.

Illustration:

    1. A and C, partners, contract with B to act as exclusive distributor of B's product in a specified territory. The terms of

the contract show that B reposes personal trust and confidence in both A and C. A term, "This agreement shall bind and benefit the respective successors and assigns of the parties hereto," may be read as inapplicable to an assignment by A or C which delegates performance unless B makes a further manifestation of assent.

c. Assent subsequent to contract. Assent to assignment or delegation may be manifested after the formation of a contract, and may have effects similar to those of a term in the contract. Indeed, such assent may be a practical construction of the contract, relevant to determine its meaning. See Uniform Commercial Code § 2–208. In addition, subsequent assent may waive a prohibition contained in the contract. Unless consideration is given or unless the circumstances are such as to make a new promise binding without consideration, however, such a manifestation of assent can be withdrawn before it has been acted on. See §§ 84, 89, 90. Assent to assignment and delegation, even though irrevocable, does not of itself establish a novation discharging duties of the assignor.

Illustrations:

2.   A and B enter into a contract binding A personally to do some delicate cabinet work. A assigns his rights and delegates performance of his duties to C. On being informed of this, B agrees with C in consideration of C's promise to do the work that B will accept C's work, if properly done, instead of the performance promised by A. Later without cause B refuses to allow C to proceed with the work, though C is ready to do so, and makes demand on A that A perform. A refuses. C can recover damages from B and B cannot recover from A.

3.   A contracts to employ B in A's business for one year at a specified salary. A contemplates selling the business, and the contract provides that the contract may be transferred with the business, but B is not informed of the identity of the purchaser. A month later A sells the business to C and assigns his rights and delegates his duties under the contract to C, who agrees to assume A's duties. After the sale B works for C and is paid by C for two weeks. C then discharges B because B refuses to accept a reduction in salary. There is a breach of contract by A as well as C.

REPORTER'S NOTE

This Section is based on former § 162. See 3 Williston, Contracts § 423 (3d ed. 1960); 4 Corbin, Contracts §§ 870–71 (1951).

Comment a. See, e.g., Abalene Pest Control Serv. v. Hall, 126 Vt. 1, 220 A.2d 717 (1966).

Comment b. Illustration 1 is based on Paige v. Faure, 229 N.Y. 114, 127 N.E. 898 (1920); cf. Standard Chau-tauqua System v. Gift, 120 Kan. 101, 242 P. 145 (1926). But cf. Mail-Well Envelope Co. v. Saley, 262 Or. 143, 497 P.2d 364 (1972); Baum v. Rock, 106 Colo. 567, 108 P.2d 230 (1940).

Comment c. Illustration 2 is based on Illustration 1 to former § 162. Illustration 3 is based on Clark v. General Cleaning Co., 345 Mass. 62, 185 N.E.2d 749 (1962).

TOPIC 2. MODE OF ASSIGNMENT OR DELEGATION

§ 324. Mode of Assignment in General

It is essential to an assignment of a right that the obligee manifest an intention to transfer the right to another person without further action or manifestation of intention by the obligee. The manifestation may be made to the other or to a third person on his behalf and, except as provided by statute or by contract, may be made either orally or by a writing.

Comment:

a. Requisites of assignment. Assignment requires an assignable right. See § 317. Aside from statute, the assignor of such a right may make an assignment by manifestation of intention without any particular formality. A manifestation of intention or a promise to make a transfer in the future is not an assignment, however. See § 330. Where the manifestation is made to a third person on behalf of the assignee, the assignment may not take effect unless there is an acceptance by the assignee; or it may take effect subject to disclaimer by the assignee. See § 327. Lack of formality may mean that the assignment is revocable (see § 332), or that it is subject to defenses or claims of the obligor which accrue subsequently (see §§ 336, 338), or that it can be defeated by creditors of the assignor or by subsequent assignees of the same right (see §§ 341, 342).

b. Statutory formalities: the Statute of Frauds. The Statute of Frauds is the subject of Chapter 5 of this Restatement. Section 4 of the Uniform Sales Act included a Statute of Frauds for "a contract to sell or a sale of any . . . choses in action of the value of five hundred dollars or upwards." The Uniform Commercial Code substitutes a general provision that "a contract for the sale of personal property is not enforceable by way of action or defense beyond five thousand dollars in amount or value of remedy" in the absence of a writing, with exceptions for the sale of goods or investment securities and for "security agreements," which are covered by more specific sections. Uniform Commercial Code § 1–206. Such provisions prevent enforcement against an assignor unless there is a memorandum in writing or some substitute formality, but under the rule stated in § 144 of this Restatement they cannot ordinarily be asserted by third persons, including the obligor of an assigned right. Notwithstanding non-compliance with the Statute, therefore, the assignment is effective against the obligor. Moreover, the obligor discharges his duty by performing in accordance with the assignment, and the assignee can keep the benefit of the performance.

c. Security agreements; wage assignments. Uniform Commercial Code § 9–203 provides that with stated exceptions "a security interest is not enforceable against the debtor or third parties" unless the collateral is in the possession of the secured party or the debtor has signed a security agreement. This provision applies not only where the "debtor" assigns contractual rights as security for an obligation, but also where the "debtor" is a "seller of accounts or chattel paper." §§ 1–201(37), 9–102(1)(b), 9–105(1)(d); see the Statutory Note at the beginning of this Chapter and the Reporter's Note to § 317. Transactions subject to this provision are not enforceable against anyone unless the statutory formalities are met. Statutes regulating assignments of wages may go further and deny all effect to a non-complying assignment.

REPORTER'S NOTE

This Section is based on former §§ 149(1) and 157. See 3 Williston, Contracts §§ 404, 430 (3d ed. 1960); 4 Corbin, Contracts §§ 861, 879 (1951).

Comment a. See Monegan v. Pacific Nat'l Bank, 16 Wash. App. 280, 556 P.2d 226 (1976); Twin Valley Motors v. Morale, 136 Vt. 115, 385 A.2d 678 (1978); Certified Collectors v. Lesnick, 116 Ariz. 601, 570 P.2d 769 (1977). Courts often speak of the requirement that the purported assignor completely divest himself of control. See, e.g., Monegan v. Pacific Nat'l Bank, supra; Miller v. Wells Fargo Int'l Bank, 540 F.2d 548 (2d Cir. 1976); S.L. Nusbaum & Co. v. Atlantic Virginia Realty Corp., 206 Va. 673, 146 S.E.2d 205 (1966).

§ 325. Order as Assignment

(1) A written order drawn upon an obligor and signed and delivered to another person by the obligee is an assignment if it is conditional on the existence of a duty of the drawee to the drawer to comply with the order and the drawer manifests an intention that a person other than the drawer is to retain the performance.

(2) An order which directs the drawee to render a performance without reference to any duty of the drawee is not of itself an assignment, even though the drawee is under a duty to the drawer to comply with the order and even though the order indicates a particular account to be debited or any other fund or source from which reimbursement is expected.

Comment:

a. Order on particular fund. The principal application of Subsection (1) is to rights to the payment of money, but it also applies to other rights. The creditor typically delivers to the assignee a written instrument addressed to the debtor, directing the debtor to pay all or part of the debt to the assignee. The instrument may be delivered instead to some other person on the assignee's behalf. See § 327. It may or may not indicate the ultimate disposition of the proceeds. Facts aside from the instrument may show that the recipient is to act as the creditor's agent rather than as assignee. An order communicated only to the debtor is not an assignment unless there is some additional manifestation of intention to assign.

Illustrations:

1. A delivers to C the following writing addressed to B, "Pay C for his own use $100 out of the amount you owe me." The writing is an assignment.

2. A gives C, acting as A's agent, an order to collect from B whatever B owes A. The order is not an assignment.

3. A writes to B, "Please pay to C the balance due me." This is insufficient to establish an assignment or to give B notice of an assignment. But the letter would be an effective assignment if delivered to C to pay or secure a debt owed by A to C.

b. Drafts and delivery orders. A check or other draft is an unconditional order for the payment of money meeting formal requisites of certainty in amount and time of payment. If payable to order or bearer, it is negotiable; whether or not negotiable, it is not of itself an assignment of a right against the drawee, and the drawee is not liable on the instrument until he accepts it. Additional facts may show that an assignment is intended, and the instrument may then be the means by which the assignment is effected. See Uniform Commercial Code §§ 3–104, 3–409, 3–805. Similar principles apply to unaccepted orders for the delivery of goods, whether or not conditional, if in negotiable form. See Uniform Commercial Code §§ 7–502, 7–503, 7–504. They also apply to any order which is treated as chargeable against the general credit of the drawer and independent of any particular fund or obligation. As to what terms render an order conditional for this purpose, see Uniform Commercial Code § 3–105.

Illustrations:

    4. A draws and delivers to C for value either a negotiable or a non-negotiable check upon his bank, B, payable to C, for the full amount of A's balance, or for part of it. B dishonors the check in violation of its duty to A. C has no right against B.

    5. In Illustration 4, B accepts the check by signing a certification on its face and redelivering it to C. There is a novation substituting C for A as B's creditor to the amount of the check.

    6. In Illustration 4, A and C agree that the check will operate as an assignment. The agreement is effective as between A and C. Its effect on B is subject to the rules relating to adverse claims to bank deposits.

REPORTER'S NOTE

This Section is based on former § 163. See 3 Williston, Contracts §§ 425–27 (3d ed. 1960); 4 Corbin, Contracts § 880 (1951); Annot., 80 A.L.R. 413, 423 (1932).

Comment a. Illustrations 1 and 2 are based on Illustrations 1 and 2 to former § 163. Illustration 3 is new; it is based on Associated Metals & Minerals Corp. v. Isletmeleri, 6 Ill. App.2d 548, 128 N.E.2d 595 (1955); James Talcott, Ltd. v. John Lewis & Co., [1940] 3 All E.R. 592 (C.A.); Halvorson v. Commerce Trust Co., 222 S.W. 897 (Mo. Ct. App. 1920);

Willow City Farmers Elevator v. Vogel, Vogel, Brantner & Kelly, 268 N.W.2d 762 (N.D. 1978); cf. Edmund W. Ginsberg Corp. v. C.D. Kepner Leather Co., 317 Mass. 581, 59 N.E.2d 253 (1945).

Comment b. Illustration 4 is based on Illustration 3 to former § 163. Illustration 5 is based on Uniform Commercial Code §§ 3–410, 3–411. Illustration 6 is based on Leach v. Mechanics Sav. Bank, 202 Iowa 899, 211 N.W. 506 (1926); cf. Willow City Farmers Elevator v. Vogel, Vogel, Brantner & Kelly, supra (relying on Uniform Commercial Code § 4–303).

See Appendix for Court Citations and Cross References

§ 326. Partial Assignment

(1) Except as stated in Subsection (2), an assignment of a part of a right, whether the part is specified as a fraction, as an amount, or otherwise, is operative as to that part to the same extent and in the same manner as if the part had been a separate right.

(2) If the obligor has not contracted to perform separately the assigned part of a right, no legal proceeding can be maintained by the assignor or assignee against the obligor over his objection, unless all the persons entitled to the promised performance are joined in the proceeding, or unless joinder is not feasible and it is equitable to proceed without joinder.

Comment:

   a. Other types of divided interests. The partial assignment covered by this Section is to be distinguished from other transactions creating divided interests in a contractual right: (1) A conditional assignment leaves the assignor with an interest if the condition is not met. (2) A total assignment may empower the assignee to enforce the entire right wholly or partially for the benefit of the assignor or others. Examples are assignment to secure an obligation and assignment to a trustee. (3) The obligee may promise to enforce the right wholly or partially for the benefit of others, or to pay to others all or part of any proceeds collected. Such a promise may amount to a declaration of trust or may create an equitable interest in the promisee by virtue of a right to specific performance of the promise.

   b. Partial assignment. The distinguishing feature of a partial assignment is a manifestation of intention to make an immediate transfer of part but not all of the assignor's right, and to confer on the assignee a direct right against the obligor to the performance of that part. Historically, the right of a partial assignee could be enforced only by a suit in a court of equity, and it was therefore sometimes described as an "equitable" right. But the right of a total assignee also had historically an "equitable" character. Under the rule stated in Subsection (1), a partial assignment and a total assignment are equally effective, subject to the protection of the obligor under the rule stated in Subsection (2).

Illustrations:

1. B owes A $100. A assigns $25 to C. With knowledge of the assignment, B pays the entire debt to A. B's duty to C is not discharged. See § 338.

2. B owes A $100. A assigns $25 to C, and later assigns the entire debt to D, who pays value without notice of the assignment to C. C has the same priority as to the $25 assigned to him as if the entire debt had been assigned to him. See § 342.

c. *Joinder.* The obligee of a right cannot bring successive actions to enforce parts of it. The right is merged in a judgment enforcing it in part, and subsequent actions are barred. See Restatement, Second, Judgments § 24. But where the obligor has notice of an assignment, a judgment for or against the assignor does not bar a subsequent action by the assignee. See Restatement, Second, Judgments §§ 37, 55; compare § 338, infra. To protect the obligor against multiple actions in a case of partial assignment, therefore, the rule stated in Subsection (2) entitles him to require joinder of all the obligees. This protection is limited by its reason: it is not available if the obligor has assented to the partial assignment. Moreover, it yields to equitable considerations if joinder is not feasible; in such cases the question whether an action may proceed depends on the probability of material prejudice to the obligor, the extent to which relief can be so shaped as to avoid such prejudice, the adequacy of the relief which can be afforded to the parties before the court, and the availability of adequate alternative remedies. See Rule 19 of the Federal Rules of Civil Procedure.

Illustrations:

3. B owes A $100. A assigns $25 to C. Neither A nor C can maintain an action against B over B's objection unless the other is joined in the proceeding.

4. The facts being otherwise as stated in Illustration 3, B pays the $75 balance to A. C can maintain an action against B for $25 without joining A.

REPORTER'S NOTE

This Section is based on former § 156. The limitation on an action by the assignor in Subsection (2) is new, following 4 Corbin, Contracts § 889 (1951). See also 3 Williston, Contracts §§ 441–44 (3d ed. 1960).

Comment b. Illustrations 1, 3 and 4 are based on Illustration 1 to former § 156. Illustration 1 is based on Graham v. Southern Ry., 173 Ga. 573, 161 S.E. 125 (1931); see Annot., 80 A.L.R. 413 (1932). Contra: Pelican

Supply Co. v. Shreveport Plumbing Co., 128 So.2d 924 (La. App. 1961). Cf. Certified Collectors v. Lesnick, 116 Ariz. 601, 570 P.2d 769 (1977). Illustration 2 follows Fairbanks v. Sargent, 104 N.Y. 108, 9 N.E. 870 (1887), 117 N.Y. 320, 22 N.E. 1039 (1889); see 3 Williston, Contracts § 435 (1960); 4 Corbin, Contracts § 902 (1951). Contra: King Bros. & Co. v. Central of Georgia Ry., 135 Ga. 225, 69 S.E. 113 (1910). Illustration 3 is based on Walter & Sullivan v. J. Murphy & Sons, [1955] 2 Q.B. 584 (C.A.); cf. First Nat'l Bank of Wayne v. Gross Real Estate Co., 162 Neb. 343, 75 N.W.2d 704 (1956). See also International Rediscount Corp. v. Hartford Accident Co., 425 F. Supp. 669, 676 n.20 (D. Del. 1977); and D'Orazi v. Bank of Canton, 254 Cal. App.2d 901, 62 Cal. Rptr. 704 (1967), discussing the use of equity procedure to avoid multiplicity of actions. Illustration 4 is based on Staples v. Rush, 99 So.2d 502 (La. App. 1958); cf. Finance Corp. v. Modern Materials Co., 312 P.2d 455 (Okl. 1957); Crane Co. v. National Heating Corp., 123 A.2d 366 (D.C. Ct. App. 1956).

§ 327.   Acceptance or Disclaimer by the Assignee

(1) A manifestation of assent by an assignee to the assignment is essential to make it effective unless

(a) a third person gives consideration for the assignment, or

(b) the assignment is irrevocable by virtue of the delivery of a writing to a third person.

(2) An assignee who has not manifested assent to an assignment may, within a reasonable time after learning of its existence and terms, render it inoperative from the beginning by disclaimer.

Comment:

a. *Necessity of acceptance.* Sale of a contractual right, like sale of goods, requires a bargain in which there is a manifestation of mutual assent to the exchange. Ordinarily the person who furnishes the consideration is the transferee of the right sold, but where consideration is given by one person for an assignment to another, it is not necessary that the assignee know of the bargain or assent to it. Compare §§ 17, 71(2). Where there is no bargain, an irrevocable gift can be made without the assent of the donee by the delivery of a written assignment or a symbolic or evidentiary writing to a third person. Compare §§ 104, 306; Restatement, Second, Trusts §§ 35, 36. The circumstances in which such a delivery makes the assignment irrevocable are stated in § 332.

See Appendix for Court Citations and Cross References

Illustrations:

1. A has a contractual right against D. For consideration received from B, A assigns the right to B's son C. C has no knowledge of the assignment. The assignment is effective immediately, subject to C's power of disclaimer.

2. A delivers his savings bank book to B, saying "I deliver this book to you as a gift to C." C has no knowledge of the gift. An attempted revocation by A before C learns of the gift is ineffective.

b. Disclaimer. As in other cases of rights created without the assent of the obligee, an assignee is entitled to reject the right, whether or not there is a related burden. Compare §§ 38, 104, 306. No particular formality is required for disclaimer, and its usual effect is the same as if no assignment had been made. But it cannot make tortious acts lawful when done, and in some cases it may give rise to a right of restitution. See Comment *a* to § 306. The effect of intervening claims of third persons is beyond the scope of this Restatement.

Illustration:

3. A, the payee of a negotiable or non-negotiable note or certificate of deposit, delivers it to B without indorsement as a gift to C, who has no knowledge of the delivery. Upon learning of the gift C refuses it. A is the owner of the note or certificate.

REPORTER'S NOTE

This Section is derived from former § 159, but is substantially rewritten. The exceptions in Subsection (1) are limited to situations involving third parties because the assignee's assent will be implicit if he gives consideration or receives without timely objection delivery of a writing making the assignment irrevocable.

See 3 Williston, Contracts §§ 424, 436–37 (1960); 4 Corbin, Contracts § 871 (1951).

Comments a and b. Illustrations 1–3 are based on Illustrations 1–3 to former § 159.

§ 328. Interpretation of Words of Assignment; Effect of Acceptance of Assignment

(1) Unless the language or the circumstances indicate the contrary, as in an assignment for security, an assignment of "the contract" or of "all my rights under the contract" or an assignment in similar general terms is an assignment of the assignor's rights and a

delegation of his unperformed duties under the contract.

(2) Unless the language or the circumstances indicate the contrary, the acceptance by an assignee of such an assignment operates as a promise to the assignor to perform the assignor's unperformed duties, and the obligor of the assigned rights is an intended beneficiary of the promise.

Caveat: **The Institute expresses no opinion as to whether the rule stated in Subsection (2) applies to an assignment by a purchaser of his rights under a contract for the sale of land.**

Comment:

    a. "Assignment" of duty. A duty cannot be "assigned" in the sense in which "assignment" is used in this Chapter. The parties to an assignment, however, may not distinguish between assignment of rights and delegation of duties. A purported "assignment" of duties may simply manifest an intention that the assignee shall be substituted for the assignor. Such an intention is not completely effective unless the obligor of the assigned right joins in a novation, but the rules of this Section give as full effect as can be given without the obligor's assent. As to contracts for the sale of goods, see Uniform Commercial Code § 2–210.

Illustration:

    1. A, an oil company, has a contract to sell and deliver oil to B. A delivers to C, another oil company, a writing assigning to C "the contract" or "all A's rights and duties under the contract." C is under a duty to B to deliver the oil called for by the contract, and A is surety for C.

    b. Contrary agreement; assignment for security. This Section states rules of presumptive interpretation which yield to a manifestation of a different intention. In particular delegation and assumption of the assignor's duties is not ordinarily implied where the contract calls for personal performance by the assignor. Again, an assignment as security does not ordinarily delegate performance to the secured party, and the secured party does not assume the assignor's duties. See Uniform Commercial Code §§ 2–210, 9–317. Under §§ 9–102 and 9–104 of the Code a sale of "accounts or chattel paper" is treated as a secured transaction unless it is part of the sale of a business or unless the assignee is to perform the contract. The quoted terms are limited by definitions in §§ 9–105 and 9–106 to "monetary obligations" or "rights to payment." See Reporter's Note to § 317.

Illustrations:

    2. In Illustration 1, A assigns "the contract" or "all A's rights under the contract" to C, a financial institution. Delivery of the oil is not delegated to C, and C is under no duty to deliver oil.

    3. A sells and delivers an automobile to B, the price to be paid in installments, and assigns to C for value "all A's rights under the contract." After B has made all the payments, the automobile is discovered to have been stolen and is retaken by the owner. C is not liable to B for breach of warranty of title; A is.

    c. Land contracts. By virtue of the right of either party to obtain specific performance of a contract for the sale of land, such contracts are treated for many purposes as creating a property interest in the purchaser and thus as partially executed. The vendor's interest resembles the interest of a mortgagee under a mortgage given as security for the purchase price. An assignment of the vendor's rights under the contract is similar to an assignment of a right to payment for goods or services: ordinarily no assumption of the vendor's duties by the assignee is implied merely from the acceptance of the assignment.

    When the purchaser under a land contract assigns his rights, the assignment has commonly been treated like a sale of land "subject to" a mortgage. In this view acceptance of the assignment does not amount to an assumption of the assignor's duties unless the contract of assignment so provides either expressly or by implication. A provision in the land contract that it will bind the "assigns" of the parties does not change this result. See Comment *b* to § 323. The assignee may, however, bind himself by later action such as bringing a suit for specific performance. Decisions refusing to infer an assumption of duties by the assignee have been influenced by doctrinal difficulties in the recognition of rights of assignees and beneficiaries. Those difficulties have now been overcome, and it is doubtful whether adherence to such decisions carries out the probable intention of the parties in the usual case. But since the shift in doctrine has not yet produced any definite change in the body of decisions, the Institute expresses no opinion on the application of Subsection (2) to an assignment by a purchaser under a land contract.

Illustration:

    4. A contracts to purchase land from B. The contract provides that it is to bind the assigns of the parties. A assigns "the contract" to C, and B assigns "the contract" to D. These facts themselves do not show a promise by D; the Institute expresses no opinion as to whether they show a promise by C.

REPORTER'S NOTE

This Section is revised from former § 164 to follow the phrasing of Uniform Commercial Code § 2–210. The application of Subsection (2) to land contracts is subjected to a new caveat because of the rejection of the rule stated in former § 164 in Langel v. Betz, 250 N.Y. 159, 164 N.E. 890 (1928).

See 3 Williston, Contracts § 418A (3d ed. 1960); 4 Corbin, Contracts § 906 (1951 & Supps. 1971 & 1980).

Comment a. Illustration 1 is based on Imperial Ref. Co. v. Kanotex Ref. Co., 29 F.2d 193 (8th Cir. 1928); cf. Art Metal Constr. Co. v. Lehigh Structural Steel Co., 116 F.2d 57 (3d Cir. 1940).

Comment b. Illustration 2 follows Uniform Commercial Code § 9–317; cf. Miller v. Wells Fargo Bank Int'l Corp., 540 F.2d 548, 558–60 (2d Cir. 1976); Stowell v. Gram, 184 Mass. 562, 69 N.E. 342 (1904). Illustration 3 is based on Daniels v. Parker, 209 Or. 419, 306 P.2d 735 (1957); cf. Chatham Pharmaceuticals, Inc. v. Angier Chem. Co., 347 Mass. 208, 196 N.E.2d 852 (1964).

Comment c. Illustration 4 is based on the facts of Langel v. Betz, 250 N.Y. 159, 164 N.E. 890 (1928), where the court refused to infer a promise by the purchaser's assignee. Cf. Goldsmith v. Deitchman, 69 N.Y.S.2d 148 (County Court 1947).

Accord: Henock v. Yeamans, 340 F.2d 503, 505 (5th Cir. 1965) (Florida and Michigan law); Kneberg v. H.L. Green Co., 89 F.2d 100 (7th Cir. 1937) (Illinois law); Treadway v. Western Cotton Oil & Ginning Co., 40 Ariz. 125, 10 P.2d 371 (1932); Maloyfsky v. Schiraldi, 108 N.J. Eq. 190, 154 A. 404 (Ch. 1931), aff'd mem., 110 N.J. Eq. 660, 160 A. 636 (Ct. Err. & App. 1932); Hardinger v. Fullerton, 165 Wash. 483, 5 P.2d 987 (1931); Lingle Water Users' Ass'n v. Occidental Bldg. & Loan Ass'n, 43 Wyo. 41, 57, 297 P. 385, 390 (1931); Annot., 59 A.L.R. 954 (1929) (California, Georgia, Indiana, Minnesota, Montana, Nevada, North Carolina, South Dakota, West Virginia). Contra: Prudential Fed. Sav. & Loan Ass'n v. King, 22 Utah 2d 379, 453 P.2d 697 (1969); Lonas v. Metropolitan Mortgage & Sec. Co., 432 P.2d 603 (Alaska 1967). See also Rose v. Vulcan Material Co., 282 N.C. 643, 194 S.E.2d 521 (1973) (rejecting Langel v. Betz in a non-land sale context, but not discussing the distinction), 10 Wake Forest L. Rev. 179 (1974); cf. Bank of America Nat'l Trust & Sav. Ass'n v. McLaughlin, 152 Cal. App.2d Supp. 911, 313 P.2d 220 (1957); Hodges v. Campbell, 211 Or. 428, 316 P.2d 312 (1957); Radley v. Smith, 6 Utah 2d 314, 313 P.2d 465 (1957).

See Appendix for Court Citations and Cross References

§ 329. Repudiation by Assignor and Novation with As-signee

(1) The legal effect of a repudiation by an assignor of his duty to the obligor of the assigned right is not limited by the fact that the assignee is a competent person and has promised to perform the duty.

(2) If the obligor, with knowledge of such a repudiation, accepts any performance from the assignee without reserving his rights against the assignor, a novation arises by which the duty of the assignor is discharged and a similar duty of the assignee is substituted.

Comment:

  a. Repudiation and its effects. In some cases a repudiation by one party to a contract discharges the duty of the other party; in some cases it requires the other to treat as total a breach which might otherwise be partial, or it may itself be a total breach. See § 253; Uniform Commercial Code § 2–610. For these purposes repudiation includes a positive statement by an assignor that he will not or cannot substantially perform his duties, or any voluntary affirmative action which renders substantial performance apparently impossible. In some circumstances a statement that he doubts whether he will substantially perform, or that he takes no responsibility for performance, or even a failure to give adequate assurance of performance may have a similar effect. See §§ 250–51.

  b. Scope of obligor's assent. The assignment of a contractual right and delegation to the assignee of the assignor's duty is often a matter of course. The obligor of the assigned right may then have a right to withhold performance until he receives adequate assurance of performance by the assignee. Section 251. Failure to demand such assurance and acceptance of performance by the assignee manifest the obligor's assent to the assignment and delegation (see § 323), but not to the discharge of the assignor's duty. However, when the obligor knows that the delegating assignor has repudiated his duty he has reason to know that the performance of the assignee is offered by way of novation, and his silent acceptance of the performance operates as acceptance of the offer of novation. Compare § 69.

Illustrations:

     1.   A is under a contract with B to build a house for $10,000. A assigns his rights under the contract to C, who agrees to assume A's duty to build the house. B is informed of the assignment and assumption, and makes no objection as C partly performs. A remains bound to B as surety for C's performance.

     2.   In Illustration 1, A withdraws from the construction business and informs B that he takes no further responsibility for C's performance. B makes no objection and C proceeds with the work. A is discharged.

    c. Reservation of rights. The obligor of an assigned right cannot be forced to assent to a repudiation by the assignor or to an offer of a substituted contract with the assignee. To avoid the implication that his silence gives assent, he must manifest either to the assignor or to the assignee his intention to retain unimpaired his rights against the assignor, but no particular form is required. See Uniform Commercial Code §§ 1–207, 3–606; § 281. If the terms of the assignment so provide, the delegation or assumption of-duty may be defeated in such a case, and the repudiation may be retracted before it has been acted on. See Uniform Commercial Code § 2–611. Where the assignee continues performance, the reservation of rights by the obligor means that the assignor, if compelled to pay for the assignee's default, will have a right over against the assignee.

Illustration:

     3.   In Illustration 2, on being informed of A's repudiation, B notifies A or C that further performance is "without prejudice." A is not discharged.

REPORTER'S NOTE

This Section is based on former § 165. See 3 Williston, Contracts § 420 (3d ed. 1960); 4 Corbin, Contracts §§ 866–67 (1951 & Supps. 1971 & 1980).

Illustrations 1–3 are based on Illustration 1 to former § 165. Illustration 2 to former § 165 is omitted.

§ 330. Contracts to Assign in the Future, or to Transfer Proceeds to be Received

(1) A contract to make a future assignment of a right, or to transfer proceeds to be received in the future by the promisor, is not an assignment.

(2) Except as provided by statute, the effect of such a contract on the rights and duties of the obligor and third persons is determined by the rules relating to specific performance of contracts.

Comment:

a. Contract to assign. As to a right in existence, it is a question of interpretation whether the obligee manifests an intention to make a present transfer or only an intention to bind himself to make a future transfer. A present assignment may be coupled with a promise to provide future evidence of the transfer, but there is no assignment if the transfer is not to take place until the obligee acts further. Whether or not there is a present assignment, the assignee may be empowered to enforce the right. Such a power is ordinarily fairly implied when there is a purported present assignment of a future right, and once the right arises in such a case the situation is substantially similar to that created by a revocable assignment. See § 321.

Illustration:

1. A holds a promissory note made by B and secured by a mortgage on Blackacre. A enters into a written agreement with C which recites that A has sold the note and mortgage to C for a price payable in installments' and that A is to hold the note and mortgage as security for the price and to indorse the note and execute an assignment of the mortgage when the price is paid. There is a present assignment to C, subject to the security interest retained by A.

b. Contract to transfer proceeds. A promise by an obligee that he will collect money due him and pay over all or part of it to the promisee is not an assignment. The same rule applies to a promise to transfer proceeds other than money. Thus if a purchaser under a contract for the sale of land contracts to resell the land, there is a subcontract rather than an assignment of the original contract. But if the prospective transferee is authorized to receive performance on behalf of the obligee-transferor and to retain it, there may be an assignment of the contractual right. The test is whether an intention is manifested to transfer present ownership of the right.

Illustrations:

2. A sells property to B and authorizes B to pay the price to X, a bank, on A's behalf. Later A borrows money from C and agrees to repay C out of the money received from B. A then

instructs X to hold for the account of A and C all sums received from B, stating "C does not claim this money as owner, but you are to hold it until you have been advised in writing by both parties." There is no assignment to C.

3. A, the holder of a note payable by B, delivers it to C, A's attorney, for collection, agreeing that C is co-owner of the claim to the extent of half of what he collects. C is a partial assignee of the right against B.

c. *Contracts specifically enforceable.* In some circumstances a contract to assign or a contract to transfer proceeds may create a right in the promisee very similar to that of an assignee. Even though there is no present assignment, the promisee may have a right to specific performance of the promise. If it can be enforced against third parties, such a right resembles that of an assignee, and it is sometimes referred to as an "equitable assignment" or "equitable lien." In general the remedy of specific performance is available if the promisee's remedy in damages would be inadequate. See §§ 359, 360. In particular, specific performance is decreed if the promise is one to transfer an interest in specific land or to transfer a specified right as security for an obligation.

Illustrations:

4. A, a real estate broker, is employed by B to find a purchaser for B's land. In consideration of C's help in finding a purchaser, A promises to pay C one-half of the commission earned. The land is sold and the commission earned. C has no right against B.

5. B, the owner of a parcel of land, contracts to sell the parcel to A. A contracts to assign the contract to C or to convey the parcel to C. Even though C is not an assignee, C can sue A and B to compel A to assert for C's benefit A's right to specific performance by B.

6. As part of a property settlement in divorce proceedings A contracts with his wife C to make an irrevocable change in the beneficiary of a policy of insurance on A's life to D, their minor child. A fails to do so and later gratuitously makes his second wife E the beneficiary of the policy. On A's death B, the insurance company, pays the amount of the policy into court and interpleads C, D and E. D is entitled to the money.

d. *After-acquired rights.* In general a contract to give security is specifically enforceable as between the parties even as to rights arising after the contract is made. By statute or decision, however, an exception has been made for contracts to assign wages under future employments. See § 321. And in some states, on the analogy of rules applied to mortgages of after-acquired tangible property, an "equitable assignment" of rights not in existence is subordinate to the claims of creditors of the assignor whose rights attach after the rights have arisen and before the assignor has made a present assignment. In the absence of statutory provision for public notice, the rights of the promisee are inferior to those of a subsequent good faith purchaser for value without notice of the prior contract.

Illustrations:

7. A "assigns" to C as security for a loan "all the book debts due and owing or which may during the continuance of this security become due and owing" to A. B subsequently becomes indebted to A on a contract made after the "assignment," and thereafter a creditor of A garnishes the debt. In the absence of a statute, C is entitled to the debt to the exclusion of the creditor.

8. The facts being otherwise as stated in Illustration 7, A assigns the debt to D after it arises. D takes the assignment in good faith as a purchaser for value, without notice of the "assignment" to C. In the absence of statute, D is entitled to the debt to the exclusion of C.

e. The Uniform Commercial Code. The provisions of Article 9 of the Uniform Commercial Code apply to "accounts" and "general intangibles," but not to insurance, bank accounts or wages. See Introductory Note to this Chapter. Under § 9–204(1) a security agreement "may provide that any or all obligations covered by the security agreement are to be secured by after-acquired collateral." When a security interest "attaches" is governed by § 9–203, "unless explicit agreement postpones the time of attaching." § 9–203(2). The security interest is subordinate to the rights of creditors of the debtor and purchasers from him if it is unperfected. See § 9–301. But if the filing provisions of the Code have been complied with beforehand, the security interest is perfected when it attaches. See § 9–303.

REPORTER'S NOTE

Subsection (1) is derived from the first sentence of Subsection (1) of former § 166. The inclusion of contracts to transfer proceeds is new. Subsection (2) is expanded from former Subsection (1) (as described in Comment *a* to former § 166), to include contracts other than those made to secure performance. The remainder of former Subsection (1) is dealt with in Comment *d*. Former Subsection (2) is replaced by the reference in present Subsection (2) to the rules relating to specific performance of contracts.

See 3 Williston, Contracts §§ 428–29 (3d ed. 1960); 4 Corbin, Contracts § 877 (1951 & Supp. 1971).

Comment a. Illustration 1 is based on Ingram v. Mandler, 56 F.2d 994 (10th Cir. 1932).

Comment b. On the question of present ownership of a right, see Twin Valley Motors v. Morale, 136 Vt. 115, 385 A.2d 678 (1978); Time Fin. Corp. v. Johnson Trucking Co., 23 Utah 2d 115, 458 P.2d 873 (1969); Trak Microwave Corp. v. Medaris Mgt., Inc., 236 So.2d 189 (Fla. Dist. Ct. App. 1970). Illustration 2 is based on Reserve Plan, Inc. v. Peters, 71 N.M. 25, 375 P.2d 576 (1962); cf. American Agency & Inv. Co. v. Gregg, 90 Colo. 142, 6 P.2d 1101 (1931) (salesman of burial lots); see Annots., 32 A.L.R. 950 (1924), 101 A.L.R. 81 (1936). Illustration 3 is based on Mirasola v. Rodgers, 120 W. Va. 685, 200 S.E. 30 (1938); see Annots., 124 A.L.R. 1508 (1940), 143 A.L.R. 204 (1943), 175 A.L.R. 1132 (1948).

Comment c. See 4 Pomeroy, Equity Jurisprudence §§ 1283a, 1288–91 (5th ed. 1941). Illustration 4 is based on Donovan v. Middlebrook, 95 A.D. 365, 88 N.Y.S. 607 (1st Dep't 1904); S.L. Nusbaum & Co. v. Atlantic Virginia Realty Corp., 206 Va. 673, 146 S.E.2d 205 (1966). Illustration 5 is based on Miller v. Dyer, 20 Cal.2d 526, 127 P.2d 901 (1942); cf. Morris v. George C. Banning, Inc., 49 Ohio L. Abs. 530, 77 N.E.2d 372 (1947); Wilmurth v. National Liberty Ins. Co., 239 Mo. App. 1177, 206 S.W.2d 730 (1947); see Annot., 141 A.L.R. 1432 (1942); 3 American Law of Property § 11.37 (1952); 4 Williston, Contracts § 954A (1964). But cf. R & R Homes, Inc. v. Gellman, 144 N.Y.S.2d 54 (Sup. Ct. 1955). Illustration 6 is based on McPhail v. John Hancock Mut. Life Ins. Co., 108 F. Supp. 902 (W.D. Ky. 1952); cf. Annot., 19 A.L.R.2d 5 (1951).

Comment d. See 1 Gilmore, Security Interests in Personal Property §§ 2.4, 7.10 (1965); Cohen & Gerber, The After-Acquired Property Clause, 87 U. Pa. L. Rev. 635 (1939), Mortgages of Accounts Receivable, 29 Georgetown L.J. 555 (1941); Annots., 72 A.L.R. 856 (1931), 116 A.L.R. 955 (1938); Note, 67 Yale L.J. 847 (1958). Illustration 7 is based on Tailby v. Official Receiver, 13 App. Cas. 523 (H.L. 1888); cf. East Lewisburg Lumber & Mfg. Co. v. Marsh, 91 Pa. 96 (1879). Contra: Taylor v. Barton-Child Co., 228 Mass. 126, 117 N.E. 43 (1917); cf. Wheeler Co. v. Abbott-Beeber Co., 64 R.I. 421, 12 A.2d 657 (1940); Manchester Nat'l Bank v. Roche, 186 F.2d 827 (1st Cir. 1951) (N.H. law); Monegan v. Pacific Nat'l Bank, 16 Wash. App. 280, 556 P.2d 226 (1976). Illustration 8 is based on State Factors Corp. v. Sales Factors Corp., 257 A.D. 101, 12 N.Y.S.2d 12 (1st Dep't 1939); cf. Stokely Bros. v. Conklin, 131 N.J. Eq. 552, 26 A.2d 147 (Ch. 1942).

Comment e. See 2 Coogan et al., Secured Transactions under the Uniform Commercial Code ch. 15 (1978); Industrial Packaging Prods. Co. v. Fort Pitt Packaging Int'l Inc., 399 Pa. 643, 161 A.2d 19 (1960).

TOPIC 3. EFFECT BETWEEN ASSIGNOR AND ASSIGNEE

§ 331. Partially Effective Assignments

An assignment may be conditional, revocable, or voidable by the assignor, or unenforceable by virtue of a Statute of Frauds.

Comment:

   a. Assignor's power to destroy assignee's right. In this Restatement "assignment" is used to refer to an act which extinguishes in whole or in part the assignor's right and creates a similar right in the assignee. See §§ 317, 324. On proof of an unconditional assignment, the assignee can recover on an assigned right; the assignor cannot. The assignor may be entitled to revoke the assignment because it is gratuitous or by virtue of a reserved power, or the assignment may be voidable for fraud or other invalidating cause. Even if destruction of the assignee's right is a violation of the assignor's duty, he retains by virtue of his former ownership certain powers which may have that effect. See §§ 338, 342.

   b. Conditional assignment; conditional and future rights. A conditional assignment does not wholly extinguish the assignor's right until the condition occurs. A conditional right may be effectively assigned either conditionally or unconditionally; a conditional assignment of a conditional right means that the rights of the assignee and assignor are both subject to one condition and that the right of the assignee is subject to an additional condition. See § 323. Strictly there cannot be an effective assignment of a right not yet in existence, but after the right arises the assignment may for some purposes be treated as if it had been effective when made. See §§ 321, 330.

Illustration:

   1. A has a right to $400 against B and assigns the right to C in payment for an automobile on condition that the car run 1,000 miles without needing repairs. The assignment is conditional and is effective according to its terms. If the car does not run 1,000 miles without needing repairs, the right to the $400 belongs to A, not to C.

REPORTER'S NOTE

This Section is modified from Subsection (2) to former § 150. See 3 Williston, Contracts § 404 (3d ed. 1960); 4 Corbin, Contracts §§ 861, 874–79 (1951).

Comment b. Illustration 1 is based on Illustration 2 to former § 150.

§ 332. Revocability of Gratuitous Assignments

(1) Unless a contrary intention is manifested, a gratuitous assignment is irrevocable if

(a) the assignment is in a writing either signed or under seal that is delivered by the assignor; or

(b) the assignment is accompanied by delivery of a writing of a type customarily accepted as a symbol or as evidence of the right assigned.

(2) Except as stated in this Section, a gratuitous assignment is revocable and the right of the assignee is terminated by the assignor's death or incapacity, by a subsequent assignment by the assignor, or by notification from the assignor received by the assignee or by the obligor.

(3) A gratuitous assignment ceases to be revocable to the extent that before the assignee's right is terminated he obtains

(a) payment or satisfaction of the obligation, or

(b) judgment against the obligor, or

(c) a new contract of the obligor by novation.

(4) A gratuitous assignment is irrevocable to the extent necessary to avoid injustice where the assignor should reasonably expect the assignment to induce action or forbearance by the assignee or a subassignee and the assignment does induce such action or forbearance.

(5) An assignment is gratuitous unless it is given or taken

(a) in exchange for a performance or return promise that would be consideration for a promise; or

(b) as security for or in total or partial satisfaction of a pre-existing debt or other obligation.

Comment:

a. Historical note. Before the assignment of a contractual right was recognized as effective by common-law courts, an assignment was treated as a power of attorney. Exercise of the power to create a new legal right in the assignee was recognized as effective by the common-law courts in the seventeenth century. But in the event of revocation by the assignor before the power was exercised, the assignee's right was enforceable only by a court of equity. See the Introductory Note to this Chapter. A power of attorney requires no consideration, but the maxim that equity will not aid a volunteer precluded relief to a gratuitous assignee in the event of revocation before the power was exercised. In modern times an assignment is recognized as an effective conveyance without regard to the distinction between law and equity. But a gratuitous conveyance remains revocable unless the formal requisites of a valid gift are met. The owner of a contractual right, like the owner of a chattel, can effectively and irrevocably declare himself trustee of it without consideration or formality, but an attempted informal gift which is ineffective does not create a trust. See Restatement, Second, Trusts §§ 28, 31. In certain cases, however, where the donor has died believing he has made an effective gratuitous conveyance to a natural object of his bounty, a constructive trust for the intended donee may arise. See Restatement of Restitution § 164.

b. Formal requisites of gift; written assignment. Historically, a gift of a chattel could be made either by delivery of the chattel or by delivery of a deed of gift under seal. This rule has been extended by analogy to gifts of intangible personal property, including contractual rights. As the seal has come to seem archaic, the delivery of a signed written assignment has by statute or decision been given the same effect. The assignment may be delivered either conditionally or unconditionally, and either to the donee or to a third person on his behalf. Compare §§ 101–103. The writing must of course fully manifest an intention to make a present transfer rather than to promise or authorize a future transfer. Compare §§ 325, 330. As to investment securities, Uniform Commercial Code § 8–309 requires delivery of a certificated security, and an attempted transfer without delivery amounts only to a promise to transfer.

Illustrations:

1. B owes A four million dollars. A signs, seals and delivers to C a deed of gift of the debt to the extent of one million dollars. There is an effective and irrevocable assignment.

2. B owes A $70,000 represented by a promissory note payable to the order of A in installments. A signs and delivers to C, his sister, a written instrument not under seal reciting that in consideration of love and affection for C A gives and assigns to C fifty per cent of the note, reserving all installments due or paid during A's life. The note is retained in A's possession. The gift is effective and irrevocable.

3. A has a savings account in the B bank which is represented by a passbook. While in the hospital and about to undergo a serious operation, A signs the following note and gives it to a nurse for her husband C: "Dear Papa, the bank book is in my letter box in the kitchen. It is yours. Look out for yourself. My will is in the lawyer's office. Your loving wife." A dies before C takes possession of the passbook. There is no effective gift.

c. Delivery of a symbolic writing. In the regular course of business certain writings are treated as adequately evidencing that a person in possession of the writing is entitled to receive performance and to dispose of the right and its proceeds. See Uniform Commercial Code § 1–201(15), defining "document of title," § 3–104, defining certain types of negotiable instrument, § 8–102, defining "security," § 9–105(1)(b), defining "chattel paper." In some circumstances the right to performance is conditional on exhibition or surrender of such a writing. See Uniform Commercial Code § 3–505 (negotiable instrument), § 5–116 (letter of credit), § 7–403(3) (negotiable document of title), § 8–401 (certificated security). A gift of a right embodied in such a writing may be made by delivery in accordance with rules governing gifts of chattels by delivery.

Illustration:

4. A gratuitously delivers to B a savings bank book, a nonnegotiable promissory note, a life insurance policy and a registered bond with the expressed intent of making B the owner of the rights of which these documents are evidence. The delivery operates as an effective and irrevocable assignment of both the rights and the documents.

d. Delivery of an evidentiary writing. Even though a right is not conditional on exhibition or surrender of a document, it may be so integrated in a writing that contradictory terms of prior agreements and contemporaneous oral agreements are superseded. See §§ 213, 216; Uniform Commercial Code § 2–202. The "best evidence" or original document rule, permitting secondary evidence to prove the contents of a writing only when an explanation is given for nonproduction of the original, has been largely eviscerated by modern evidence practice. See, e.g., Fed. R. Evidence 1001–04. Even though the traditional rule does not apply, an evidentiary writing may be of such importance in the enforcement of the right that its delivery is an appropriate formality to validate a gift of the right. Accordingly, the rule validating a gift by delivery of an essential instrument has been extended to some evidentiary writings. The test is whether the writing is of a type customarily accepted as evidence of the right.

Illustrations:

    5. A makes a written contract with B to convey land to B for $25,000. Later A gratuitously delivers to C the written contract, signed by B, with the expressed intent of making C the owner of the right to the purchase money. The gift is effective and irrevocable.

    6. A deposits a draft with B bank for collection and is given a receipt signed by B which describes the draft and recites that it is "received from A for collection." A writes on the receipt, "Pay this to C," signs his name, and delivers the receipt to C with the expressed intent of making a gift to C of the proceeds of the draft. The gift is effective and irrevocable.

    7. A has a checking account in B bank and delivers the bank pass book to C with the expressed intent of making a gift to C of the balance in the account. The gift is revocable in view of the customary practice of making withdrawals without notation in the pass book, even though A has in fact made no such withdrawals.

    8. A deposits various sums of money with B, and keeps a list of the amounts on a sheet of paper. A delivers the list, bearing a total and a date but no signature or other writing, to C with the expressed intent of making a gift to C of the amount due. The gift is revocable.

    e. What constitutes delivery. Where a gift of a contractual right by delivery of a symbolic or evidentiary writing is in issue, the concept of delivery is the same as that employed with respect to gifts of tangible personal property. Delivery may be made either conditionally or unconditionally, and either to the donee or to a third person on his behalf. Compare §§ 101–03. A writing in the possession of a third person may be delivered by means of a symbolic or evidentiary writing or by means of a token or symbol such as a key to a safe deposit box. Or the third person may agree to hold on behalf of the donee. A gift of a writing already in the possession of the donee for another purpose may be made by mere oral manifestation of intention. Redelivery to the donor for safekeeping does not defeat the delivery. Where a different rule is applied to gifts of chattels, it is applied equally to gifts of contractual rights by delivery: thus if it is held that a gift *causa mortis* by mere spoken words is ineffective in the case of a chattel in the donee's possession, the same rule is applied to a gift of a contractual writing.

   f.   Effect of acts subsequent to assignment. A gratuitous assignment, even though revocable, may authorize the assignee to take action which will complete the gift. If, pursuant to the authority given, the assignee obtains performance or other satisfaction from the obligor or a judgment against the obligor or a new contract by novation, the assignor's power of revocation terminates and the assignee may keep for his own benefit what he has acquired. Whatever he obtains after revocation can be recovered from him by the assignor. Revocation is also precluded to the extent that it would be unjust in view of a material change of position in reliance on the assignment. Compare § 90.

Illustration:

   9.   A draws a check on his account in B bank payable to the order of C and delivers it to C with the expressed intent of making a gift to C of part of the account. C negotiates the check to D for value, or obtains payment from B. Meanwhile A dies. C can retain what he received before the death, but A's personal representative can recover what C received thereafter.

   g.   Effect of bankruptcy. Under § 541 of the Bankruptcy Reform Act of 1978, 11 U.S.C. § 541 (1978), the commencement of a case under the Act creates an estate, which includes with certain inapplicable exceptions all legal or equitable interests of the debtor in property as of the commencement of the case. Hence if a gratuitous assignment is revocable by an assignor at the time when he becomes bankrupt, his trustee in bankruptcy may exercise the power of revocation. Even if the assignment is otherwise irrevocable, the trustee in bankruptcy has the right of any creditor to set it aside if the assignor is insolvent or is rendered insolvent or if it is made with actual intent to hinder, delay, or defraud creditors. See Uniform Fraudulent Conveyance Act §§ 4, 7; Bankruptcy Reform Act of 1978, 11 U.S.C. § 548 (1978).

h. Gratuitous assignment. Whether an assignment is gratuitous for the purposes of the rules stated in this Section is not necessarily the same question as whether the assignment is for value so as to constitute the assignee a bona fide purchaser for value within such rules as that stated in § 342. See Comment *c* to § 338. For example, where an assignment is made in exchange for a return promise which would be consideration under the rule stated in § 75, the assignment is not gratuitous, whether or not the promise is value under the rules stated in Restatement, Second, Trusts § 302. A new loan or other obligation is consideration for this purpose if bargained for and given in exchange for the assignment. Moreover, an assignment as security for or in total or partial satisfaction of a pre-existing obligation is not gratuitous, whether or not there is consideration under § 73 or value under Restatement, Second, Trusts § 304 and Restatement of Restitution § 173. Such an assignment is not gratuitous even if the pre-existing obligation is unenforceable, to the extent that in the circumstances a promise to pay the obligation would be binding under §§ 82–85.

REPORTER'S NOTE

Subsection (1) is based on Subsections (1)(a) and (b) to former § 158, broadened to give effect to gifts by written assignment not under seal and by delivery of an evidentiary document. Subsections (2)–(4) are reworded from Subsections (1), (3) and (1)(c), respectively to former § 158. Subsection (5) is new; compare Subsection (4) to former § 149. See 3 Williston, Contracts §§ 438A–40 (3d ed. 1960); 4 Corbin, Contracts §§ 909–22 (1951); Brown, Personal Property §§ 8.1–8.8 (3d ed. 1975).

Comment a. See Gulliver & Tilson, Classification of Gratuitous Transfers, 51 Yale L.J. 1 (1941); Costigan, Gifts Inter Vivos of Choses in Action, 27 L.Q. Rev. 326 (1911).

Comment b. See Stone, Delivery in Gifts of Personal Property, 20 Colum. L. Rev. 196 (1920); Mechem, The Requirement of Delivery in Gifts of Chattels, 21 Ill. L. Rev. 341, 457,

568 (1926); Annots., 63 A.L.R. 537 (1929), 48 A.L.R.2d 1405 (1956). Illustration 1 is based on Chase Nat'l Bank v. Sayles, 11 F.2d 948 (1st Cir.), cert. denied, 273 U.S. 708 (1926). Illustration 2 is based on Thatcher v. Merriam, 121 Utah 191, 240 P.2d 266 (1952). Illustration 3 is based on Foster v. Reiss, 18 N.J. 41, 112 A.2d 553 (1955). See also Cassiday v. Cassiday, 256 Md. 5, 259 A.2d 299 (1969) (finding no intent to make a gift or assignment on fairly similar facts).

Comment c. See Annots., 40 A.L.R. 1249 (1926), 84 A.L.R. 558 (1933) (savings bank pass book); 23 A.L.R.2d 1171 (1952) (stock); 33 A.L.R.2d 273 (1954) (life insurance). Illustration 4 is based on Illustration 1 to former § 158, followed in Brooks v. Mitchell, 163 Md. 1, 161 A. 261 (1932); Hileman v. Hulver, 243 Md. 527, 221 A.2d 693 (1966).

Comment d. See Bruton, The Requirement of Delivery as Applied to Gifts of Choses in Action, 39 Yale L.J. 837 (1930); Williston, Gifts of Rights under Contracts in Writing by Delivery of the Writing, 40 Yale L.J. 1 (1930); Annots., 3 A.L.R. 933 (1919), 14 A.L.R. 707 (1921); cf. 63 A.L.R.2d 259 (1959) (gift to debtor). As to the original document rule, see McCormick, Evidence §§ 229–43 (2d ed. 1972 & Supp. 1978); 4 Wigmore, Evidence § 1177 et seq. (Chadbourn rev. 1972). Illustration 5 rejects the conclusion of Illustration 2 to former § 158; it is based on In re Huggins' Estate, 204 Pa. 167, 53 A. 746 (1902); cf. Davie v. Davie, 47 Wash. 231, 91 P. 950 (1907); Moore v. Darton, 4 De G. & S. 517 (Ch. 1851). Illustration 6 is based on Cronin v. Chelsea Sav. Bank, 201 Mass. 146, 87 N.E. 484 (1909). But cf. Matter of Cassola,

183 Misc. 66, 47 N.Y.S.2d 90 (Surr. Ct. 1944) (broker's statement of account). Illustration 7 is based on Burrows v. Burrows, 240 Mass. 485, 137 N.E. 923 (1922). Illustration 8 is based on Cook v. Lum, 55 N.J.L. 373, 26 A. 803 (1893).

Comment e. See Brown, Personal Property §§ 7.2–7.9 (3d ed. 1975); Mechem, The Requirement of Delivery in Gifts of Chattels, 21 Ill. L. Rev. 341, 457, 568 (1926).

Comment f. Illustration 9 is based on Burrows v. Burrows, 240 Mass. 485, 137 N.E. 923 (1922); Armstrong v. Armstrong, 142 Ill. App. 507 (1908); see Annot., 38 A.L.R.2d 594 (1954).

Comment h. Subsection (5) and Comment *h* depart from former § 149 (5) and (6), following instead Comment *b* to former § 166.

§ 333. Warranties of an Assignor

(1) Unless a contrary intention is manifested, one who assigns or purports to assign a right by assignment under seal or for value warrants to the assignee

(a) that he will do nothing to defeat or impair the value of the assignment and has no knowledge of any fact which would do so;

(b) that the right, as assigned, actually exists and is subject to no limitations or defenses good against the assignor other than those stated or apparent at the time of the assignment;

(c) that any writing evidencing the right which is delivered to the assignee or exhibited to him to induce him to accept the assignment is genuine and what it purports to be.

(2) An assignment does not of itself operate as a warranty that the obligor is solvent or that he will perform his obligation.

(3) An assignor is bound by affirmations and promises to the assignee with reference to the right assigned in the same way and to the same extent that one who transfers goods is bound in like circumstances.

(4) An assignment of a right to a sub-assignee does not operate as an assignment of the assignee's rights under his assignor's warranties unless an intention is manifested to assign the rights under the warranties.

Comment:

a. Implied warranties. The warranties of an assignor of a contractual right arise by operation by law and are similar to those of one who transfers a negotiable instrument without indorsement or who transfers a document of title or investment security. See Uniform Commercial Code §§ 3–417, 7–507, 8–306. Unlike an indorser of commercial paper or a collecting bank or its customer, an assignor is not liable for defaults of the obligor and does not warrant his solvency. Compare Uniform Commercial Code §§ 3–414, 4–207 with § 7–505 (document of title), § 8–308(9) (certificated investment security). An assignor does warrant his lack of knowledge of facts and his future abstention from conduct which would impair the value of the assigned right.

Illustrations:

1. A has a right against B and assigns it for value to C. Thereafter A gives B a release. C can recover damages from A for any harm this causes C. The amount of harm may be greater if B is released for value before he receives notification of the assignment than if B remains liable to C.

2. A has a right against B, performance of which B has repudiated without excuse. A assigns his right to C for value without disclosing B's repudiation. C can recover from A damages for any harm the repudiation causes C.

3. A reasonably and in good faith believes he has a right against B, and assigns it to C for value as an actual right. In fact the right does not exist. C can recover damages from A.

b. Express warranties and disclaimers. The rules stated in this Section can be varied by express or implied agreement. Express warranties are created in the same ways as express warranties in the transfer of goods, and implied warranties may be excluded or modified in the same ways. See Uniform Commercial Code §§ 2–312, 2–313, 2–316, 2–317. The words "without recourse" may be ambiguous in this context: ordinarily they are used to disclaim the liability of an indorser but do not eliminate implied warranties. See Uniform Commercial Code §§ 3–414, 3–417(3).

Illustration:

4. A believes that there is only a slight possibility that he may have a right against B. A assigns to C for value "Any claim or right" which he may have against B without disclosing how seriously he doubts the validity of the claim. A is under no duty to C if the claim is invalid.

c. *Warranty to a sub-assignee.* A sub-assignee may be an intended beneficiary of an assignor's warranty to an intermediate assignee, or the intermediate assignee may assign to the sub-assignee a claim for breach of warranty. But unless such an intention is manifested, the warranties of an assignor run only to his assignee, and are not transferred by a sub-assignment. Compare Uniform Commercial Code §§ 2–318, 2–607(5), 3–803.

d. *Remedies.* When a warranty of an assignor is broken, the assignee is entitled to the usual remedies for breach of contract. He can recover damages not only for harm caused but also for the amount by which he would have been benefited if the assigned right had been as warranted. But if the assigned right would have been worthless aside from the breach of warranty, there are no damages. The assignor is also subject to liability, at the assignee's election, for the value of anything received by him from the assignee on account of the assignment, or for any amount wrongfully collected from the obligor. In an appropriate case such equitable remedies as injunction and constructive trust are also available.

REPORTER'S NOTE

This Section is based on former § 175. See 3 Williston, Contracts § 445 (3d ed. 1960); 4 Corbin, Contracts § 904 (1951).

Comment a. That assignment, as opposed to endorsement, of a promissory note does not warrant that the obligor is solvent or that he will perform, see Lopez v. Puzina, 239 Cal. App.2d 708, 49 Cal. Rptr. 122 (1966). Illustrations 1–3 are based on Illustrations 1–3 to former § 175.

Comment b. Illustration 4 is based on Illustration 4 to former § 175.

TOPIC 4.   EFFECT ON THE OBLIGOR'S DUTY

§ 334.   Variation of Obligor's Duty by Assignment

(1) If the obligor's duty is conditional on the personal cooperation of the original obligee or another person, an assignee's right is subject to the same condition.

(2) If the obligor's duty is conditional on cooperation which the obligee could properly delegate to an agent, the condition may occur if there is similar cooperation by an assignee.

Comment:

a. Scope. This Section relates to the consequences of assignment of a right, stating corollaries of the statement in § 317 that a right cannot be assigned if the effect would be to change materially the duty of the obligor. Delegation of the performance of a duty or requirement of a condition is the subject of §§ 318 and 319. Those Sections apply the same principles applied by this Section to determine when the obligor's duty is conditional on the obligee's personal cooperation and when the obligee could properly delegate cooperation to an agent. See also Restatement, Second, Agency § 17.

b. Terms of assignment. Whether there is a material change in the obligor's duty depends not only on the terms of the contract creating the duty and on the circumstances, but also on the terms of the assignment. Commonly an assignment manifests an intention that the obligor render performance to the assignee rather than to the assignor. Such a change is immaterial in the usual case of a duty to pay money, but material where personal cooperation is made a condition of the duty. Even in the latter case, however, it is at least theoretically possible to assign the right without departing from the requirement.

Illustrations:

1.   B contracts to sell A specified goods for a stated price. A effectively assigns his right to C. On tender of the agreed price, C has a right to take delivery of the goods at the agreed time and place.

2.   B contracts to sell and deliver 100 gallons of fuel oil to A at A's house. C lives next door to A and has equal facility for receiving delivery of oil. A assigns his right under the contract to C and directs B to deliver the oil at C's house. B is under a duty to do so. The change in the required performance is too slight to give B a valid objection.

3. B contracts with A to furnish A's family with all the oil it shall need for the ensuing year at a fixed price. A assigns his rights under the contract to C. C can acquire no right against B that C's family shall be supplied with oil, but may acquire a right that A's family shall be supplied, if such is the intention of the parties.

4. B contracts with A to serve A as a valet. A, for value, assigns his rights under the contract to C. C acquires no right to have B act as valet to C. If the assignment manifests an intent to give C a right to have B act as valet to A, C acquires such a right.

c. *Conditions of cooperation.* This Section refers to conditions of cooperation, and does not apply to performances which do not involve the cooperation of anyone, such as going to Rome, forbearing from suit, or refraining from competition. Performances involving the cooperation of third persons, such as paying money to, selling to, buying from, or working for a third person, may bring into play the same principles as conditions of cooperation by the obligee. Contracts to pay money to the obligee or to sell to or buy from him seldom require his personal cooperation, but may do so. Typically, Subsection (1) applies to contracts to serve under the personal direction of the obligee or to give personal direction to his work.

Illustrations:

5. B, a silver mining company, contracts with A, a smelting company, to deliver B's ore to A for smelting. A contracts to smelt the ore and to deliver the metal thereby obtained to B, receiving an agreed price for the work. A's right to receive the ore is assigned for value by him to C. A remains financially responsible but ceases to operate a smelter. The assignment is ineffective. The contract to deliver valuable ore to the assignor involves a degree of personal confidence which precludes the substitution of an assignee to receive the ore. C, therefore, has no right to have the ore delivered to himself, and as A has ceased to carry on the smelting business, C has no right to require B to deliver the ore to A.

6. B contracts to sell to A, an ice cream manufacturer, the amount of ice A may need in his business for the ensuing three years, to the extent of not more than 250 tons a week, at a stated price a ton. A makes a corresponding promise to B to buy such an amount of ice. A sells his ice cream plant to C and assigns to C all A's rights under the contract with B. Whether the assignment is effective depends on the terms of the contract between A and B

and on the likelihood that C's requirements will be different from A's. If the contract is read as a contract to furnish such ice as the plant requires, B is bound to furnish C ice up to the agreed maximum even though C requires more or less ice than B would have required.

7. B contracts to build a wall on A's land at a place to be selected by A personally. A sells the land and assigns his rights under the contract to C and joins C in selecting the place. B is bound to build the wall.

REPORTER'S NOTE

Subsection (1) is based in part on former § 161; Subsection (2) is based on Subsection (2) of former § 152. See 3 Williston, Contracts §§ 412, 421–21A (3d ed. 1960); 4 Corbin, Contracts §§ 868–69 (1951).

Comments b and c. Illustrations 1–6 were in substance Illustrations 1, 6, 2, 3, 4 and 5 to former § 152. As to Illustration 6, see Crane Ice Cream Co. v. Terminal Freezing & Heating Co., 147 Md. 588, 128 A. 280 (1925). Illustration 7 is new; it is based on Elting v. Clinton Mills, 36 Conn. 296 (1869).

§ 335.   Assignment by a Joint Obligee

A joint obligee may effectively assign his right, but the assignee can enforce it only in the same manner and to the same extent as the assignor could have enforced it.

Comment:

a. The extent to which the rights of obligees of the same performance are joint depends on the intention manifested and on the extent to which their interests in the performance or in the remedies for breach are distinct. See § 297(2). In an action based on a joint right, the obligor can require joinder of all surviving joint obligees, but any joint obligee may sue in the name of all. See § 298. This power to enforce the joint right, the related power to discharge the obligor, and any right to receive and retain the proceeds as against the co-obligees are assignable, subject to limitations imposed by the relationship of the obligees. See §§ 299–301.

REPORTER'S NOTE

This Section is based on former § 153, but replaces a specific rule of joinder with reference in commentary to §§ 297–301. See 3 Williston, Contracts § 432 (1960); 4 Corbin, Contracts §§ 817–18 (1951 & Supp. 1980).

---

§ 336.   Defenses Against an Assignee

(1) By an assignment the assignee acquires a right against the obligor only to the extent that the obligor is under a duty to the assignor; and if the right of the assignor would be voidable by the obligor or unenforceable against him if no assignment had been made, the right of the assignee is subject to the infirmity.

(2) The right of an assignee is subject to any defense or claim of the obligor which accrues before the obligor receives notification of the assignment, but not to defenses or claims which accrue thereafter except as stated in this Section or as provided by statute.

(3) Where the right of an assignor is subject to discharge or modification in whole or in part by impracticability, public policy, non-occurrence of a condition, or present or prospective failure of performance by an obligee, the right of the assignee is to that extent subject to discharge or modification even after the obligor receives notification of the assignment.

(4) An assignee's right against the obligor is subject to any defense or claim arising from his conduct or to which he was subject as a party or a prior assignee because he had notice.

Comment:

a. Negotiable instruments and documents. The rules stated in this Section do not apply to the negotiation or transfer of a negotiable instrument or document. See § 316. The Uniform Commercial Code provides for the rights of a holder in due course of a negotiable instrument, a holder to whom a negotiable document has been duly negotiated and a purchaser for value who has taken an investment security without notice of a particular defense. Such a holder or purchaser takes free of many defenses of the obligor. See §§ 3–305, 7–502, 8–202. Compare Comment *f*. Where those provisions do not apply, transfer of a negotiable instrument or document vests in the transferee the rights which the transferor had or had authority to convey. See §§ 3–201, 3–306, 7–504, 8–301.

b. Accrued defenses. Unlike the negotiation of a negotiable instrument, the assignment of a non-negotiable contractual right ordinarily transfers what the assignor has but only what he has. The assignee's right depends on the validity and enforceability of the contract creating the right, and is subject to limitations imposed by the terms of that contract and to defenses which would have been available against the obligee had there been no assignment. Until the obligor receives notification of an assignment, he is entitled to treat the obligee as owner of the right, and the assignee's right is subject to defenses and claims arising from dealings between assignor and obligor in relation to the contract before notification. See § 338.

Illustrations:

1. A holds B's unsealed written promise, unenforceable because given without consideration. A assigns this to C, who pays value on the faith of the writing, with reasonable belief that A had given B consideration and that the promise is legally binding. C has no right against B.

2. A has a right against B voidable because created when B was an infant. A assigns his right to C, who is ignorant of the facts making the right voidable. C's right against B is voidable.

3. A lends money to B and assigns his right to C. C's right is barred by the Statute of Limitations when A's right would have been.

4. A, who is not C's agent, fraudulently induces B to buy lumber from C. C does not know of the fraud and acts in good faith. C later assigns his rights under the contract to D, who knows of the fraud but was not a party to it. B cannot avoid the contract against D.

c. Accrued claims. Statutes or rules of court commonly permit an obligor when sued to assert by way of set-off or counterclaim in the same action such claims as he has against the plaintiff, whether related to the plaintiff's claim or not. See, e.g., Rule 13 of the Federal Rules of Civil Procedure. In appropriate circumstances the obligor may use defensively against an assignee an offsetting claim against the assignor, although the assignee is not subject to affirmative liability on such a claim unless he contracts to assume such liability. See § 328; Uniform Commercial Code §§ 2–210, 9–317. Courts of equity exercised jurisdiction in set-off at an early date, but set-off in actions at law stems from an English statute enacted in 1729 and applicable to "mutual debts"; counterclaim statutes first appeared in the nineteenth century. Set-off against an assignee has sometimes been limited to cases where both offsetting claims were fully matured at the time of assignment. The modern rule, however, unless a statute provides otherwise, turns on the time the obligor receives notification of assignment and applies even though the assigned right has not then matured. See Uniform Commercial Code § 9–318.

Illustration:

5.   A lends money to B, who regularly sells goods to A on credit and expects to repay the loan by making such sales. A assigns his right to C. Thereafter B sells goods to A as expected, and the price becomes due before B receives notification of the assignment. Unless a statute provides otherwise, B can set off his claim for the price in an action by C as assignee.

d. *Defenses and claims accruing after notification.* After receiving notification of an assignment, an obligor must treat the assignee as owner of the right and cannot assert against him a defense or claim arising out of a subsequent transaction except as stated in § 338. Moreover, the obligor cannot under the usual statute or rule of court set off an unrelated claim which matures after notification is received. Section 553 of the Bankruptcy Reform Act of 1978, 11 U.S.C. § 553 (1978), provides for the set-off of unmatured claims. The extent to which a similar rule is applicable to assignment for the benefit of creditors or to other insolvency proceedings is often affected by statute and is beyond the scope of this Restatement. Notification, however, does not enlarge the obligor's duty, and the possibility remains that the assigned right will become subject to a defense or to a claim by way of recoupment. The assignee's right is subject to such a defense or claim if it arises from the terms of the contract between the assignor and the obligor. See Uniform Commercial Code § 9–318.

Illustrations:

6.   A contracts to market goods for B in return for payment to be made by B. A then assigns his right to payment to C, and B receives notification of the assignment. Subsequently A becomes insolvent and wholly fails to perform the contract. B has a defense against C.

7.   A contracts to build a structure for B, and becomes entitled to progress payments. A assigns the money due to C, and B receives notification of the assignment. Thereafter, in breach of his contract, A abandons the work. In an action by C against B, B is entitled to recoup damages caused by A's breach.

e. *Claims against a prior assignee.* The rules stated in this Section apply to a sub-assignee. Just as an assignee is subject to defenses and claims accruing before the obligor receives notification, so a sub-assignee is subject to defenses and claims accruing between assignee and obligor before the obligor receives notification of a sub-assignment. Defenses and claims arising from the terms of the contract creating the right are available to the obligor regardless of when they accrue.

Illustration:

> 8. B owes A $100. A assigns the right to C, and C assigns it to D. C owes B $50. Unless a statute provides otherwise, B can set off against D the debt owed by C only if it becomes due before B receives notification of the assignment by C.

f. Agreement not to assert defenses. The obligor may undertake a greater obligation to an assignee than to the assignor by direct contract with the assignee, and may confer on the assignor an agency power to bind him to such an agreement. Section 9–206 of the Uniform Commercial Code gives effect to an agreement by a buyer or lessee that he will not assert against an assignee any claim or defense which he may have against the seller or lessor, making it enforceable by a good faith assignee for value without notice of a claim or defense, except as to defenses of a type which may be asserted against a holder in due course of a negotiable instrument. The Assignment of Claims Act of 1940, 31 U.S.C. § 203 (1979), contains a more limited authorization for a no-setoff agreement by the United States. The Code provision is subject to any statute or decision which establishes a different rule for buyers or lessees of consumer goods, and a number of retail installment sales acts limit the power of a buyer to make such an agreement. In addition, the Federal Trade Commission has issued a Trade Regulation Rule barring such agreements with respect to consumers. See 16 C.F.R. §§ 433.1–.3 (1975). In the absence of statute, administrative rule or court decision, such an agreement can take effect to give the assignee greater rights than the assignor as to matters governed by the terms of the contract; but if the agreement not to assert defenses or claims is itself voidable or unenforceable, the assignee takes subject to the defect.

Illustrations:

> 9. B, doing business under the name A, executes a purported contract with A reciting the delivery of goods by A to B and B's promise to pay A for them. B then executes on behalf of A an assignment to C of A's rights under the contract and delivers it to C for consideration. Whether or not C knows the facts, B's purported promise is binding in favor of C.

10.   A sells and delivers goods to B, and B agrees that in the event of an assignment to C, B will pay the price to C without asserting any defense or claim based on breach of warranty by A. A assigns his rights under the contract to C, who takes in good faith and without notice of any defense or claim.   In the absence of statute or administrative rule, B is barred from asserting against C a defense or claim based on breach of warranty by A.

11.   A contracts to sell goods to B, and B agrees that in the event of an assignment to C B will pay the price to C without asserting any defense or claim that B has against A.   A assigns his rights under the contract to C and absconds without delivering any goods to B.   In the absence of statute, administrative rule or of facts giving rise to an estoppel, B has a defense against C.

g.   *Estoppel.*   Even though an obligor's agreement not to assert a defense or claim is not binding or is voidable or unenforceable, he may be estopped to assert the claim or defense against an assignee. Where he makes a representation of fact with the intention of inducing an assignee or prospective assignee to act in reliance on the representation, and an assignee does so act, the doctrine of estoppel bars the obligor from contradicting the representation in litigation against the assignee if contradiction would be inequitable.   Compare § 90.   Application of the doctrine depends on all the circumstances.   The representation may be express or it may be implied from conduct, in unusual cases even from failure to act.   In some circumstances estoppel may rest on the obligor's reason to know that the assignee may rely, even though there is no intention to induce reliance.

Illustrations:

12.   A contracts to do construction work for B, a subcontractor, and becomes entitled to progress payments.   A assigns the progress payments to C, who advances money to A in reliance on B's assertion to C that the work has been done and that the payments will be made when received from the general contractor. In an action by C for the payments, B is estopped to offset B's claim against A for A's defaults subsequent to the assignment.

13.   A contracts to sell furniture to B for a price payable in installments.   A assigns his rights under the contract to C, who buys the rights and pays for them in reliance on B's written statement addressed to C that the furniture has been received and accepted by B.   In an action by C for the balance due on the price, B is estopped to assert that no furniture had been received.   But there is no such estoppel if at the time of the assignment C has

reason to know that A has made a practice of obtaining false statements of receipt and acceptance.

14. In May A contracts to deliver described goods to B on credit in October. In June A assigns his rights and delegates his duties under the contract to C. With knowledge of the assignment B accepts the goods from C in October, making no claim of an offset. B is estopped to assert against C claims for prior defective deliveries by A.

h. Conduct of the assignee. The conduct of the assignee or his agents may, like that of any obligee, give rise to defenses and claims which may be asserted against him by the obligor. An obligee who is subject to such a defense or claim cannot improve his position by assigning the right to an assignee who is not subject to the defense or claim and then taking a reassignment. Compare Uniform Commercial Code § 3–201.

Illustration:

15. A is fraudulently induced by B, the agent of C, to sell goods to C. C assigns his rights to D, who pays value in good faith and without notice. D assigns to E, who knows of the fraud. A cannot avoid the contract as against E, who succeeded to D's rights. But if E assigns to C, A's power of avoidance will revive.

REPORTER'S NOTE

Former § 167 is here revised in the light of § 309 and Uniform Commercial Code § 9–318. Former § 167(3) is omitted because contrary to § 9–318(1) and other statutes and to some decisions.

See 3 Williston, Contracts §§ 432, 33 (3d ed. 1960); 4 Corbin, Contracts §§ 892–99 (1951 & Supp. 1980); Gilmore, The Assignee of Contract Rights and His Precarious Security, 74 Yale L.J. 217 (1964).

Comment a. See Gilmore, The Commercial Doctrine of Good Faith Purchase, 63 Yale L.J. 1057 (1954).

Comment b. That the assignment of a non-negotiable contract right cannot transfer more than what the assignor has, see Beacon Constr. Co. v. Prepakt Concrete Co., 375 F.2d 977 (1st Cir. 1967). Illustrations 1 and 2 are carried forward from former § 167. Illustration 3 is new. Illustration 4 is Illustration 1 to former § 478. On the obligor's privilege to treat the obligee as owner of the right until the obligor receives notification of assignment, see Time Fin. Corp. v. Johnson Trucking Co., 23 Utah 2d 115, 458 P.2d 873 (1969).

Comment c. See Clark, Code Pleading §§ 100, 106 (2d ed. 1947); Loyd, The Development of Set-Off, 64 U. Pa. L. Rev. 541 (1916). Illustration 5 is based on Illustration 4 to former § 167 and Uniform Commercial Code § 9–318(1)(b); cf. Maryland Coop. Milk Producers, Inc. v. Bell, 206 Md. 168, 110 A.2d 661 (1955); Petters & Co. v. School Dist. No. 5, 37 Wyo. 237, 260 P. 678 (1927); Greene v. Reed, 15 Ariz. App. 110, 486 P.2d 222 (1971) (dictum). Contra: N.Y. Civil Practice Law & Rules § 3019(c); cf. Stadler v. First Nat'l Bank, 22 Mont. 190, 56 P. 111 (1899). In Massey-Ferguson Credit Corp. v. Brown, 173 Mont. 253, 567 P.2d 440 (1977), an assignee-manufacturer was held subject to the affirmative liability of the assignor-dealer because of the close connection between the assignee and assignor, and because the assignee was found to have participated in the underlying transaction between the assignor and the obligor-buyer. See also Comment *f*.

Comment d. Set-off of an unrelated claim not matured at the time notification of assignment was received was denied in Cronkleton v. Hastings Theatre & Realty Corp., 134 Neb. 168, 278 N.W. 144 (1938); Northwestern Nat'l Bank v. Commonwealth, 345 Pa. 192, 27 A.2d 20 (1942). Contra: St. Louis Nat'l Bank v. Gay, 101 Cal. 286, 35 P. 876 (1894). Permitting such set-off in cases of insolvent assignors, see N.Y. Debtor & Creditor Law §§ 13, 151, 192; Eigenman v. Clark, 21 Ind. App. 129, 51 N.E. 725 (1898); Clark, Set-Off in Cases of Immature Claims in Insolvency and Receivership, 34 Harv. L. Rev. 178 (1920). Illustration 6 is based on Bliss v. California Co-Op. Producers, 30 Cal.2d 240, 181 P.2d 369 (1947); cf. Sponge Divers' Ass'n v. Smith, Kline & French Co., 263 F. 70 (3d Cir. 1920); Illustration 3 to former § 167. Illustration 7 is based on American Bridge Co. v. City of

Boston, 202 Mass. 374, 88 N.E. 1089 (1909); see Annot., 87 A.L.R. 187 (1933). See also Greene v. Reed, 15 Ariz. App. 110, 486 P.2d 222 (1971) (underlying contract was unenforceable as against public policy). Cf. United States Nat'l Bank v. Madison Nat'l Bank, 355 F. Supp. 165 (D.D.C. 1973), aff'd mem., 489 F.2d 1273 (D.C. Cir. 1974); Glassman Constr. Co. v. Fidelity & Cas. Co., 356 F.2d 340 (D.C. Cir.), cert. denied, 384 U.S. 987 (1966) (both involving defenses not arising from the underlying transaction).

Comment e. The rule stated in former § 167(3) is abandoned as contrary to Uniform Commercial Code § 9–318(1)(b). Illustration 8 is Illustration 5 to former § 167, revised accordingly; it is based on Union Nat'l Bank of Fremont v. Village of Beemer, 123 Neb. 778, 244 N.W. 303 (1932); see also United States Nat'l Bank v. Madison Nat'l Bank, 355 F. Supp. 165 (D.D.C. 1973), aff'd mem., 489 F.2d 1273 (D.C. Cir. 1974) (citing this Illustration in Tentative Draft); cf. Produce Exch. Bank v. School Dist., 138 Kan. 834, 28 P.2d 742 (1934); Martin v. Richardson, 68 N.C. 255 (1873); Metzgar v. Metzgar, 1 Rawle 227 (Pa. 1829). Contra: Downey v. Tharp, 63 Pa. 322 (1869).

Comment f. Illustration 9 is based on Forest Inv. Corp. v. Chaplin, 55 Ill. App.2d 429, 205 N.E.2d 51 (1965); cf. State Sav. Bank v. Universal Credit Corp., 233 Iowa 247, 8 N.W.2d 719 (1943); General Credit Corp. v. First Nat'l Bank, 74 Wyo. 1, 283 P.2d 1009 (1955). Illustration 10 is based on Anglo-California Trust Co. v. Hall, 61 Utah 223, 211 P. 991 (1922); cf. Young v. John Deere Plow Co., 102 Ga. App. 132, 115 S.E.2d 770 (1960);

Walter J. Hieb Sand & Gravel, Inc. v. Universal C.I.T. Credit Corp., 332 S.W.2d 619 (Ky. 1960); see Annot., 44 A.L.R.2d 8, 162–169 (1955). But cf. San Franscisco Sec. Corp. v. Phoenix Motor Co., 25 Ariz. 531, 220 P. 229 (1923). Illustration 11 is based on American Nat'l Bank v. A.G. Somerville, Inc., 191 Cal. 364, 216 P. 376 (1923); Quality Fin. Co. v. Hurley, 337 Mass. 150, 148 N.E.2d 385 (1958); see Annots., 39 A.L.R.3d 518 (1971) (consumer goods), 44 A.L.R.2d 8, 162–172 (1955); cf. Dearborn Motors Credit Corp. v. Neel, 184 Kan. 437, 337 P.2d 992 (1959) (fraud); Hudiburg Imported Cars, Inc. v. Hart, 383 P.2d 650 (Okla. 1963) (fraud). Contra: Unico v. Owen, 50 N.J. 101, 232 A.2d 405 (1967) (consumer goods); Fairfield Credit Corp. v. Donnelly, 158 Conn. 543, 264 A.2d 547 (1969) (same); Commercial Credit Corp. v. Biagi, 11 Ill. App.2d 80, 136 N.E.2d 580 (1956); First Nat'l Bank of Elgin v. Husted, 57 Ill. App.2d 227, 205 N.E.2d 780 (1965) (under Uniform Commercial Code § 9–206).

Comment g. Illustration 12 is based on Commerce Union Bank v. Blalock, 38 Tenn. App. 260, 273 S.W.2d 487 (1954); cf. Simmons v. Smith County Bank, 225 Miss. 384, 83 So.2d 441 (1955). Illustration 13 is based on Thorp Fin. Corp. v. LeMire, 264 Wis. 220, 58 N.W.2d 641 (1953); see Annot., 44 A.L.R.2d 196 (1955). Illustration 14 is based on the decision but not the reasoning in King v. West Coast Grocery Co., 72 Wash. 132, 129 P. 1081 (1913); cf. Annot., 78 A.L.R. 824 (1932) (set-off against rent). Illustration 15 is based on Illustration 2 to former § 478.

§ 337. Elimination of Defenses by Subsequent Events

Where the right of an assignor is limited or voidable or unenforceable or subject to discharge or modification, subsequent events which would eliminate the limitation or defense have the same effect on the right of the assignee.

Comment:

a. Rationale. The rule of this Section is the converse of the rules stated in § 336. An assignment ordinarily transfers only what the assignor has, but limitations and defenses are not enlarged by the transfer. If a condition of the obligor's duty is met or excused, for example, the condition ceases to limit the assignee's right just as it would have ceased to limit the right of the assignor in the absence of assignment.

Illustrations:

1. A has a right against B, voidable for A's fraud. A assigns the right to C. Thereafter B learns of the fraud but does not within a reasonable time notify either A or C of his intention to

avoid the transaction. Whether or not B knows of the assignment, C's right ceases to be voidable.

2. A has a right against B, unenforceable because of noncompliance with the Statute of Frauds. A assigns the right to C. Thereafter B makes a memorandum sufficient to satisfy the Statute. Whether or not B knows of the assignment, C's right is enforceable.

b. New promises. The rule of this Section does not apply to new transactions between the obligor and the assignor after the obligor has received notification of the assignment. See § 338. Moreover, the effect of a new promise by the obligor of a kind referred to in §§ 82–85 is governed by those Sections. A new promise of such a kind, made to the assignor, is binding only if the assignor is then an obligee of the antecedent duty or is acting as agent for the assignee. See § 92.

Illustration:

3. A is the payee of B's negotiable note for $200. A indorses and delivers the note to C. After maturity, without knowledge of C's rights, B pays A $50 on account of the note. The part payment is not effective to extend the period of the statute of limitations in favor of C. If the part payment were made before assignment, the period would be so extended.

REPORTER'S NOTE

The phrasing of former § 168 is here revised to fit that of new § 336, and the cross-reference to § 92 is left to Comment.

See 3 Williston, Contracts § 432 (3d ed. 1960); 4 Corbin, Contracts § 893 (1951).

Comment a. Illustrations 1 and 2 are based on Illustrations 1 and 2 to former § 168.

Comment b. Illustration 3 is based on Stamford, Spalding & Boston Banking Co. v. Smith, [1892] 1 Q.B. 765. That case may have been influenced by the fact that the part payment would not have reduced the obligor's liability to the holder of the note.

§ 338.   Discharge of an Obligor After Assignment

(1) Except as stated in this Section, notwithstanding an assignment, the assignor retains his power to discharge or modify the duty of the obligor to the extent that the obligor performs or otherwise gives value until but not after the obligor receives notification

that the right has been assigned and that performance is to be rendered to the assignee.

(2) So far as an assigned right is conditional on the performance of a return promise, and notwithstanding notification of the assignment, any modification of or substitution for the contract made by the assignor and obligor in good faith and in accordance with reasonable commercial standards is effective against the assignee. The assignee acquires corresponding rights under the modified or substituted contract.

(3) Notwithstanding a defect in the right of an assignee, he has the same power his assignor had to discharge or modify the duty of the obligor to the extent that the obligor gives value or otherwise changes his position in good faith and without knowledge or reason to know of the defect.

(4) Where there is a writing of a type customarily accepted as a symbol or as evidence of the right assigned, a discharge or modification is not effective

(a) against the owner or an assignor having a power of avoidance, unless given by him or by a person in possession of the writing with his consent and any necessary indorsement or assignment;

(b) against a subsequent assignee who takes possession of the writing and gives value in good faith and without knowledge or reason to know of the discharge or modification.

Comment:

a. Discharge by true obligee. Rules governing the discharge of a contractual right by one who is actually the owner of the right are stated in Chapter 12. Such a discharge is effective against the obligee who gives it, whether he is the original promisee, a beneficiary, or an assignee, and against any person who has no greater rights. Under § 336 a subsequent assignee is ordinarily such a person; but the law governing negotiable instruments and documents in some circumstances gives to a bona fide holder a greater right than his transferor had. See Uniform Commercial Code §§ 3–305, 7–502, 8–202. Estoppel and related doctrines have a similar effect. See Subsection (4)(b); § 336 Comments *f, g;* Uniform Commercial Code § 9–206.

Illustration:

 1. B owes A $100. A assigns the right to C. C gives B a gratuitous release under seal and subsequently assigns the right to D for value. D acquires no right against B.'

 b. Discharge by apparent obligee. This Section covers discharge by one who reasonably seems to the obligor to own the right, though in fact he does not. The obligor is ordinarily protected in such a case of a discharge wrongfully given, but only if he renders performance or otherwise gives value or changes his position in good faith and without knowledge or reason to know that the appearance is false.

Illustrations:

 2. B owes A $100. A assigns the right to C. C assigns it to D, and D assigns it to E. Before receiving notification of the assignment to E, B pays D. B is discharged.

 3. B owes A $100. A assigns the right for value to C and subsequently by way of oral gift to D. Before receiving notification of the assignment to C, B pays D. B is discharged.

 c. Value; antecedent debt. The rules as to what constitutes value in this Chapter are the same as the rules stated in §§ 298–309 of the Restatement, Second, of Trusts, except as stated in § 173 of the Restatement of Restitution and except as modified by statute. See also Restatement of Security § 10 Comment *e.* The exception, which conforms to the provisions of Uniform Commercial Code §§ 1–201(44) and 3–303 and earlier uniform acts, is that a transfer of property other than land in satisfaction of or as security for a preexisting debt or other obligation is a transfer for value. Compare § 332.

 d. Promise as value. Restatement, Second, Trusts § 302 and Restatement of Restitution § 173 state that a transfer of property in consideration of a promise to make payment in the future is not a transfer for value unless the transferee would be liable upon his promise even if he were compelled to surrender the property, or unless he has so changed his position that it would be inequitable to compel him to surrender the property. Uniform Commercial Code § 3–303 embodies a similar rule for some transactions in negotiable instruments. But for other transactions Uniform Commercial Code § 1–201(44) provides that value is given for rights acquired "in return for a binding commitment to extend credit or for the extension of immediately available credit whether or not drawn upon and whether or not a charge-back is provided for in the event of difficulties in collection"; or "generally, in return for any consideration sufficient to support a simple contract." Compare §§ 4–208 and 4–209 on bank collections. Under those provisions an executory promise is value for the purposes of bona fide purchase of goods, negotiable documents, or investment securities from a person with voidable title. Uniform Commercial Code §§ 2–403(1), 7–501(4), 7–502, 8–301, 8–302. The extent to which by analogy this statutory rule may be applicable to purchases of contractual rights not subject to the statutory provisions is beyond the scope of this Restatement.

e. Receipt of notification. Subsection (1), like § 336, follows Uniform Commercial Code § 9–318 in stating that the assignor's power to discharge terminates when the obligor "receives notification." This phrase is used with the meaning prescribed by Uniform Commercial Code § 1–201(26): a person receives a notification when it comes to his attention or is duly delivered at a place held out by him as the place for receipt of such communications. No particular formality is required, but under § 9–318 the notification must reasonably identify the rights assigned, and if the assignee fails upon request to furnish reasonable proof an account debtor may pay the assignor. For the greater protection given to banks of deposit, see § 339 Comment *c*. Receipt of notification does not include all facts which would give "reason to know." See Restatement, Second, Agency §§ 9, 268.

Illustration:

   4. A assigns to C a debt owed by B. Pursuant to Uniform Commercial Code §§ 9–401 and 9–402, C files a financing statement describing the collateral as "debt owed by B." Without knowledge of the filing and without any other reason to know of the assignment, B pays A. B is discharged.

f. Modification of executory contract. Subsection (2) follows Uniform Commercial Code § 9–318 in stating that so far as a contract is executory the assignor and obligor retain power to make good faith modifications without the assignee's consent even after notification. The assignee is protected by automatic corresponding rights in the modified or substituted contract. As in the case of a discharge by the assignor before notification, exercise of the power may be a breach of the contract of assignment. See § 333. Contrary agreement between obligor and assignee is effective.

Illustrations:

   5. A contracts to do construction work for B, and assigns to C the payments to become due. C notifies B of the assignment. A becomes financially unable to perform, and B makes advance payments to A which are necessary to enable A to perform. B is

liable to C only for the balance due after deducting the amount of the advances.

   6. A Company contracts to supply electricity to B for twenty years. Later A assigns to C for value certain fixed monthly payments to be made by B under the contract. After ten years B ceases to require electricity and A and B agree in good faith to terminate all performance under the contract. B is not liable to C for payments which would have accrued thereafter.

   g. Revocable or voidable assignment. Where an assignment is revocable because gratuitous or is voidable because of infancy, insanity, fraud, duress, mistake, or public policy, the assignee nevertheless has power to discharge or modify the duty of an obligor who pays value in good faith and without notice. In the case of a revocable gratuitous assignment, the obligor may assume until he has reason to know otherwise that the assignor desires him to complete the gift by performance or novation. See § 332. But if the obligor has reason to know that a revocable assignment has been revoked or that the assignment is voidable by the assignor, he cannot safely perform. If the facts or law are in dispute in such a case, or if the assignor has not yet exercised a power to avoid, the obligor is entitled to protection by interpleader or like remedy. See § 339. Where an assignor's right is voidable by or held in trust for a third person, an assignee may or may not take subject to the defect. See § 343. If he is subject to it, the same principles apply as in a case of voidable assignment.

Illustrations:

   7. B owes A $100. A makes a revocable gratuitous assignment to C, and subsequently makes a similar assignment to D. B with knowledge of the facts pays C. B is not discharged. The assignment to D gives B reason to know that A intends to revoke the assignment to C.

   8. B owes A $100. A is induced by C's fraud to assign the right to C. B in good faith and without notice of the fraud enters into a novation with C in satisfaction of the debt. B's duty under the original contract is discharged. But if C holds a substituted right under the novation in constructive trust for A, performance by B with reason to know the facts does not discharge his duty to A.

   9. A, as trustee for X, has a right against B. A, in violation of his trust, assigns his right to C gratuitously. B pays C with reason to know of A's breach of trust. B's duty to X is not discharged.

h. Symbolic writings. Certain writings are treated in the ordinary course of business as symbols of contractual rights. See Comment *c* to § 332. Discharge of duties under some such writings is affected by statute. See Uniform Commercial Code §§ 3–601 (commercial paper), 7–403 (document of title), 8–207 (registered investment security). These and other writings are "chattel paper", "documents" or "instruments" under Uniform Commercial Code § 9–105; still others, such as insurance policies are excluded from Article 9 by § 9–104. In either case they are not subject to § 9–318 on assignment of "accounts." See § 9–106.

Aside from statute, an obligor who renders performance without requiring production of such a symbolic writing takes the risk that the person receiving performance does not have possession of the writing either because he has assigned it or because his right is defective. Non-production has the same effect as receipt of notification of assignment or reason to know of a defect in an assignee's right. In addition, the obligor who performs without surrender or cancellation of or appropriate notation on the writing takes the risk of further obligation to an assignee who takes possession of the writing as a bona fide purchaser. The latter rule may be regarded as an application of a broader doctrine of estoppel. See Restatement, Second, Agency §§ 8B, 176.

Illustrations:

10. A gives or sells to C a savings bank book on the B bank and delivers the book to C. C gives or sells the book to D, but D allows C to retain or resume possession of it. The B bank pays C in good faith and before receipt of notification of the assignment from C to D. B's debt is discharged.

11. The facts being otherwise as stated in Illustration 10, the B bank pays A in good faith and before notification of any assignment. B's debt is not discharged.

12. The facts being otherwise as stated in Illustration 10, B pays C without surrender or cancellation of or notation in the book. Subsequently C sells and delivers the book to E, a bona fide purchaser for value. B owes the debt to E.

13. B owes A $100. A executes and delivers a written assignment of the debt to C, but a separate written agreement provides that the assignment shall only take effect if C renders a specified service. C does not render the service, but presents the assignment to B, who pays C in good faith. A is estopped to deny the effectiveness of the assignment to support discharge of B, though A may recover the payment from C.

REPORTER'S NOTE

The Section is based on former § 170, revised to omit as superfluous statements that discharge by the true owner of a right is effective. Subsection (1) follows Uniform Commercial Code § 9–318(3). Subsection (2) is new; it follows Uniform Commercial Code § 9–318(2). Subsection (3) is a revision of the balance of Subsection (2) to former § 170 in the interest of simplification. Subsection (4) covers the subject matter of former Subsections (3) and (4).

See 3 Williston, Contracts §§ 432, 433 (3d ed. 1960); 4 Corbin, Contracts §§ 890, 894, 899 (1951 & Supps. 1971 & 1980). Gilmore, The Assignee of Contract Rights and His Precarious Security, 74 Yale L.J. 217 (1964).

Comment a. Illustration 1 is based on Illustration 1 to former § 170.

Comment b. Illustrations 2 and 3 are based on Illustrations 2 and 3 to former § 170.

Comments c and d. Compare former § 149(5) and (6) and Comment *b* to former § 166.

Comment e. Illustration 4 is new. On what constitutes notification under the Code, see, e.g., First Nat'l Bank v. Mountain States Tel. & Tel. Co., 91 N.M. 126, 571 P.2d 118 (1977); Valley Nat'l Bank v. Flagstaff Dairy, 116 Ariz. 513, 570 P.2d 200 (1977) (both construing the pre-1972 text of Uniform Commercial Code § 9–318, see Reporter's Note to Introductory Note to this Chapter, but nonetheless containing useful discussions of it); in non-Code situations,

see, e.g., Time Fin. Corp. v. Johnson Trucking Co., 23 Utah 2d 115, 458 P.2d 873 (1969); Cooper v. Holder, 21 Utah 2d 40, 440 P.2d 15 (1968). Cf. Annots., 89 A.L.R. 171, 197 (1934), 104 A.L.R. 1301, 1309 (1936).

Comment f. See Gilmore, The Assignee of Contract Rights and His Precarious Security, 74 Yale L.J. 217, 243–60 (1964). Illustration 5 is based on St. Paul Fire & Marine Ins. Co. v. James I. Barnes Constr. Co., 59 Cal.2d 691, 31 Cal. Rptr. 52, 381 P.2d 932 (1963); cf. Fricker v. Uddo & Taormina Co., 48 Cal.2d 696, 312 P.2d 1085 (1957); Homer v. Shaw, 212 Mass. 113, 98 N.E. 697 (1912); Peden Iron & Steel Co. v. McKnight, 60 Tex. Civ. App. 45, 128 S.W. 156 (1910); Stansbery v. Medo-Land Dairy, Inc., 5 Wash.2d 328, 105 P.2d 86 (1940); St. Mary's Bank v. Cianchette, 99 F. Supp. 994 (D. Me. 1951). But cf. Brice v. Bannister, L.R. 3 Q.B.D. 569 (1878). Illustration 6 is based on Babson v. Village of Ulysses, 155 Neb. 492, 52 N.W.2d 320 (1952).

Comment g. Illustrations 7 and 8 are based on Illustrations 5 and 4, respectively, to former § 170; the reference to a possible constructive trust in Illustration 8 is new. See Restatement of Restitution § 202. Illustration 9 is suggested by Illustration 2 to former § 174.

Comment h. Illustration 10 is based on Illustration 7 to former § 170; Illustrations 11 and 12 are variations. Illustration 13 is based on Illustration 6 to former § 170.

§ 339. Protection of Obligor in Cases of Adverse Claims

Where a claim adverse to that of an assignee subjects the obligor to a substantial risk beyond that imposed on him by his contract, the obligor will be granted such relief as is equitable in the circumstances.

Comment:

a. Rationale. Like the rules stated in §§ 317 and 334, the rule of this Section rests on the basic principle that rights based on agreement are limited by the agreement. An obligor who has contracted to render a performance should not be required to render it twice because of uncertainties of law and fact relating to the person entitled to receive it, or because a person having a power of avoidance has not yet elected whether to exercise it. In most situations the obligor is protected against double liability by the rules permitting him to disregard an assignment until he receives notification of it and to honor it thereafter. See §§ 336, 338. But additional safeguards may be needed when the obligor has received such notification and also has reason to know of an adverse claim.

b. Proof of assignment. Even in the absence of an adverse claim, the obligor may request that the assignee furnish reasonable proof that the assignment has been made. Uniform Commercial Code § 9–318(3) permits an account debtor to pay the assignor in such a case unless the proof is seasonably furnished. Compare § 5–116 (letters of credit). Where the obligation is embodied in a commercial instrument or document, the obligor may without dishonor require its production. See Uniform Commercial Code §§ 3–505 (commercial paper), 5–116 (letters of credit), 7–403(3) (negotiable document of title). If it is lost, security may be required indemnifying the obligor against loss by reason of further claims. See Uniform Commercial Code §§ 3–804 (commercial paper), 7–601 (documents of title), 8–405 (investment securities).

Illustration:

1. A assigns to C a debt owed A by B, and C notifies B of the assignment. B requests C to furnish reasonable proof of the assignment, but C fails to do so. After a reasonable time B pays A. B's duty to C is discharged.

c. Bank deposits; commercial instruments. In the absence of statute, a bank of deposit pays at its peril on its depositor's order after it has received a proper notification of an adverse claim. To be safe, the bank must promptly notify its depositor and must hold the deposit for a reasonable time to permit the adverse claimant to bring an action. If no process is served within a reasonable time it may pay its depositor or honor his order. By statute in many states the bank is permitted to continue to honor the depositor's instructions even with knowledge of an adverse claim, unless the adverse claimant supplies indemnity or obtains an injunction. Similar provisions are made by the Uniform Commercial Code for payments to holders of certain commercial instruments. See §§ 3–603 (commercial paper), 5–114(2) (letters of credit), 8–403 (investment securities). Such statutes may expressly or by implication limit the right of the obligor to defend on the basis of the claim of a third person. See Uniform Commercial Code § 3–306(d).

Illustrations:

    2. A deposits money in the B bank and later assigns the deposit to C. C notifies B of the assignment, but does not serve B with process or supply B with indemnity or deliver to B an instrument of assignment signed by A. After nine days B pays A. In the absence of statute B is discharged from liability to C only if nine days is found to be a reasonable time.

    3. A deposits money in the B bank and orally assigns the deposit to C. C applies for an injunction against payment by B to A. A denies making the assignment. The injunction should be granted only if C gives security to protect both A and B.

    d. Interpleader and like remedies. The classical remedy for an innocent and neutral stakeholder confronted by conflicting claims was a bill in equity to compel the claimants to interplead. That remedy was subject to a number of technical restrictions, and was ineffective if one or more claimants were not within the jurisdiction of the court. A distinct remedy, the bill in the nature of interpleader, was sometimes available when the obligor had an interest in the dispute between claimants but could establish an independent basis of equity jurisdiction. The extent to which such restrictions and distinctions survive modern procedural reforms is beyond the scope of this Restatement. Under Rule 22 of the Federal Rules of Civil Procedure and 28 U.S.C. §§ 1335, 1397, 2361, for example, interpleader is an appropriate remedy for an obligor confronted by a claim adverse to that of an assignee.

    Where no statute like those relating to adverse claims to bank deposits is applicable, the obligor is excused from performance until he has had a reasonable time to ascertain the validity of adverse claims or to compel the claimants to interplead. See Uniform Commercial Code

§ 7–603 (documents of title). Even though an adverse-claims statute applies, interpleader is appropriate if it is otherwise available, either by way of defense or by original action. The effect of interpleader can also be obtained if an adverse claimant takes over the defense of an action against the obligor in such a way that he is bound by the judgment. See Restatement, Second, Judgments § 39. In many situations an adverse claimant who receives a notification by the obligor thus to take over the defense and who fails to do so is barred by a judgment against the obligor from making further claim against the obligor. See, e.g., Restatement, Second, Judgments § 57. If the situation is such that the adverse claimant cannot be so barred by a judgment against the obligor, the obligor is entitled to equitable protection.

Illustrations:

4. A deposits money with B and later makes an irrevocable gratuitous assignment of the deposit to C, who gives notice to B. X notifies B that A held the money as X's agent. If sued by either C or X, B can protect himself by notifying the other to take over the defense. If the other unreasonably refuses to do so, and judgment is rendered against B, the other is barred by the judgment from making further claim against B.

5. The facts being otherwise as stated in Illustration 4, the circumstances are such that the other claimant is not subject to the jurisdiction of the court and cannot be barred by a judgment against B from making further claim against B. Such a judgment will be denied or its enforcement restrained unless the plaintiff gives security to protect B against the outstanding claim.

6. A is drilling a well for B under contract. C notifies B that A has assigned to C his rights under the contract. X, claiming that A is indebted to X, serves B with garnishment process in an action against A. B files an answer alleging the assignment, and promptly notifies A and C of the proceedings. C then sues B in an adjoining state. C's action will be stayed until X's action is determined.

e. Types of adverse claim; voidable assignment. The rule stated in this Section applies to all the cases suggested by §§ 338–43: to disputes between assignee and assignor, between assignee and attaching creditor of the assignor, between successive assignees, and between assignee and a claimant against an assignor. In particular, when the obligor has reason to know that an assignment is voidable by the assignor, he renders performance to the assignee at his peril. See

§ 338(3). In such a case he may by interpleader or like remedy ascertain whether the assignor desires to exercise his power of avoidance. If the assignor elects to exercise his power the obligor is under no duty to the assignee.

REPORTER'S NOTE

Former § 169 dealt only with interpleader in cases of voidable assignment. Here it has been broadened to deal more generally with adverse claims. Voidable assignment is now the subject of Comment *e*. See 3 Williston, Contracts §§ 432–34 (3d ed. 1960); 4 Corbin, Contracts § 892 (1951 & Supp. 1980).

Comment b. As to assertion of the claim of a third person as a defense to the obligor, see Britton, Bills and Notes §§ 157–60 (2d ed. 1951); Chafee, Rights in Overdue Paper, 31 Harv. L. Rev. 1104, 1141–42 (1918). Illustration 1 is based on Seger v. Farmers' Loan & Trust Co., 176 N.Y. 589, 68 N.E. 1124 (1903), reversing on dissenting opinions in 73 A.D. 293, 76 N.Y.S. 721 (1902) (assignment by trust beneficiary). See also First Nat'l Bank v. Mountain States Tel. & Tel. Co., 91 N.M. 126, 571 P.2d 118 (1977).

Comment c. As to interpleader by banks, see Annot., 60 A.L.R. 719 (1929). For statutes on adverse claims to bank deposits, see 2 Paton, Digest of Legal Opinions 1656 (1942 & 1957 Supp.); 3 Scott, Trusts § 324.3 (1956); Annot., 62 A.L.R.2d 1116 (1958). Illustration 2 is based on Huff v. Oklahoma State Bank, 87 Okla. 7, 207 P. 963 (1922); cf. Gendler v. Sibley State Bank, 62 F. Supp. 805 (D. Iowa 1945); Gibraltar Realty Corp. v. Mount Vernon Trust Co., 276 N.Y. 353, 12 N.E.2d 438 (1938). Illustration 3 is based on Leeds v.

Guaranty Trust Co., 193 Misc. 681, 85 N.Y.S.2d 70 (Sup. Ct. 1948).

Comment d. On interpleader, see generally, 3A Moore, Federal Practice ch. 22 (1979); 7 Wright & Miller, Federal Practice and Procedure §§ 1701–21 (1972). As to traditional restrictions on interpleader and statutory revision, see Chafee, Modernizing Interpleader, 30 Yale L.J. 814 (1921), Interstate Interpleader, 33 Yale L.J. 685 (1924), Interpleader in the United States Courts, 41 Yale L.J. 1134, 42 Yale L.J. 41 (1932), The Federal Interpleader Act of 1936, 45 Yale L.J. 963, 1161 (1936), Federal Interpleader Since the Act of 1936, 49 Yale L.J. 377 (1940), Broadening the Second Stage of Interpleader, 56 Harv. L. Rev. 541, 929 (1943). Illustration 4 is based on Third Nat'l Bank v. Skillings, Whitneys & Barnes Lumber Co., 132 Mass. 410 (1882) (dictum); cf. First Nat'l Bank of Broken Bow v. Bank of Horatio, 161 Ark. 259, 255 S.W. 881 (1923); Morgan v. Mutual Benefit Life Ins. Co., 16 Cal. App. 85, 116 P. 385 (1911); Ely v. Hartford Life Ins. Co., 128 Ky. 799, 110 S.W. 265 (1908); see Comment 5 to Uniform Commercial Code § 3–306(d), making cross reference to § 3–803. But cf. New York Life Ins. Co. v. Dunlevy, 241 U.S. 518 (1916). Illustration 5 is based on the principle stated in Western Union Tel. Co. v. Pennsylvania, 368 U.S. 71, 75 (1961); cf. Atkinson v. Superior Court, 49 Cal.2d 338, 347–48, 316 P.2d 960, 966

(1957), cert. denied, 357 U.S. 569 (1958). Illustration 6 is based on Whan v. Hope Natural Gas Co., 81 W. Va. 338, 94 S.E. 365 (1917).

TOPIC 5. PRIORITIES BETWEEN ASSIGNEE AND ADVERSE CLAIMANTS

§ 340. Effect of Assignment on Priority and Security

(1) An assignee is entitled to priority of payment from the obligor's insolvent estate to the extent that the assignor would have been so entitled in the absence of assignment.

(2) Where an assignor holds collateral as security for the assigned right and does not effectively transfer the collateral to the assignee, the assignor is a constructive trustee of the collateral for the assignee in accordance with the rules stated for pledges in §§ 29–34 of the Restatement of Security.

Comment:

a. Priority. The principle that an assignment transfers to the assignee the same right held by the assignor, with its advantages and disadvantages, applies to priority of payment in insolvency proceedings.

Illustration:

1. By the Bankruptcy Reform Act of 1978, the wages of employees in certain cases are given priority of payment over most other provable claims. A, an employee of B of the class entitled to priority, effectively assigns his wages to C either before or after B's bankruptcy. C is entitled to priority of payment from B's estate.

b. Security follows the debt. Where a secured claim is assigned, the collateral is ordinarily assigned as well. The obligor then has the same right to redeem from the assignee that he previously had to redeem from the assignor. If the assignor retains the collateral, he has no right to hold it as security for any other claim without the consent of the owner of the collateral. An attempt so to hold it or to dispose of it for the assignor's own benefit is a breach of the assignor's duty to the obligor, and the obligor can offset his damages against the assignee just as he could have against the assignor. See § 336; compare Restatement of Security §§ 20, 24. Such an impairment of the assignee's right is a breach of the assignor's warranty to the assignee. See § 333. To avoid these difficulties and the unjust enrichment of either assignor or obligor, a constructive trust for the assignee is imposed on the collateral.

Illustrations:

2. A is entitled to receive $1000 from B, and as security for the right has a certificate for 25 shares of the X railroad, indorsed by B in blank. A effectively assigns his right to C, who is ignorant of the existence of the security. C is entitled to the shares as security.

3. A holds a bond issued by B, secured by collateral held by X as trustee for the benefit of the bondholders. X wrongfully fails to preserve the collateral. Later A sells the bond to C, who does not know of the wrong. When the wrong is discovered, B is insolvent. C is entitled to A's claim against X.

c. Agreements affecting security. A constructive trust arises by operation of law and does not depend on agreement. Even though a transfer of collateral is articulated in the agreement between assignor and assignee, a constructive trust arises to the extent that the transfer by agreement is inoperative. But the constructive trust can be avoided by agreement. If the assignment is a breach of a condition of the assignor's interest in the collateral, that interest is terminated and the beneficial owner of the collateral is the obligor rather than the assignee. An agreement between assignor and assignee or between obligor and assignee that the collateral is not to be transferred has a similar effect. On the other hand, with the obligor's consent the collateral can be held as security for another claim of the assignor. See Restatement of Security § 29.

Illustration:

4. The facts being otherwise as stated in Illustration 2, A and C agree that the pledge of shares is not to be transferred to C. B is entitled to return of the shares.

d. Rights of creditors and purchasers. Where an assignor wrongfully exercises dominion over collateral for the assigned right, he and those who succeed only to his rights remain subject to the rights of both the assignee and the obligor. Both his creditors and purchasers of the collateral with notice remain subject both to any constructive trust for an assignee and to the obligor's rights to redeem and to offset his claim for damages. Even a bona fide purchaser of the collateral gets no greater rights than the assignor unless the collateral is negotiable or there is an agreement or estoppel binding the assignee or obligor or both. But where negotiable collateral is duly negotiated by the assignor, the purchaser takes free of the rights of assignee and obligor, and estoppel or agreement may have similar consequences. In such cases the assigned right is subject to the obligor's offsetting claim unless the offset is barred by the law of negotiable instruments or documents or by estoppel or agreement.

Illustrations:

5. The facts being otherwise as stated in Illustration 2, A sells and delivers the share certificate to D, a bona fide purchaser. D acquires it free of any adverse claim. Uniform Commercial Code §§ 8–302, 9–309. C's right against B is subject to the offset of B's claim for damages against A for conversion.

6. A has a right to receive $1,000 from B for money lent, secured by a pledge of B's savings bank book on the X bank, with an unconditional written assignment of the bank account to A signed by B. A sells and assigns 25 per cent of the right to C for value, but retains possession of the savings bank book and the assignment by B. Later A sells the savings bank account to D, who takes possession of the book as a bona fide purchaser for value. D's right is prior to C's under § 342, and B is estopped to redeem from D. C's right against B is subject to the offset of B's claim for damages against A.

REPORTER'S NOTE

This Section is based on former § 171. Subsection (2) of former § 171 is here modified to refer to the fuller statement of rules in §§ 29–34 of the Restatement of Security. See 3 Williston, Contracts § 432A (3d ed. 1960); 4 Corbin, Contracts § 907 (1951).

Comment a. Illustration 1 is largely unchanged from Illustration 1 to former § 171. See Bankruptcy Reform Act of 1978, 11 U.S.C. § 507(a)(3) (1978); Shropshire, Woodliff & Co. v. Bush, 204 U.S. 186 (1907).

Comment b. Illustration 2 was Illustration 2 to former § 171; see Schram v. Sage, 46 F. Supp. 381,

reh. denied, 47 F. Supp. 94 (E.D. Mich. 1942); Lesnik v. Public Indus. Corp., 144 F.2d 968, 973 (2d Cir. 1944). Illustration 3 is based on Phelan v. Middle States Oil Corp., 154 F.2d 978 (2d Cir. 1946). Contra: Smith v. Continental Bank & Trust Co., 292 N.Y. 275, 54 N.E.2d 823 (1944), overruled by N.Y. Gen. Oblig. Law § 13–107 (1978). See 1950 Report N.Y. Law Rev. Comm. 67; Corbin, The Subsequent Bondholder and the Delinquent Trustee, 51 Colum. L. Rev. 813 (1951).

Comment c. As to the effect of the Uniform Commercial Code on an equitable right "articulated by the contract," see Jacobs v. Northeastern Corp., 416 Pa. 417, 206 A.2d 49, 55 (1965). Illustration 4 is based on Restatement of Security § 29(2) and Comment *e*.

Comment d. Illustration 5 is based on Weinress v. Bland, 31 Del. Ch. 269, 283, 71 A.2d 59, 67 (1950). Illustration 6 is new; compare Restatement of Security § 31. See Miller v. Wells Fargo Bank Int'l Corp., 540 F.2d 548, 561–63 (2d Cir. 1976), containing a sophisticated discussion of whether a telex key and key code in an international banking transaction was an "indispensable instrument" equivalent to a passbook in a pledge involving a passbook savings account. The developing field of electronic funds transfers can be expected to raise similar issues.

§ 341. Creditors of an Assignor

(1) Except as provided by statute, the right of an assignee is superior to a judicial lien subsequently obtained against the property of the assignor, unless the assignment is ineffective or revocable or is voidable by the assignor or by the person obtaining the lien or is in fraud of creditors.

(2) Notwithstanding the superiority of the right of an assignee, an obligor who does not receive notification of the assignment until after he has lost his opportunity to assert the assignment as a defense in the proceeding in which the judicial lien was obtained is discharged from his duty to the assignee to the extent of his satisfaction of the lien.

Comment:

a. Priority of assignee. An effective assignment extinguishes the assignor's right without any notification of the obligor. Any proceeds of the assigned right received by the assignor thereafter are held in constructive trust for the assignee. See Restatement of Restitution § 165. A creditor of the assignor who claims the assigned right by garnishment, levy of execution or like process is not a bona fide purchaser, even though he has no notice of the assignment. Unless protected by statute or by estoppel or like doctrine, he is subject to the assignee's right. Compare § 342; see Restatement of Restitution § 173. "Judicial lien," as used in this Section, has the same meaning as it does in the Bankruptcy Reform Act of 1978.

b. Defective assignment. An assignor's trustee in bankruptcy can in general reach all of the assignor's legal or equitable interest in any of his property, including powers that he might have exercised for his own benefit and property transferred by him in fraud of creditors. See Bankruptcy Reform Act of 1978, 11 U.S.C. §§ 541(a), (b), 548 (1978). In addition, a person against whom a transfer is voidable can reach the property transferred. In such cases, therefore, the assignee's right is not superior to that of the lien obtained by garnishment or like process. A revocable gratuitous assignment, for example, does not limit the power of the assignor's creditors to levy on the assigned claim. See § 332.

c. Protection of obligor. An obligor garnished by a creditor of the assignor cannot safely pay even in response to a judgment if he has received notification of the assignment, but he is entitled to protection against double liability by interpleader or like remedy. See § 339. If the garnished obligor has not received notification, the assignee's right against him is discharged to the same extent as the assignor's right would have been in the absence of assignment. See §§ 336, 338.

Such a discharge of the obligor does not necessarily terminate the assignee's rights against the assignor and the garnishing creditor. The assignee is entitled to restitution from the assignor to the extent that the assignor has been unjustly enriched by the discharge of his debt. See Restatement of Restitution § 118. The garnishing creditor takes free of the assignee's right to the extent that he becomes a bona fide purchaser or that the assignee is barred by estoppel, laches, *res judicata*, or other defense. See Restatement of Restitution §§ 131, 173, 179.

Illustration:

1. A has a right against B and assigns it to C for value. X, a creditor of A, serves garnishment process on B in an action against A, and obtains judgment against B before B receives notification of the assignment. A month later, before any payment or satisfaction or issue of execution and within the time specified in local procedural rules, B and C move to reopen the judgment. The motion should be granted, and C is entitled to judgment against B to the exclusion of X.

d. Filing statutes. Creditors are commonly among the beneficiaries of statutes requiring public filing of notices of certain types of transactions. The Uniform Commercial Code makes a general requirement of filing to "perfect" a nonpossessory "security interest" in personal property, including "any sale of accounts or chattel paper." See §§ 9–102, 9–302. An unperfected security interest is subordinate to the rights of "a person who becomes a lien creditor before the security interest is perfected." See § 9–301. Transfers of wage claims, rights under insurance policies or deposit accounts, and various other transactions are excluded from coverage. See § 9–104. With respect to certain international open accounts receivable, § 9–103(3)(c) provides alternatives of the application of the filing law of the American jurisdiction in which the debtor has its executive offices or perfection "by notification to the account debtor." Wage assignment statutes also often provide for public filing or for notification of the obligor or both. See Statutory Note preceding § 316.

REPORTER'S NOTE

Subsection (1) of former § 172 is here rephrased. Cf. Bankruptcy Reform Act of 1978, 11 U.S.C. § 547(e)(1)(B) (1978). Former § 172(2) is revised to follow the rule of McDowell, Pyle & Co. v. Hopfield, 148 Md. 84, 128 A. 742 (1925), stated as Illustration 1.

See 3 Williston Contracts § 434 (3d ed. 1960); 4 Corbin, Contracts § 903 (1951); Annot., 52 A.L.R. 109 (1928).

Comment a. On the respective rights of a surety and an assignee in different types of proceeds of construction contracts, compare First Nat'l Bank v. McHasco Elec., Inc., 273 Minn. 407, 141 N.W.2d 491 (1966), and Royal Indem. Co. v. United States, 178 Ct. Cl. 46, 371 F.2d 462, cert. denied, 389 U.S. 833 (1967); with Fidelity & Deposit Co. v. Scott Bros. Constr. Co., 461 F.2d 640 (5th Cir. 1972). For discussions of disputes between assignees and judgment creditors, see Stathos v. Murphy, 26 A.D.2d 500, 276 N.Y.S.2d 727 (1966), aff'd, 19 N.Y.2d 833, 281 N.Y.S.2d 81, 227 N.E.2d 880 (1967); Willow City Farmers Elevator v. Vogel, Vogel, Brantner & Kelly, 268 N.W.2d 762 (N.D. 1978). For a particularly lucid discussion of the complex problem of subordination among assignees when there is an intervening attachment, see Grise v. White, 355 Mass. 698, 247 N.E.2d 385 (1969), and authorities cited therein; 2 Gilmore, Security Interests in Personal Property §§ 37.1–.3, 39.1 (1965).

Comment c. Illustration 1 is based on McDowell, Pyle & Co. v. Hopfield, 148 Md. 84, 128 A. 742 (1925).

Comment d. See 2 Coogan et al., Secured Transactions under the Uniform Commercial Code ch. 15 (1978); Conwill & Ellis, Much Ado About Nothing: The Real Effect of Amended 60(a) on Accounts Receivable Financing, 64 Harv. L. Rev. 62 (1950); Craig, Accounts Receivable Financing: A Reappraisal of Validation Statutes in the Light of Amended 60(a), 65 Harv. L. Rev. 627 (1952).

§ 342. Successive Assignees from the Same Assignor

Except as otherwise provided by statute, the right of an assignee is superior to that of a subsequent assignee of the same right from the same assignor, unless

(a) the first assignment is ineffective or revocable or is voidable by the assignor or by the subsequent assignee; or

(b) the subsequent assignee in good faith and without knowledge or reason to know of the prior assignment gives value and obtains

(i) payment or satisfaction of the obligation,

(ii) judgment against the obligor,

(iii) a new contract with the obligor by novation, or

(iv) possession of a writing of a type customarily accepted as a symbol or as evidence of the right assigned.

Comment:

a. Scope. No attempt is made in this Section to state the effect of statutory changes, which often make priority depend on filing in a public office. In the absence of statute, the rules stated in this Section are applicable to both total and partial assignments and to assignments as security for an obligation as well as to outright sales of contractual rights. If the first assignment is partial, or if the assignor retains a beneficial interest, the subsequent assignee is entitled to any balance after the first assignee has been satisfied.

b. Dearle v. Hall. In England and in a number of states, aside from statute, a different rule has been followed, giving priority to the assignee who first gives notice to the obligor, regardless of the order in which the assignments were made. That rule stems from the leading case of Dearle v. Hall, 3 Russ. 1, 48 (1828), involving successive assignments of the interest of a beneficiary of a trust. The English rule has consequences similar to that of a system of public filing, except that the obligor acts as the filing office; it is somewhat more convenient where a single obligor is involved such as a trustee or the owner or prime contractor on a construction project than in cases of multiple obligors, as where a business concern assigns its accounts receivable. The English rule was not adopted in Restatement, Second, Trusts § 163.

c. Filing statutes. In modern times the rules of this Section have been greatly affected by statute. From 1938 to 1950 Section 60 of the Bankruptcy Act made the validity of an assignment in the assignor's bankruptcy turn on perfection of the assignment as against a hypothetical subsequent assignee. As a result numerous state statutes were enacted, directed particularly at assignments of accounts receivable. In 1950 amendments to the Bankruptcy Act reduced the significance of the problem of successive assignments. The current formulation is found in Bankruptcy Reform Act of 1978, 11 U.S.C. § 547(e)(1)(B) (1978):

> a transfer of a fixture or property other than real property is perfected when a creditor on a simple contract cannot acquire a judicial lien that is superior to the interest of the transferee.

The subject is now largely governed by the Uniform Commercial Code, except in cases of wage claims, some rights under insurance policies, deposit accounts, and certain other excluded types of transactions. See § 9–104.

Under the Code, filing or the taking of possession is generally required to "perfect" a "security interest," which includes the interest of a buyer of accounts or chattel paper. Sections 1–201(37), 9–302. An unperfected security interest is subordinate to the rights of a person who is not a secured party to the extent that he gives value for accounts or general intangibles without knowledge of the security interest and before it is perfected. Section 9–301. As between secured parties, priority is determined by the order of filing or perfection, or if neither security interest is filed or perfected, by the order of attachment. Sections 9–312(5) and (6).

d. Defective assignment. If the prior assignment is revocable or voidable by the assignor a subsequent assignment is an effective manifestation of an intent to revoke or avoid. The subsequent assignment therefore has priority. A subsequent assignment may be similarly used to effectuate a power of avoidance of the subsequent assignee.

Illustrations:

1. A has a right to the payment of $100 by B, and orally assigns it to C by way of gift. Subsequently A assigns the right to D, who gives value but knows of the assignment to C. Unless B has paid C without notice of D's assignment, B must pay D.

2. B owes A $100. A is an infant in a state where an infant may avoid his contract without restoring any consideration received. A assigns his right to C for value. Subsequently, on becoming of age, A assigns his right to D, who gives value but knows of the assignment to C. Unless B has paid C without notice of D's assignment, B must pay D.

e. Payment, judgment or novation. Where the subsequent assignee as a bona fide purchaser for value obtains performance by the obligor, judgment against him, or a new contract with him by novation, he is entitled to retain what he has received and to enforce the judgment or novation against the obligor, free of any obligation to account to the prior assignee. Historically, this rule was justified on the ground that the right of an assignee was equitable and was not enforceable against a bona fide purchaser of the legal right. In modern times the doctrine of bona fide purchase has been extended in the interest of the security of transactions. But where the interest of the first assignee has been perfected pursuant to statute, whether by filing or otherwise, subsequent bona fide purchasers are not protected unless the statute so provides or there is an estoppel. See Uniform Commercial Code §§ 1–103, 9–306, 9–309, 9–312.

Illustration:

3. B owes $100 to A. A assigns the right to C for value. Later A assigns it for value to D, who takes it in good faith. D notifies B of the assignment to him before C notifies B of his assignment. C's right is superior to D's. But if D, still without knowledge or reason to know of the assignment to C, receives $50 from B, D can retain what he receives.

f. Symbolic writings. Certain writings are treated in the ordinary course of business as symbols of contractual rights. See Comment *c* to § 332; Comment *h* to § 338. To the extent that such writings are negotiable by common law or by statute, they are beyond the scope of this Section. The rights of bona fide purchasers of some such writings, both negotiable and non-negotiable, are governed by the Uniform Commercial Code. See, *e.g.*, § 9–308 (chattel paper). Aside from statute, a person who takes possession of such a writing as a bona fide purchaser is protected in his reasonable expectations arising from the apparent ownership of his assignor. This rule may be regarded as an application of a broader doctrine of estoppel. See Restatement, Second, Agency §§ 8B, 176.

Illustrations:

4. A, the holder of a savings bank book which records a deposit of $100 in the B savings bank, assigns the deposit to C for value without delivering the book. A then delivers the book to D, who pays value therefore in ignorance of the assignment to C. D is entitled to the deposit.

5. A holds a life insurance policy issued by the B insurance company. By written assignment A assigns the policy to C as security for a debt, but does not deliver the policy. Later A assigns the policy to D as security for a loan of $3,000, and delivers the policy to D. Still later D lends an additional $1,000 to A on A's note, relying in good faith on a notation added to the note without A's authority that the note is secured by the policy. C is entitled to redeem the policy from D on payment of $3,000.

g. *Relation to discharge of obligor.* Priority between successive assignees is independent of the protection of the obligor under § 338. An assignee who acts in good faith may take priority under this Section by receiving payment from an obligor who acts in bad faith and hence is not discharged. Conversely, an assignee who receives a payment with knowledge of a prior assignment must account to the prior assignor even though the obligor acts in good faith and is discharged to the extent of the payment.

h. *Value.* As to what constitutes value, see Comments *c* and *d* to § 338.

REPORTER'S NOTE

Former § 173 is here rephrased without change of substance. See 3 Williston, Contracts § 435 (3d ed. 1960); 4 Corbin, Contracts § 902 (1951); Annots., 31 A.L.R. 876 (1924), 110 A.L.R. 774 (1937).

Comments a and b. Compare Restatement, Second, Trusts § 163. As to the first-to-notify rule, see American Fire & Cas. Co. v. First Nat'l City Bank, 411 F.2d 755 (1st Cir. 1969), cert. denied, 396 U.S. 1007 (1970).

Comment c. See the authorities in the Reporter's Note to § 341, Comment *d*.

Comment d. Illustrations 1 and 2 are based on Illustrations 1 and 2 to former § 173.

Comment e. For analysis in terms of equitable and legal title, see Judson v. Corcoran, 58 U.S. (17 How.) 612 (1854); In re Rosen, 157 F.2d 997 (3d Cir. 1946), cert. denied, 330 U.S. 835 (1947). Illustration 3 is based on Illustration 3 to former § 173; cf. Rabinowitz v. People's Nat'l Bank, 235 Mass. 102, 126 N.E. 289 (1920); Evans v. Joyner, 195 Va. 85, 77 S.E.2d 420 (1953). Contra: Superior Brassiere Co. v. Zimetbaum, 214 A.D. 525, 212 N.Y.S. 473 (1st Dep't 1925). For a debate over the interpretation of two carefully drafted assignments in light of perceived equities, see Terry Contracting, Inc. v. Levitt, 54 A.D.2d 1, 386 N.Y.S.2d 233 (1976), aff'd mem., 42 N.Y.2d 833, 397 N.Y.S.2d 382, 366 N.E.2d 83 (1977).

Comment f. Illustration 4 is based on Illustration 4 to former § 173. Illustration 5 is based on Herman v. Connecticut Mut. Life Ins. Co., 218 Mass. 181, 105 N.E. 450 (1914).

§ 343. Latent Equities

If an assignor's right against the obligor is held in trust or constructive trust for or subject to a right of avoidance or equitable lien of another than the obligor, an assignee does not so hold it if he gives value and becomes an assignee in good faith and without notice of the right of the other.

Comment:

a. Scope. The rule stated in this Section is an application to contractual rights of the rules stated in Restatement, Second, Trusts §§ 284–85 and Restatement of Restitution § 172 as applying to property generally. See also Restatement, Second, Agency § 307A. The rule does not apply to defenses or claims of the obligor, but protects the bona fide purchaser against all other equitable claims adverse to the right of the assignor. The bona fide purchaser may be a purchaser for value of the entire right or only of a fractional or otherwise limited interest, such as a security interest. But the rule does not apply to cases of successive assignments by the same assignor, and does not protect a promisee or beneficiary of a contract to assign or a declaration of trust until he becomes an assignee. See Restatement, Second, Trusts § 286; Restatement of Restitution § 175.

Illustrations:

1. A, as trustee for X, has a right against B. In violation of his trust A assigns the right gratuitously to C. C assigns to D, a purchaser for value in good faith and without notice of the breach of trust. D holds the right free of the trust.

2. A has a right against B and is induced to assign it to C by C's fraud. C assigns it to D, a purchaser for value in good faith and without notice of the fraud. Even after discovering the fraud D can enforce the right against B and retain the proceeds free of A's claim.

b. Equities of the obligor. The rule of this Section is not applied where the protection of the bona fide purchaser would impair the rights of the obligor. Thus where the assignor of a debt holds collateral in constructive trust for the assignee under the rule stated in § 340, a subsequent bona fide purchaser of the collateral from the assignor takes subject to the debtor's right to redeem the collateral by paying the debt to the assignee; the rule of this Section is not applicable unless the collateral is negotiable or the debtor is bound by agreement or estoppel. See Restatement of Security §§ 29, 31. Again, where a surety for the assignor is subrogated to the rights of the obligor, the assignee does not have priority by virtue of the rule stated in this Section. Priorities in such cases arising in connection with public construction contracts are affected by statute and are beyond the scope of this Restatement. Compare Restatement of Restitution § 162; Restatement of Security §§ 141, 165–68.

c. Negotiable instruments and documents. The rule of this Section is negated with respect to negotiable instruments and documents of title which are transferred but not duly negotiated by Uniform Commercial Code §§ 3–306, 7–504, 8–301. Compare § 9–308 (chattel paper).

d. Value. As to what constitutes value, see Comments *c* and *d* to § 338.

REPORTER'S NOTE

This Section is substantially the same as former § 174. See 3 Williston, Contracts § 438 (3d ed. 1960); 4 Corbin, Contracts §§ 900–01 (1951 & Supp. 1980); Note, 20 U. Chi. L. Rev. 693 (1953).

Comment a. Illustration 1 is based on Illustration 2 to former § 174; cf. Lasser v. Philadelphia Nat'l Bank, 321 Pa. 189, 183 A. 791 (1936). Contra: Levenbaum v. Hanover Trust Co., 253 Mass. 19, 148 N.E. 227 (1925). Illustration 2 is based on Illustration 1 to former § 174; cf. Peo-

ple's Banking Co. v. Fidelity & Deposit Co., 165 Md. 657, 170 A. 544, 171 A. 345 (1934).

Comment b. Former § 174 was relied on to support a decision for an assignee bank against a construction surety in Maryland Cas. Co. v. National Bank, 320 Pa. 129, 182 A. 362 (1936); compare Aetna Cas. & Sur. Co. v. Harvard Trust Co., 344 Mass. 169, 181 N.E.2d 673 (1962); see Notes, 20 U. Chi. L. Rev. 119 (1952), 71 Yale L.J. 1274 (1962).

Chapter 16

REMEDIES

Introductory Note

TOPIC 1. IN GENERAL

TOPIC 2. ENFORCEMENT BY AWARD OF DAMAGES

TOPIC 3. ENFORCEMENT BY SPECIFIC PERFORMANCE AND INJUNCTION

TOPIC 4. RESTITUTION

Introductory Note

TOPIC 5. PRECLUSION BY ELECTION AND AFFIRMANCE

Introductory Note: This Chapter deals with remedies that are of special importance in disputes arising out of contracts, including restitution as well as damages and equitable relief. Topic 1 sets out the interests protected by these remedies and enumerates the remedies themselves. The next two topics deal with the enforcement of contracts, by the award of damages under the rules stated in Topic 2 and by specific performance or injunction under the rules in Topic 3. Topic 4 is concerned with restitution when an agreement is, for some reason, not to be enforced under the rules stated in Topics 2 and 3. Finally, Topic 5 deals with those circumstances in which a party is precluded from pursuing a remedy by conduct inconsistent with it.

This Chapter is not exhaustive. It does not treat in detail those forms of relief, such as declaration of the rights of the parties or enforcement of an arbitration award, that are largely statutory and are not limited to contracts cases. See Comments *d* and *e* to § 345. It does not deal with some specialized remedies, such as reformation of a writing or replevin of property. Nor does it deal with the extent to which a party to a contract is empowered to protect himself or to obtain satisfaction by methods not involving recourse to a court, such as deducting damages that he claims from the price that he owes, retaking goods, or foreclosing on security. See Uniform Commercial Code §§ 2–717, 9–503, 9–504. Also omitted are the rights of third parties such as those of a good faith purchaser against one who has a power to avoid a contract through which the purchaser derives his title. See Uniform Commercial Code §§ 2–403, 3–305.

The important role that the institution of contract plays in the economy has drawn the attention of economists to the law of contract remedies. In classic economic theory the mechanism of exchange resulting from bargain is essential to the voluntary reallocation of goods, labor and other resources in a socially desirable manner. However, a party may err in calculating the net benefit to be expected from the performance of a bargain, or circumstances may so change as to disappoint his expectations. A contract that he once thought would be profitable may therefore become unprofitable for him. If the contract is still profitable for the other party, however, a question arises as to whether the reluctant party should be compelled to perform. The answer provided by at least some economic analysis tends to confirm the traditional response of common-law judges in dealing with this question.

The traditional goal of the law of contract remedies has not been compulsion of the promisor to perform his promise but compensation of the promisee for the loss resulting from breach. "Willful" breaches have not been distinguished from other breaches, punitive damages have not been awarded for breach of contract, and specific performance has not been granted where compensation in damages is an adequate substitute for the injured party. In general, therefore, a party may find it advantageous to refuse to perform a contract if he will still have a net gain after he has fully compensated the injured party for the resulting loss.

This traditional response is not without its shortcomings. Its focus on the pecuniary aspects of breach fails to take account of notions of the sanctity of contract and the resulting moral obligation to honor one's promises. The analysis of breach of contract in purely economic terms assumes an ability to measure value with a certainty that is not often possible in the judicial process. The analysis also ignores the "transaction costs" inherent in the bargaining process and in the resolution of disputes, a defect that is especially significant where the amount in controversy is small. However, the main thrust of the preceding economic analysis lends some support to traditional contract doctrine in this area.

REPORTER'S NOTE

This Chapter is based largely on former Chapter 12, Judicial Remedies for Breach of Contract and on parts of Chapter 15, Fraud and Misrepresentation, relating to avoidance. See 5 Corbin, Contracts chs. 55–61 (1964 & Supp. 1980); 5A id. chs. 62–66 (1964 & Supp. 1980); 11 Williston, Contracts chs. 41–43 (3d ed. 1968); 12 id. ch. 44 (3d ed. 1970); Dobbs, Remedies (1973); McCormick, Damages (1935); Farnsworth, Legal Remedies for Breach of Contract, 70 Colum. L. Rev. 1145 (1970); Peters, Remedies for Breach of Contracts Relating to the Sale of Goods Under the Uniform Commercial Code: A Roadmap for Article Two, 73 Yale L.J. 199 (1963); Wright, The Law of Remedies as a Social Institution, 18 U. Det. L.J. 376 (1955).

According to economic theory, if available goods and resources are to be utilized in their most productive manner, each good must be consumed by the person who values it most highly, and each "factor of production" must be employed in the way that produces the most valued output. Voluntary agreements in which individuals exchange assets for those that they value more are necessary to bring about this result. A bargain from which both parties benefit results in a gain in "economic efficiency" by moving the exchanged assets to higher valued uses. Economic theory assumes that the parties to an agreement strive to maximize their own welfare and that, absent some impediment such as mistake, misrepresentation or duress, each party places a value on the other's performance that is greater than the anticipated cost to him of his own performance. At the time the agreement is made, then, each party has a reasonable expectation that he will benefit from its performance.

If one party later concludes that a contract that he originally thought would be profitable will be unprofitable for him, his non-performance cannot be said to result in a gain in efficiency unless the value to him of the gain can be said to be greater than the value to the other party of the loss. Since individuals make different value judgments, the gain and the loss cannot be simply compared in absolute terms. However, a leading principle of economic theory can be applied to overcome this difficulty.

According to this principle, a breach of contract will result in a gain in "economic efficiency" if the party contemplating breach evaluates his gains at a higher figure than the value that the other party puts on his losses, and this will be so if the party contemplating breach will gain enough from the breach to have a net benefit even though he compensates the other party for his resulting loss, calculated according to the subjective preferences of that party. If this requirement is met, breach with such compensation will be advantageous to one party and not disadvantageous to the other. To prevent it by compelling performance, it is argued, would result in a less efficient distribution of wealth since the party in breach would lose more than the injured party would gain.

This conclusion accords well with the assumption of contract law that the principal purpose of the rules relating to breach is to place the injured party in as good a position as he would have been in had the contract been performed. Awarding damages on this basis to protect the injured party's "expectation interest" gives the other party an incentive to break the contract if, but only if, he gains enough from the breach that he can compensate the injured party for his losses and still retain some of the benefits from the breach.

For economic analyses in recent legal literature of the law relating to breach of contract, see Kronman & Posner (eds.), The Economics of Contract Law (1979); Posner, Economic Analysis of Law, Ch. 4 (2d ed. 1977); Barton, The Economic Basis of Damages for Breach of Contract, 1 J. Leg. Studies 277 (1972); Birmingham, Breach of Contract, Damage Measures, and Economic Efficiency, 24 Rutgers L. Rev. 273 (1970); Birmingham, Damage Measures and Economic Rationality: The Geometry of Contract Law, 1969 Duke L.J. 49 (1969); Kronman, Specific Performance, 45 U. Chi. L. Rev. 351 (1978). For a statement of the limitations of this approach, see Polinsky, Economic Analysis as a Potentially Defective Product: A Buyer's Guide to Posner's Economic Analysis of Law, 87 Harv. L. Rev. 1655 (1974). Economics treatises that explore the concept of "economic efficiency" and the role played by bargained for exchanges include: Bowden, Economics: The Science of Common Sense (1974); Samuelson, Economics (10th Ed. 1976); Mansfield, Microeconomics (2d ed. 1975); Henderson & Quandt, Microeconomic Theory: A Mathematical Approach (2d ed. 1971). The principle discussed here in relation to breach is known as the "Kaldor Compensation Principle" and was initially stated in Kaldor, Welfare Propositions of Economics and Interpersonal Comparisons, 49 Econ. J. 549 (1939); Hicks, The Foundations of Welfare Economics, 49 Econ. J. 696 (1939).

TOPIC 1. IN GENERAL

§ 344. Purposes of Remedies

Judicial remedies under the rules stated in this Restatement serve to protect one or more of the following interests of a promisee:

(a) his "expectation interest," which is his interest in having the benefit of his bargain by being put in as good a position as he would have been in had the contract been performed,

(b) his "reliance interest," which is his interest in being reimbursed for loss caused by reliance on the contract by being put in as good a position as he would have been in had the contract not been made, or

(c) his "restitution interest," which is his interest in having restored to him any benefit that he has conferred on the other party.

Comment:

a. Three interests. The law of contract remedies implements the policy in favor of allowing individuals to order their own affairs by making legally enforceable promises. Ordinarily, when a court concludes that there has been a breach of contract, it enforces the broken promise by protecting the expectation that the injured party had when he made the contract. It does this by attempting to put him in as good a position as he would have been in had the contract been performed, that is, had there been no breach. The interest protected in this way is called the "expectation interest." It is sometimes said to give the injured party the "benefit of the bargain." This is not, however, the only interest that may be protected.

The promisee may have changed his position in reliance on the contract by, for example, incurring expenses in preparing to perform, in performing, or in foregoing opportunities to make other contracts. In that case, the court may recognize a claim based on his reliance rather than on his expectation. It does this by attempting to put him back in the position in which he would have been had the contract not been made. The interest protected in this way is called "reliance interest." Although it may be equal to the expectation interest, it is ordinarily smaller because it does not include the injured party's lost profit.

In some situations a court will recognize yet a third interest and grant relief to prevent unjust enrichment. This may be done if a party has not only changed his own position in reliance on the contract but has also conferred a benefit on the other party by, for example, making a part payment or furnishing services under the contract. The court may then require the other party to disgorge the benefit that he has received by returning it to the party who conferred it. The interest of the claimant protected in this way is called the "restitution interest." Although it may be equal to the expectation or reliance interest, it is ordinarily smaller because it includes neither the injured party's lost profit nor that part of his expenditures in reliance that resulted in no benefit to the other party.

The interests described in this Section are not inflexible limits on relief and in situations in which a court grants such relief as justice requires, the relief may not correspond precisely to any of these interests. See §§ 15, 87, 89, 90, 139, 158 and 272.

Illustrations:

1. A contracts to build a building for B on B's land for $100,000. B repudiates the contract before either party has done anything in reliance on it. It would have cost A $90,000 to build the building. A has an expectation interest of $10,000, the difference between the $100,000 price and his savings of $90,000 in not having to do the work. Since A has done nothing in reliance, A's reliance interest is zero. Since A has conferred no benefit on B, A's restitution interest is zero.

2. The facts being otherwise as stated in Illustration 1, B does not repudiate until A has spent $60,000 of the $90,000. A has been paid nothing and can salvage nothing from the $60,000 that he has spent. A now has an expectation interest of $70,000, the difference between the $100,000 price and his saving of $30,000 in not having to do the work. A also has a reliance interest of $60,000, the amount that he has spent. If the benefit to B of the partly finished building is $40,000, A has a restitution interest of $40,000.

b. *Expectation interest.* In principle, at least, a party's expectation interest represents the actual worth of the contract to him rather than to some reasonable third person. Damages based on the expectation interest therefore take account of any special circumstances that are peculiar to the situation of the injured party, including his personal values and even his idiosyncracies, as well as his own needs and opportunities. See Illustration 3. In practice, however, the injured party is often held to a more objective valuation of his expectation interest because he may be barred from recovering for loss resulting from such special circumstances on the ground that it was not foreseeable or cannot be shown with sufficient certainty. See §§ 351 and 352. Furthermore, since he cannot recover for loss that he could have avoided by arranging a substitute transaction on the market (§ 350), his recovery is often limited by the objective standard of market price. See Illustration 4. The expectation interest is not based on the injured party's hopes when he made the contract but on the actual value that the contract would have had to him had it been performed. See Illustration 5. It is therefore based on the circumstances at the time for performance and not those at the time of the making of the contract.

Illustrations:

3. A, who is about to produce a play, makes a contract with B, an actor, under which B is to play the lead in the play at a

stated salary for the season. A breaks the contract and has the part played by another actor. B's expectation interest includes the extent to which B's reputation would have been enhanced if he had been allowed to play the lead in A's play, as well as B's loss in salary, both subject to the limitations stated in Topic 2.

4. A contracts to construct a monument in B's yard for $10,000 but abandons the work after the foundation has been laid. It will cost B $6,000 to have another contractor complete the work. The monument planned is so ugly that it would decrease the market price of the house. Nevertheless, B's expectation interest is the value of the monument to him, which, under the rule stated in § 348(2)(b), would be measured by the cost of completion, $6,000.

5. A makes a contract with B under which A is to pay B for drilling an oil well on B's land, adjacent to that of A, for development and exploration purposes. Both A and B believe that the well will be productive and will substantially enhance the value of A's land in an amount that they estimate to be $1,000,000. Before A has paid anything, B breaks the contract by refusing to drill the well. Other exploration then proves that there is no oil in the region. A's expectation interest is zero.

c. *Reliance interest.* If it is reliance that is the basis for the enforcement of a promise, a court may enforce the promise but limit the promisee to recovery of his reliance interest. See §§ 87, 89, 90, 139. There are also situations in which a court may grant recovery based on the reliance interest even though it is consideration that is the basis for the enforcement of the promise. These situations are dealt with in §§ 349 and 353.

d. *Restitution interest.* Since restitution is the subject of a separate Restatement, this Chapter is concerned with problems of restitution only to the extent that they arise in connection with contracts. Such problems arise when a party, instead of seeking to enforce an agreement, claims relief on the ground that the other party has been unjustly enriched as a result of some benefit conferred under the agreement. In some cases a party's choice of the restitution interest is dictated by the fact that the agreement is not enforceable, perhaps because of his own breach (§ 374), as a result of impracticability of performance or frustration of purpose (§ 377(1)), under the Statute of Frauds (§ 375), or in consequence of the other party's avoidance for some reason as misrepresentation, duress, mistake or incapacity (§ 376). Occasionally a party chooses the restitution interest even though the contract is enforceable because it will give a larger recovery than will enforcement based on either the expectation or reliance interest. These rare instances are dealt with in § 373. Sometimes the restitution interest can be protected by requiring restoration of the specific thing, such as goods or land, that has resulted in the benefit. See § 372. Where restitution in kind is not appropriate, however, a sum of money will generally be allowed based on the restitution interest. See § 371.

REPORTER'S NOTE

This Section is new. Paragraph (1)(a) is based on Uniform Commercial Code § 1–106(1). See Fuller & Perdue, The Reliance Interest in Contract Damages, 46 Yale L.J. 52 (1936), 46 id. 373 (1937); 5 Corbin, Contracts § 992 (1964 & Supp. 1980); 11 Williston, Contracts § 1338 (3d ed. 1968).

Comment a. Illustrations 1 and 2 are new. For an exceptional case in which the benefit to the defendant exceeded the loss to the claimant, see Olwell v. Nye & Nissen Co., 26 Wash.2d 282, 173 P.2d 652 (1946) (plaintiff "waived" conversion and claimed restitution).

Comment b. Illustration 3 is based on Herbert Clayton & Jack Waller Ltd. v. Oliver, [1930] A.C. 209 (H.L.); cf. Tolvey v. Criterion Film Prods., [1936] 2 All. E.R. 1625 (K.B.); see also Restatement, Second, Agency § 433. Contra: Quinn v. Straus Broadcasting Group, 309 F. Supp. 1208 (S.D.N.Y. 1970). See Note, 27 U. Miami L. Rev. 465 (1973). Illustration 4 is based on Illustration 4 to former § 346. Illustration 5 is based on Illustration 3 to former § 346; cf. Guardian Trust Co. v. Brothers, 59 S.W.2d 343 (Tex. Civ. App. 1933), error refused.

§ 345.　Judicial Remedies Available

The judicial remedies available for the protection of the interests stated in § 344 include a judgment or order

(a) awarding a sum of money due under the contract or as damages,

(b) requiring specific performance of a contract or enjoining its non-performance,

(c) requiring restoration of a specific thing to prevent unjust enrichment,

(d) awarding a sum of money to prevent unjust enrichment,

(e) declaring the rights of the parties, and

(f) enforcing an arbitration award.

Comment:

a. Nature of remedies. This Section enumerates the principal judicial remedies available for the protection of the interests defined in the preceding section. It is not intended to be exhaustive, since other remedies such as replevin of a chattel or reformation or cancellation of a writing supplement those listed here. As to reformation, see §§ 155, 166. Nor are the remedies listed mutually exclusive, since a court may in the same action, for example, both require specific performance of a promise and award a sum of money as damages for delay in its performance. The details of the procedure by which such remedies are obtained and enforced vary from one jurisdiction to another and are beyond the scope of this Restatement. In some circumstances a party to a contract is empowered to protect himself or to obtain satisfaction by methods not involving recourse to a court, such as retaking goods or foreclosing on security. The exercise of such a power, whether under a term of the contract or otherwise, is not a judicial remedy and is not dealt with in this Section. But see Topic 5 as to election and avoidance.

b. Enforcement. In most contract cases, what is sought is enforcement of a contract. Enforcement usually takes the form of an award of a sum of money due under the contract or as damages. Damages may be based on either the expectation or reliance interest of the injured party. See § 344. They are subject to the rules stated in Topic 2. A court may also enforce a promise by ordering that it be specifically performed or, in the alternative, by enjoining its nonperformance. In doing so, it protects the promisee's expectation interest. The rules governing the granting of such relief are stated in Topic 3.

c. Restitution. Sometimes a party, instead of seeking to enforce a contract under the rules stated in Topics 2 and 3, seeks protection of his restitution interest. If this can be accomplished by requiring the other party to restore a specific thing that is in his hands, a court may order restoration or make restoration a condition of granting relief to the other party. If restoration of the specific thing is not appropriate, the restitution interest may be protected by requiring the other party to pay a sum of money equivalent to the benefit that he has derived from that thing. The rules relating to the prevention of unjust enrichment by restitution, in either kind or money, are stated in Topic 4.

d. Declaratory judgments. Declaratory judgments play an important and growing role in the resolution of disputes arising out of contracts. Courts may render declaratory judgments under statutes adopted in nearly all states, and, in some instances, without the aid of statute. Such a judgment declares the legal relations between the parties but does not award damages or order other relief and may be rendered even though no breach of contract has occurred. In most states, including those that have adopted the Uniform Declaratory Judgment Act, courts may also render declaratory judgments in conjunction with other relief. In all states, and in the federal courts under the Federal Declaratory Judgment Act, the decision whether to render a declaratory judgment is discretionary. Because questions relating to declaratory judgments depend largely on statute and are not confined to contract cases, they are not considered in detail in this Restatement.

    e. Enforcement of arbitration awards. Arbitration also plays an important and growing role in the resolution of contract disputes. Although arbitration is not in itself a judicial remedy, enforcement by a court of an award of an arbitral tribunal is. Statutes relating to the enforcement of such awards, based on either an agreement to arbitrate a future dispute or a submission of an existing dispute, have been enacted in many states. These statutes provide for the transformation of an award into a judgment by means of a summary procedure, without the necessity of bringing an action on the award as was required at common law. This transformation permits the use of the regular judicial process to enforce the arbitration award. The passage of these statutes reflects the increasing use of arbitration to settle private disputes and a decline in the judicial hostility to arbitration that had limited its effectiveness. Because questions concerning the enforcement of arbitration awards depend largely on statute, they are not considered in detail in this Restatement. But see Comment *a* Illustration 2 to § 366.

REPORTER'S NOTE

    This Section is based on former § 326. See 5 Corbin, Contracts §§ 990–91, 994 (1954); 11 Williston, Contracts § 1314 (3d ed. 1968).

    On declaratory judgments, see Borchard, Declaratory Judgments (2d ed. 1941); 6A Moore, Federal Practice ch. 57 (1974); 3 Weinstein, Korn & Miller, New York Civil Practice § 3001 (1977); 10 Wright & Miller, Federal Practice and Procedure §§ 2751–80 (1973); Wright, Law of Federal Courts 497–503 (3d ed. 1976). See also Uniform Declaratory Judgments Act; Federal Declaratory Judgments Act, 28 U.S.C. §§ 2201, 2202 (1976). On the enforcement of arbitration awards see Domke, The Law and Practice of Commercial Arbitration § 37 (1968); 16 Williston, Contracts § 1923A (3d ed. 1976). See also Uniform Arbitration Act; United States Arbitration Act, 9 U.S.C. § 1 et seq., and, for examples of modern

state enforcement procedures, see
Cal. Civ. Proc. Code § 1285 et seq.
and N.Y. Civ. Prac. Law § 7510.

TOPIC 2. ENFORCEMENT BY AWARD OF DAMAGES

Introductory Note: This Topic contains rules for enforcement
of contracts by means of the award of damages. The initial assumption is that the injured party is entitled to full compensation for his
actual loss. This is reflected in the general measure of damages set
out in § 347. However, important limitations including those of avoidability, unforeseeability and uncertainty follow in §§ 350–53. The limitation of certainty can sometimes be overcome, at least in part,
through the use of alternative bases for measuring damages (§ 348) or
through the use of reliance as a measure of damages (§ 349). Other
sections deal with nominal damages (§ 346), punitive damages (§ 355)
and liquidated damages and penalties (§ 356). Except for the restrictions imposed by the rule that proscribes the fixing of penalties (§ 356),
parties are free to vary the rules governing damages, subject to the
usual limitations on private agreement such as that on unconscionable
contracts or terms (§ 208). Although interest may be awarded as
damages under the rule stated in § 354, for the sake of simplicity specific references to interest have generally been omitted from the illustrations in this Chapter.

Under the rule stated in § 346, a breach of contract ordinarily
gives rise to a claim for damages. For the sake of convenience, the
term "a claim for damages" is used in other chapters of this Restatement to refer to a right arising out of breach whether or not it includes
a right to specific performance or an injunction as well as damages.
See, for example, the use of that term in §§ 243 and 251. Although a
claim to the price promised to be paid for something or to a sum of
money promised to be repaid is, strictly speaking, not a claim for damages, such money claims are generally enforceable in the same way as
those for damages. As to the right of a seller of land to recover the
price, see Comment *e* to § 360.

REPORTER'S NOTE

This Topic is based on Topic 2,
Damages, of former Chapter 12. See
5 Corbin, Contracts chs. 55–60 (1964
& Supp. 1980); 11 Williston, Con-
tracts chs. 41–42 (3d ed. 1968);
Dobbs, Remedies chs. 3, 12 (1973);
McCormick, Damages chs. 4–8,
22–28 (1935); Farnsworth, Judicial
Remedies for Breach of Contract, 70
Colum L. Rev. 1145 (1970); Peters,
Remedies for Breach of Contracts
Relating to the Sale of Goods Under

the Uniform Commercial Code: A
Roadmap for Article Two, 73 Yale
L.J. 199 (1963); Vernon, Expectancy

Damages for Breach of Contract: A
Primer and Critique, 1976 Wash.
U.L.Q. 179.

§ 346. Availability of Damages

(1) The injured party has a right to damages for any breach by a party against whom the contract is enforceable unless the claim for damages has been suspended or discharged.

(2) If the breach caused no loss or if the amount of the loss is not proved under the rules stated in this Chapter, a small sum fixed without regard to the amount of loss will be awarded as nominal damages.

Comment:

a. Right to damages. Every breach of contract gives the injured party a right to damages against the party in breach, unless the contract is not enforceable against that party, as where he is not bound because of the Statute of Frauds. The resulting claim may be one for damages for total breach or one for damages for only partial breach. See § 236. Although a judgment awarding a sum of money as damages is the most common judicial remedy for breach of contract, other remedies, including equitable relief in the form of specific performance or an injunction, may be also available, depending on the circumstances. See Topic 3. In the exceptional situation of a contract for transfer of an interest in land that is unenforceable under the Statute of Frauds, action in reliance makes the contract enforceable by specific performance even though it gives rise to no claim for damages for breach. See Comment *c* to § 129. A duty to pay damages may be suspended or discharged by agreement or otherwise, and if it is discharged the claim for damages is extinguished. See Introductory Note to Chapter 12. When this happens, the right to enforcement by other means such as specific performance or an injunction is also extinguished. If the duty of performance, as distinguished from the duty to pay damages, has been suspended or discharged, as by impracticability of performance or frustration of purpose, there is then no breach and this Section is not applicable.

The parties can by agreement vary the rules stated in this Section, as long as the agreement is not invalid for unconscionability (§ 208) or on other grounds. The agreement may provide for a remedy such as repair or replacement in substitution for damages. See Uniform Commercial Code § 2–719.

---

b. Nominal damages. Although a breach of contract by a party against whom it is enforceable always gives rise to a claim for damages, there are instances in which the breach causes no loss. See Illustration 1. There are also instances in which loss is caused but recovery for that loss is precluded because it cannot be proved with reasonable certainty or because of one of the other limitations stated in this Chapter. See §§ 350–53. In all these instances the injured party will nevertheless get judgment for nominal damages, a small sum usually fixed by judicial practice in the jurisdiction in which the action is brought. Such a judgment may, in the discretion of the court, carry with it an award of court costs. Costs are generally awarded if a significant right was involved or the claimant made a good faith effort to prove damages, but not if the maintenance of the action was frivolous or in bad faith. Unless a significant right is involved, a court will not reverse and remand a case for a new trial if only nominal damages could result.

Illustration:

    1.   A contracts to sell to B 1,000 shares of stock in X Corporation for $10 a share to be delivered on June 1, but breaks the contract by refusing on that date to deliver the stock. B sues A for damages, but at trial it is proved that B could have purchased 1,000 shares of stock in X Corporation on the market on June 1 for $10 a share and therefore has suffered no loss. In an action by B against A, B will be awarded nominal damages.

c. Beneficiaries of gift promises. If a promisee makes a contract, intending to give a third party the benefit of the promised performance, the third party may be an intended beneficiary who is entitled to enforce the contract. See § 302(1)(b). Such a gift promise creates overlapping duties, one to the beneficiary and the other to the promisee. If the performance is not forthcoming, both the beneficiary and the promisee have claims for damages for breach. If the promisee seeks damages, however, he will usually be limited to nominal damages: although the loss to the beneficiary may be substantial, the promisee cannot recover for that loss and he will ordinarily have suffered no loss himself. In such a case the remedy of specific performance will often be an appropriate one for the promisee. See § 307.

Illustration:

    2.   As part of a separation agreement B promises his wife A not to change the provision in B's will for C, their son. A dies and B changes his will to C's detriment, adding also a provision that C

will forfeit any bequest if he questions the change before any tribunal. In an action by A's personal representative against B, the representative can get a judgment for nominal damages. As to the representative's right to specific performance, see Illustration 2 to § 307.

REPORTER'S NOTE

This Section consolidates the rules stated in former §§ 327 and 328. See 5 Corbin, Contracts §§ 992–96, 1001 (1964 & Supp. 1980); 11 Williston, Contracts §§ 1338–39A (3d ed. 1968).

Comment b. Illustration 1 is based on Illustration 1 to former § 328.

Comment c. This Comment replaces former § 345(1). The facts in Illustration 2 are taken from Illustration 2 to § 307.

§ 347. Measure of Damages in General

Subject to the limitations stated in §§ 350–53, the injured party has a right to damages based on his expectation interest as measured by

(a) the loss in the value to him of the other party's performance caused by its failure or deficiency, plus

(b) any other loss, including incidental or consequential loss, caused by the breach, less

(c) any cost or other loss that he has avoided by not having to perform.

Comment:

a. Expectation interest. Contract damages are ordinarily based on the injured party's expectation interest and are intended to give him the benefit of his bargain by awarding him a sum of money that will, to the extent possible, put him in as good a position as he would have been in had the contract been performed. See § 344(1)(a). In some situations the sum awarded will do this adequately as, for example, where the injured party has simply had to pay an additional amount to arrange a substitute transaction and can be adequately compensated by damages based on that amount. In other situations the sum awarded cannot adequately compensate the injured party for his disappointed expectation as, for example, where a delay in performance has caused him to miss an invaluable opportunity. The measure of damages stated in this Section is subject to the agreement of the parties, as where they provide for liquidated damages (§ 356) or exclude liability for consequential damages.

b. Loss in value. The first element that must be estimated in attempting to fix a sum that will fairly represent the expectation interest is the loss in the value to the injured party of the other party's performance that is caused by the failure of, or deficiency in, that performance. If no performance is rendered, the loss in value caused by the breach is equal to the value that the performance would have had to the injured party. See Illustrations 1 and 2. If defective or partial performance is rendered, the loss in value caused by the breach is equal to the difference between the value that the performance would have had if there had been no breach and the value of such performance as was actually rendered. In principle, this requires a determination of the values of those performances to the injured party himself and not their values to some hypothetical reasonable person or on some market. See Restatement, Second, Torts § 911. They therefore depend on his own particular circumstances or those of his enterprise, unless consideration of these circumstances is precluded by the limitation of foreseeability (§ 351). Where the injured party's expected advantage consists largely or exclusively of the realization of profit, it may be possible to express this loss in value in terms of money with some assurance. In other situations, however, this is not possible and compensation for lost value may be precluded by the limitation of certainty. See § 352. In order to facilitate the estimation of loss with sufficient certainty to award damages, the injured party is sometimes given a choice between alternative bases of calculating his loss in value. The most important of these are stated in § 348. See also §§ 349 and 373.

Illustrations:

1. A contracts to publish a novel that B has written. A repudiates the contract and B is unable to get his novel published elsewhere. Subject to the limitations stated in §§ 350–53, B's damages include the loss of royalties that he would have received had the novel been published together with the value to him of the resulting enhancement of his reputation. But see Illustration 1 to § 352.

2. A, a manufacturer, contracts to sell B, a dealer in used machinery, a used machine that B plans to resell. A repudiates and B is unable to obtain a similar machine elsewhere. Subject to the limitations stated in §§ 350–53, B's damages include the net profit that he would have made on resale of the machine.

c. Other loss. Subject to the limitations stated in §§ 350–53, the injured party is entitled to recover for all loss actually suffered. Items of loss other than loss in value of the other party's performance are often characterized as incidental or consequential. Incidental losses include costs incurred in a reasonable effort, whether successful or not, to avoid loss, as where a party pays brokerage fees in arranging or attempting to arrange a substitute transaction. See Illustration 3. Consequential losses include such items as injury to person or property resulting from defective performance. See Illustration 4. The terms used to describe the type of loss are not, however, controlling, and the general principle is that all losses, however described, are recoverable.

Illustrations:

3. A contracts to employ B for $10,000 to supervise the production of A's crop, but breaks his contract by firing B at the beginning of the season. B reasonably spends $200 in fees attempting to find other suitable employment through appropriate agencies. B can recover the $200 incidental loss in addition to any other loss suffered, whether or not he succeeds in finding other employment.

4. A leases a machine to B for a year, warranting its suitability for B's purpose. The machine is not suitable for B's purpose and causes $10,000 in damage to B's property and $15,000 in personal injuries. B can recover the $25,000 consequential loss in addition to any other loss suffered. See Uniform Commercial Code § 2–715(2)(b).

d. Cost or other loss avoided. Sometimes the breach itself results in a saving of some cost that the injured party would have incurred if he had had to perform. See Illustration 5. Furthermore, the injured party is expected to take reasonable steps to avoid further loss. See § 350. Where he does this by discontinuing his own performance, he avoids incurring additional costs of performance. See Illustrations 6 and 8. This cost avoided is subtracted from the loss in value caused by the breach in calculating his damages. If the injured party avoids further loss by making substitute arrangements for the use of his resources that are no longer needed to perform the contract, the net profit from such arrangements is also subtracted. See Illustration 9. The value to him of any salvageable materials that he has acquired for performance is also subtracted. See Illustration 7. Loss avoided is subtracted only if the saving results from the injured party not having to perform rather than from some unrelated event. See

Illustration 10. If no cost or other loss has been avoided, however, the injured party's damages include the full amount of the loss in value with no subtraction, subject to the limitations stated in §§ 350–53. See Illustration 11. The intended "donee" beneficiary of a gift promise usually suffers loss to the full extent of the value of the promised performance, since he is ordinarily not required to do anything, and so avoids no cost on breach. See § 302(1)(b).

Illustrations:

5. A contracts to build a hotel for B for $500,000 and to have it ready for occupancy by May 1. B's occupancy of the hotel is delayed for a month because of a breach by A. The cost avoided by B as a result of not having to operate the hotel during May is subtracted from the May rent lost in determining B's damages.

6. A contracts to build a house for B for $100,000. When it is partly built, B repudiates the contract and A stops work. A would have to spend $60,000 more to finish the house. The $60,000 cost avoided by A as a result of not having to finish the house is subtracted from the $100,000 price lost in determining A's damages. A has a right to $40,000 in damages from B, less any progress payments that he has already received. See Illustration 2 to § 344.

7. The facts being otherwise as stated in Illustration 6, A has bought materials that are left over and that he can use for other purposes, saving him $5,000. The $5,000 cost avoided is subtracted in determining A's damages, resulting in damages of only $35,000 rather than $40,000.

8. A contracts to convey land to B in return for B's working for a year. B repudiates the contract before A has conveyed the land. The value to A of the land is subtracted from the value to A of B's services in determining A's damages.

9. A contracts to employ B for $10,000 to supervise the production of A's crop, but breaks his contract by firing B at the beginning of the season. B instead takes another job as a supervisor at $9,500. The $9,500 is subtracted from the $10,000 loss of earnings in determining B's damages. See Illustration 8 to § 350.

10. A contracts to build a machine for B and deliver it to be installed in his factory by June 30. A breaks the contract and does not deliver the machine. B's factory is destroyed by fire on December 31 and the machine, if it had been installed there, would also have been destroyed. The fact that the factory was burned is not considered in determining B's damages.

11.   A contracts to send his daughter to B's school for $5,000 tuition.   After the academic year has begun, A withdraws her and refuses to pay anything.   A's breach does not reduce B's instructional or other costs and B is unable to find another student to take the place of A's daughter.   B has a right to damages equal to the full $5,000.

e. Actual loss caused by breach.   The injured party is limited to damages based on his actual loss caused by the breach.   If he makes an especially favorable substitute transaction, so that he sustains a smaller loss than might have been expected, his damages are reduced by the loss avoided as a result of that transaction.   See Illustration 12.   If he arranges a substitute transaction that he would not have been expected to do under the rules on avoidability (§ 350), his damages are similarly limited by the loss so avoided.   See Illustration 13. Recovery can be had only for loss that would not have occurred but for the breach.   See § 346.   If, after the breach, an event occurs that would have discharged the party in breach on grounds of impracticability of performance or frustration of purpose, damages are limited to the loss sustained prior to that event.   See Illustration 15.   Compare § 254(2).   The principle that a party's liability is not reduced by payments or other benefits received by the injured party from collateral sources is less compelling in the case of a breach of contract than in the case of a tort.   See Restatement, Second, Torts § 920A.   The effect of the receipt of unemployment benefits by a discharged employee will turn on the court's perception of legislative policy rather than on the rule stated in this Section.   See Illustration 14.

Illustrations:

12.   A contracts to build a house for B for $100,000, but repudiates the contract after doing part of the work and having been paid $40,000.   Other builders would charge B $80,000 to finish the house, but B finds a builder in need of work who does it for $70,000.   B's damages are limited to the $70,000 that he actually had to pay to finish the work less the $60,000 cost avoided or $10,000, together with damages for any loss caused by the delay. See Illustration 2 to § 348.

13.   A contracts to employ B for $10,000 to supervise the production of A's crop.   A breaks the contract by firing B at the beginning of the season, and B, unable to find another job, instead takes a job as a farm laborer for the entire season at $6,000.   The $6,000 that he made as a farm laborer is subtracted from the $10,000 loss of earnings in determining B's damages.   See Illustration 8 to § 350.

14. A contracts to employ B for $10,000 to supervise the production of A's crop, but breaks his contract by firing B at the beginning of the season. B is unable to find another similar job but receives $3,000 in state unemployment benefits. Whether the $3,000 will be subtracted from the $10,000 loss of earnings depends on the state legislation under which it was paid and the policy behind it.

15. On April 1, A and B make a personal service contract under which A is to employ B for six months beginning July 1 and B is to work for A during that period. On May 1, B repudiates the contract. On August 1, B falls ill and is unable to perform the contract for the remainder of the period. A can only recover damages based on his loss during the month of July since his loss during subsequent months was not caused by B's breach. Compare Illustration 2 to § 254.

f. Lost volume. Whether a subsequent transaction is a substitute for the broken contract sometimes raises difficult questions of fact. If the injured party could and would have entered into the subsequent contract, even if the contract had not been broken, and could have had the benefit of both, he can be said to have "lost volume" and the subsequent transaction is not a substitute for the broken contract. The injured party's damages are then based on the net profit that he has lost as a result of the broken contract. Since entrepreneurs try to operate at optimum capacity, however, it is possible that an additional transaction would not have been profitable and that the injured party would not have chosen to expand his business by undertaking it had there been no breach. It is sometimes assumed that he would have done so, but the question is one of fact to be resolved according to the circumstances of each case. See Illustration 16. See also Uniform Commercial Code § 2–708(2).

Illustration:

16. A contracts to pave B's parking lot for $10,000. B repudiates the contract and A subsequently makes a contract to pave a similar parking lot for $10,000. A's business could have been expanded to do both jobs. Unless it is proved that he would not have undertaken both, A's damages are based on the net profit he would have made on the contract with B, without regard to the subsequent transaction.

REPORTER'S NOTE

This Section consolidates former §§ 329 and 335. The rules stated in former § 346, Damages for Breach of a Construction Contract, are presented as applications of the general rules on damages, and that section is omitted. See 5 Corbin, Contracts §§ 992–98, 1089 (1964 & Supp. 1980); 11 Williston, Contracts §§ 1338–57 (3d ed. 1968); Birmingham, Breach of Contract, Damage Measures, and Economic Efficiency, 24 Rutgers L. Rev. 273 (1970); Farnsworth, Legal Remedies for Breach of Contract, 70 Colum. L. Rev. 1145 (1970); Leff, Injury, Ignorance and Spite–The Dynamics of Coercive Collection, 80 Yale L.J. 1 (1970); Nordstrom, Damages as Compensation for Loss, 2 N.C. Central L.J. 1 (1970); Nordstrom, Toward a Law of Damages, 18 W. Res. L. Rev. 86 (1966); Vernon, Expectancy Damages for Breach of Contract: A Primer and Critique, 1976 Wash. U.L.Q. 179.

Comment b. Illustration 1 is suggested by Freund v. Washington Square Press, 34 N.Y.2d 379, 314 N.E.2d 419, 357 N.Y.S.2d 857 (1974). For analogous cases recognizing a right to recover under the Uniform Commercial Code for loss of good will resulting from the sale of defective goods, see Isenberg v. Lemon, 84 Ariz. 340, 327 P.2d 1016, modified on rehearing, 84 Ariz. 364, 329 P.2d 882 (1958) (dictum); Sol-O-Lite Laminating Corp. v. Allen, 223 Or. 80, 353 P.2d 843 (1960). Illustration 2 is based on Murarka v. Bachrack Bros., 215 F.2d 547 (2d Cir. 1954); see Uniform Commercial Code §§ 2–713, 2–715.

Comment c. See former § 336(2). Illustration 3 is based on Mr. Eddie,

Inc. v. Ginsberg, 430 S.W.2d 5 (Tex. Civ. App. 1968). As to Illustration 4, see Uniform Commercial Code § 2–715.

Comment d. See Patterson, Builder's Measure of Recovery for Breach of Contract, 31 Colum. L. Rev. 1286 (1931). The last sentence of this Comment is based on former § 345(1)(b). Illustration 5 is based on Illustration 6 to former § 346; see also Illustration 7 to former § 346; see State ex rel. Schilling v. Baird, 65 Wis.2d 394, 222 N.W.2d 666 (1974). Illustration 6 is based on Illustration 1 to former § 335 and Illustrations 11 and 12 to former § 346. As to the treatment of A's fixed costs, such as rent or property taxes on office space, see Vitex v. Caribtex, 377 F.2d 795 (3d Cir. 1967). Illustration 7 is based on Illustration 1 to former § 335. Illustration 8 is based on Illustration 3 to former § 335. Illustration 9 is based on Erler v. Five Point Motors, 249 Cal. App.2d 560, 57 Cal. Rptr. 516 (1967); Sutherland v. Wyer, 67 Me. 64 (1877); cf. Allen, Heaton & McDonald v. Castle Farm Amusement Co., 151 Ohio St. 522, 86 N.E.2d 782 (1949). Illustration 10 is based on Illustration 6 to former § 335; Clydebank Eng'r & Sb. Co. v. Castenada, [1905] A.C. 6. Illustration 11 is based on Illustration 5 to former § 335; see also Illustration 4 to former § 335.

Comment e. Illustration 12 is based on Fleming v. Twine, 58 A.2d 498 (D.C. Ct. App. 1948); cf. Illinois Central R.R. Co. v. Crail, 281 U.S. 57 (1930); Bowes v. Saks and Co., 397 F.2d 113 (7th Cir. 1968). Illustration 13 is based on Allgeyer v. Rutherford, 45 S.W. 628 (Tex. Civ. App.

1898). As to Illustration 14, compare Billeter v. Posell, 94 Cal. App.2d 858, 211 P.2d 621 (1949), with United Protective Workers of America v. Ford Motor Co., 223 F.2d 49 (7th Cir. 1955); see Sporn v. Celebrity, Inc., 129 N.J. Super. 449, 324 A.2d 71 (1974). Illustration 15 is based on Illustration 4 to § 457; Model Vending v. Stanisci, 74 N.J. Super. 12, 180 A.2d 393 (1962).

Comment f. On the problem of "lost volume," see Goetz & Scott, Measuring Seller's Damages: the Lost-Profits Puzzle, 31 Stan. L. Rev. 323 (1979); Nordstrom, Handbook of the Law of Sales § 177 (1970); White & Summers, Handbook of the Law Under the Uniform Commercial Code §§ 7–9 to 7–13 (1972); Harris, A Radical Restatement of the Law of Seller's Damages: Sales Act and Commercial Code Results Compared, 18 Stan. L. Rev. 66 (1965); Speidel & Clay, Seller's Recovery of Overhead Under UCC Section 2–708(2): Economic Cost Theory and Contract Remedial Policy, 57 Cornell L. Rev. 681 (1972); Comments, 24 Case W. Res. L. Rev. 684 (1973). Illustration 16 is based on Distribu-Dor v. Karadnis, 11 Cal. App.3d 463, 90 Cal. Rptr. 231 (1970); Torkomian v. Russell, 90 Conn. 481, 97 A. 760 (1916); Locks v. Wade, 36 N.J. Super. 128, 114 A.2d 875 (1955); Neri v. Retail Marine Co., 30 N.Y.2d 393, 334 N.Y.S.2d 165, 285 N.E.2d 311 (1972); Stewart v. Hansen, 62 Utah 281, 218 P. 959 (1923). See also Snyder v. Herbert Greenbaum & Assocs., 38 Md. App. 144, 380 A.2d 618 (1977) (applying lost volume rule but saying that burden of proving lost volume is on seller). But cf. Famous Knitwear Corp. v. Drug Fair, 493 F.2d 251 (4th Cir. 1974); Charles Street Garage Co. v. Kaplan, 312 Mass. 624, 45 N.E.2d 928 (1942). As to the situation in which the breach enables the injured party to make a new contract to do the same work, see Massengale v. Transitron Elec. Corp., 385 F.2d 83 (1st Cir. 1967); Grinnell Co. v. Voorhees, 1 F.2d 693 (3d Cir.), cert. denied, 266 U.S. 629 (1924); Olds v. Mapes–Reeve Constr. Co., 177 Mass. 41, 58 N.E. 478 (1900); Kunkle v. Jaffe, 71 N.E.2d 298 (Ohio App. 1946).

§ 348.   Alternatives to Loss in Value of Performance

(1) If a breach delays the use of property and the loss in value to the injured party is not proved with reasonable certainty, he may recover damages based on the rental value of the property or on interest on the value of the property.

(2) If a breach results in defective or unfinished construction and the loss in value to the injured party is not proved with sufficient certainty, he may recover damages based on

(a) the diminution in the market price of the property caused by the breach, or

(b) the reasonable cost of completing perform-ance or of remedying the defects if that cost is not clearly disproportionate to the probable loss in value to him.

(3) If a breach is of a promise conditioned on a fortui-tous event and it is uncertain whether the event would have occurred had there been no breach, the injured party may recover damages based on the value of the conditional right at the time of breach.

Comment:

a. Reason for alternative bases. Although in principle the in-jured party is entitled to recover based on the loss in value to him caused by the breach, in practice he may be precluded from recovery on this basis because he cannot show the loss in value to him with sufficient certainty. See § 352. In such a case, if there is a reasonable alternative to loss in value, he may claim damages based on that alter-native. This Section states the rules that have been developed for three such cases.

b. Breach that delays the use of property. If the breach is one that prevents for a period of time the use of property from which profits would have been made, the loss in value to the injured party is based on the profits that he would have made during that period. If those profits cannot be proved with reasonable certainty (§ 352), two other bases for recovery are possible. One is the fair rental value of the property during the period of delay. Damages based on fair rental value include an element of profit since the fair rental value of prop-erty depends on what it would command on the market and this turns on the profit that would be derived from its use. For this reason, uncertainty as to profits may result in uncertainty in fair rental value. Another possible basis for recovery, as a last resort, is the interest on the value of the property that has been made unproductive by the breach, if that value can be shown with reasonable certainty. Al-though these two other bases will ordinarily give a smaller recovery than loss in value, it is always open to the party in breach to show that this is not so and to hold the injured party to a smaller recovery based on loss in value to him.

Illustration:

1. A contracts with B to construct an outdoor drive-in the-atre, to be completed by June 1. A does not complete the work until September 1. If B cannot prove his lost profits with reason-

able certainty, he can recover damages based on the rental value of the theatre property or based on the interest on the value of the theatre property itself if he can prove either of these values with reasonable certainty. See Illustration 2 to § 352.

c. Incomplete or defective performance. If the contract is one for construction, including repair or similar performance affecting the condition of property, and the work is not finished, the injured party will usually find it easier to prove what it would cost to have the work completed by another contractor than to prove the difference between the values to him of the finished and the unfinished performance. Since the cost to complete is usually less than the loss in value to him, he is limited by the rule on avoidability to damages based on cost to complete. See § 350(1). If he has actually had the work completed, damages will be based on his expenditures if he comes within the rule stated in § 350(2).

Sometimes, especially if the performance is defective as distinguished from incomplete, it may not be possible to prove the loss in value to the injured party with reasonable certainty. In that case he can usually recover damages based on the cost to remedy the defects. Even if this gives him a recovery somewhat in excess of the loss in value to him, it is better that he receive a small windfall than that he be undercompensated by being limited to the resulting diminution in the market price of his property.

Sometimes, however, such a large part of the cost to remedy the defects consists of the cost to undo what has been improperly done that the cost to remedy the defects will be clearly disproportionate to the probable loss in value to the injured party. Damages based on the cost to remedy the defects would then give the injured party a recovery greatly in excess of the loss in value to him and result in a substantial windfall. Such an award will not be made. It is sometimes said that the award would involve "economic waste," but this is a misleading expression since an injured party will not, even if awarded an excessive amount of damages, usually pay to have the defects remedied if to do so will cost him more than the resulting increase in value to him. If an award based on the cost to remedy the defects would clearly be excessive and the injured party does not prove the actual loss in value to him, damages will be based instead on the difference between the market price that the property would have had without the defects and the market price of the property with the defects. This diminution in market price is the least possible loss in value to the injured party, since he could always sell the property on the market even if it had no special value to him.

Illustrations:

   2.   A contracts to build a house for B for $100,000 but repudiates the contract after doing part of the work and having been paid $40,000.   Other builders will charge B $80,000 to finish the house.   B's damages include the $80,000 cost to complete the work less the $60,000 cost avoided or $20,000, together with damages for any loss caused by delay.   See Illustration 12 to § 347.

   3.   A contracts to build a house for B for $100,000.   When it is completed, the foundations crack, leaving part of the building in a dangerous condition.   To make it safe would require tearing down some of the walls and strengthening the foundation at a cost of $30,000 and would increase the market value of the house by $20,000.   B's damages include the $30,000 cost to remedy the defects.

   4.   A contracts to build a house for B for $100,000 according to specifications that include the use of Reading pipe.   After completion, B discovers that A has used Cohoes pipe, an equally good brand.   To replace the Cohoes pipe with Reading pipe would require tearing down part of the walls at a cost of over $20,000 and would not affect the market price of the house.   In an action by B against A, A gives no proof of any special value that Reading pipe would have to him.   B's damages do not include the $20,000 cost to remedy the defects because that cost is clearly disproportionate to the loss in value to B.   B can recover only nominal damages.

   d.   Fortuitous event as condition.   In the case of a promise conditioned on a fortuitous event (see Comment *a* to § 379), a breach that occurs before the happening of the fortuitous event may make it impossible to determine whether the event would have occurred had there been no breach.   It would be unfair to the party in breach to award damages on the assumption that the event would have occurred, but equally unfair to the injured party to deny recovery of damages on the ground of uncertainty.   The injured party has, in any case, the remedy of restitution (see § 373).   Under the rule stated in Subsection (3) he also has the alternative remedy of damages based on the value of his conditional contract right at the time of breach, or what may be described as the value of his "chance of winning."   The value of that right must itself be proved with reasonable certainty, as it may be if there is a market for such rights or if there is a suitable basis for determining the probability of the occurrence of the event.

   The rule stated in this Subsection is limited to aleatory promises and does not apply if the promise is conditioned on some event, such as return performance by the injured party, that is not fortuitous.   If, for example, an owner repudiates a contract to pay for repairs to be done by a contractor and then maintains that the contractor could not or would not have done the work had he not repudiated, the contractor must prove that he could and would have performed. If he fails to do this, he has no remedy in damages. He is not entitled to claim damages under the rule stated in Subsection (3).

Illustration:

5. A offers a $100,000 prize to the owner whose horse wins a race at A's track. B accepts by entering his horse and paying the registration fee. When the race is run, A wrongfully prevents B's horse from taking part. Although B cannot prove that his horse would have won the race, he can prove that it was considered to have one chance in four of winning because one fourth of the money bet on the race was bet on his horse. B has a right to damages of $25,000 based on the value of the conditional right to the prize.

REPORTER'S NOTE

This Section consolidates rules stated in three former sections. Subsection (1) replaces former § 331(2). Subsection (2) replaces former § 346(1)(a). Subsection (3) replaces former § 332(a). See 5 Corbin, Contracts §§ 1029–30, 1089–92 (1964 & Supp. 1980); 11 Williston, Contracts §§ 1363, 1400 (3d ed. 1968).

Comment b. Illustration 1 is based on Illustrations 11 and 12 to former § 331; Evergreen Amusement Corp. v. Milstead, 206 Md. 610, 112 A.2d 901 (1955); Hill v. Willett, 281 S.W. 1110 (Tex. Civ. App. 1926).

Comment c. Illustration 2 is based on Illustration 1 to former § 346. For a rare case in which cost to complete was greater than the loss in value, see Bowes v. Saks & Co., 397 F.2d 113 (7th Cir. 1968). Illustration 3 is based on Illustration 5 to former § 346; Prier v. Refrigeration Eng'r Co., 74 Wash.2d 25, 442 P.2d 621 (1968); cf. Groves v. John Wunder

Co., 205 Minn. 163, 286 N.W. 235 (1939); Dimick v. J.K. Noonan, 242 S.W.2d 599 (Mo. Ct. App. 1951); P.G. Lake, Inc. v. Sheffield, 438 S.W.2d 952 (Tex. Civ. App. 1969); Gory Assoc. Indus., Inc. v. Jupiter Roofing & Sheet Metal, Inc., 358 So.2d 93 (Fla. Dist. Ct. App. 1978). Illustration 4 is based on Illustration 2 to former § 346; Jacob & Youngs v. Kent, 230 N.Y. 239, 129 N.E. 889 (1921); cf. Avery v. Fredericksen & Westbrook, 67 Cal. App.2d 334, 154 P.2d 41 (1944); Hansen v. Andersen, 246 Iowa 1310, 71 N.W.2d 921 (1955); Emery v. Caledonia Sand & Gravel Co., 117 N.H. 441, 374 A.2d 929 (1977); Peevyhouse v. Garland Coal & Mining Co., 382 P.2d 109 (Okl.), cert. denied, 375 U.S. 906 (1963); J.G. Jansen, Inc. v. Rilling, 203 Wis. 193, 232 N.W. 887 (1931); Gory Assoc. Indus., Inc. v. Jupiter Roofing & Sheet Metal, Inc., 358 So.2d 93 (Fla. Dist. Ct. App. 1978).

Comment d. Illustration 5 is based on Illustration 3 to former § 332.

§ 349. Damages Based on Reliance Interest

As an alternative to the measure of damages stated in § 347, the injured party has a right to damages based on his reliance interest, including expenditures made in preparation for performance or in performance, less any loss that the party in breach can prove with reasonable certainty the injured party would have suffered had the contract been performed.

Comment:

a. Reliance interest where profit uncertain. Loss in value and cost or other loss avoided are key components of contract damages. See § 347. If the injured party was to supply services such as erecting a building, for example, the difference between loss in value of the other party's performance and the cost or other loss avoided by the injured party will be equal to the cost of the injured party's expenditures in reliance, up to the time of breach, plus the profit that would have been made had the contract been fully performed. To the extent that "overhead" costs are fixed costs, they are not included in the cost of expenditures in reliance for this purpose. See Illustration 6 to § 347. Under the rule stated in this Section, the injured party may, if he chooses, ignore the element of profit and recover as damages his expenditures in reliance. He may choose to do this if he cannot prove his profit with reasonable certainty. He may also choose to do this in the case of a losing contract, one under which he would have had a loss rather than a profit. In that case, however, it is open to the party in breach to prove the amount of the loss, to the extent that he can do so with reasonable certainty under the standard stated in § 352, and have it subtracted from the injured party's damages. The resulting damages will then be the same as those under the rule stated in § 347. If the injured party's expenditures exceed the contract price, it is clear that at least to the extent of the excess, there would have been a loss. For this reason, recovery for expenditures under the rule stated in this section may not exceed the full contract price. As to the possibility of restitution in such a case, see § 373. Often the reliance consists of preparation for performance or actual performance of the contract, and this is sometimes called "essential reliance." See, for example,

Illustration 3. It may, however, also consist of preparation for collateral transactions that a party plans to carry out when the contract in question is performed, and this is sometimes called "incidental" reliance. See Illustration 4.

Illustrations:

    1. A gives B a "dealer franchise" to sell A's products in a stated area for one year. In preparation for performance, B spends money on advertising, hiring sales personnel, and acquiring premises that cannot be used for other purposes. A then repudiates before performance begins. If neither party proves with reasonable certainty what profit or loss B would have made if the contract had been performed, B can recover as damages his expenditures in preparation for performance. See Illustration 8 to § 90.

    2. A contracts with B to stage a series of performances in B's theater, each to have 50 per cent of the gross receipts. After A has spent $20,000 in getting ready for the performances, B rents the theater to others and repudiates the contract, and A stages the performance at another theater. A's expenditures in preparation for performance of the contract with B are worth $8,000 to him in connection with staging the performances at the other theater. If neither party proves with reasonable certainty what profit or loss A would have made if the contract had been performed, A can recover as damages the $12,000 balance of his expenditures in preparation for performance.

    3. A contracts to build for B a factory of experimental design for $1,000,000. After A has spent $250,000 and been paid $150,000 in progress payments, B repudiates the contract and A stops work. A's expenditures include materials worth $10,000 that he can use on other jobs. If neither party proves with reasonable certainty what profit or loss A would have made if the contract had been performed, A can recover as damages the $90,000 balance of his expenditures in preparation for performance.

    4. A contracts to sell his retail store to B. After B has spent $100,000 for inventory, A repudiates the contract and B sells the inventory for $60,000. If neither party proves with reasonable certainty what profit or loss B would have made if the contract had been performed, B can recover as damages the $40,000 loss that he sustained on the sale of the inventory.

b. Reliance interest in other cases. There are other instances in which damages may be based on the reliance interest. Under the rules stated in §§ 87, 89, 90 and 139, if a promise is enforceable because it has induced action or forbearance, the remedy granted for breach may be limited as justice requires. Under these rules, relief may be limited to damages measured by the extent of the promisee's reliance rather than by the terms of the promise. See Comment *e* to § 87, Comment *d* to § 89, Comment *d* to § 90 and Comment *d* to § 139. Furthermore, even when the contract is enforceable because of consideration, a court may, under the rule stated in § 353, conclude that the circumstances require that damages be limited to losses incurred in reliance. See Comment *a* to § 353.

REPORTER'S NOTE

This Section is based on former § 333. See 5 Corbin, Contracts § 1031 (1964 & Supp. 1980); 11 Williston, Contracts §§ 1363, 1363A (3d ed. 1968); Patterson, Builder's Measure of Recovery for Breach of Contract, 31 Colum. L. Rev. 1286, 1296–99 (1931).

Comment a. Illustration 1 is based on Illustrations 1 and 2 to former § 333; Wells v. National Life Ass'n, 99 F. 222 (5th Cir. 1900); cf. General Tire & Rubber Co. v. Distributors, Inc., 253 N.C. 459, 117 S.E.2d 479 (1960). Illustration 2 is based on Illustration 4 to former § 333; cf. Security Stove & Mfg. Co. v. American Ry. Express Co., 227 Mo. App. 175, 51 S.W.2d 572 (1932). Illustration 3 is based on Illustration 14 to former § 346; United States v. Behan, 110 U.S. 338 (1884). Illustration 4 is based on Nurse v. Barns, Haym. Sir T. 77, 83 Eng. Rep. 43 (1664); L. Albert & Son v. Armstrong Rubber Co., 178 F.2d 182 (2d Cir. 1949). On the effect of divisibility, see Shapiro Eng'r Co. v. Francis O. Day Co., 215 Md. 373, 137 A.2d 695 (1958).

§ 350. Avoidability as a Limitation on Damages

(1) Except as stated in Subsection (2), damages are not recoverable for loss that the injured party could have avoided without undue risk, burden or humiliation.

(2) The injured party is not precluded from recovery by the rule stated in Subsection (1) to the extent that he has made reasonable but unsuccessful efforts to avoid loss.

Comment:

a. *Rationale.* The rules stated in this Section reflect the policy of encouraging the injured party to attempt to avoid loss. The rule stated in Subsection (1) encourages him to make such efforts as he can to avoid loss by barring him from recovery for loss that he could have avoided if he had done so. See Comment b. The exception stated in Subsection (2) protects him if he has made actual efforts by allowing him to recover, regardless of the rule stated in Subsection (1), if his efforts prove to be unsuccessful. See Comment h. See also Comment c to § 347.

b. *Effect of failure to make efforts to mitigate damages.* As a general rule, a party cannot recover damages for loss that he could have avoided by reasonable efforts. Once a party has reason to know that performance by the other party will not be forthcoming, he is ordinarily expected to stop his own performance to avoid further expenditure. See Illustrations 1, 2, 3 and 4. Furthermore, he is expected to take such affirmative steps as are appropriate in the circumstances to avoid loss by making substitute arrangements or otherwise. It is sometimes said that it is the "duty" of the aggrieved party to mitigate damages, but this is misleading because he incurs no liability for his failure to act. The amount of loss that he could reasonably have avoided by stopping performance, making substitute arrangements or otherwise is simply subtracted from the amount that would otherwise have been recoverable as damages.

Illustrations:

1. A contracts to build a bridge for B for $100,000. B repudiates the contract shortly after A has begun work on the bridge, telling A that he no longer has need for it. A nevertheless spends an additional $10,000 in continuing to perform. A's damages for breach of contract do not include the $10,000.

2. A contracts to lease a machine to B and to deliver it at B's factory. B repudiates the contract, but A nevertheless ships the machine to B, who refuses to receive it. A's damages for breach of contract do not include the cost of shipment of the machine.

3. A sells oil to B in barrels. B discovers that some of the barrels are leaky, in breach of warranty, but does not transfer the oil to good barrels that he has available. B's damages for breach of contract do not include the loss of the oil that could have been saved by transferring the oil to the available barrels.

4. A contracts to sell flour to B. The flour is defective, in breach of warranty, as B discovers after delivery. B neverthe-

less uses it to bake bread to supply his customers. B's damages for breach of contract do not include his loss of business caused by delivering inferior bread made from the flour.

c. Substitute transactions. When a party's breach consists of a failure to deliver goods or furnish services, for example, it is often possible for the injured party to secure similar goods or services on the market. If a seller of goods repudiates, the buyer can often buy similar goods elsewhere. See Illustration 5. If an employee quits his job, the employer can often find a suitable substitute. See Illustration 6. Similarly, when a party's breach consists of a failure to receive goods or services, for example, it is often possible for the aggrieved party to dispose of the goods or services on the market. If a buyer of goods repudiates, the seller can often sell the goods elsewhere. See Illustration 7. If an employer fires his employee, the employee can often find a suitable job elsewhere. See Illustration 8. In such cases as these, the injured party is expected to make appropriate efforts to avoid loss by arranging a substitute transaction. If he does not do so, the amount of loss that he could have avoided by doing so is subtracted in calculating his damages. In the case of the sale of goods, this principle has inspired the standard formulas under which a buyer's or seller's damages are based on the difference between the contract price and the market price on that market where the injured party could have arranged a substitute transaction for the purchase or sale of similar goods. See Uniform Commercial Code §§ 2–708, 2–713. Similar rules are applied to other contracts, such as contracts for the sale of securities, where there is a well-established market for the type of performance involved, but the principle extends to other situations in which a substitute transaction can be arranged, even if there is no well-established market for the type of performance. However, in those other situations, the burden is generally put on the party in breach to show that a substitute transaction was available, as is done in the case in which an employee has been fired by his employer.

Illustrations:

     5. A contracts to sell to B a used machine to be delivered at B's factory by June 1 for $10,000. A breaks the contract by repudiating it on May 1. By appropriate efforts B could buy a similar machine from another seller for $11,000 in time to be delivered at his factory by June 1, but he does not do so and loses a profit of $25,000 that he would have made from use of the machine. B's damages do not include the loss of the $25,000 profit, but he can recover $1,000 from A. See Uniform Commercial Code §§ 2–713(1), 2–715(2)(a).

6. A contracts to supervise the production of B's crop for $10,000, but breaks his contract and leaves at the beginning of the season. By appropriate efforts, B could obtain an equally good supervisor for $11,000, but he does not do so and the crop is lost. B's damages for A's breach of contract do not include the loss of his crop, but he can recover $1,000 from A.

7. A contracts to buy from B a used machine from B's factory for $10,000. A breaks the contract by refusing to receive or pay for the machine. By appropriate efforts, B could sell the machine to another buyer for $9,000, but he does not do so. B's damages for A's breach of contract do not include the loss of the $10,000 price, but he can recover $1,000 from A. See Uniform Commercial Code § 2–708(1).

8. A contracts to employ B for $10,000 to supervise the production of A's crop, but breaks his contract by firing B at the beginning of the season. By appropriate efforts, B could obtain an equally good job as a supervisor at $100 less than A had contracted to pay him, but he does not do so and remains unemployed. B's damages for A's breach of contract do not include his $10,000 loss of earnings, but he can recover $100 from A. See Illustration 9 to § 347.

d. *"Lost volume."* The mere fact that an injured party can make arrangements for the disposition of the goods or services that he was to supply under the contract does not necessarily mean that by doing so he will avoid loss. If he would have entered into both transactions but for the breach, he has "lost volume" as a result of the breach. See Comment f to § 347. In that case the second transaction is not a "substitute" for the first one. See Illustrations 9 and 10.

Illustrations:

9. A contracts to buy grain from B for $100,000, which would give B a net profit of $10,000. A breaks the contract by refusing to receive or pay for the grain. If B would have made the sale to A in addition to other sales, B's efforts to make other sales do not affect his damages. B's damages for A's breach of contract include his $10,000 loss of profit.

10. A contracts to pay B $20,000 for paving A's parking lot, which would give B a net profit of $3,000. A breaks the contract by repudiating it before B begins work. If B would have made the contract with A in addition to other contracts, B's efforts to obtain other contracts do not affect his damages. B's damages for A's breach of contract include his $3,000 loss of profit.

e. What is a "substitute." Whether an available alternative transaction is a suitable substitute depends on all the circumstances, including the similarity of the performance and the times and places that they would be rendered. See Illustration 11. If discrepancies between the transactions can be adequately compensated for in damages, the alternative transaction is regarded as a substitute and such damages are awarded. See Illustrations 12 and 13. If the party in breach offers to perform the contract for a different price, this may amount to a suitable alternative. See Illustration 14. But this is not the case if the offer is conditioned on surrender by the injured party of his claim for breach. See Illustration 15.

Illustrations:

11.   The facts being otherwise as stated in Illustration 8, by appropriate efforts B could only obtain a job as a farm laborer at $6,000, but he does not do so and remains unemployed. B's damages for breach of contract include his $10,000 loss of earnings.

12.   The facts being otherwise as stated in Illustration 5, the other seller will not deliver the similar machine to B's factory, and insists that B take possession of it two weeks earlier than he can install it in his factory, but B can arrange to have it stored for two weeks and shipped to his factory for $1,500. B's damages do not include the loss of the $25,000 profit, but he can recover the $1,500 as well as the $1,000 from A.

13.   A contracts to bale hay on B's farm so that B can use it later to feed his livestock. A does the work so defectively that the hay is worthless. B can buy similar hay in bales in Central City, 100 miles from his farm, for $10,000. The cost to ship the bales between Central City and his farm is $1,000. B's damages include the $10,000 market price and the $1,000 cost of shipment. If B had intended to ship his bales of hay to Central City for sale there, rather than to feed it to his livestock, the $1,000 cost of shipment would be subtracted from the $10,000 market price as cost avoided under § 347(c).

14.   A contracts to sell to B a used machine from A's factory for $10,000. A breaks the contract by refusing to deliver the machine at that price, but offers to sell it to B for $11,000 without prejudice to B's right to damages. B refuses to buy it at that price and, since he cannot find a similar machine elsewhere, loses a profit of $25,000 that he would have made from use of the machine. B's damages do not include the loss of the $25,000 profit, but he can recover $1,000 from A.

15. The facts being otherwise as stated in Illustration 14, A's offer to sell the machine at $11,000 is conditioned on B's surrendering any claim that he may have against A for breach of contract. B's damages may include the loss of the $25,000 profit.

f. Time for arranging substitute transaction. The injured party is expected to arrange a substitute transaction within a reasonable time after he learns of the breach. He is expected to do this even if the breach takes the form of an anticipatory repudiation, since under the rule stated in Subsection (2) he is then protected against the possibility of a change in the market before the time for performance. See Comment *g*. The injured party may, however, make appropriate efforts to urge the repudiating party to perform in spite of his repudiation or to retract his repudiation, and these efforts will be taken into account in determining what is a reasonable time. Although the injured party is expected to arrange a substitute transaction without unreasonable delay following the anticipatory repudiation, the time for performance under the substitute transaction will ordinarily be the same time as it would have been under the original contract.

Illustrations:

16. On May 1, A contracts to sell to B a stated quantity of grain for $100,000, delivery and payment to be made on July 1. On July 1, A breaks the contract by refusing to deliver the grain, but B does not buy substitute grain on the market on that date although he could do so for $110,000. On July 10, B buys substitute grain on the market for $120,000. B's damages for A's breach of contract do not include the $20,000 above the contract price that he paid on July 10, but he can recover $10,000 from A.

17. The facts being otherwise as stated in Illustration 16, A breaks the contract by repudiating it on June 1 and on the same day B tells A that he considers the repudiation final. B does not buy substitute grain on the market on that date although he could do so for $105,000 for delivery and payment on July 1. B's damages for A's breach of contract do not include the $20,000 above the contract price that he paid on July 10, but he can recover $5,000 from A.

g. Efforts expected. In some situations, it is reasonable for the injured party to rely on performance by the other party even after breach. This may be true, for example, if the breach is accompanied by assurances that performance will be forthcoming. In such a situation the injured party is not expected to arrange a substitute transaction although he may be expected to take some steps to avoid loss due to a delay in performance. Nor is it reasonable to expect him to take steps to avoid loss if those steps may cause other serious loss. He need not, for example, make other risky contracts, incur unreasonable expense or inconvenience or disrupt his business. In rare instances the appropriate course may be to complete performance instead of stopping. Finally the aggrieved party is not expected to put himself in a position that will involve humiliation, including embarrassment or loss of honor and respect.

Illustrations:

18. A contracts to build a building for B for $100,000. B repudiates the contract shortly before A has finished work. Because A has duties to subcontractors and will have difficulty in calculating his damages, A spends an additional $10,000 and completes the building. If stopping work would not have been reasonable in the circumstances, A can recover the full $100,000, including the $10,000 that he spent after B's repudiation. Compare Illustration 1.

19. A contracts to supervise the production of B's crop for $10,000, but commits a material breach of the contract by failing to begin on time. By appropriate efforts, B could obtain an equally good supervisor for $1,000 more than he had contracted to pay A, but he does not do so because A assures him that the delay is only temporary. By the time that B discovers that A will be unavailable for the entire season, it is too late to hire another supervisor and the crop is lost. If B's delay in hiring another supervisor was reasonable in the circumstances, B's damages for A's breach of contract may include the loss of his crop.

20. A, a motion picture company, contracts to have B star in a musical comedy for $100,000. A breaks the contract and engages C, a rival of B, to star in the musical comedy, but offers B an equally good role under an identical contract as a star in another musical comedy for $100,000. Because B would be humiliated to work for A after A hired a rival in B's place, B refuses to accept the offer. If rejection of the offer was reasonable in the circumstances, B can recover the full $100,000. Compare Illustration 8.

h. Actual efforts to mitigate damages. Sometimes the injured party makes efforts to avoid loss but fails to do so. The rule stated in Subsection (2) protects the injured party in that situation if the efforts were reasonable. If, for example, a seller who is to manufacture goods for a buyer decides, on repudiation by the buyer, "in the exercise of reasonable commercial judgment for the purpose of avoiding loss" to complete manufacture of the goods, he is protected under Uniform Commercial Code § 2–704(2) even if it later appears that he could have better avoided loss by stopping manufacture. Similarly, if a buyer of goods who decides, on repudiation by the seller, to " 'cover' by making in good faith and without unreasonable delay any reasonable purchase of or contract to purchase goods in substitution for those due from the seller," he is protected under Uniform Commercial Code § 2-712. See also Uniform Commercial Code § 2–706 for the seller's comparable right of resale. The rule stated in Subsection (2) reflects the policy underlying these Code provisions, one encouraging the injured party to make reasonable efforts to avoid loss by protecting him even when his efforts fail. To this extent, his failure to avoid loss does not have the effect stated in Subsection (1). Under the rule stated in § 347, costs incurred in a reasonable but unsuccessful effort to avoid loss are recoverable as incidental losses. See Comment *c* to § 347.

Illustrations:

21. A contracts to sell to B a used machine to be delivered at A's factory by June 1 for $10,000. A breaks the contract by repudiating it on May 1. B makes a reasonable purchase of a similar machine for $12,000 in time to be delivered at his factory by June 1. It later appears that, unknown to B, a similar machine could have been found for only $11,000. Nevertheless, B can recover $2,000 from A. Compare Illustration 5. See Uniform Commercial Code § 2–712.

22. A contracts to supervise the production of B's crop for $10,000, but breaks his contract and leaves at the beginning of the season. B makes a reasonable substitute contract with another supervisor for $12,000 in time to save his crop. It later appears that, unknown to B, a suitable supervisor could have been found for only $11,000. Nevertheless, B can recover $2,000 from A. Compare Illustration 6.

23. A pays a premium to B, an insurance company, for a policy of fire insurance on his house for a period of five years. B later repudiates the policy and A reasonably gets a similar policy from another insurer for the balance of the period. A has a right to damages against B based on the cost of the new policy.

REPORTER'S NOTE

Subsection (1) is based on former § 336(1). Subsection (2) states the principle underlying Uniform Commercial Code §§ 2–706, 2–712. See 5 Corbin, Contracts §§ 1039–44 (1964 & Supp. 1980); 11 Williston, Contracts

§§ 1353–54 (3d ed. 1968); Childres, Buyer's Remedies: The Danger of Section 2–713, 72 Nw. U.L. Rev. 837 (1978); Jackson, "Anticipatory Repudiation" and the Temporal Element of Contract Law: An Economic Inquiry into Contract Damages in Cases of Prospective Nonperformance, 31 Stan. L. Rev. 69 (1978).

Comment b. Illustration 1 is based on Rockingham County v. Luten Bridge Co., 35 F.2d 301 (4th Cir. 1929); Clark v. Marsiglia, 1 Denio 317 (N.Y. Sup. Ct. 1845). Illustrations 2, 3 and 4 are based on Illustrations 5, 2 and 9 to former § 336.

Comment c. Illustration 5 is based on Uniform Commercial Code §§ 2–713(1), 2–715(2)(a). But cf. Anchorage Centennial Dev. Co. v. Van Wormer & Rodrigues, 443 P.2d 596 (Alaska 1968). Illustration 6 is based on Illustration 1 to former § 336; but cf. Roth v. Speck, 126 A.2d 153 (D.C. Ct. App. 1956). Illustration 7 is based on Uniform Commercial Code § 2–708(1). Illustration 8 is based on Sutherland v. Wyer, 67 Me. 64 (1877).

Comment d. Illustration 9 is based on Illustration 6 to former § 336; see Neri v. Retail Marine Corp., 30 N.Y.2d 393, 334 N.Y.S.2d 165, 285 N.E.2d 311 (1972); Snyder v. Herbert Greenbaum & Assoc., Inc., 38 Md. App. 144, 380 A.2d 618 (1977). Illustration 10 is based on Illustration 7 to former § 336; Coast Indus. v. Noonan, 4 Conn. Cir. Ct. 333, 231 A.2d 663 (1966); Wired Music v. Clark, 26 Ill. App.2d 413, 168 N.E.2d 736 (1960); Koplin v. Faulkner, 293 S.W.2d 467 (Ky. 1956); Mount Pleasant Stable Co. v. Steinberg, 238 Mass. 567, 131 N.E. 295 (1921); Locks v. Wade, 36 N.J. Super. 128, 114 A.2d 875 (1955).

Compare Stern v. Satra Corp., 539 F.2d 1305 (2d Cir. 1976).

Comment e. Illustration 11 is based on Hussey v. Holloway, 217 Mass. 100, 104 N.E. 471 (1914); State ex rel. Freeman v. Sierra County Bd. of Educ., 49 N.M. 54, 157 P.2d 234 (1945); Mr. Eddie v. Ginsberg, 430 S.W.2d 5 (Tex. Civ. App. 1968); cf. Parker v. Twentieth Century-Fox Co., 3 Cal.3d 176, 89 Cal. Rptr. 737, 474 P.2d 689 (1970). Illustration 12 is new. Illustration 13 is suggested by Watt v. Nevada Central R.R. Co., 23 Nev. 154, 44 P. 423, modified, 23 Nev. 154, 46 P. 52 (1896). Illustration 14 is based on Lawrence v. Porter, 63 F. 62 (6th Cir. 1894). Illustration 15 is based on Gilson v. F.S. Royster Guano Co., 1 F.2d 82 (3d Cir. 1924); Billetter v. Posell, 94 Cal. App.2d 858, 211 P.2d 621 (1947).

Comment f. This comment follows the reasoning of Uniform Commercial Code §§ 2–708 and 2–713 rather than that of former § 338. Illustration 16 is based on Uniform Commercial Code § 2–713. Illustration 17 is based on Oloffson v. Coomer, 11 Ill. App.3d 918, 296 N.E.2d 871 (1973); Cargill, Inc. v. Stafford, 553 F.2d 1222 (10th Cir. 1977). But cf. Olsen v. Scholl, 38 Ill. App.3d 340, 347 N.E.2d 195 (1976). See Renner Co. v. McNeff Bros., 102 F.2d 664, cert. denied, 308 U.S. 576 (1939), and Mays Mills v. McRae, 187 N.C. 707, 122 S.E. 762 (1924), decided before the adoption of the Uniform Commercial Code. But cf. Reliance Cooperage Co. v. Treat, 195 F.2d 977 (8th Cir. 1952), also decided before the adoption of the Code.

Comment g. Illustration 18 is based on Bomberger v. McKelvey, 35 Cal.2d 607, 220 P.2d 729 (1950);

Northern Helex Co. v. United States, 197 Ct. Cl. 118, 455 F.2d 546 (1972); Dowling v. Whites Lumber & Supply Co., 170 Miss. 267, 154 So. 703 (1934); see also Uniform Commercial Code § 2–704(2). Illustration 19 is supported by Steele v. J.I. Case Co., 197 Kan. 554, 419 P.2d 902 (1966). Illustration 20 is new; see

Western Grain Co. v. Barron G. Collier, Inc., 163 Ark. 369, 258 S.W. 979 (1924).

Comment h. Illustration 21 is based on Uniform Commercial Code § 2–712. Illustration 22 is new. Illustration 23 is based on Illustration 5 to former § 332.

§ 351. Unforeseeability and Related Limitations on Damages

(1) Damages are not recoverable for loss that the party in breach did not have reason to foresee as a probable result of the breach when the contract was made.

(2) Loss may be foreseeable as a probable result of a breach because it follows from the breach

(a) in the ordinary course of events, or

(b) as a result of special circumstances, beyond the ordinary course of events, that the party in breach had reason to know.

(3) A court may limit damages for foreseeable loss by excluding recovery for loss of profits, by allowing recovery only for loss incurred in reliance, or otherwise if it concludes that in the circumstances justice so requires in order to avoid disproportionate compensation.

Comment:

a. Requirement of foreseeability. A contracting party is generally expected to take account of those risks that are foreseeable at the time he makes the contract. He is not, however, liable in the event of breach for loss that he did not at the time of contracting have reason to foresee as a probable result of such a breach. The mere circumstance that some loss was foreseeable, or even that some loss of the same general kind was foreseeable, will not suffice if the loss that actually occurred was not foreseeable. It is enough, however, that the loss was foreseeable as a probable, as distinguished from a necessary, result of his breach. Furthermore, the party in breach need not have made a "tacit agreement" to be liable for the loss. Nor must he have had the loss in mind when making the contract, for the test is an objective one based on what he had reason to foresee. There is no requirement of foreseeability with respect to the injured party. In spite of these qualifications, the requirement of foreseeability is a more severe limitation of liability than is the requirement of substantial or "proximate" cause in the case of an action in tort or for breach of warranty. Compare Restatement, Second, Torts § 431; Uniform Commercial Code § 2–715(2)(b). Although the recovery that is precluded by the limitation of foreseeability is usually based on the expectation interest and takes the form of lost profits (see Illustration 1), the limitation may also preclude recovery based on the reliance interest (see Illustration 2).

Illustrations:

1. A, a carrier, contracts with B, a miller, to carry B's broken crankshaft to its manufacturer for repair. B tells A when they make the contract that the crankshaft is part of B's milling machine and that it must be sent at once, but not that the mill is stopped because B has no replacement. Because A delays in carrying the crankshaft, B loses profit during an additional period while the mill is stopped because of the delay. A is not liable for B's loss of profit. That loss was not foreseeable by A as a probable result of the breach at the time the contract was made because A did not know that the broken crankshaft was necessary for the operation of the mill.

2. A contracts to sell land to B and to give B possession on a stated date. Because A delays a short time in giving B possession, B incurs unusual expenses in providing for cattle that he had already purchased to stock the land as a ranch. A had no reason to know when they made the contract that B had planned to purchase cattle for this purpose. A is not liable for B's expenses in providing for the cattle because that loss was not foreseeable by A as a probable result of the breach at the time the contract was made.

b. *"General" and "special" damages.* Loss that results from a breach in the ordinary course of events is foreseeable as the probable result of the breach. See Uniform Commercial Code § 2–714(1). Such loss is sometimes said to be the "natural" result of the breach, in the sense that its occurrence accords with the common experience of ordinary persons. For example, a seller of a commodity to a wholesaler usually has reason to foresee that his failure to deliver the commodity as agreed will probably cause the wholesaler to lose a reasonable profit on it. See Illustrations 3 and 4. Similarly, a seller of a machine to a manufacturer usually has reason to foresee that his delay in delivering the machine as agreed will probably cause the manufacturer to lose a reasonable profit from its use, although courts have been somewhat more cautious in allowing the manufacturer recovery for loss of such profits than in allowing a middleman recovery for loss of profits on an intended resale. See Illustration 5. The damages recoverable for such loss that results in the ordinary course of events are sometimes called "general" damages.

If loss results other than in the ordinary course of events, there can be no recovery for it unless it was foreseeable by the party in breach because of special circumstances that he had reason to know when he made the contract. See Uniform Commercial Code § 2–715(2)(a). For example, a seller who fails to deliver a commodity to a wholesaler is not liable for the wholesaler's loss of profit to the extent that it is extraordinary nor for his loss due to unusual terms in his resale contracts unless the seller had reason to know of these special circumstances. See Illustration 6. Similarly, a seller who delays in delivering a machine to a manufacturer is not liable for the manufacturer's loss of profit to the extent that it results from an intended use that was abnormal unless the seller had reason to know of this special circumstance. See Illustration 7. In the case of a written agreement, foreseeability is sometimes established by the use of recitals in the agreement itself. The parol evidence rule (§ 213) does not, however, preclude the use of negotiations prior to the making of the contract to show for this purpose circumstances that were then known to a party. The damages recoverable for loss that results other than in the ordinary course of events are sometimes called "special" or "consequential" damages. These terms are often misleading, however, and it is not necessary to distinguish between "general" and "special" or "consequential" damages for the purpose of the rule stated in this Section.

Illustrations:

     3. A and B make a written contract under which A is to recondition by a stated date a used machine owned by B so that it will be suitable for sale by B to C. A knows when they make the contract that B has contracted to sell the machine to C but knows nothing of the terms of B's contract with C. Because A delays in returning the machine to B, B is unable to sell it to C and loses the profit that he would have made on that sale. B's loss of reasonable profit was foreseeable by A as a probable result of the breach at the time the contract was made.

4. A, a manufacturer of machines, contracts to make B his exclusive selling agent in a specified area for the period of a year. Because A fails to deliver any machines, B loses the profit on contracts that he would have made for their resale. B's loss of reasonable profit was foreseeable by A as a probable result of the breach at the time the contract was made.

5. A and B make a contract under which A is to recondition by a stated date a used machine owned by B so that it will be suitable for use in B's canning factory. A knows that the machine must be reconditioned by that date if B's factory is to operate at full capacity during the canning season, but nothing is said of this in the written contract. Because A delays in returning the machine to B, B loses its use for the entire canning season and loses the profit that he would have made had his factory operated at full capacity. B's loss of reasonable profit was foreseeable by A as a probable result of the breach at the time the contract was made.

6. The facts being otherwise as stated in Illustration 3, the profit that B would have made under his contract with A was extraordinarily large because C promised to pay an exceptionally high price as a result of a special need for the machine of which A was unaware. A is not liable for B's loss of profit to the extent that it exceeds what would ordinarily result from such a contract. To that extent the loss was not foreseeable by A as a probable result of the breach at the time the contract was made.

7. The facts being otherwise as stated in Illustration 5, the profit that B would have made from the use of the machine was unusually large because of an abnormal use to which he planned to put it of which A was unaware. A is not liable for B's loss of profit to the extent that it exceeds what would ordinarily result from the use of such a machine. To that extent the loss was not foreseeable by A at the time the contract was made as a probable result of the breach.

c. Litigation or settlement caused by breach. Sometimes a breach of contract results in claims by third persons against the injured party. The party in breach is liable for the amount of any judgment against the injured party together with his reasonable expenditures in the litigation, if the party in breach had reason to foresee such expenditures as the probable result of his breach at the time he made the contract. See Illustrations 8, 10, 11 and 12. This is so even if the judgment in the litigation is based on a liquidated damage clause in the injured party's contract with the third party. See Illustration 8. A failure to notify the party in breach in advance of the litigation may prevent the result of the litigation from being conclusive as to him. But to the extent that the injured party's loss resulting from litigation is reasonable, the fact that the party in breach was not notified does not prevent the inclusion of that loss in the damages assessed against him. In furtherance of the policy favoring private settlement of disputes, the injured party is also allowed to recover the reasonable amount of any settlement made to avoid litigation, together with the costs of settlement. See Illustration 9.

Illustrations:

    8. The facts being otherwise as stated in Illustration 3, B not only loses the profit that he would have made on sale of the machine to C, but is held liable for damages in an action brought by C for breach of contract. The damages paid to C and B's reasonable expenses in defending the action were also foreseeable by A as a probable result of the breach at the time he made the contract with B. The result is the same even though they were based on a liquidated damage clause in the contract between B and C if A knew of the clause or if the use of such a clause in the contract between B and C was foreseeable by A at the time he made the contract with B.

    9. The facts being otherwise as stated in Illustration 3, B not only loses the profit that he would have made on sale of the machine to C, but settles with C by paying C a reasonable sum of money to avoid litigation. The amount of the settlement paid to C and B's reasonable expenses in settling were also foreseeable by A at the time he made the contract with B as a probable result of the breach.

    10. A contracts to supply B with machinery for unloading cargo. A, in breach of contract, furnishes defective machinery, and C, an employee of B, is injured. C sues B and gets a judgment, which B pays. The amount of the judgment and B's reasonable expenditures in defending the action were foreseeable by A at the time the contract was made as a probable result of the breach.

    11. A contracts to procure a right of way for B, for a railroad. Because A, in breach of contract, fails to do this, B has to acquire the right of way by condemnation proceedings. B's reasonable expenditures in those proceedings were foreseeable by A at the time the contract was made as a probable result of the breach.

---

12. A leases land to B with a covenant for quiet enjoyment. C brings an action of ejectment against B and gets judgment. B's reasonable expenditures in defending the action were foreseeable by A as the probable result of the breach at the time the contract was made.

d. Unavailability of substitute. If several circumstances have contributed to cause a loss, the party in breach is not liable for it unless he had reason to foresee all of them. Sometimes a loss would not have occurred if the injured party had been able to make substitute arrangements after breach, as, for example, by "cover" through purchase of substitute goods in the case of a buyer of goods (see Uniform Commercial Code § 2–712). If the inability of the injured party to make such arrangements was foreseeable by the party in breach at the time he made the contract, the resulting loss was foreseeable. See Illustration 13. On the impact of this principle on contracts to lend money, see Comment *e.*

Illustration:

13. A contracts with B, a farmer, to lease B a machine to be used harvesting B's crop, delivery to be made on July 30. A knows when he makes the contract that B's crop will be ready on that date and that B cannot obtain another machine elsewhere. Because A delays delivery until August 10, B's crop is damaged and he loses profit. B's loss of profit was foreseeable by A at the time the contract was made as a probable result of the breach.

e. Breach of contract to lend money. The limitation of foreseeability is often applied in actions for damages for breach of contracts to lend money. Because credit is so widely available, a lender often has no reason to foresee at the time the contract is made that the borrower will be unable to make substitute arrangements in the event of breach. See Comment *d.* In most cases, then, the lender's liability will be limited to the relatively small additional amount that it would ordinarily cost to get a similar loan from another lender. However, in the less common situation in which the lender has reason to foresee that the borrower will be unable to borrow elsewhere or will be delayed in borrowing elsewhere, the lender may be liable for much heavier damages based on the borrower's inability to take advantage of a specific opportunity (see Illustration 14), his having to postpone or abandon a profitable project (see Illustration 15), or his forfeiture of security for failure to make prompt payment (see Illustration 16).

Illustrations:

14. A contracts to lend B $100,000 for one year at eight percent interest for the stated purpose of buying a specific lot of goods for resale. B can resell the goods at a $20,000 profit. A delays in making the loan, and although B can borrow money on the market at ten percent interest, he is unable to do so in time and loses the opportunity to buy the goods. Unless A had reason to foresee at the time that he made the contract that such a delay in making the loan would probably cause B to lose the opportunity, B can only recover damages based on two percent of the amount of the loan.

15. A contracts to lend $1,000,000 to B for the stated purpose of enabling B to build a building and takes property of B as security. After construction is begun, A refuses to make the loan or release the security. Because B lacks further security, he is unable to complete the building, which becomes a total loss. B's loss incurred in partial construction of the building was foreseeable by A at the time of the contract as a probable result of the breach.

16. A, who holds B's land as security for a loan, contracts to lend B a sum of money sufficient to pay off other liens on the land at the current rate of interest. A repudiates and informs B in time to obtain money elsewhere on the market, but B is unable to do so. The liens are foreclosed and the land sold at a loss. Unless A knew when he made the contract that B would probably be unable to borrow the money elsewhere, B's loss on the foreclosure sale was not foreseeable as a probable result of A's breach.

f. Other limitations on damages. It is not always in the interest of justice to require the party in breach to pay damages for all of the foreseeable loss that he has caused. There are unusual instances in which it appears from the circumstances either that the parties assumed that one of them would not bear the risk of a particular loss or that, although there was no such assumption, it would be unjust to put the risk on that party. One such circumstance is an extreme disproportion between the loss and the price charged by the party whose liability for that loss is in question. The fact that the price is relatively small suggests that it was not intended to cover the risk of such liability. Another such circumstance is an informality of dealing, including the absence of a detailed written contract, which indicates that there was no careful attempt to allocate all of the risks. The fact that the parties did not attempt to delineate with precision all of the risks justifies a court in attempting to allocate them fairly. The limitations dealt with in this Section are more likely to be imposed in connection with contracts that do not arise in a commercial setting. Typical examples of limitations imposed on damages under this discretionary power involve the denial of recovery for loss of profits and the restriction of damages to loss incurred in reliance on the contract. Sometimes these limits are covertly imposed, by means of an especially demanding requirement of foreseeability or of certainty. The rule stated in this Section recognizes that what is done in such cases is the imposition of a limitation in the interests of justice.

Illustrations:

17. A, a private trucker, contracts with B to deliver to B's factory a machine that has just been repaired and without which B's factory, as A knows, cannot reopen. Delivery is delayed because A's truck breaks down. In an action by B against A for breach of contract the court may, after taking into consideration such factors as the absence of an elaborate written contract and the extreme disproportion between B's loss of profits during the delay and the price of the trucker's services, exclude recovery for loss of profits.

18. A, a retail hardware dealer, contracts to sell B an inexpensive lighting attachment, which, as A knows, B needs in order to use his tractor at night on his farm. A is delayed in obtaining the attachment and, since no substitute is available, B is unable to use the tractor at night during the delay. In an action by B against A for breach of contract, the court may, after taking into consideration such factors as the absence of an elaborate written contract and the extreme disproportion between B's loss of profits during the delay and the price of the attachment, exclude recovery for loss of profits.

19. A, a plastic surgeon, makes a contract with B, a professional entertainer, to perform plastic surgery on her face in order to improve her appearance. The result of the surgery is, however, to disfigure her face and to require a second operation. In an action by B against A for breach of contract, the court may limit damages by allowing recovery only for loss incurred by B in reliance on the contract, including the fees paid by B and expenses for hospitalization, nursing care and medicine for both operations, together with any damages for the worsening of B's appearance if these can be proved with reasonable certainty, but not including any loss resulting from the failure to improve her appearance.

REPORTER'S NOTE

Subsections (1) and (2) are based on former § 330, with changes in language to conform to the language of Uniform Commercial Code §§ 2–714(1) and 2–715(2)(a). Subsection (3) is new. See 5 Corbin, Contracts §§ 1006–19 (1964 & Supp. 1980); 11 Williston, Contracts §§ 1344–44A, 1347, 1355–57 (3d ed. 1968); Danzig, *Hadley v. Baxendale: A Study in the Industrialization of the Law*, 4 J. Legal Stud. 249 (1975).

Comment a. This Comment rejects the "tacit agreement" test of Globe Ref. Co. v. Landa Cotton Oil Co., 190 U.S. 540 (1903). See Comment 2 to Uniform Commercial Code § 2–715; R.I. Lampus Co. v. Neville Cement Prods. Corp., 474 Pa. 199, 378 A.2d 288 (1977). When parties expressly exclude or limit consequential damages, the basic principles of freedom of contract counsel that the agreed upon provision should be enforced. Nonetheless, courts are often asked after the fact not to enforce such provisions and may construe a provision narrowly or find it unenforceable because of lack of bargain, bad faith, unconscionability or public policy. See Note, "No Damage" Clauses in Construction Contracts: A Critique, 53 Wash. L. Rev. 471 (1978); Annot., 74 A.L.R.3d 187 (1976). See also Siefford v. Housing Auth., 192 Neb. 643, 223 N.W.2d 816 (1974); American Elec. Power Co. v. Westinghouse Elec. Corp., 418 F. Supp. 435 (S.D.N.Y. 1976). Illustration 1 is based on Hadley v. Baxendale, 9 Exch. 341, 156 Eng. Rep. 145 (1854); cf. Kerr S.S. Co. v. Radio Corp. of America, 245 N.Y. 284, 157 N.E. 140, cert. denied, 275 U.S. 557 (1927). But cf.

Armstrong v. Bangor Mill Supply Corp., 128 Me. 75, 145 A. 741 (1929). Illustration 2 is based on Sitlington v. Fulton, 281 F.2d 552 (10th Cir. 1960); see also Rochester Lantern Co. v. Stiles & Parker Co., 135 N.Y. 209, 31 N.E. 1018 (1892).

Comment b. Illustration 3 is based on Illustration 9 to former § 330; see also Brewer v. Custom Builders Corp., 42 Ill. App.3d 668, 1 Ill. Dec. 377, 356 N.E.2d 565 (1976) (builder liable for water damage to drywall installed by homeowner after assurance by builder that roof was watertight). But cf. Berlin Dev. Corp. v. Vermont Structural Steel Corp., 127 Vt. 367, 250 A.2d 189 (1968). Illustration 4 is based on Illustration 3 to former § 330; see Appliances v. Queen Stove Works, 228 Minn. 55, 36 N.W.2d 121 (1949). Illustration 5 is based on Illustration 6 to former § 330; Victoria Laundry (Windsor) v. Newman Indus., [1949] 2 K.B. 528; cf. Spang Indus. v. Aetna Cas. and Sur. Co., 512 F.2d 365 (2d Cir. 1975); Armstrong v. Bangor Mill Supply Corp., 128 Me. 75, 145 A. 741 (1929). Illustration 6 is based on Illustration 7 to former § 330; Guetzkow Bros. v. A.H. Andrews & Co., 92 Wis. 214, 66 N.W. 119 (1896); cf. Booth v. Spuyten Duyvil Rolling Mill Co., 60 N.Y. 487 (1875). But cf. Hill's, Inc. v. William B. Kessler, Inc., 41 Wash.2d 42, 246 P.2d 1099 (1952). Illustration 7 is based on Cory v. Thames Ironworks & Shipbuilding Co., L.R. 3 Q.B. 181 (1868); see Adams Express Co. v. Allen, 125 Va. 530, 100 S.E. 473 (1919).

Comment c. This Comment is based on former § 334. Illustration 8 is based on Illustration 1 to former §

334; see also Verhagen v. Platt, 1 N.J. 85, 61 A.2d 892 (1948). As to liquidated damages, it is based on Illustration 11 to former § 330; Krauss v. Greenbarg, 137 F.2d 569 (3d Cir.), cert. denied, 320 U.S. 791 (1943). But cf. Albany Phosphate Co. v. Hugger Bros., 4 Ga. App. 771, 62 S.E. 533 (1908); Longview Constr. and Dev. v. Loggins Constr. Co., 523 S.W.2d 771 (Tex. Civ. App. 1975). Illustration 9 is supported by Verhagen v. Platt, supra. But cf. Chrysler Corp. v. E. Shavitz & Sons, 536 F.2d 743 (7th Cir. 1976); Czarnikow-Rionda Co. v. Federal Sugar Ref. Co., 255 N.Y. 33, 173 N.E. 913 (1930). Illustrations 10, 11 and 12 are based on Illustrations 5, 4 and 2 to former § 334. See also Stone, Recovery of Consequential Damages for Product Recall Expenditures, 1980 B.Y.U.L. Rev. 485.

Comment d. Illustration 13 is based on Illustration 10 to former § 330; see also Murarka v. Bachrack Bros., 215 F.2d 547 (2d Cir. 1954); Kelley, Maus & Co. v. La Crosse Carriage Co., 120 Wis. 84, 97 N.W. 674 (1903). But cf. Marcus & Co. v. K.L.G. Baking Co., 122 N.J.L. 202, 3 A.2d 627 (1939).

Comment e. This Comment is based on former § 343. Illustration 14 is based on Illustration 1 to former § 343. Illustration 15 is based on Illustration 3 to former § 343; Stanish v. Polish Roman Catholic Union of America, 484 F.2d 713 (7th Cir. 1973); Spiese v. Mutual Trust Co., 258 Pa. 414, 102 A. 119 (1917). But cf. McMillain Lumber Co. v. First Nat'l Bank of Eutaw, 215 Ala. 379, 110 So. 602 (1926). Illustration 16 is based on Illustration 2 to former § 343; Doushkess v. Burger Brewing Co., 20 A. D. 375, 47 N.Y.S. 312 (1897).

Comment f. Illustration 17 is suggested by Kerr S.S. Co. v. Radio Corp. of America, 245 N.Y. 284, 157 N.E. 140, cert. denied, 275 U.S. 557 (1927); Newsome v. Western Union Tel. Co., 153 N.C. 153, 69 S.E. 10 (1910). Reasoning such as that in Harper Furniture Co. v. Southern Express Co., 148 N.C. 87, 62 S.E. 145 (Super. Ct. 1908), aff'd by equally divided ct., 151 N.C. 739, 67 S.E. 1132 (1909), is rejected. Illustration 18 is based on Lamkins v. International Harvester Co., 207 Ark. 637, 182 S.W.2d 203 (1944). Illustration 19 is based on Sullivan v. O'Connor, 363 Mass. 579, 296 N.E.2d 183 (1973).

§ 352. Uncertainty as a Limitation on Damages

Damages are not recoverable for loss beyond an amount that the evidence permits to be established with reasonable certainty.

Comment:

a. Requirement of certainty. A party cannot recover damages for breach of a contract for loss beyond the amount that the evidence permits to be established with reasonable certainty. See Illustration

1. Courts have traditionally required greater certainty in the proof of damages for breach of a contract than in the proof of damages for a tort. The requirement does not mean, however, that the injured party is barred from recovery unless he establishes the total amount of his loss. It merely excludes those elements of loss that cannot be proved with reasonable certainty. The main impact of the requirement of certainty comes in connection with recovery for lost profits. Although the requirement of certainty is distinct from that of foreseeability (§ 351), its impact is similar in this respect. Although the requirement applies to damages based on the reliance as well as the expectation interest, there is usually little difficulty in proving the amount that the injured party has actually spent in reliance on the contract, even if it is impossible to prove the amount of profit that he would have made. In such a case, he can recover his loss based on his reliance interest instead of on his expectation interest. See § 349 and Illustrations 1, 2 and 3.

Doubts are generally resolved against the party in breach. A party who has, by his breach, forced the injured party to seek compensation in damages should not be allowed to profit from his breach where it is established that a significant loss has occurred. A court may take into account all the circumstances of the breach, including willfulness, in deciding whether to require a lesser degree of certainty, giving greater discretion to the trier of the facts. Damages need not be calculable with mathematical accuracy and are often at best approximate. See Comment 1 to Uniform Commercial Code § 1–106. This is especially true for items such as loss of good will as to which great precision cannot be expected. See Illustration 4. Furthermore, increasing receptiveness on the part of courts to proof by sophisticated economic and financial data and by expert opinion has made it easier to meet the requirement of certainty.

Illustrations:

    1. A contracts to publish a novel that B has written. A repudiates the contract and B is unable to get his novel published elsewhere. If the evidence does not permit B's loss of royalties and of reputation to be estimated with reasonable certainty, he cannot recover damages for that loss, although he can recover nominal damages. See Illustration 1 to § 347.

    2. A contracts to sell B a tract of land on which B plans to build an outdoor drive-in theatre. A breaks the contract by selling the land to C, and B is unable to build the theatre. If, because of the speculative nature of the new enterprise the evidence does

not permit B's loss of profits to be estimated with reasonable certainty, his recovery will be limited to expenses incurred in reliance or, if none can be proved with reasonable certainty, to nominal damages.

3. A and B make a contract under which A is to construct a building of radical new design for B for $5,000,000. After A has spent $3,000,000 in reliance, B repudiates the contract and orders A off the site. If the evidence does not permit A's lost profits to be estimated with reasonable certainty, he can recover the $3,000,000 that he has spent in reliance. He must, however, then prove that amount with reasonable certainty.

4. A, a manufacturer, makes a contract with B, a wholesaler, to sell B a quantity of plastic. B resells the plastic to dealers. The plastic is discovered to be defective and B has many complaints from dealers, some of which refuse to place further orders with him. B can recover the loss of good will if his loss can be estimated with reasonable certainty by such evidence as his business records before and after the transaction and the testimony of his salespersons and that of dealers.

b. Proof of profits. The difficulty of proving lost profits varies greatly with the nature of the transaction. If, for example, it is the seller who claims lost profit on the ground that the buyer's breach has caused him to lose a sale, proof of lost profit will ordinarily not be difficult. If, however, it is the buyer who claims lost profit on the ground that the seller's breach has caused him loss in other transactions, the task of proof is harder. Furthermore, if the transaction is more complex and extends into the future, as where the seller agrees to furnish all of the buyer's requirements over a period of years, proof of the loss of profits caused by the seller's breach is more difficult. If the breach prevents the injured party from carrying on a well-established business, the resulting loss of profits can often be proved with sufficient certainty. Evidence of past performance will form the basis for a reasonable prediction as to the future. See Illustration 5. However, if the business is a new one or if it is a speculative one that is subject to great fluctuations in volume, costs or prices, proof will be more difficult. Nevertheless, damages may be established with reasonable certainty with the aid of expert testimony, economic and financial data, market surveys and analyses, business records of similar enterprises, and the like. See Illustration 6. Under a contract of exclusive agency for the sale of goods on commission, the agent can often prove with sufficient certainty the profits that he would have made had he not been discharged. Proof of the sales made by the agent in the agreed territory before the breach, or of the sales made there by the principal after the breach, may permit a reasonably accurate estimate of the agent's loss of commissions. However, if the agency is not an exclusive one, so that the agent's ability to withstand competition is in question, such a showing will be more difficult, although the agent's past record may give a sufficient basis for judging this. See Illustration 7.

Illustrations:

    5. A contracts with B to remodel B's existing outdoor drive-in theatre, work to be completed on June 1. A does not complete the work until September 1. B can use records of the theatre's prior and subsequent operation, along with other evidence, to prove his lost profits with reasonable certainty.

    6. A contracts with B to construct a new outdoor drive-in theatre, to be completed on June 1. A does not complete the theatre until September 1. Even though the business is a new rather than an established one, B may be able to prove his lost profits with reasonable certainty. B can use records of the theatre's subsequent operation and of the operation of similar theatres in the same locality, along with other evidence including market surveys and expert testimony, in attempting to do this.

    7. A contracts with B to make B his exclusive agent for the sale of machine tools in a specified territory and to supply him with machine tools at stated prices. After B has begun to act as A's agent, A repudiates the agreement and replaces him with C. B can use evidence as to sales and profits made by him before the repudiation and made by C after the repudiation in attempting to prove his lost profits with reasonable certainty. It would be more difficult, although not necessarily impossible, for B to succeed in this attempt if his agency were not exclusive.

    c. Alternative remedies. The necessity of proving damages can be avoided if another remedy, such as a decree of specific performance or an injunction, is granted instead of damages. Although the availability of such a remedy does not preclude an award of damages as an alternative, it may justify a court in requiring greater certainty of proof if damages are to be awarded. See Illustration 8.

Illustration:

    8. A, a steel manufacturer, and B, a dealer in scrap steel, contract for the sale by A to B of all of A's output of scrap steel for five years at a price fixed in terms of the market price. B's profit

will depend largely on the amount of A's output and the cost of transporting the scrap to B's purchasers. A repudiates the contract at the end of one year. Whether B can recover damages based on lost profits over the remaining four years will depend on whether he can prove A's output and the transportation costs with reasonable certainty. If he can do so for part of the remaining four years, he can recover damages based on lost profits for that period. The availability of the remedy of specific performance is a factor that will influence a court in requiring greater certainty.

REPORTER'S NOTE

This Section continues the rule stated in former § 331. See 5 Corbin, Contracts §§ 1020–25 (1964 & Supp. 1980); 11 Williston, Contracts §§ 1345–46A (3d ed. 1968); Notes, 64 Harv. L. Rev. 317 (1950); 56 N.C.L. Rev. 693 (1978); 65 Yale L.J. 992 (1956).

Comment a. Illustration 1 is based on Freund v. Washington Square Press, 34 N.Y.2d 379, 357 N.Y.S.2d 857, 314 N.E.2d 419 (1974). Illustration 2 is based on Illustrations 6 and 8 to former § 331; Evergreen Amusement Corp. v. Milstead, 206 Md. 610, 112 A.2d 901 (1955); see also Gerwin v. Southeastern Cal. Ass'n of Seventh Day Adventists, 14 Cal. App.3d 209, 92 Cal. Rptr. 111 (1971); Paola Gas Co. v. Paola Glass Co., 56 Kan. 614, 44 P. 621 (1896); Cramer v. Grand Rapids Show Case Co., 223 N.Y. 63, 119 N.E. 227 (1918); Winston Cigarette Mach. Co. v. Wells-Whitehead Tobacco Co., 141 N.C. 284, 53 S.E. 885 (1906). Illustration 3 is supported by Illustrations 3, 4 and 5 to former § 333; United States v. Behan, 110 U.S. 338 (1884); Dade County, Florida v. Palmer & Baker Eng'rs, 339 F.2d 208 (5th Cir. 1964); Sperry & Hutchinson Co. v. O'Neill-Adams Co., 185 F. 231 (2d Cir. 1911); L. Albert & Son v. Armstrong Rub-

ber Co., 178 F.2d 182 (2d Cir. 1949); Gruber v. S-M News Co., 126 F. Supp. 442 (S.D.N.Y. 1954); Security Stove & Mfg. Co. v. American Ry. Express Co., 227 Mo. App. 175, 51 S.W.2d 572 (1932); Holt v. United Security Life Ins. & Trust Co., 76 N.J.L. 585, 72 A. 301 (1909). But cf. Beefy Trail v. Beefy King Internat'l, 267 So.2d 853 (Fla. Dist. Ct. App. 1972). Illustration 4 is based on Sol-O-Lite Laminating Corp. v. Allen, 223 Or. 80, 353 P.2d 843 (1960); Stott v. Johnston, 36 Cal.2d 864, 229 P.2d 348 (1951); see Comment, 75 Dick. L. Rev. 63 (1970). Compare Brewer v. Customer Builders Corp., 42 Ill. App.3d 668, 1 Ill. Dec. 377, 356 N.E.2d 565 (1976).

Comment b. Illustration 5 is based on Illustration 7 to former § 331; Rombola v. Cosindas, 351 Mass. 382, 220 N.E.2d 919 (1966). As to Illustration 6, compare Evergreen Amusement Co. v. Milstead, supra, with Ferrell v. Elrod, 63 Tenn. App. 129, 469 S.W.2d 678 (1971); cf. El Fredo Pizza v. Roto-Flex Oven Co., 199 Neb. 697, 261 N.W.2d 358 (1978). Illustration 7 is based on Illustration 9 to former § 331; Excelsior Motor Mfg. & Supply Co. v. Sound Equip., 73 F.2d 725 (7th Cir.), cert. denied, 294 U.S. 706 (1934).

See Appendix for Court Citations and Cross References

Comment c. Illustration 8 is supported by Locke v. United States, 151 Ct. Cl. 262, 283 F.2d 521 (1960); facts are taken from Eastern Rolling Mill Co. v. Michlovitz, 157 Md. 51, 145 A. 378 (1929); cf. Peterson v. Colorado Potato Flake & Mfg. Co., 164 Colo. 304, 435 P.2d 237 (1967).

§ 353.   Loss Due to Emotional Disturbance

Recovery for emotional disturbance will be excluded unless the breach also caused bodily harm or the contract or the breach is of such a kind that serious emotional disturbance was a particularly likely result.

Comment:

a. Emotional disturbance. Damages for emotional disturbance are not ordinarily allowed. Even if they are foreseeable, they are often particularly difficult to establish and to measure. There are, however, two exceptional situations where such damages are recoverable. In the first, the disturbance accompanies a bodily injury. In such cases the action may nearly always be regarded as one in tort, although most jurisdictions do not require the plaintiff to specify the nature of the wrong on which his action is based and award damages without classifying the wrong. See Restatement, Second, Torts §§ 436, 905. In the second exceptional situation, the contract or the breach is of such a kind that serious emotional disturbance was a particularly likely result. Common examples are contracts of carriers and innkeepers with passengers and guests, contracts for the carriage or proper disposition of dead bodies, and contracts for the delivery of messages concerning death. Breach of such a contract is particularly likely to cause serious emotional disturbance. Breach of other types of contracts, resulting for example in sudden impoverishment or bankruptcy, may by chance cause even more severe emotional disturbance, but, if the contract is not one where this was a particularly likely risk, there is no recovery for such disturbance.

Illustrations:

1. A contracts to construct a house for B. A knows when the contract is made that B is in delicate health and that proper completion of the work is of great importance to him. Because of delays and departures from specifications, B suffers nervousness and emotional distress. In an action by B against A for breach of contract, the element of emotional disturbance will not be included as loss for which damages may be awarded.

2. A, a hotel keeper, wrongfully ejects B, a guest, in breach of contract. In doing so, A uses foul language and accuses B of immorality, but commits no assault. In an action by B against A for breach of contract, the element of B's emotional disturbance will be included as loss for which damages may be awarded.

3. A makes a contract with B to conduct the funeral for B's husband and to provide a suitable casket and vault for his burial. Shortly thereafter, B discovers that, because A knowingly failed to provide a vault with a suitable lock, water has entered it and reinterment is necessary. B suffers shock, anguish and illness as a result. In an action by B against A for breach of contract, the element of emotional disturbance will be included as loss for which damages may be awarded.

4. The facts being as stated in Illustration 19 to § 351, the element of emotional disturbance resulting from the additional operation will be included as loss for which damages may be awarded.

REPORTER'S NOTE

This Section is based on former § 341. See 5 Corbin, Contracts §§ 1076 (1964); 11 Williston, Contracts §§ 1338, 1341 (3d ed. 1968); Comments, 55 Canadian B. Rev. 169, 333 (1977).

Comment a. Illustration 1 is based on Jankowski v. Mazzotta, 7 Mich. App. 483, 152 N.W.2d 49 (1967); cf. Carpel v. Saget Studios, 326 F. Supp. 1331 (E.D. Pa. 1971). Illustration 2 is based on Illustration 1 to former § 341. Illustration 3 is based on Lamm v. Shingleton, 231 N.C. 10, 55 S.E.2d 810 (1949); Hirst v. Elgin Metal Casket Co., 438 F. Supp. 906 (D. Mont. 1977); cf. Stewart v. Rudner, 349 Mich. 459, 84 N.W.2d 816 (1957); Illustrations 3 and 4 to former § 341. Illustration 4 is based on Sullivan v. O'Connor, 363 Mass. 579, 296 N.E.2d 183 (1973); see also Heywood v. Wellers, [1976], 1 All E.R. 300 (C.A.), 55 Canadian B. Rev. 169 (1977).

§ 354. Interest as Damages

(1) If the breach consists of a failure to pay a definite sum in money or to render a performance with fixed or ascertainable monetary value, interest is recoverable from the time for performance on the amount due less all deductions to which the party in breach is entitled.

(2) In any other case, such interest may be allowed as justice requires on the amount that would have been

just compensation had it been paid when performance was due.

Comment:

a. Scope. This Section deals with an injured party's right to interest as damages in compensation for the deprivation of a promised performance. Had the performance been rendered when it was due, the injured party would have been able to make use of it. Interest is a standardized form of compensation to the injured party for the loss of that use, in the absence of agreement to the contrary. It is payable without compounding at the rate, commonly called the "legal rate," fixed by statute for this purpose.

This Section does not deal with the injured party's right to interest to compensate him for expenditures occasioned by the breach. If, following an anticipatory repudiation, he loses the use of money through making reasonable substitute arrangements, he is entitled to interest as incidental damages under the rule stated in § 347. Nor does this Section deal with the injured party's right to interest under the terms of the contract. If the parties have agreed on the payment of interest, it is payable not as damages but pursuant to a contract duty that is enforceable as is any other such duty, subject to legal restrictions on the rate of interest. Nor does this Section deal with interest on a judgment once rendered.

b. Performance must be due. Interest is not payable as damages for non-performance until performance is due. If there is a period of time before performance is due, such as a definite or indefinite period of credit, interest does not begin to run until the period is over. If the performance is to be rendered on demand, interest does not begin to run until a demand is made, even though an action might be maintained without a demand. See Illustration 3 to § 226. If the action itself is considered to be the required demand, interest begins to run from the time the action is brought. If the performance is subject to the occurrence of an event as a condition, interest does not begin to run until that condition occurs or is excused.

c. Where amount due is sufficiently definite. Under the rule stated in Subsection (1), a party is not chargeable with interest on a sum unless its amount is fixed by the contract or he could have determined its amount with reasonable certainty so that he could have made a proper tender. Unless otherwise agreed, interest is always recoverable for the non-payment of money once payment has become due and there has been a breach. This rule applies to debts due for money lent, goods sold or services performed, including installments due on a construction contract. The fact that the breach has spared some expense that is uncertain in amount does not prevent the recovery of interest. The sum due is sufficiently definite if it is ascertainable from the terms of the contract, as where the contract fixes a price per unit of performance, even though the number of units performed must be proved and is subject to dispute. The same is true, even if the contract does not of itself create a money debt, if it fixes a money equivalent of the performance. It is also true, even if the contract does not fix a money equivalent of the performance, if such an equivalent can be determined from established market prices. The fact that the extent of the performance rendered and the existence of the market price must be proved by evidence extrinsic to the contract does not prevent the application of these rules.

Illustrations:

1. A lends B $10,000 to be repaid in 30 days without interest. B fails to pay the debt. A sues B and recovers $10,000. A is also entitled to simple interest on the $10,000 at the legal rate from the date of maturity.

2. A contracts to sell B goods for $10,000 on 30 days credit, nothing being said as to interest. A delivers the goods but B fails to pay for them at the end of 30 days. A sues B and recovers $10,000. A is also entitled to simple interest on the $10,000 at the legal rate from the expiration of the credit period.

3. A contracts to sell B all the berries to be grown on A's farm during one year for $5 a quart. A delivers 2,000 quarts. No part of the price is paid. B wrongly claims that only 1,000 quarts were delivered and that they were all paid for when received. A sues B and recovers $10,000. A is also entitled to simple interest on the $10,000 at the legal rate from the date when payment was due.

4. A contracts to sell machinery to B for $10,000, the price to be paid by B in wheat at the market price on July 1. A delivers the machinery but B fails to deliver the wheat. A sues B and recovers $10,000. A is also entitled to simple interest on the $10,000 at the legal rate from July 1. The result would be the same if the price were not expressed in dollars but in terms of 1,000 bushels of wheat to be delivered on July 1 and the market price on that day was $10 a bushel.

5. On February 1 A makes a contract to sell a ship to B for $10,000,000, payment and delivery to be October 1. On September 1, B repudiates the contract and A promptly makes a reasona-

ble contract to resell the ship for $8,000,000, payment and delivery to take place on October 1. A sues B and recovers $2,000,000. A is entitled to simple interest on the $2,000,000 at the legal rate from October 1.

6. A contracts to cut and deliver to B 1 million feet of lumber from trees on B's land. Delivery is to be by June 1 and the price is $100 per thousand feet payable on delivery. After A has spent $30,000 in cutting the timber, but before he has delivered any of it, B repudiates the contract. As a result of his expenditure, A has $1,000 worth of materials left over that he can use on other contracts. It would have cost A an additional $60,000 to cut and deliver all of the timber. A sues B and recovers $39,000. See § 347. A is entitled to simple interest on the $39,000 at the legal rate from June 1.

7. A contracts to work for B at a weekly salary of $2,000. B wrongfully discharges A ten weeks before the contract ends and refuses to pay A anything for the four weeks preceding the discharge. By reasonable efforts, A can find similar work paying $1,500 a week for the last ten weeks. A sues B and recovers $2,000 for each of the first four weeks and $500 for each of the last ten, or $13,000. A is entitled to simple interest on each instalment at the legal rate from the date that it was payable.

d. Discretionary in other cases. Damages for breach of contract include not only the value of the promised performance but also compensation for consequential loss. The amount to be awarded for such loss is often very difficult to estimate in advance of trial and cannot be determined by the party in breach with sufficient certainty to enable him to make a proper tender. In such cases, the award of interest is left to judicial discretion, under the rule stated in Subsection (2), in the light of all the circumstances, including any deficiencies in the performance of the injured party and any unreasonableness in the demands made by him.

Illustrations:

8. A sells seed to B, warranting that it is Bristol cabbage seed. It is an inferior type of cabbage seed instead, and B suffers a loss of profit. B sues A and recovers $10,000, the difference between the value to B of a crop of Bristol cabbage and the crop actually grown. That amount was not, however, sufficiently definite to give B a right to interest on it. The allowance of interest is in the discretion of the court.

9.   A contracts to build a bungalow for B for $30,000. After completion but before B has paid the final $6,000, B occupies the bungalow but refuses to pay the balance because the workmanship and materials are unsatisfactory. A sues B and recovers only $4,000 on the ground that B's claim entitles him to compensation in the amount of $2,000. The sum of $4,000 was not sufficiently definite to give A a right to interest on it. The allowance of interest is within the discretion of the court. The fact that A was himself in breach will be considered.

REPORTER'S NOTE

This Section is based on former § 337. See 5 Corbin, Contracts § 1045–52 (1964 & Supp. 1980); 11 Williston, Contracts § 1412–17 (3d ed. 1968); Note, 8 Cum. L. Rev. 521 (1977).

Comment c. Illustrations 1 and 2 are based on Illustrations 1 and 2 to former § 337. Illustration 3 is based on Illustration 3 to former § 337; cf. Paradise Homes v. Central Sur. & Ins. Co., 84 Nev. 109, 437 P.2d 78

(1968). Illustration 4 is based on Illustrations 4 and 5 to former § 337. Illustrations 5, 6 and 7 are based on Illustrations 6, 7 and 8 to former § 337.

Comment d. Illustrations 8 and 9 are based on Illustrations 9 and 10 to former § 337. See also Hussey Metals Div. v. Lectromelt Furnace Div., 417 F. Supp. 964 (W.D. Pa. 1976), aff'd mem., 556 F.2d 566 (3d Cir. 1977).

§ 355. Punitive Damages

Punitive damages are not recoverable for a breach of contract unless the conduct constituting the breach is also a tort for which punitive damages are recoverable.

Comment:

a. Compensation not punishment. The purposes of awarding contract damages is to compensate the injured party. See Introductory Note to this Chapter. For this reason, courts in contract cases do not award damages to punish the party in breach or to serve as an example to others unless the conduct constituting the breach is also a tort for which punitive damages are recoverable. Courts are sometimes urged to award punitive damages when, after a particularly aggravated breach, the injured party has difficulty in proving all of the loss that he has suffered. In such cases the willfulness of the breach may be taken into account in applying the requirement that damages be proved with reasonable certainty (Comment *a* to § 352); but the purpose of awarding damages is still compensation and not punishment, and punitive damages are not appropriate. In exceptional instances, departures have been made from this general policy. A number of states have enacted statutes that vary the rule stated in this Section, notably in situations involving consumer transactions or arising under insurance policies.

Illustrations:

1. A is employed as a school teacher by B. In breach of contract and without notice B discharges A by excluding him from the school building and by stating in the presence of the pupils that he is discharged. Regardless of B's motive in discharging A, A cannot recover punitive damages from B. A can recover compensatory damages under the rule stated in § 347, including any damages for emotional disturbance that are allowable under the rule stated in § 353.

2. A and B, who are neighbors, make a contract under which A promises to supply water to B from A's well for ten years in return for B's promise to make monthly payments and share the cost of repairs. After several years, the relationship between A and B deteriorates and A, in breach of contract and to spite B, shuts off the water periodically. B cannot recover punitive damages from A. B can recover compensation damages under the rule stated in § 347 if he can prove them with reasonable certainty (§ 352), and the court may take into account the willfulness of A's breach in applying that requirement. See Comment *a* to § 352.

b. Exception for tort. In some instances the breach of contract is also a tort, as may be the case for a breach of duty by a public utility. Under modern rules of procedure, the complaint may not show whether the plaintiff intends his case to be regarded as one in contract or one in tort. The rule stated in this Section does not preclude an award of punitive damages in such a case if such an award would be proper under the law of torts. See Restatement, Second, Torts § 908. The term "tort" in the rule stated in this Section is elastic, and the effect of the general expansion of tort liability to protect additional interests is to make punitive damages somewhat more widely available for breach of contract as well. Some courts have gone rather far in this direction.

Illustrations:

3. A, a telephone company, contracts with B to render uninterrupted service. A, tortiously as well as in breach of contract,

fails to maintain service at night and B is unable to telephone a doctor for his sick child. B's right to recover punitive damages is governed by Restatement, Second, Torts § 908.

4. A borrows money from B, pledging jewelry as security for the loan. B, tortiously as well as in breach of contract, sells the jewelry to a good faith purchaser for value. A's right to recover punitive damages is governed by Restatement, Second, Torts § 908.

REPORTER'S NOTE

This Section is based on former § 342. See 5 Corbin, Contracts § 1077 (1964 & Supp. 1980); 11 Williston, Contracts § 1340 (3d ed. 1968); Rice, Exemplary Damages in Private Consumer Actions, 55 Iowa L. Rev. 307 (1969); Simpson, Punitive Damages for Breach of Contract, 20 Ohio St. L.J. 284 (1959); Sullivan, Punitive Damages in the Law of Contract: The Reality and the Illusion of Legal Change, 61 Minn. L. Rev. 207 (1977); Notes, 45 Fordham L. Rev. 164 (1976); 8 Ind. L. Rev. 668 (1975); 46 U. Cin. L. Rev. 170 (1977). As to the impact of Uniform Commercial Code § 1–106(1) on the availability of punitive damages, compare Waters v. Trenckmann, 503 P.2d 1187 (Wyo. 1972), with Z.D. Howard Co. v. Cartwright, 537 P.2d 345 (Okl. 1975).

Comment a. See generally, First Nat'l State Bank v. Commonwealth Fed'l Sav. & Loan Ass'n, 455 F. Supp. 464 (D.N.J. 1978). For an example of a state statute varying the rule stated in this Section in consumer transactions, see Wis. Stat. Ann. §§ 425.107, 425.303. For examples varying the rule in situations arising under insurance policies, see Ark. Stat. Ann. § 66–3228; Ga. Code Ann. § 56–1206; Idaho Code § 41–1839; Ill. Ann. Stat. ch. 73 § 767;

Mo. Ann. Stat. § 375.420; Neb. Rev. Stat. § 44–359; Tex. Ins. Code Ann. art. 3.62. See also the unusual opinion of the United States Supreme Court in Snepp. v. United States, 444 U.S. 507 (1980). Illustration 1 is based on Illustration 1 to former § 342; cf. Hess v. Jarboe, 201 Kan. 705, 443 P.2d 294 (1968); Addis v. Gramophone, [1909] A.C. 488 (H.L.); Illustration 2 is based on White v. Benkowski, 37 Wis.2d 285, 155 N.W.2d 74 (1967); see also J.J. White, Inc. v. Metropolitan Merchandise Mart, 48 Del. 526, 107 A.2d 892 (Super. Ct. 1954); Den v. Den, 222 A.2d 647 (D.C. 1966).

Comment b. Illustration 3 is based on Illustration 2 to former § 342; see Birmingham Waterworks Co. v. Keiley, 2 Ala. App. 629, 56 So. 838 (1911). Illustration 4 is based on Welborn v. Dixon, 70 S.C. 108, 49 S.E. 232 (1904); cf. Wright v. Public Sav. Life Ins. Co., 262 S.C. 285, 204 S.E.2d 57 (1974); see also Hibschman Pontiac, Inc. v. Batchelor, 266 Ind. 310, 362 N.E.2d 845 (1977); Vernon Fire & Cas. Ins. Co. v. Sharp, 264 Ind. 599, 349 N.E.2d 173 (1976); Gruenberg v. Aetna Ins. Co., 9 Cal.3d 566, 108 Cal. Rptr. 480, 510 P.2d 1032 (1973).

§ 356.   Liquidated Damages and Penalties

(1) **Damages for breach by either party may be liquidated in the agreement but only at an amount that is reasonable in the light of the anticipated or actual loss caused by the breach and the difficulties of proof of loss. A term fixing unreasonably large liquidated damages is unenforceable on grounds of public policy as a penalty.**

(2) **A term in a bond providing for an amount of money as a penalty for non-occurrence of the condition of the bond is unenforceable on grounds of public policy to the extent that the amount exceeds the loss caused by such non-occurrence.**

Comment:

    a. Liquidated damages or penalty. The parties to a contract may effectively provide in advance the damages that are to be payable in the event of breach as long as the provision does not disregard the principle of compensation. The enforcement of such provisions for liquidated damages saves the time of courts, juries, parties and witnesses and reduces the expense of litigation. This is especially important if the amount in controversy is small. However, the parties to a contract are not free to provide a penalty for its breach. The central objective behind the system of contract remedies is compensatory, not punitive. Punishment of a promisor for having broken his promise has no justification on either economic or other grounds and a term providing such a penalty is unenforceable on grounds of public policy. See Chapter 8. The rest of the agreement remains enforceable, however, under the rule stated in § 184(1), and the remedies for breach are determined by the rules stated in this Chapter. See Illustration 1. A term that fixes an unreasonably small amount as damages may be unenforceable as unconscionable. See § 208. As to the liquidation of damages and modification or limitation of remedies in contracts of sale, see Uniform Commercial Code §§ 2–718, 2–719.

    b. Test of penalty. Under the test stated in Subsection (1), two factors combine in determining whether an amount of money fixed as damages is so unreasonably large as to be a penalty. The first factor is the anticipated or actual loss caused by the breach. The amount fixed is reasonable to the extent that it approximates the actual loss that has resulted from the particular breach, even though it may not approximate the loss that might have been anticipated under other possible breaches. See Illustration 2. Furthermore, the amount fixed is reasonable to the extent that it approximates the loss anticipated at the time of the making of the contract, even though it may not approximate the actual loss. See Illustration 3. The second factor is the difficulty of proof of loss. The greater the difficulty either of proving that loss has occurred or of establishing its amount with the requisite certainty (see § 351), the easier it is to show that the amount fixed is reasonable. To the extent that there is uncertainty as to the harm, the estimate of the court or jury may not accord with the principle of compensation any more than does the advance estimate of the parties. A determination whether the amount fixed is a penalty turns on a combination of these two factors. If the difficulty of proof of loss is great, considerable latitude is allowed in the approximation of anticipated or actual harm. If, on the other hand, the difficulty of proof of loss is slight, less latitude is allowed in that approximation. If, to take an extreme case, it is clear that no loss at all has occurred, a provision fixing a substantial sum as damages is unenforceable. See Illustration 4.

Illustrations:

1. A and B sign a written contract under which A is to act in a play produced by B for a ten week season for $4,000. A term provides that "if either party shall fail to perform as agreed in any respect he will pay $10,000 as liquidated damages and not as a penalty." A leaves the play before the last week to take another job. The play is sold out for that week and A is replaced by a suitable understudy. The amount fixed is unreasonable in the light of both the anticipated and the actual loss and, in spite of the use of the words "liquidated damages," the term provides for a penalty and is unenforceable on grounds of public policy. The rest of the agreement is enforceable (§ 184(1)), and B's remedies for A's breach are governed by the rules stated in this Chapter.

2. A, B and C form a partnership to practice veterinary medicine in a town for ten years. In the partnership agreement, each promises that if, on the termination of the partnership, the practice is continued by the other two members, he will not practice veterinary medicine in the same town during its continuance up to a maximum of three years. A term provides that for breach of this duty "he shall forfeit $50,000 to be collected by the others as damages." A leaves the partnership, and the practice is continued by B and C. A immediately begins to practice veterinary medicine in the same town. The loss actually caused to B and C is

difficult of proof and $50,000 is not an unreasonable estimate of it. Even though $50,000 may be unreasonable in relation to the loss that might have resulted in other circumstances, it is not unreasonable in relation to the actual loss. Therefore, the term does not provide for a penalty and its enforcement is not precluded on grounds of public policy. See Illustration 14 to § 188.

3. A contracts to build a grandstand for B's race track for $1,000,000 by a specified date and to pay $1,000 a day for every day's delay in completing it. A delays completion for ten days. If $1,000 is not unreasonable in the light of the anticipated loss and the actual loss to B is difficult to prove, A's promise is not a term providing for a penalty and its enforcement is not precluded on grounds of public policy.

4. The facts being otherwise as stated in Illustration 3, B is delayed for a month in obtaining permission to operate his race track so that it is certain that A's delay of ten days caused him no loss at all. Since the actual loss to B is not difficult to prove, A's promise is a term providing for a penalty and is unenforceable on grounds of public policy.

c. Disguised penalties. Under the rule stated in this Section, the validity of a term providing for damages depends on the effect of that term as interpreted according to the rules stated in Chapter 9. Neither the parties' actual intention as to its validity nor their characterization of the term as one for liquidated damages or a penalty is significant in determining whether the term is valid. Sometimes parties attempt to disguise a provision for a penalty by using language that purports to make payment of the amount an alternative performance under the contract, that purports to offer a discount for prompt performance, or that purports to place a valuation on property to be delivered. Although the parties may in good faith contract for alternative performances and fix discounts or valuations, a court will look to the substance of the agreement to determine whether this is the case or whether the parties have attempted to disguise a provision for a penalty that is unenforceable under this Section. In determining whether a contract is one for alternative performances, the relative value of the alternatives may be decisive.

Illustration:

5. A contracts to build a house for B for $50,000 by a specified date or in the alternative to pay B $1,000 a week during any period of delay. A delays completion for ten days. If $1,000 a

week is unreasonable in the light of both the anticipated and actual loss, A's promise to pay $1,000 a week is, in spite of its form, a term providing for a penalty and is unenforceable on grounds of public policy.

d. *Related types of provisions.* This Section does not purport to cover the wide variety of provisions used by parties to control the remedies available to them for breach of contract. A term that fixes as damages an amount that is unreasonably small does not come within the rule stated in this Section, but a court may refuse to enforce it as unconscionable under the rule stated in § 208. A mere recital of the harm that may occur as a result of a breach of contract does not come within the rule stated in this Section, but may increase damages by making that harm foreseeable under the rule stated § 351. As to the effect of a contract provision on the right to equitable relief, see Comment *a* to § 359. As to the effect of a term requiring the occurrence of a condition where forfeiture would result, see § 229. Although attorneys' fees are not generally awarded to the winning party, if the parties provide for the award of such fees the court will award a sum that it considers to be reasonable. If, however, the parties specify the amount of such fees, the provision is subject to the test stated in this Section.

e. *Penalties in bonds.* Bonds often fix a flat sum as a penalty for non-occurrence of the condition of the bond. A term providing for a penalty is not unenforceable in its entirety but only to the extent that it exceeds the loss caused by the non-occurrence of the condition.

Illustration:

6. A executes a bond obligating himself to pay B $10,000, on condition that the bond shall be void, however, if C, who is B's cashier, shall properly account for all money entrusted to him. C defaults to the extent of $500. A's promise is unenforceable on grounds of public policy to the extent that it exceeds the actual loss, $500.

REPORTER'S NOTE

This Section is based on former §§ 339 and 579, but Subsection (1) has been redrafted to harmonize with Uniform Commercial Code § 2–718(1). The Code's reference to "the inconvenience or nonfeasibility of otherwise obtaining an adequate remedy" has been omitted as already being expressed by the language of Subsection (1), as explained in the Comment. See 5 Corbin, Contracts ch. 58 (1964 & Supp. 1980); 5 Williston, Contracts §§ 776–89 (3d ed. 1961); Clarkson, Miller & Muris, Liquidated Damages v. Penalties: Sense or Nonsense, 1978 Wis. L. Rev. 351;

Goetz & Scott, Liquidated Damages, Penalties and the Just Compensation Principle: Some Notes on an Enforcement Model and a Theory of Efficient Breach, 77 Colum. L. Rev. 554 (1977); Macneil, Power of Contract and Agreed Remedies, 47 Cornell L.Q. 495 (1962); Sweet, Liquidated Damages in California, 60 Calif. L. Rev. 84 (1972); The [English] Law Commission, Penalty Clauses and Forfeiture of Monies Paid (Law of Contract Working Paper No. 61, 1975). Notes, 45 Fordham L. Rev. 1349 (1977); 72 Nw. U.L. Rev. 1055 (1978).

Comment b. Illustration 1 is based on Illustration 1 to former § 339; H.J. McGrath Co. v. Wisner, 189 Md. 260, 55 A.2d 793 (1947). Illustration 2 is based on Illustration 2 to former § 339; Jaquith v. Hudson, 5 Mich. 123 (1858). It is supported by 5 Corbin, Contracts § 1066 (1964 & Supp. 1980); McCormick, Damages § 151 (1935); and is consistent with the rationale behind § 184(2). But cf. Bauer v. Sawyer, 8 Ill.2d 351, 134 N.E.2d 329 (1956); Management, Inc. v. Schassberger, 39 Wash.2d 321, 235 P.2d 293 (1951). Illustration 3 is based on Illustration 3 to former § 339; United States v. Bethlehem Steel Co., 205 U.S. 105 (1907); Banta v. Stamford Motor Co., 89 Conn. 51, 92 A. 665 (1914); Dave Gustafson & Co. v. State, 83 S.D. 160, 156 N.W.2d 185 (1968). But cf. Priebe & Sons v. United States, 332 U.S. 407 (1947); Hungerford Constr. Co. v. Florida Citrus Exposition, Inc., 410 F.2d 1229 (5th Cir.), cert. denied, 396 U.S. 928 (1969). Illustration 4 is supported by Massman Constr. Co. v. City Council of Greenville, Miss., 147 F.2d 925 (5th Cir. 1945); Northwest Fixture Co. v. Kilbourne & Clark Co., 128 F. 256 (9th Cir. 1904); Norwalk Door Closer Co. v. Eagle Lock and Screw Co., 153 Conn. 681, 220 A.2d 263 (1966). It rejects the view of Illustration 7 to former § 339; Southwest Eng'r Co. v. United States, 341 F.2d 998 (8th Cir.), cert. denied, 382 U.S. 819 (1965); McCarthy v. Tally, 46 Cal.2d 577, 297 P.2d 981 (1956); cf. Bethlehem Steel Corp. v. Chicago, 350 F.2d 649 (7th Cir. 1965). That the difficulties of proof of loss are to be determined at the time the contract is made, not at the time of the breach, see Hutchison v. Tompkins, 259 So.2d 129 (Fla. 1972). As to whether the actual loss must be reasonably foreseeable, compare comment, 45 Fordham L. Rev. 1349, 1357 (1977), with 1 N.Y.L. Rev'n Comm'n, Study of the Uniform Commercial Code, Leg. Doc. (1955) No. 65, p. 581 n. 468.

Comment c. Illustration 5 is based on Illustration 5 to former § 339.

Comment d. Allowing attorneys' fees, see Puget Sound Mutual Sav. Bank v. Lillions, 50 Wash.2d 799, 314 P.2d 935 (1957), cert. denied, 357 U.S. 926 (1958). As to whether a specified sum as attorney's fees is a penalty, see Equitable Lumber Corp. v. IPA Land Dev. Corp., 38 N.Y.2d 516, 381 N.Y.S.2d 459, 344 N.E.2d 391 (1976).

Comment e. Illustration 6 is based on Illustration 8 to former § 339.

TOPIC 3. ENFORCEMENT BY SPECIFIC PERFORMANCE AND INJUNCTION

Introductory Note: Specific performance and injunction are alternatives to the award of damages as means of enforcing contracts. Specific performance is by definition limited to the enforcement of contract duties. The remedy of injunction is used in many fields of law, but is dealt with here in connection with contracts only. The general availability of these remedies in contract cases is affirmed in § 357. The power of the court to shape the remedy is stressed in § 358. These remedies originated in courts of equity, and their use is within the discretion of the court and is subject to a number of limitations that are dealt with in §§ 359–69. The most significant is the rule that specific performance or an injunction will not be granted if damages are an adequate remedy (§ 359). This rule, the product of the historical division of jurisdiction between law and equity, has been preserved under the Uniform Commercial Code. See Uniform Commercial Code § 2–716(1) and Official Comment; Introductory Note to this Chapter. Nevertheless, there has been an increasing disposition to find that damages are not adequate and the commentary to the Code reflects this "more liberal attitude." Comment 1 to Uniform Commercial Code § 2–716. Courts have been increasingly willing to order performance in a wide variety of cases involving output and requirements contracts, contracts for the sale of a business or of an interest in a business represented by shares of stock, and covenants not to compete. Factors that bear on the adequacy of damages are listed in § 360. Other limitations on the availability of such equitable relief go to such matters as the need for certainty of terms (§ 362) and for security as to the completion of the agreed exchange (§ 363), and to the impact of unfairness (§ 364), of public policy (§ 365) and of difficulty of enforcement of the decree (§ 366). This Chapter does not deal with other equitable remedies such as reformation or cancellation. See Introductory Note to this Chapter and, as to reformation, §§ 155, 166.

REPORTER'S NOTE

This Topic is based on Topic 4, Specific Performance, of former Chapter 12. See 5A Corbin, Contracts chs. 63–65 (1964 & Supp. 1980); 11 Williston, Contracts ch. 43 (3d ed. 1968); Dobbs, Remedies ch. 2 (1973); McClintock, Equity ch. 5 (2d ed. 1948); Walsh, Equity chs. 12–19 (1930); Kronman, Specific Performance, 45 U. Chi. L. Rev. 351 (1978); Van Hecke, Changing Emphases in Specific Performance, 40 N.C.L. Rev. 1 (1961).

§ 357.   Availability of Specific Performance and Injunction

(1) **Subject to the rules stated in §§ 359–69, specific performance of a contract duty will be granted in the discretion of the court against a party who has committed or is threatening to commit a breach of the duty.**

(2) **Subject to the rules stated in §§ 359–69, an injunction against breach of a contract duty will be granted in the discretion of the court against a party who has committed or is threatening to commit a breach of the duty if**

(a) **the duty is one of forbearance, or**

(b) **the duty is one to act and specific performance would be denied only for reasons that are inapplicable to an injunction.**

Comment:

  a. Specific performance. An order of specific performance is intended to produce as nearly as is practicable the same effect that the performance due under a contract would have produced. It usually, therefore, orders a party to render the performance that he promised. (On the form of the order, see § 358.) Such relief is seldom granted unless there has been a breach of contract, either by non-performance or by repudiation. In unusual circumstances, however, it may be granted where there is merely a threatened breach. See Subsection (1).

  b. Injunction. A court may by injunction direct a party to refrain from doing a specified act. This is appropriate in two types of cases.

  In the first, the performance due under the contract consists simply of forbearance, and the injunction in effect orders specific performance. See Paragraph (2)(a). Duties of forbearance are often imposed not as a matter of agreement but as a matter of law, as is usually the case for the duty not to interfere with the other party's performance of the contract. Duties of forbearance are ordinarily accompanied by other duties that require affirmative action by both parties. The presence of such other duties does not, of itself, preclude issuance of an injunction ordering forbearance only, but an injunction will not be issued if the performance of those other duties cannot be secured. See § 363.

In the second type of case, the performance due under the contract consists of the doing of an act rather than of forbearance, and the injunction is used as an indirect means of enforcing the duty to act. See Paragraph (2)(b). Instead of ordering that the act be done, the court orders forbearance from inconsistent action. This is appropriate in situations where an injunction will afford a measure of relief and the duty to act would have been specifically enforced were it not for some objection that can be avoided by ordering forbearance from inconsistent action. For example, the difficulties involved in supervising compliance with the order may be less in the case of an injunction that in the case of specific performance. See § 366. An injunction will not be issued, however, if the reason for refusing specific performance is not merely that the practical difficulties of such relief are too great but that compelling performance of the duty is itself undesirable. For example, an injunction is not ordinarily appropriate as an indirect means of enforcing a duty to render personal service. See Comment c to § 367.

Illustrations:

1. A contracts with B to give B the "first refusal" of A's house on stated terms. A later offers to sell the house to others without first offering it to B and B sues A to enjoin him from doing this. An injunction may properly be granted.

2. A, B and C form a partnership to practice veterinary medicine in a town for ten years. In the partnership agreement each makes an enforceable promise that if, on the termination of the partnership, the practice is continued by the other two members, he will not practice veterinary medicine in the same town during its continuance up to a maximum of three years. See Illustration 11 to § 188. A leaves the partnership and the practice is continued by B and C. A immediately threatens to begin the practice of veterinary medicine in the same town, and B and C sue to enjoin A from doing so. An injunction may properly be granted.

3. A, the owner of a large factory, contracts to take all of his requirements of electricity from B, who promises to build a new electric plant at a place where it would not otherwise be profitable. A repudiates the contract and B sues A to enjoin him from using electricity that is not supplied by B. An injunction may properly be granted.

4. A makes a contract with B under which A promises to sell exclusively B's dress patterns in A's stores for a period of five

years. The contract provides details as to manner of exhibition
and division of profits. On anticipatory repudiation of the contract by A, B sues A for specific performance of his duty to sell B's
patterns and to enjoin him from selling competing dress patterns. Even if the court refuses specific performance on the
ground that enforcement and supervision would be too difficult (§
366), it may properly grant an injunction.

    5. A, a fruit growers' cooperative, contracts to sell to B, a
fruit processor, 1,000 tons of loganberries a year for five years.
In reliance on the contract, B substantially expands his plant and
engages in an extensive advertising campaign. A then repudiates
the contract. The loss to B is difficult to estimate but will probably exceed $500,000. A's entire assets do not exceed $100,000. B
sues A for specific performance and to enjoin A from selling loganberries to anyone other than B. Even if the court refuses specific
performance on the ground that enforcement and supervision
would be too difficult (§ 366), it may properly grant an injunction.

    c. Discretionary nature of relief. The granting of equitable re-
lief has traditionally been regarded as within judicial discretion. The
exercise of that discretion is subject to the rules stated in §§ 359–69.
It is also subject to general principles of equity that are not peculiar to
contract disputes, such as those that bar relief to one who has been
guilty of laches or who has come into court with unclean hands. Furthermore, it is subject to principles of common sense so that, for example, a court will not order a performance that is impossible. In granting relief, as well as in denying it, a court may take into consideration
the public interest.

REPORTER'S NOTE

Subsection (1) is based on former §
359(1). Subsection (2) is based on
former § 380(1). See 5A Corbin,
Contracts §§ 1136, 1205–07 (1964 &
Supp. 1980); 11 Williston, Contracts
§§ 1418, 1418B, 1425–25B, 1445 (3d
ed. 1968).

Comment b. Illustrations 1, 3 and
4 are based on Illustrations 1, 3 and 4
to former § 380. Illustration 2 is
based on Bauer v. Sawyer, 8 Ill.2d
351, 134 N.E.2d 329 (1956); see also
Illustration 7 to former § 380; Morgan's Home Equip. Corp. v. Martucci,
390 Pa. 618, 136 A.2d 838 (1957). Illustration 5 is based on Illustration 4
to former § 359.

Comment c. For a brief survey of
when courts have granted specific
performance, see First Nat'l State
Bank v. Commonwealth Fed. Sav. &
Loan Ass'n, 455 F. Supp. 464 (D.N.J.
1978). The rule that a court will not
order an impossible performance is
taken from former § 368. As to the
public interest, see Pennsylvania
R.R. v. City of Louisville, 277 Ky.
402, 126 S.W.2d 840 (1939); Schmidt
v. Louisville & N.R. Co., 101 Ky.
441, 41 S.W. 1015 (1897).

§ 358.   Form of Order and Other Relief

(1) An order of specific performance or an injunction will be so drawn as best to effectuate the purposes for which the contract was made and on such terms as justice requires. It need not be absolute in form and the performance that it requires need not be identical with that due under the contract.

(2) If specific performance or an injunction is denied as to part of the performance that is due, it may nevertheless be granted as to the remainder.

(3) In addition to specific performance or an injunction, damages and other relief may be awarded in the same proceeding and an indemnity against future harm may be required.

Comment:

a. Flexibility of order. The objective of the court in granting equitable relief is to do complete justice to the extent that this is feasible. Under the rule stated in Subsection (1), the court has the power to mold its order to this end. The form and terms of the order are to a considerable extent within the discretion of the court. Its order may be directed at the injured party as well as at the party in breach. It may be conditional on some performance to be rendered by the injured party or a third person, such as the payment of money to compensate for defects or the giving of security. It may even be conditional on the injured party's assent to the modification of the contract that he seeks to enforce.

The exact performance that is promised in a contract may be, in whole or in part, very difficult of enforcement, or it may have become unreasonably burdensome or unlawful. Nevertheless, by exercising its discretion in fashioning the order, the court may be able substantially to assure the expectations of the parties, without undue difficulty of enforcement, unreasonable hardship to the party in breach, or violation of the law. It may command a performance by the party in breach that is not identical with the one that he promised to render. It may indirectly induce the party in breach to do an act by enjoining him from doing inconsistent acts. See § 357(2)(b). If a court cannot, because of the promisor's death or disability, compel performance of a contract to give a child rights as an heir, whether by adoption or otherwise, it may nevertheless be able to give the child those rights. Statutes in most states empower the court to transfer the title to land by

---

virtue of its own decree or the deed of an officer of the court without the execution of a deed by the previous owner. In appropriate cases, a court may issue a preliminary injunction to prevent an undesirable change in the situation.

Illustrations:

1. A, a water company, contracts with B, a city, to construct a water supply system and to supply sufficient water for public and private use, including any increase in demand. In return B gives A the exclusive right to supply water at rates fixed according to a schedule. A constructs the system substantially as agreed with the exception of a few defects, which can be corrected. B repudiates and A sues B for specific performance. Specific performance may properly be granted, conditional on correction of the defects. See § 369. If changing circumstances require it, the order may also be conditional on A's consent to modification of the terms of the contract, if this should become necessary to avoid unreasonable hardship to B.

2. A contracts to sell land to B, who promises to pay the price in eight installments on stated dates. Conveyance is to be made on payment of the third installment, and the balance is to be secured by a mortgage and paid with interest in five annual installments. After B has paid the third installment, A delays and finally refuses to convey, and B sues for specific performance. Specific performance may properly be granted. The order will be conditional on execution of the mortgage for the balance and may provide for equitable adjustment of rents and profits, interest on the unpaid part of the price, and extension of the times fixed for the last five payments to allow for time lost by A's delay.

b. Order as to part. Sometimes the requirements are met for specific performance of part of the performance due from the party in breach, but the remaining part of the performance has become impracticable or is otherwise of such a character as to preclude such relief. A court may properly issue an order as to the first part, together with any compensation that is appropriate for non-performance of the second part. This will not be done, however, if compelling performance of only part would impose unreasonable hardship on the party in breach.

c. Damages and other relief. In addition to any equitable relief granted, a court may also award damages or other relief. Since an order seldom results in performance within the time the contract requires, damages for the delay will usually be appropriate. A seller of land who cannot perform as agreed because of a deficiency in area or a defect in title may be ordered to transfer all that he can, with compensation for the resulting claim for partial breach. The compensation may take the form of damages, restitution of money already paid or an abatement of the price not yet paid. A claimant who sues for specific performance or an injunction and who is denied that relief, may be awarded damages or restitution in the same proceeding. In appropriate cases, an indemnity may be required against future harm, and in some cases such an indemnity may be the only remedy that is necessary.

Illustrations:

3. A contracts to sell B a tract of land warranted to contain 200 acres for $100,000. The tract contains only 160 acres, substantially uniform in value. A refuses to perform and B sues for specific performance. Specific performance will be granted with an abatement of $20,000, conditional on B paying $80,000. See Illustration 1 to § 369. If the price had already been paid in full, the decree would order the restitution of $20,000.

4. A contracts to transfer land to B and to make specified repairs and complete an unfinished building on the land. A repudiates and B sues for specific performance. Specific performance of A's duty to transfer the land may be granted with an abatement in the price or other compensation sufficient to enable him to make the repairs and complete the building himself.

REPORTER'S NOTE

Subsection (1) is based on former § 359(2). Subsections (2) and (3) are based on former § 365. See 5A Corbin, Contracts §§ 1137, 1160 (1964 & Supp. 1980); 11 Williston, Contracts §§ 1425–25B, 1430–31 (3d ed. 1968).

Comment a. Illustrations 1 and 2 are based on Illustrations 1 and 2 to former § 359.

Comment c. Former § 363 is incorporated in this Comment. Illustration 3 is based on Illustration 1 to former § 365; Nelson v. Gibe, 162 Mich. 410, 127 N.W. 304 (1911). Illustration 4 is based on Illustration 2 to former § 365. For a case holding that damages incident to a grant of specific performance are not subject to the limitation of foreseeability, see Reis v. Sparks, 547 F.2d 236 (4th Cir. 1976). For a discussion of the measure of delay damages in connection with specific performance of a land sale contract, see Meyer v. Benko, 55 Cal. App.3d 937, 127 Cal. Rptr. 846 (1976).

§ 359. Effect of Adequacy of Damages

(1) Specific performance or an injunction will not be ordered if damages would be adequate to protect the expectation interest of the injured party.

(2) The adequacy of the damage remedy for failure to render one part of the performance due does not preclude specific performance or injunction as to the contract as a whole.

(3) Specific performance or an injunction will not be refused merely because there is a remedy for breach other than damages, but such a remedy may be considered in exercising discretion under the rule stated in § 357.

Comment:

a. Bases for requirement. The underlying objective in choosing the form of relief to be granted is to select a remedy that will adequately protect the legally recognized interest of the injured party. If, as is usually the case, that interest is the expectation interest, the remedy may take the form either of damages or of specific performance or an injunction. As to the situation in which the interest to be protected is the restitution interest, see § 373.

During the development of the jurisdiction of courts of equity, it came to be recognized that equitable relief would not be granted if the award of damages at law was adequate to protect the interests of the injured party. There is, however, a tendency to liberalize the granting of equitable relief by enlarging the classes of cases in which damages are not regarded as an adequate remedy. This tendency has been encouraged by the adoption of the Uniform Commercial Code, which "seeks to further a more liberal attitude than some courts have shown in connection with the specific performance of contracts of sale." Comment 1 to Uniform Commercial Code § 2–716. In accordance with this tendency, if the adequacy of the damage remedy is uncertain, the combined effect of such other factors as uncertainty of terms (§ 362), insecurity as to the agreed exchange (§ 363) and difficulty of enforcement (§ 366) should be considered. Adequacy is to some extent relative, and the modern approach is to compare remedies to determine which is more effective in serving the ends of justice. Such a comparison will often lead to the granting of equitable relief. Doubts should be resolved in favor of the granting of specific performance or injunction.

Because the availability of equitable relief was historically viewed as a matter of jurisdiction, the parties cannot vary by agreement the requirement of inadequacy of damages, although a court may take appropriate notice of facts recited in their contract. See also Comment *b* to § 361.

b. Damages adequate as to part. The fact that damages would be an adequate remedy for failure to render one part of the promised performance does not preclude specific performance of the contract as a whole. In such a case, complete relief should be granted in a single action and that relief may properly be a decree ordering performance of the entire contract if the other requisites for such relief are met.

Illustration:

1. A contracts to sell his business, including land, buildings and stock in trade, to B. A repudiates the contract and B sues for specific performance. Specific performance of the entire contract may be granted, even though the stock in trade is of a kind that could be purchased elsewhere. However, in that case it is also within the court's discretion to require A to convey the land and buildings and to pay damages for failure to deliver the stock in trade.

c. Other legal remedies. Common-law remedies other than damages may be available to the injured party, but they will seldom afford as complete relief as will specific performance. Restitution of the value in money of the performance rendered by the injured party is one of those remedies, but it does not purport to be the equivalent of a promised performance, and its availability is not a sufficient reason for denying specific enforcement. Replevin is another of those remedies, but its effectiveness is reduced by rules allowing the giving of a bond in place of surrendering of the goods sought to be replevied. The availability of such a remedy will not preclude the granting of equitable relief, although it may be considered by a court in the exercise of its discretion in that regard. The availability of other forms of equitable relief, such as a decree for specific restitution, for reformation, and for rescission or cancellation, may also be considered in choosing the remedy best suited to the circumstances of the case.

REPORTER'S NOTE

Subsections (1) and (3) are based on former § 358. Subsection (2) is based on former § 364. See 5A Corbin, Contracts §§ 1136, 1139 (1964 & Supp. 1980); 11 Williston, Contracts § 1418 (3d ed. 1968); Kronman, Specific Performance, 45 U. Chi. L. Rev. 351 (1978); Schmitt & Pasterczyk, Specific Performance Under the Uniform Commercial Code—Will Liberalism

Prevail?, 26 De Paul L. Rev. 54 (1976); Van Hecke, Changing Emphases in Specific Performance, 40 N.C.L. Rev. 1 (1961); Comments, 51 Mich. L. Rev. 408 (1953), 33 U. Pitt. L. Rev. 243 (1971). As to the practical effect of denial of equitable relief, see Frank & Endicott, Defenses in Equity and "Legal Rights," 14 La. L. Rev. 380 (1954).

Comment a. The historical limitation on the availability of specific performance and injunction has persisted in spite of the merger of law and equity and can be justified on economic as well as historical grounds. See Introductory Note to this Chapter.

Comment b. Illustration 1 is based on Illustration 1 to former § 364.

§ 360. Factors Affecting Adequacy of Damages

In determining whether the remedy in damages would be adequate, the following circumstances are significant:

    (a) the difficulty of proving damages with reasonable certainty,

    (b) the difficulty of procuring a suitable substitute performance by means of money awarded as damages, and

    (c) the likelihood that an award of damages could not be collected.

Comment:

a. Principal factors. Under the rule stated in § 359, specific performance or an injunction will not be ordered if damages would be adequate to protect the injured party's expectation interest. This Section lists the principal factors that enter into a decision as to the adequacy of damages. The enumeration does not purport to be exclusive of other factors. A court may also consider, for example, the probability that full compensation cannot be had without multiple litigation, although this is an unusual circumstance in contract cases.

b. Difficulty in proving damages. The damage remedy may be inadequate to protect the injured party's expectation interest because the loss caused by the breach is too difficult to estimate with reasonable certainty (§ 352). If the injured party has suffered loss but cannot sustain the burden of proving it, only nominal damages will be awarded. If he can prove some but not all of his loss, he will not be compensated in full. In either case damages are an inadequate remedy. Some types of interests are by their very nature incapable of being valued in money. Typical examples include heirlooms, family

---

treasures and works of art that induce a strong sentimental attachment. Examples may also be found in contracts of a more commercial character. The breach of a contract to transfer shares of stock may cause a loss in control over the corporation. The breach of a contract to furnish an indemnity may cause the sacrifice of property and financial ruin. The breach of a covenant not to compete may cause the loss of customers of an unascertainable number or importance. The breach of a requirements contract may cut off a vital supply of raw materials. In such situations, equitable relief is often appropriate.

Illustrations:

1. A contracts to sell to B a painting by Rembrandt for $1,000,000. A repudiates the contract and B sues for specific performance. Specific performance will be granted.

2. A contracts to sell to B the racing sloop "Columbia," this sloop being one of a class of similar boats manufactured by a particular builder. Although other boats of this class are easily obtainable, their racing characteristics differ considerably and B has selected the "Columbia" because she is regarded as a witch in light airs and, therefore, superior to most of the others. A repudiates the contract and B sues for specific performance. Specific performance may properly be granted.

3. A contracts to sell to B his interest as holder of a franchise to operate a hamburger stand. Because A has not yet opened his stand for business, it would be difficult to prove his expected profits with reasonable certainty. A repudiates the contract and B sues for specific performance. Specific performance may properly be granted.

4. A, a manufacturer of steel, contracts to sell B all of its output of steel scrap for a period of five years. After one year, A repudiates the contract and B sues A for specific performance. The uncertainty in A's output over the remaining four years would make it very difficult for B to prove damages. Specific performance may properly be granted.

5. A contracts to supply B with water for irrigation. In reliance on his contract, B sows his land with rice. A repudiates the contract although he has water that he can supply and B sues for specific performance. The loss that B will suffer as a result of A's failure to supply water is difficult of estimation. Specific performance may properly be granted.

c. Difficulty of obtaining substitute. If the injured party can readily procure by the use of money a suitable substitute for the promised performance, the damage remedy is ordinarily adequate. Entering into a substitute transaction is generally a more efficient way to prevent injury than is a suit for specific performance or an injunction and there is a sound economic basis for limiting the injured party to damages in such a case. Furthermore, the substitute transaction affords a basis for proving damages with reasonable certainty, eliminating the factor stated in Paragraph (a). The fact that the burden of financing the transaction is cast on the injured party can usually be sufficiently compensated for by allowing interest. There are many situations, however, in which no suitable substitute is obtainable, and others in which its procurement would be unreasonably difficult or inconvenient or would impose serious financial burdens or risks on the injured party. A suitable substitute is never available for a performance that consists of forbearance, such as that under a contract not to compete. If goods are unique in kind, quality or personal association, the purchase of an equivalent elsewhere may be impracticable, and the buyer's "inability to cover is strong evidence of" the propriety of granting specific performance. Comment 2 to Uniform Commercial Code § 2–716. Shares of stock in a corporation may not be obtainable elsewhere. Patents and copyrights are unique. In all these situations, damages may be regarded as inadequate.

Illustrations:

    6. A contracts to sell B 10,000 bales of cotton. A repudiates the contract on the day for delivery. B can buy cotton on the market at a somewhat higher price. B will not be granted specific performance.

    7. A contracts to sell to B 1,000 shares of stock in the X Corporation for $10,000. A repudiates the contract and B sues for specific performance. Other shares of X Corporation are not readily obtainable and B will suffer an uncertain loss as a result of diminished voting power. Specific performance may properly be granted. If other shares were readily obtainable, even though at a considerably higher price, specific performance would be refused.

    8. A contracts to obtain a patent for his invention and to assign a half interest in it to B, who promises to pay A's expenses and $100,000. A repudiates the contract and threatens to assign the patent when it is issued to others. B sues A for specific performance. Specific performance may properly be granted. The decree may enjoin A from assigning the patent to others and order

him to proceed with the application and, on its issuance to execute an assignment to B, all conditional on appropriate payment by B.

d. Difficulty of collecting damages. Even if damages are adequate in other respects, they will be inadequate if they cannot be collected by judgment and execution. The party in breach may be judgment proof or may conceal his assets. Statutes may exempt some or all of his property from execution. If he is insolvent, specific performance may result in a preferential transfer to the party seeking relief and will then be denied on grounds of public policy. See Comment *b* to § 365 and Illustration 4 to that Section. If, however, the contract is unperformed on both sides and provides for a fair exchange, performance will not result in a preferential transfer and may benefit other creditors and help prevent insolvency.

Illustrations:

9. A contracts to sell his stock of goods together with good will to B for $100,000, a fair price, payable on delivery. Before the time for performance, A becomes insolvent and repudiates the contract. B sues A for specific performance. A's insolvency is a factor tending to show that damages are inadequate. But see Illustration 4 to § 365.

10. A owns an interest in a shop, the title to which is held by B in trust for A and others. B is insolvent. A assigns his interest to C and B contracts with C to effectuate the transfer of that interest to C and to terminate his own power. B then refuses to do so and C sues B for specific performance. B's insolvency is a factor tending to show that damages are inadequate.

e. Contracts for the sale of land. Contracts for the sale of land have traditionally been accorded a special place in the law of specific performance. A specific tract of land has long been regarded as unique and impossible of duplication by the use of any amount of money. Furthermore, the value of land is to some extent speculative. Damages have therefore been regarded as inadequate to enforce a duty to transfer an interest in land, even if it is less than a fee simple. Under this traditional view, the fact that the buyer has made a contract for the resale of the land to a third person does not deprive him of the right to specific performance. If he cannot convey the land to his purchaser, he will be held for damages for breach of the resale contract, and it is argued that these damages cannot be accurately determined without litigation. Granting him specific performance enables him to perform his own duty and to avoid litigation and damages.

Similarly, the seller who has not yet conveyed is generally granted specific performance on breach by the buyer. Here it is argued that, because the value of land is to some extent speculative, it may be difficult for him to prove with reasonable certainty the difference between the contract price and the market price of the land. Even if he can make this proof, the land may not be immediately convertible into money and he may be deprived of funds with which he could have made other investments. Furthermore, before the seller gets a judgment, the existence of the contract, even if broken by the buyer, operates as a clog on saleability, so that it may be difficult to find a purchaser at a fair price. The fact that specific performance is available to the buyer has sometimes been regarded as of some weight under the now discarded doctrine of "mutuality of remedy" (see Comment c to § 363), but this is today of importance only because it enables a court to assure the vendee that he will receive the agreed performance if he is required to pay the price. The fact that legislation may have prohibited imprisonment as a means of enforcing a decree for the payment of money does not affect the seller's right to such a decree. After the seller has transferred the interest in the land to the buyer, however, and all that remains is for the buyer to pay the price, a money judgment for the amount of the price is an adequate remedy for · the seller.

Illustrations:

11. On February 1, A contracts to sell his farm to B for $500,000, of which $100,000 is paid when the contract is signed and $400,000 is to be paid on A's delivery of a deed on August 1. On March 1, A repudiates the contract. B sues A for specific performance. Specific performance will be granted immediately, A's performance not to take place until August 1 and to be conditional on the simultaneous payment by B of the $400,000 balance when the deed is tendered at that time. A may also be enjoined from making a conveyance to anyone else.

12. The facts being otherwise as stated in Illustration 11, B rather than A repudiates the contract on March 1 and A sues B for specific performance. Specific performance will be granted immediately, B's performance not to take place until August 1 and to be conditional on the simultaneous tender by A of the deed when the $400,000 balance is tendered at that time.

13. A contracts to sell land to B, a dealer in land, who contracts to sell it to C. C plans to build a home on the land and would be granted specific performance against B if B refused to

convey the land to him. A repudiates the contract and refuses to convey the land to B and B sues A for specific performance. Specific performance will be granted.

REPORTER'S NOTE

This Section is based on former § 361. Former § 362, which dealt with the effect of the insolvency of the party against whom relief is sought is now dealt with in commentary as a specific example of the general rule stated in this Section. See also § 365. Former § 360, which dealt with contracts for the transfer of interests in land, has also been dealt with in commentary as another specific example of the general rule stated in this Section. See 5A Corbin, Contracts §§ 1142–61 (1964 & Supp. 1980); 11 Williston, Contracts §§ 1418–21A (3d ed. 1968); Kronman, Specific Performance. 45 U. Chi. L. Rev. 351 (1978); Schmitt & Pasterczyk, Specific Performance Under the Uniform Commercial Code—Will Liberalism Prevail?, 26 De Paul L. Rev. 54 (1976); Van Hecke, Changing Emphases in Specific Performance, 40 N.C.L. Rev. 1 (1961); Comments, 51 Mich. L. Rev. 408 (1953), 33 U. Pitt. L. Rev. 243 (1971).

Comment b. Illustration 1 is based on Illustration 1 to former § 361. Illustration 2 is based on Illustration 3 to former § 361. Illustration 3 is based on Hogan v. Norfleet, 113 So.2d 437 (Dist. Ct. App. 1959), aff'd per curiam, 143 So.2d 384 (Fla. 1962); Cochrane v. Szpakowski, 355 Pa. 357, 49 A.2d 692 (1946). Illustration 4 is based on Eastern Rolling Mill Co. v. Michlovitz, 157 Md. 51, 145 A. 378 (1929); cf. Curtice Bros. v. Catts, 72 N.J. Eq. 831, 66 A. 935 (1907). Illustration 5 is based on Illustration 8 to former § 361; cf. Laclede Gas Co. v.

Amoco Oil Co., 522 F.2d 33 (8th Cir. 1975).

Comment c. Illustration 6 is based on Block v. Shaw, 78 Ark. 511, 95 S.W. 806 (1906); Weathersby v. Gore, 556 F.2d 1247 (5th Cir. 1977); Duval & Co. v. Malcom, 233 Ga. 784, 214 S.E.2d 356 (1975); cf. McCallister v. Patton, 214 Ark. 293, 215 S.W.2d 701 (1948); Fortner v. Wilson, 202 Okl. 563, 216 P.2d 299 (1950). But cf. Mitchell-Huntley Cotton Co. v. Waldrep, 377 F. Supp. 1215 (N.D. Ala. 1974). Illustration 7 is based on Illustration 2 to former § 361. Illustration 8 is based on Illustration 5 to former § 361. Illustration 9 is based on Illustration 3 to former § 362; see also Clark v. Snelling, 205 F. 240 (1st Cir. 1913). Illustration 10 is based on Illustration 5 to former § 363.

Comment e. Illustration 11 is based on Illustrations 1 and 4 to former § 360; Gartrell v. Stafford, 12 Neb. 545, 11 N.W. 732 (1882). Illustration 12 is based on Illustration 1 to former § 360; Prichard v. Mulhall, 140 Iowa 1, 118 N.W. 43 (1908). But cf. Suchan v. Rutherford, 90 Idaho 288, 410 P.2d 434 (1966) (specific performance denied seller where the tract of irrigated farm land was not unique and its market price could be determined without difficulty); Centex Homes Corp. v. Boag, 128 N.J. Super. 385, 320 A.2d 194 (1974) (specific performance denied seller of condominium apartment unit). Illustration 13 is suggested by Mier Co. v. Hadden, 148 Mich. 488, 111 N.W. 1040 (1907); see also Loveless v.

Diehl, 235 Ark. 805, 364 S.W.2d 317 (1963). But cf. Watkins v. Paul, 95 Idaho 499, 511 P.2d 781 (1973); Schmid v. Whitten, 114 S.C. 245, 103 S.E. 553 (1920).

§ 361.   Effect of Provision for Liquidated Damages

Specific performance or an injunction may be granted to enforce a duty even though there is a provision for liquidated damages for breach of that duty.

Comment:

a. Rationale. A contract provision for payment of a sum of money as damages may not afford an adequate remedy even though it is valid as one for liquidated damages and not a penalty (§ 356). Merely by providing for liquidated damages, the parties are not taken to have fixed a price to be paid for the privilege not to perform. The same uncertainty as to the loss caused that argues for the enforceability of the provision may also argue for the inadequacy of the remedy that it provides. Such a provision does not, therefore, preclude the granting of specific performance or an injunction if that relief would otherwise be granted. If the provision is unenforceable as one for a penalty, the same result follows, but because of the ineffectiveness of the clause rather than the operation of the rule here stated. If equitable relief is granted, damages for such breach as has already occurred may also be awarded in accordance with the rule stated in § 358. These damages will ordinarily be limited to the actual loss suffered unless the provision for liquidated damages affords a suitable basis for calculating such damages.

Illustration:

1. A, B and C form a partnership to practice veterinary medicine in a town for ten years. In the partnership agreement each makes an enforceable promise that if, on the termination of the partnership, the practice is continued by the other two members, he will not practice veterinary medicine in the same town during its continuance up to a maximum of three years. See Illustration 11 to § 188 and Illustration 2 to § 357. Each also makes an enforceable promise that for breach of this duty he will pay $50,000 as liquidated damages. See Illustration 2 to § 356. A leaves the partnership, and the practice is continued by B and C. A immediately begins to practice veterinary medicine in the same town. B and C sue A for an injunction and damages. In spite of the liquidated damage clause, A will be enjoined from practicing

veterinary medicine in violation of his promise not to compete. B and C may not then recover damages under the liquidated damage clause but may recover damages for any actual loss caused by A's breach, but not more than $50,000.

b. Provision for alternative performance distinguished. Although parties who merely provide for liquidated damages are not taken to have fixed a price for the privilege not to perform, there is no reason why parties may not fix such a price if they so choose. If a contract contains a provision for the payment of such a price as a true alternative performance, specific performance or an injunction may properly be granted on condition that the alternative performance is not forthcoming. But if the obligor chooses to pay the price, equitable relief will not be granted.

Illustration:

2. A sells his grocery business to B for $200,000, of which $100,000 is payable immediately and $100,000 at the end of a year. Under the agreement A makes an enforceable promise not to engage in a business of the same kind within a hundred miles for three years unless he reduces the balance from $100,000 to $50,000. See Illustration 1 to § 188. Before the end of the year, A writes B that the balance is reduced to $50,000 and immediately opens a competing business. A will not be enjoined from operating the competing business.

REPORTER'S NOTE

This Section is based on former § 378. See 5A Corbin, Contracts § 1213 (1964 & Supp. 1980); 11 Williston, Contracts § 1444 (3d ed. 1968).

Comment a. Illustration 1 is based on Illustration 1 to former § 378; Bauer v. Sawyer, 8 Ill.2d 351, 134 N.E.2d 329 (1956); Armstrong v. Stiffler, 189 Md. 630, 56 A.2d 808 (1948); Karpinski v. Ingrasci, 28 N.Y.2d 45, 320 N.Y.S.2d 1, 268 N.E.2d 751 (1971); cf. Stokes v. Moore, 262 Ala. 59, 77 So.2d 331 (1955); Manchester Dairy Sys. v.

Hayward, 82 N.H. 193, 132 A. 12 (1926).

Comment b. Illustration 2 is based on Illustration 2 to former § 378, cf. Davis v. Isenstein, 257 Ill. 260, 100 N.E. 940 (1913); Duckwall v. Rees, 119 Ind. App. 474, 86 N.E.2d 460 (1949); In re Heckman's Estate, 236 Pa. 193, 84 A. 689 (1912); Moss & Raley v. Wren, 102 Tex. 567, 113 S.W. 739 (1908), opinion on rehearing, 102 Tex. 567, 120 S.W. 847 (1909).

§ 362.　Effect of Uncertainty of Terms

Specific performance or an injunction will not be granted unless the terms of the contract are sufficiently certain to provide a basis for an appropriate order.

Comment:

a. Reason for requirement. One of the fundamental requirements for the enforceability of a contract is that its terms be certain enough to provide the basis for giving an appropriate remedy. See § 33. If this minimum standard of certainty is not met, there is no contract at all. It may be, however, that the terms are certain enough to provide the basis for the calculation of damages but not certain enough to permit the court to frame an order of specific performance or an injunction and to determine whether the resulting performance is in accord with what has been ordered. In that case there is a contract but it is not enforceable by specific performance or an injunction.

b. Degree of certainty required. If specific performance or an injunction is to be granted, it is important that the terms of the contract are sufficiently certain to enable the order to be drafted with precision because of the availability of the contempt power for disobedience. Before concluding that the required certainty is lacking, however, a court will avail itself of all of the usual aids in determining the scope of the agreement. See Chapter 9, The Scope of Contractual Obligations. Apparent difficulties of enforcement due to uncertainty may disappear in the light of courageous common sense. Expressions that at first appear incomplete may not appear so after resort to usage (§ 221) or the addition of a term supplied by law (§ 204). A contract is not too uncertain merely because a promisor is given a choice of performing in several ways, whether expressed as alternative performances or otherwise. He may be ordered to make the choice and to perform accordingly, and, if he fails to make the choice, the court may choose for him and order specific performance. Even though subsidiary terms have been left to determination by future agreement, if performance has begun by mutual consent, equitable relief may be appropriate with the court supplying the missing terms so as to assure the promisor all advantages that he reasonably expected.

Illustrations:

1. A and B make a contract under which A promises to convey part of a tract of land to B and B promises to pay $100,000 and to build "a first class theatre" on it. Building the theatre will

enhance the value of A's remaining land. A conveys the land to B, who pays the price but refuses to build the theatre. A sues B for specific performance. Specific performance will be refused because of the uncertainty of the terms of the contract, although A can receive damages from B based on the failure to enhance the value of his land if he can prove them with reasonable certainty (§ 352). See also § 366 on the effect of difficulty in supervision.

2. A leases land to B for three years, with an option to buy for $100,000 on terms of payment to be agreed upon. B occupies the land, making substantial repairs and improvements, and then accepts the option, tendering $100,000 in cash. A repudiates and B sues A for specific performance. Specific performance will not be refused on the ground of uncertainty. Although the terms of payment are uncertain and the parties may have contemplated a period of credit, refusal of specific performance would result in a forfeiture because B has made improvements and the payment tendered is on terms sufficiently favorable to A. See Illustration 2 to § 33.

3. A contracts to lease an apartment, with heat and light, to B as soon as the apartment building is completed. After the building is completed, A refuses to install sufficient equipment for heat and light. B sues A for specific performance. Specific performance will not be refused on the ground of uncertainty.

REPORTER'S NOTE

This Section is based on former § 370. See also Uniform Commercial Code § 2–204(3). See 5A Corbin, Contracts § 1174 (1964 & Supp. 1980); 11 Williston, Contracts § 1424 (3d ed. 1968).

Comment b. The facts in Illustration 1 are taken from Bettancourt v. Gilroy Theatre Co., 120 Cal. App.2d 364, 261 P.2d 351 (1953); Ferrara v. Silver, 138 Cal. App.2d 616, 292 P.2d 251 (1956). Illustration 2 is based on Illustration 1 to former § 370; cf. City Stores Co. v. Ammerman, 266 F. Supp. 766 (D.D.C. 1967), aff'd per curiam, 394 F.2d 950 (D.C. Cir. 1968); Illustration 3 is based on Illustration 3 to former § 370.

§ 363.   Effect of Insecurity as to the Agreed Exchange

Specific performance or an injunction may be refused if a substantial part of the agreed exchange for the performance to be compelled is unperformed and its performance is not secured to the satisfaction of the court.

Comment:

a. Importance of security. The rule stated in this Section is intended to make sure that a party is not compelled to render his own performance without receiving substantially the agreed exchange from the other party. This problem does not arise in an action for damages for total breach because the party in breach is only required to pay money, and the amount is always reduced by the amount the injured party saves by not having to proceed with his own performance. If the party in breach is to be required to perform specifically, however, the injured party is expected to do the same, and some security to assure that performance is desirable. Even if performance by the party in breach would have been due under the contract before that of the injured party, such security is desirable since, after controversy has developed, the risk of non-performance is increased. In some situations, the injured party may already have so far partly performed and so committed his funds and labor that his own self-interest furnishes adequate security. In other situations, however, it will be reasonable, in the exercise of judicial discretion, to require the injured party to furnish further security.

b. Means of securing performance. The desired security can often be afforded by the terms of the order itself. If performance by the injured party is already due or will be due simultaneously with the performance of the party in breach, the order may be made conditional on the injured party's rendition of his performance. This can be done even if a series of simultaneous exchanges is involved. If performance by the injured party is not due under the contract until after performance by the party in breach or is not due until an undetermined time, the injured party may nevertheless consent to have the order conditioned on his simultaneous performance, and even absent his consent it may be just to require him to perform simultaneously if he is to be granted equitable relief rather than damages. In such situations a discount may be allowed to compensate the injured party for the advancement in the time for his performance. If security cannot be afforded by fashioning the order in one of these ways, it may be made conditional on the injured party's execution of a mortgage as security for future performance or on his giving other collateral.

If it is impossible to assure performance by the injured party, an order may be refused, especially if there is reason to fear that the injured party will not perform. For example, a contract to render personal service exclusively for one employer will not be indirectly enforced by an injunction against serving another employer unless the court is convinced that the employer is ready and willing to perform his part of the contract.

See Appendix for Court Citations and Cross References

The question of security does not arise until the time for issuance of an order. At the pleading stage, a mere allegation by the plaintiff that he is ready and willing to perform is usually sufficient in a suit for specific performance or an injunction. Actual performance or tender is not generally required.

Illustrations:

1. A contracts to sell land to B, part of the purchase price to be paid in installments after the time fixed for the conveyance of the land. A refuses to convey the land and B sues for specific performance. Specific performance may properly be granted, conditional on B executing a mortgage or giving other satisfactory security that the payments will be made. This is so even though the contract provides for no security.

2. A contracts to transfer land to B immediately in return for B's promise to render personal services to A for ten years. A dispute between them causes unfriendly relations, A refuses to convey the land, and B sues for specific performance. Specific performance will be refused because of the increased risk that B's services will not be rendered and because sufficient security that they will be rendered is lacking.

3. A contracts to transfer land to B on performance by B of his promise to render personal services to A for ten years. After B has performed for six years, A repudiates the contract and B, who is able and willing to finish performance, sues for specific performance. A may properly be enjoined from conveying the land to anyone else and ordered to convey it to B upon full performance by B. But see § 367(2).

4. A contracts to transfer land to B for $100,000. B promises to pay $20,000 in cash on conveyance, to pay the balance in four annual installments secured by a mortgage and, immediately on conveyance, to improve the land by building a suitable brick residence. The contract provides that if B does not build the residence, title to the land will revert to A. A refuses to convey and B sues for specific performance. Specific performance may properly be granted. Even though B's promise to build the residence may not be specifically enforceable, the provision for reversion of title affords A sufficient security. The order may be made defeasible if B does not build the residence.

5. A, a fruit growers cooperative association, organized to improve economic conditions in the industry, contracts with its members to market their fruit, each member promising to deal

exclusively with the association.　B, one of the members, threatens to deal with others, imperilling the association's success. There is no indication that A will fail to market B's fruit as agreed.　A sues to enjoin B from dealing with others.　The injunction may properly be granted without requiring additional security.

c. "Mutuality of remedy."　It has sometimes been said that there is a requirement of "mutuality of remedy."　However, the law does not require that the parties have similar remedies in case of breach, and the fact that specific performance or an injunction is not available to one party is not a sufficient reason for refusing it to the other party.　The rationale of the supposed requirement of "mutuality of remedy" is to make sure that the party in breach will not be compelled to perform without being assured that he will receive any remaining part of the agreed exchange from the injured party.　It is therefore enough if adequate security can be furnished.

Illustrations:

6.　A contracts to sell a tract of land to B for $100,000.　The contract when made is unenforceable against B because the only memorandum of the contract is signed by A but not B.　A repudiates the contract and B sues for specific performance.　Specific performance may properly be granted because the commencement of the action by B makes the contract enforceable against him.

7.　A contracts to sell a tract of land to B for $100,000.　A is unable to convey the agreed title because C owns a part interest in the tract.　A repudiates the contract and B sues for specific performance.　Specific performance as to A's interest may properly be granted even though A could not have obtained such a decree against B because of his own breach.　See § 369.

d. Assignments.　A special application of the rule stated in this Section occurs where a party to a contract assigns his rights to an assignee.　The assignee can get specific performance or an injunction on the same terms that the assignor could.　The fact that the other party to the contract cannot get such relief against the assignee is not in itself a sufficient reason for refusing it when it is sought by the assignee.　The assignment does not relieve the assignor from his contractual duty and may not make it less likely that the agreed exchange will be rendered.　However, specific performance or an injunction may be refused if there is no satisfactory security that it will be rendered.　The order may, as in any other case, be fashioned to provide this security. Furthermore, if the assignee assumes the assignor's duty, the other party acquires additional security for the performance due him. Even if the assignor repudiates his duty or becomes unable to perform it, the assignee may be able to get an order by making a tender and keeping it good.

REPORTER'S NOTE

This Section is based on former § 373. See 5A Corbin, Contracts § 1137 (1964); 11 Williston, Contracts § 1440 (3d ed. 1968). Former § 372 on mutuality of remedy has been replaced by Comment c. Former § 380(2)(a) has been omitted since it is covered by the general rule stated here and is dealt with in Comment b.

Comment b. Illustration 1 is based on Illustration 1 to former § 373. Illustration 2 is based on Illustration 2 to former § 373; see also Illustration 4 to former § 379; cf. Illustration 4 to former § 373. Illustration 3 is based on Illustration 3 to former § 373; see also Illustration 1 to former § 372. Illustrations 4 and 5 are based on Illustrations 5 and 6 to former § 373.

Comment c. Illustration 6 is based on Safeway Sys. v. Manuel Bros., 102 R.I. 136, 228 A.2d 851 (1967); cf. Tombari v. Griepp, 55 Wash.2d 771, 350 P.2d 452 (1960); see also Illustration 5 to former § 372. Illustration 7 is based on Illustration 4 to former § 372; M & D Robinson Co. v. Dunitz, 12 Mich. App. 5, 162 N.W.2d 318 (1968); cf. Morad v. Silva, 331 Mass. 94, 117 N.E.2d 290 (1954).

§ 364. Effect of Unfairness

(1) Specific performance or an injunction will be refused if such relief would be unfair because

(a) the contract was induced by mistake or by unfair practices,

(b) the relief would cause unreasonable hardship or loss to the party in breach or to third persons, or

(c) the exchange is grossly inadequate or the terms of the contract are otherwise unfair.

(2) Specific performance or an injunction will be granted in spite of a term of the agreement if denial of such relief would be unfair because it would cause unreasonable hardship or loss to the party seeking relief or to third persons.

Comment:

a. Types of unfairness. Courts have traditionally refused equitable relief on grounds of unfairness or mistake in situations where they would not necessarily refuse to award damages. Some of these situations involve elements of mistake (§§ 152, 153), misrepresentation (§ 164), duress (§ 175) or undue influence (§ 177) that fall short of what is required for avoidance under those doctrines. See Paragraph (a) and Illustrations 1, 2 and 3. Others involve elements of impracticability of performance or frustration of purpose that fall short of what is required for relief under those doctrines. See Paragraph (b) and Illustration 4. Still others involve elements of substantive unfairness in the exchange itself or in its terms that fall short of what is required for unenforceability on grounds of unconscionability (§ 208). See Paragraph (c) and Comment *b*. The gradual expansion of these doctrines to afford relief in an increasing number of cases has resulted in a contraction of the area in which this traditional distinction is made between the availability of equitable and legal relief. Nevertheless, the discretionary nature of equitable relief permits its denial when a variety of factors combine to make enforcement of a promise unfair, even though no single legal doctrine alone would make the promise unenforceable. Such general equitable doctrines as those of laches and "unclean hands" supplement the rule stated in this Section. See Comment *c* to § 357.

Illustrations:

    1. A is an aged, illiterate farmer, inexperienced in business. B is an experienced speculator in real estate who knows that a developer wants to acquire a tract of land owned by A and will probably pay a price considerably above the previous market price. B takes advantage of A's ignorance of this fact and of his general inexperience and persuades A not to seek advice. He induces A to contract to sell the land at the previous market price, which is considerably less than the developer later agrees to pay B. A refuses to perform, and B sues A for specific performance. Specific performance may properly be refused on the ground of unfairness.

    2. A and B make a contract under which A is to sell B a tract of land for $100,000. B does not tell A that he intends to combine the tract with others as part of a large development in order to prevent A from asking a higher price. $100,000 is a fair price for the tract at existing market prices. A refuses to perform and B sues A for specific performance. Specific performance will not be refused on the ground of unfairness. Cf. Illustration 2 to § 171.

    3. A writes B offering to sell for $100,000 a tract of land that A owns known as "201 Lincoln Street." B, who mistakenly be-

lieves that this description contains an additional tract of land worth $30,000, accepts A's offer. On discovery of his mistake, B refuses to perform and A sues for specific performance. Even if the court determines that enforcement of the contract would not be unconscionable under the rule stated in § 153, specific performance may properly be refused on the ground of unfairness. Cf. Illustration 5 to § 153.

4. A, a milkman, and B, a dairy farmer make a contract under which B is to sell and A to buy all of A's requirements of milk, but not less than 200 quarts a day, for one year. B may deliver milk from any source but expects to deliver milk from his own herd. B's herd is destroyed because of hoof and mouth disease and he fails to deliver any milk. A sues B for specific performance. Even though B's duty to deliver milk is not discharged and B is liable to A for breach of contract, specific performance may properly be refused on the ground of unfairness. Cf. Illustration 12 to § 261.

b. Unfairness in the exchange. Unfairness in the exchange does not of itself make an agreement unenforceable. See Comment *c* to § 208. If it is extreme, however, it may be a sufficient ground, without more, for denying specific performance or an injunction. See Illustration 5. A contract, other than an option contract on fair terms (§§ 25, 87), that is binding solely because of a nominal payment or by reason of some formality such as a seal or a signed writing will not ordinarily be enforced by specific performance or an injunction. It is, however, unusual to find such unfairness in the exchange itself without some mistake or unfairness in its inducement. In determining the fairness of an exchange, account will be taken of the risks taken by both parties at the time the agreement was made. An exchange that might otherwise seem unfairly favorable to one party may in fact be fair if there is a substantial risk that the other party's performance may never become due. This is so for insurance and other aleatory contracts. See also Illustration 6. Where the agreement is one of modification between parties who are already bound by a contract (§ 89), the overriding duty of good faith and fair dealing (§ 205) imposes a requirement of fairness.

Illustrations:

5. A, an individual, contracts in June to sell at a fixed price per ton to B, a large soup manufacturer, carrots to be grown on A's farm. The contract, written on B's standard printed form, is obviously drawn to protect B's interests and not A's; it contains

numerous provisions to protect B against various contingencies and none giving analogous protection to A. Each of the clauses can be read restrictively so that it is not unconscionable, but several can be read literally to give unrestricted discretion to B. In January, when the market price has risen above the contract price, A repudiates the contract, and B seeks specific performance. In the absence of justification by evidence of commercial setting, purpose or effect, the court may determine that the contract as a whole was unconscionable when made and may properly deny specific performance on the ground of unfairness regardless of whether it would award B damages for breach.

6. A, a childless widow in her seventies suffering from Parkinson's disease, contracts with B, her niece, to leave B her farm in her will in return for B's promise to care for A for the rest of her life. B immediately resigns her job and begins to care for A, but deterioration of A's condition requires her to go to the hospital within a week and she dies without changing her will. B sues A's estate for specific performance. If the court concludes that the contract was fair when made, in view of the burden of caring for A in her condition and the risk that she might live for a considerable time, it will order specific performance.

c. *Unfair term.* Sometimes a party relies upon an unfair term as a defense in a suit for specific performance or injunction. Even if the term is not unconscionable (§ 208), the court may disregard it and grant the relief sought. See Illustration 7.

Illustration:

7. A contracts to sell land to B for $100,000, payable in five annual $20,000 installments with conveyance to be at the time of the last payment. The contract contains a term providing that "time is of the essence with respect to each installment, and B shall lose all his rights under the contract if he fails to pay any installment when due." See Comment *d* to § 242. B pays the first installment and takes possession, making improvements and paying the next two installments on time. When he tenders the fourth payment one month late, A refuses it and brings an action of ejectment. B sues for specific performance. The court may refuse to enforce the quoted term on the ground of unfairness. Specific performance may then properly be granted conditional on payment into court of the fourth installment with interest from maturity and on payment of the last installment on conveyance.

REPORTER'S NOTE

This Section is based on former § 367. Former § 366 has been dealt with in Comment b. See 5A Corbin, Contracts §§ 1162–68 (1964 & Supp. 1980); 11 Williston, Contracts §§ 1427, 1428, 1435 (3d ed. 1968).

Comment a. Illustration 1 is based on Illustration 2 to former § 367; Woollums v. Horsley, 93 Ky. 582, 20 S.W. 781 (1892); McKinnon v. Benedict, 38 Wis.2d 607, 157 N.W.2d 665 (1968). Illustration 2 is based on Illustration 3 to former § 367. Illustration 3 is supported by Perlmutter v. Bacas, 219 Md. 406, 149 A.2d 23 (1959); Brooks v. Towson Realty, 223 Md. 61, 162 A.2d 431 (1960). Illus-

tration 4 is supported by Waite v. O'Neil, 76 F. 408 (6th Cir. 1896).

Comment b. This comment is based in part on former § 366. Illustration 5 is based on Campbell Soup Co. v. Wentz, 172 F.2d 80 (3d Cir. 1948). Illustration 6 is based on Tuckwiller v. Tuckwiller, 413 S.W.2d 274 (Mo. 1967); see also Meyer v. Benko, 55 Cal. App.3d 937, 127 Cal. Rptr. 846 (1976).

Comment c. Illustration 7 is based on Illustrations 5 and 6 to former § 374; McFadden v. Walker, 5 Cal.3d 809, 97 Cal. Rptr. 537, 488 P.2d 1353 (1971).

§ 365.   Effect of Public Policy

Specific performance or an injunction will not be granted if the act or forbearance that would be compelled or the use of compulsion is contrary to public policy.

Comment:

a. Act or forbearance against public policy. If the performance of a contract is contrary to public policy, the contract will often be unenforceable under the rules stated in Chapter 8, Unenforceability on Grounds of Public Policy. Its performance may, for example, involve a breach of a duty to a third person arising under tort law, out of a fiduciary relation or under a contract. See §§ 192, 193 and 194. There are, however, situations in which the contract is enforceable but it would be an improper use of judicial power to grant specific performance or an injunction because the act or forbearance that would be compelled would adversely affect some aspect of the public interest or would otherwise be contrary to public policy. In such situations, equitable relief will be refused even though a judgment for damages will be granted. See Illustration 1.

Illustration:

1. A is induced to make a contract to sell land to B, to be paid for out of funds of C that B holds as trustee, by B's false

representation that such use of C's money is within B's authority as trustee. A sues B for specific performance. Specific performance will be refused on grounds of public policy, since the act that would be ordered would involve a breach of trust, even though B will be held liable in damage for breach of contract.

b. Compulsion against public policy. Even though the act or forbearance that would be compelled is not contrary to public policy, the use of compulsion to require that act or forbearance may be contrary to public policy. One example of this general principle is the rule under which a court will refuse to grant specific performance if the character of performance is such that enforcement will impose a disproportionate burden on the court (§ 366). Another is the rule under which a court will refuse to grant specific performance of a promise to render personal services or supervision (§ 367). The general principle is not, however, limited to these situations and another important application occurs where equitable relief is denied on the ground that to grant it would give a preference with respect to the assets of an insolvent party.

Illustrations:

2. A contracts to give B, a railroad company, a right of way in return for B's promise to locate a station and stop its express trains at a designated place. It later turns out that that place is an inconvenient one for the public and that the disadvantage to B as well as the public of B's promise is performed will be disproportionate to any advantage to A. B refuses to locate the station as promised, and A sues B for specific performance. Specific performance will be refused on grounds of public policy, even though B will be held liable in damages for breach of contract.

3. A borrows money from B and contracts to transfer to him as security 100 shares of stock in X Corporation but does not create a security interest in specific shares. A dies insolvent without having kept his promise. B sues A's administrator for specific performance. Specific performance will be refused on grounds of public policy because it would compel the administrator to commit a breach of his duty as trustee of the asset in his charge, even though A's estate will be held liable in damages for breach of contract.

4. A contracts to manufacture and deliver to B, for a price paid in advance, 100 articles as to which A has a monopoly under a patent. A manufactures 1,000 such articles but refuses to deliver any of them to B. B sues A for specific performance. A becomes

insolvent and his other creditors file a petition in bankruptcy. A's trustee intervenes in the suit to protect A's assets. Specific performance will be refused because it would result in a preference, even though A will be held liable for breach of contract. But see Uniform Commercial Code § 2–502.

REPORTER'S NOTE

This Section is based on former § 369 and on parts of former §§ 362 and 368. See 5A Corbin, Contracts § 1169 (1964); 11 Williston, Contracts § 1429 (3d ed. 1968).

Comment a. Illustration 1 is based on Illustration 2 to former § 368.

Comment b. As to the policy against preferences, see former § 362. Illustration 2 is based on Illustration 2 to former § 369. Illustration 3 is based on Illustration 1 to former § 362. Illustration 4 is based on Illustration 2 to former § 362; Jamison Coal & Coke Co. v. Gottra, 143 F.2d 889 (8th Cir.), cert. denied, 323 U.S. 769 (1944).

§ 366.   Effect of Difficulty in Enforcement or Supervision

A promise will not be specifically enforced if the character and magnitude of the performance would impose on the court burdens in enforcement or supervision that are disproportionate to the advantages to be gained from enforcement and to the harm to be suffered from its denial.

Comment:

a. Burden on court as a factor. Granting specific performance may impose on the court heavy burdens of enforcement or supervision. Difficult questions may be raised as to the quality of the performance rendered under the decree. Supervision may be required for an extended period of time. Specific relief will not be granted if these burdens are disproportionate to the advantages to be gained from enforcement and the harm to be suffered from its denial. A court will not, however, shrink from assuming these burdens if the claimant's need is great or if a substantial public interest is involved. In such cases, for example, structures may be ordered to be built and facilities may be required to be maintained. Experience has shown that potential difficulties in enforcement or supervision are not always realized and the significance of this factor is peculiarly one for judicial discretion. Because of the limited scope appropriate to judicial review of arbitration awards, a court will be less hesitant in confirming such an award that grants specific performance than it would in granting specific performance itself.

Illustrations:

1. A contracts to modernize and expand B's steel fabricating plant at a cost of $50,000,000. A falls behind the schedule fixed in the agreement, and B seeks specific performance to compel A to requisition 300 more workmen for the night shift and take other steps to speed up the work. A court may properly refuse specific performance on the ground that the difficulty of supervision by the court would be disproportionate to the benefits to be gained from enforcement.

2. The facts being otherwise as stated in Illustration 1, the dispute between A and B is referred, under a clause in the contract or a subsequent submission, to arbitration pursuant to rules stating that the arbitrator may grant any appropriate remedy including specific performance. The arbitrators award B specific performance. A court may properly confirm the award even though it would not have granted specific performance itself.

3. A, a real estate developer, sells a lot to B, contracting with him to build a sewer system to serve it. B pays the price and builds a house on the lot. A builds a sewer system that is inadequate and endangers the health and comfort of B's family. Specific performance will not be refused on the grounds that supervision by the court would be disproportionately difficult.

4. A, a manufacturer of steel, contracts to sell B all of its output of steel scrap for a period of five years. After one year, A repudiates the contract and B sues A for specific performance. Specific performance will not be refused on the ground that supervision by the court over the balance of the five-year period would be disproportionately difficult.

REPORTER'S NOTE

This Section is based on former § 371. See 5A Corbin, Contracts § 1171 (1964); 11 Williston, Contracts § 1422A (3d ed. 1968); Van Hecke, Changing Emphases in Specific Performance, 40 N.C.L. Rev. 1, 13–16 (1961).

Comment a. Illustration 1 is based on Northern Delaware Indus. Dev. Corp. v. E.W. Bliss Co., 245 A.2d 431 (Del. Ch. 1968); cf. Illustration 3 to former § 371; London Bucket Co. v. Stewart, 314 Ky. 832, 237 S.W.2d 509 (1951); see also Blanchard v. Detroit, Lansing & Lake Michigan R.R., 31 Mich. 43 (1875). But cf. Lane v. Pacific & I.N. R.R., 8 Idaho 230, 67 P. 656 (1902). Illustration 2 is based on Matter of Grayson-Robinson Stores (Iris Constr. Corp.), 8 N.Y.2d

133, 202 N.Y.S.2d 303, 168 N.E.2d 377 (1960). Illustration 3 is based on Illustration 4 to former § 371; City Stores Co. v. Ammerman, 266 F. Supp. 766 (D.D.C. 1967), aff'd, 394 F.2d 950 (D.C. Cir. 1968); Fran Realty v. Thomas, 30 Md. App. 362, 354 A.2d 196 (1976). Illustration 4 is based on Eastern Rolling Mill v. Michlovitz, 157 Md. 51, 145 A. 378 (1929). But cf. Edelen v. Samuels, 126 Ky. 295, 103 S.W. 360 (1907); Manchester Dairy Sys. v. Hayward, 82 N.H. 193, 132 A. 12 (1926).

§ 367. Contracts for Personal Service or Supervision

(1) A promise to render personal service will not be specifically enforced.

(2) A promise to render personal service exclusively for one employer will not be enforced by an injunction against serving another if its probable result will be to compel a performance involving personal relations the enforced continuance of which is undesirable or will be to leave the employee without other reasonable means of making a living.

Comment:

   a. Rationale of refusal of specific performance. A court will refuse to grant specific performance of a contract for service or supervision that is personal in nature. The refusal is based in part upon the undesirability of compelling the continuance of personal association after disputes have arisen and confidence and loyalty are gone and, in some instances, of imposing what might seem like involuntary servitude. To this extent the rule stated in Subsection (1) is an application of the more general rule under which specific performance will not be granted if the use of compulsion is contrary to public policy (§ 365). The refusal is also based upon the difficulty of enforcement inherent in passing judgment on the quality of performance. To this extent the rule stated in Subsection (1) is an application of the more general rule on the effect of difficulty of enforcement (§ 366).

   b. What is personal service. A performance is not a personal service under the rule stated in Subsection (1) unless it is personal in the sense of being non-delegable (§ 318). However, not every non-delegable performance is properly described as a service. An act such as the writing of an autograph or the signing of a diploma may be personal in the sense of being non-delegable even though it is not a personal service, and if that is so specific performance is not precluded. In determining what is a personal service, the policies reflected in the more general rules on the effect of public policy (§ 365) and of the difficulty of enforcement (§ 366) are relevant. The importance of trust and confidence in the relation between the parties, the difficulty of judging the quality of the performance rendered and the length of time required for performance are significant factors. Among the parties that have been held to render what are personal services within the rule stated in Subsection (1) are actors, singers and athletes, and the rule applies generally to contracts of employment that create the intimate relation traditionally known as master and servant. See Restatement, Second, Agency § 2.

The rule that bars specific enforcement of the employee's promise to render personal service has sometimes been extended to bar specific enforcement of the employer's promise where personal supervision is considered to be involved. The policies against compelling an employer to retain an employee have not, however, prevented courts from ordering reinstatement of employees discharged in contravention of statutes prohibiting discrimination or in violation of collective bargaining agreements.

Illustrations:

1. A, a noted opera singer, contracts with B to sing exclusively at B's opera house during the coming season. A repudiates the contract before the time for performance in order to sing at C's competing opera house, and B sues A for specific performance. Even though A's singing at C's opera house will cause B great loss that he cannot prove with reasonable certainty, and even though A can find suitable jobs singing at opera houses not in competition with B's, specific performance will be refused.

2. The facts being otherwise as stated in Illustration 1, B discharges A and A sues for specific performance. Even though singing at B's opera house would have greatly enhanced A's reputation and earning power in an amount that A cannot prove with reasonable certainty, specific performance will be refused.

c. Availability of injunction. A contract for personal service is usually exclusive in the sense that it imposes not only a duty to render the service to the other party but also a duty to forbear from rendering it to anyone else. Because specific performance of the duty to render the service is precluded by the rule stated in Subsection (1), the availability of injunctive relief to enforce the duty of forbearance takes on special importance. Subsection (2) indicates the application of the general rule on injunctive relief stated in § 357(2) to this important situation. Under that general rule, an injunction will not be ordered if the remedy in damages would be adequate (§ 359). Damages are likely to be adequate to protect the employer's interest unless the employee's services are unique or extraordinary, either because of special skill that he possesses or because of special knowledge that he has acquired of the employer's business.

Even if damages are not adequate, however, an injunction will not be granted if its probable result will be to leave the employee without other reasonable means of making a living. It is not the purpose in granting the injunction to enforce the duty to render the service and, to justify granting it, it should appear that the employee is not being forced to perform the contract as the only reasonable means of making a living. Furthermore, if the probable result of an injunction will be the employee's performance of the contract, it should appear that the employer is prepared to continue the employment in good faith so that performance will not involve personal relations the enforced continuance of which is undesirable. These issues are for the exercise of judicial discretion based on such factors as the character and duration of the service, the probability of the renewal of good relations, the extent to which other remedies are adequate, and the probable hardship that will result from an injunction.

Illustrations:

3. A contracts to serve exclusively as sales manager in B's clothing store for a year. A repudiates the contract shortly after beginning performance and goes to work for C, a competitor of B. B sues A for an injunction ordering A not to work for C. Unless A's services are unique or extraordinary, the injunction will be refused. If, however, A has special knowledge of B's customers that will cause a substantial number of them to leave B and patronize C, the injunction may properly be granted.

4. The facts being otherwise as stated in Illustration 1, B sues A for an injunction ordering A not to sing in C's opera house. The injunction may properly be granted. If, however, C is not a competitor of B, the injunction will not be granted because its principal effect would be indirectly to compel A to continue in B's service.

REPORTER'S NOTE

Subsection (1) is based on former § 379, but the reference to "supervision" has been deleted. Subsection (2) is based on former § 380(2). See 5A Corbin, Contracts §§ 1204–09 (1964 & Supp. 1980); 11 Williston, Contracts § 1423 (3d ed. 1968); Van Hecke, Changing Emphases in Specific Performance, 40 N.C.L. Rev. 1, 16–22 (1961).

Comment b. Illustration 1 is based on Illustrations 1 and 3 to former § 379; DeRivafinoli v. Corsetti, 4 Paige 264 (N.Y. Ch. 1833). Illustration 2 is based on Illustrations 1 and 5 to former § 379; Fitzpatrick v. Michael, 177 Md. 248, 9 A.2d 639 (1939). For cases refusing specific performance of an employer's promise on the ground that personal supervision is involved, see Felch v. Findlay College, 119 Ohio App. 357, 200 N.E.2d 353 (1963); State ex rel. Schoblom v. Anacortes Veneer, 42 Wash. 2d 338, 255 P.2d 379 (1953); cf. Hoffman Candy & Ice Cream Co. v. Dep't of Liquor Control, 154 Ohio St. 357, 96 N.E.2d 203 (1950).

Comment c. Illustration 3 is based on H.W. Gossard Co. v. Crosby, 132 Iowa 155, 109 N.W. 483 (1906). The last sentence is based on Illustration 9 to former § 380. Illustration 4 is based on Illustration 6 to former § 380; Lumley v. Wagner, 1 Deg. M. & G. 604, 42 Eng. Rep. 687 (Ch. 1852); Shubert Theatrical Co. v. Rath, 271 F. 827 (2d Cir. 1921); Philadelphia Ball Club v. Lajoie, 202 Pa. 210, 51 A. 973 (1902). The last sentence is based on Illustration 8 to former § 380.

§ 368.　Effect of Power of Termination

(1) Specific performance or an injunction will not be granted against a party who can substantially nullify the effect of the order by exercising a power of termination or avoidance.

(2) Specific performance or an injunction will not be denied merely because the party seeking relief has a power to terminate or avoid his duty unless the power could be used, in spite of the order, to deprive the other party of reasonable security for the agreed exchange for his performance.

Comment:

a. Power in party against whom relief is sought. Specific performance or an injunction will not be granted against a party who, by exercising a power of termination or avoidance, can substantially nullify the effect of the order. The power of termination or avoidance may be derived from a term of the agreement or from a rule of law. If a term of the agreement allows the party to terminate at will so as to make his promise illusory, no contract is created and no question of enforcement arises. See Comment *e* to § 2. Even if the term requires that notice of termination be given some period of time before it takes effect, so that the promise is not illusory and the contract is enforceable, the period may be so short that specific performance or an injunction would be pointless. If, however, the period is a substantial one, for example thirty days, and the performance that would have to be rendered during that period would be substantial even if notice were given immediately, equitable relief may properly be granted.   As to the situation in which the power can be exercised only at the cost of rendering some significant alternative performance, see Comment *b* to § 361.

Illustrations:

1.   A, a noted opera singer, contracts with B to sing exclusively at B's opera house for two seasons, reserving the power to terminate the contract at any time after the end of the first season by giving 24 hours' written notice.   A repudiates the contract when the second season is half over in order to sing at C's competing opera house, and B sues to enjoin A from doing so.   The injunction will not be granted.   If, however, A repudiates when the first season is half over, the injunction may be granted.

2.   A sells his business to B and makes a valid promise not to carry on a competing business, reserving the power to terminate his duty not to compete by paying B $50,000.   A repudiates his duty not to compete and threatens to operate a competing business, and B sues A to enjoin him from doing so.   The injunction may be granted, conditional on A not having paid the $50,000.

b.   Power in party seeking relief.   The existence of a power of termination or avoidance in the party who seeks specific performance or an injunction does not preclude such relief unless the power will seriously threaten the other party's security that the agreed exchange will be rendered.   This is a specific application of the general rule stated in § 363.   If the power is reserved by a term of the agreement, the court can protect the other party by providing that either the decree itself or the other party's performance shall extinguish the power.   If the party seeking relief has already rendered part performance or otherwise materially changed his position in reliance on the contract, this may give him a stronger economic interest in carrying out the agreement and thus increase the other party's security.   If the other party's security cannot be reasonably assured, however, equitable relief will be refused.

Illustrations:

3.   A, a minor, makes a contract to transfer a farm to B for $100,000.   B repudiates the contract and A sues B for specific performance.   Specific performance, even on condition of payment of the $100,000, will be refused if A has not reached the age

of majority, unless the jurisdiction is one in which the court's decree is conclusive on A so as to terminate his power of avoidance. After A reaches the age of majority and has ratified the contract, specific performance will be granted.

4. A makes a contract with B under which B obtains rights to all the oil and gas that he can produce from A's land for 10 years and promises to sink specific wells and pay A a fixed royalty on all oil and gas produced. The contract provides that B may at any time surrender his rights and terminate his duties on payment of $1. After B has sunk one well, A repudiates the contract and threatens to make a similar contract with C. B sues to enjoin A from interfering with his right to oil and gas as long as he continues to render substantial performance. The injunction may be granted. The result would be different if A repudiated before any performance by B and there was no way reasonably to secure B's performance.

5. A, a noted opera singer, contracts with B to sing exclusively at B's opera house during the coming season, B reserving the right to terminate the contract on 10 days' written notice. A repudiates the contract when the season is half over, after having been paid for that part of the season, in order to sing at C's competing opera house, and B sues to enjoin A from singing at C's opera house. The injunction may be granted, conditional on B's continued readiness and willingness to perform his part of the contract.

REPORTER'S NOTE

Subsection (1) is based on former § 377. Subsection (2) is based on former § 376. See 5A Corbin, Contracts §§ 1201–02 (1964); 11 Williston, Contracts § 1442 (3d ed. 1968).

Comment a. Illustration 1 is based on Illustration 1 to former § 377; see also Peru Wheel Co. v. Union Coal Co., 295 Ill. App. 276, 14 N.E.2d 998 (1938); Childs v. Columbia, 87 S.C. 566, 70 S.E. 296 (1911). Illustration 2 is based on Illustration 3 to former § 377.

Comment b. Illustrations 3 and 4 are based on Illustrations 1 and 4 to former § 376. The first sentence of Illustration 4 is based on Illustration 2 to former § 376. Illustration 5 is based on Illustration 3 to former § 376.

§ 369. Effect of Breach by Party Seeking Relief

Specific performance or an injunction may be granted in spite of a breach by the party seeking relief, unless the breach is serious enough to discharge the other party's remaining duties of performance.

See Appendix for Court Citations and Cross References

Comment:

a. Seriousness of breach. If a party has himself committed such a serious breach of contract, whether by non-performance or repudiation, as to discharge the other party's remaining duties under the contract, the party in breach is not entitled to relief, equitable or otherwise, if the other party refuses further performance. Whether a breach is serious enough to have this effect is determined by the rules stated in Chapter 10, Performance and Non-Performance. However, the fact that a party has committed a minor breach, one not serious enough to discharge the other party's remaining duties, does not preclude specific performance or an injunction. The party seeking relief may be required to cure the breach as a condition of the decree (see Illustration 1 to § 358) or may be held accountable for damages caused by his breach, either through a payment of money to the other party or by an abatement in the price that the other party is compelled to pay.

Illustrations:

1. A contracts to sell B his farm, said to contain 150 acres and to have a house on it in good repair. The farm contains 149 acres and the house is in slight disrepair. A tenders a deed but B refuses to accept it or pay although the defects are not such as would discharge his remaining duties of performance (see § 241), and A sues B for specific performance. Specific performance may properly be granted with an abatement of the price in an amount equal to damages for the defects. See Illustration 3 to § 358.

2. A contracts to sell to B his farm, conveyance and payment to be made on May 1. A tenders a deed on May 1 but B is not then able to pay. B tenders payment on May 10 but A refuses to convey although the delay is not such as would discharge his remaining duties of performance (see § 242), and B sues A for specific performance. Specific performance may properly be granted, conditional on B paying A any damages caused by the delay.

3. The facts being otherwise as stated in Illustration 2, B does not tender payment until September 1, a delay sufficient to discharge A's remaining duties of performance (see § 242). Specific performance will be refused on the ground of B's breach.

REPORTER'S NOTE

This Section is based on former § 375. See 5A Corbin, Contracts §§ 1175–76 (1964 & Supp. 1980); 12 Williston, Contracts §§ 1473–77 (3d ed. 1970). The exception in former § 375(1) permitting specific enforcement in the case of even a serious breach if this is necessary to avoid an unjust penalty or forfeiture has been omitted as unnecessary in the light of the merger of law and equity and the greater flexibility of legal rules that deal with penalties and forfeitures. See, for example, § 208 on unconscionable terms, § 227(1) on interpretation to avoid forfeiture, and § 229 on excuse of a condition to avoid forfeiture.

Comment a. Illustration 1 is based on Illustrations 5 and 7 to former § 375. Illustration 2 is based on Illustration 6 to former § 375. Illustration 3 is supported by Illustrations 1, 2 and 3 to former § 375; see also Durden v. Furniture Fair, 348 So.2d 1375 (Ala. 1977).

TOPIC 4. RESTITUTION

Introductory Note: Restitution is a common form of relief in contract cases. It has as its objective not the enforcement of contracts through the protection of a party's expectation or reliance interests but the prevention of unjust enrichment through the protection of his restitution interest. See § 344. A party who has received a benefit at the expense of the other party to the agreement is required to account for it, either by returning it in kind or by paying a sum of money. General rules that govern restitution in this context are set out in §§ 370–77.

This Chapter does not deal with restitution in general, because that subject is covered by the Restatement of Restitution. This Topic treats restitution in five situations that are closely related to contracts. The first is that in which the other party is in breach and the party seeking restitution has chosen it as an alternative to the enforcement of the contract between them (§ 373). In the second the party seeking restitution claims the benefit that he has conferred under the contract because he is precluded by his own breach from enforcing the contract (§ 374). In the third situation the party seeking restitution claims the benefit that he has conferred under the contract because he is precluded from enforcing it against the other party because of the Statute of Frauds (§ 375). The fourth situation is that in which a party claims restitution upon avoidance of a contract on the ground, for example, of mistake, misrepresentation or duress (§ 376). The fifth is that in which he claims restitution on the ground that his duty of performance did not arise or was discharged as a result of impracticability of performance, frustration of purpose, non-occurrence of a condition or disclaimer by a beneficiary (§ 377). A party's right to restitution under an agreement that is unenforceable on grounds of public policy is the subject of Topic 5 of Chapter 8, Unenforceability on Grounds of Public Policy. As to the right to restitution following an agreement of rescission, see Comment c to § 283. This Chapter does not deal with restitution for benefits during negotiations that do not result in an agreement or under an agreement that is not enforceable because its terms are not sufficiently certain (§ 33). See generally Restatement of Restitution §§ 15, 40, 47, 53.

REPORTER'S NOTE

This Topic is based on Topic 3, Restitution, of former Chapter 12 and on former §§ 468 and 488. See 5 Corbin, Contracts ch. 61 (1964 & Supp. 1980); 11 Williston, Contracts ch. 44 (3d ed. 1970); Palmer, Law of Restitution chs. 3–7, 9, 12 (1978); Dawson, Unjust Enrichment (1951); Dobbs, Remedies ch. 4 (1973); Palmer, Mistake and Unjust Enrichment (1962).

§ 370.   Requirement That Benefit Be Conferred

A party is entitled to restitution under the rules stated in this Restatement only to the extent that he has conferred a benefit on the other party by way of part performance or reliance.

Comment:

a. Meaning of requirement. A party's restitution interest is his interest in having restored to him any benefit that he has conferred on the other party. See § 344(2). Restitution is, therefore, available to a party only to the extent that he has conferred a benefit on the other party. The benefit may result from the transfer of property or from services, including forbearance. See Restatement of Restitution § 1, Comment *b*. The benefit is ordinarily conferred by performance by the party seeking restitution, and receipt by the other party of performance that he bargained for is regarded as a benefit. However, a benefit may also be conferred if the party seeking restitution relies on the contract in some other way, as where he makes improvements on property that does not ultimately become his. However, a party's expenditures in preparation for performance that do not confer a benefit on the other party do not give rise to a restitution interest. See Illustration 1. If, for example, the performance consists of the manufacture and delivery of goods and the buyer wrongfully prevents its completion, the seller is not entitled to restitution because no benefit has been conferred on the buyer. See Illustration 2. The injured party may, however, have an action for damages, including one for recovery based on his reliance interest (§ 349). The requirement of this Section is generally satisfied if a benefit has been conferred, and it is immaterial that it was later lost, destroyed or squandered. See Illustration 3. The benefit must have been conferred by the party claiming restitution. It is not enough that it was simply derived from the breach. See Illustration 4. The other party is considered to have had a benefit conferred on him if a performance was rendered at his request to a third person. See Illustration 5. If the contract is for the benefit of a third person, the promisee is entitled to restitution unless the duty to the beneficiary cannot be varied under the rule stated in § 311.

Illustrations:

1. A, who holds a mortgage on B's house, makes a contract with B under which A promises not to foreclose the mortgage for a year. In reliance on this promise, B invests money that he would have used to pay the mortgage in improving other land that he owns. A repudiates the contract and forecloses. B cannot get restitution based on the improvements since making them conferred no benefit on A. But see Illustration 4 to § 373 and Illustration 11 to § 90.

2. A contracts to sell B a machine for $100,000. After A has spent $40,000 on the manufacture of the machine but before its completion, B repudiates the contract. A cannot get restitution of the $40,000 because no benefit was conferred on B.

3. A promises to deposit $100,000 to B's credit in the X Bank in return for B's promise to render services. A deposits the $100,000, the X Bank fails, and B refuses to perform. A can get restitution of the $100,000 because a benefit was to that extent conferred on B even though it was lost by B when the X Bank failed. See § 373.

4. A contracts to work full time for B as a bookkeeper. In breach of this contract, A uses portions of the time that he should spend working for B in keeping books for C, who pays him an additional salary. B sues A for breach of contract. B cannot recover from A the amount of the salary paid by C because it was not a benefit conferred by B.

5. A, a social worker, promises B to render personal services to C in return for B's promise to educate A's children. B repudiates the contract after A has rendered part of the services. A can get restitution from B for the services, even though they were not rendered to B, because they conferred a benefit on B. See Illustration 3 to § 371.

REPORTER'S NOTE

This Section is based on former § 348. See 5 Corbin, Contracts §§ 1107–09 (1964 & Supp. 1980); 12 Williston, Contracts §§ 1480–83 (3d ed. 1970); Sullivan, The Concept of Benefit in the Law of Quasi-Contract, 64 Geo. L.J. 1 (1975); Notes, 19 Hastings L.J. 1259 (1968); 46 Mich. L. Rev. 543 (1948); cf. Ottenweller, Right of a Subcontractor to Make Claim Under a Payment Bond Where the Measure of Damage is Based on the Theory of Quantum Meruit, 14 Forum 1161 (1978).

Comment a. The last sentence of this Comment is based on former § 356(1). Illustration 1 is based on Illustration 4 to former § 348; cf. Boone v. Coe, 153 Ky. 233, 154 S.W. 900 (1913). Illustration 2 is based on Illustration 7 to former § 348. But cf. Acme Process Equip. Co. v. United States, 171 Ct. Cl. 324, 347 F.2d 509 (1965), rev'd on other grounds, 385 U.S. 138, rehearing denied, 385 U.S. 1032 (1966). Illustration 3 is based on Illustration 1 to former § 348. Illustration 4 is based on Illustration 2 to Restatement, Second, Agency § 404. Illustration 5 is based on Illustration 2 to former § 348.

§ 371. Measure of Restitution Interest

If a sum of money is awarded to protect a party's restitution interest, it may as justice requires be measured by either

(a) the reasonable value to the other party of what he received in terms of what it would have cost him to obtain it from a person in the claimant's position, or

(b) the extent to which the other party's property has been increased in value or his other interests advanced.

Comment:

a. Measurement of benefit. Under the rules stated in §§ 344 and 370, a party who is liable in restitution for a sum of money must pay an amount equal to the benefit that has been conferred upon him. If the benefit consists simply of a sum of money received by the party from whom restitution is sought, there is no difficulty in determining this amount. If the benefit consists of something else, however, such as services or property, its measurement in terms of money may pose serious problems.

Restitution in money is available in a wide variety of contexts, and the resolution of these problems varies greatly depending on the circumstances. If, for example, the party seeking restitution has himself committed a material breach (§ 374), uncertainties as to the amount of the benefit may properly be resolved against him.

A particularly significant circumstance is whether the benefit has been conferred by way of performance or by way of reliance in some other way. See Comment *a* to § 370. Recovery is ordinarily more generous for a benefit that has been conferred by performance. To the extent that the benefit may reasonably be measured in different ways, the choice is within the discretion of the court. Thus a court may take into account the value of opportunities for benefit even if they have not been fully realized in the particular case.

An especially important choice is that between the reasonable value to a party of what he received in terms of what it would have cost him to obtain it from a person in the claimant's position and the addition to the wealth of that party as measured by the extent to which his property has been increased in value or his other interests advanced. In practice, the first measure is usually based on the market price of such a substitute. Under the rule stated in this Section, the court has considerable discretion in making the choice between these two measures of benefit. Under either choice, the court may properly consider the purposes of the recipient of the benefit when he made the contract, even if those purposes were later frustrated or abandoned.

b. Choice of measure. The reasonable value to the party against whom restitution is sought (Paragraph (a)) is ordinarily less than the cost to the party seeking restitution, since his expenditures are excluded to the extent that they conferred no benefit. See Comment *a* to § 344. Nor can the party against whom restitution is sought reduce the amount for which he may himself be liable by subtracting such expenditures from the amount of the benefit that he has received. See Illustration 5 to § 377. The reasonable value to the party from whom restitution is sought (Paragraph (a)), is, however, usually greater than the addition to his wealth (Paragraph (b)). If this is so, a party seeking restitution for part performance is commonly allowed the more generous measure of reasonable value, unless that measure is unduly difficult to apply, except when he is in breach (§ 374). See Illustration 1. In the case of services rendered in an emergency or to save life, however, restitution based on addition to wealth will greatly exceed that based on expense saved and recovery is invariably limited to the smaller amount. See Illustration 2. In the case of services rendered to a third party as the intended beneficiary of a gift promise, restitution from the promisee based on his enrichment is generally not susceptible of measurement and recovery based on reasonable value is appropriate. See Illustration 3.

Illustrations:

1. A, a carpenter, contracts to repair B's roof for $3,000. A does part of the work at a cost of $2,000, increasing the market price of B's house by $1,200. The market price to have a similar carpenter do the work done by A is $1,800. A's restitution interest is equal to the benefit conferred on B. That benefit may be measured either by the addition to B's wealth from A's services in terms of the $1,200 increase in the market price of B's house or the reasonable value to B of A's services in terms of the $1,800 that it would have cost B to engage a similar carpenter to do the same work. If the work was not completed because of a breach by A and restitution is based on the rule stated in § 374, $1,200 is appropriate. If the work was not completed because of a breach by B and restitution is based on the rule stated in § 373, $1,800 is appropriate.

2. A, a surgeon, contracts to perform a series of emergency operations on B for $3,000. A does the first operation, saving B's life, which can be valued in view of B's life expectancy at $1,000,000. The market price to have an equally competent surgeon do the first operation is $1,800. A's restitution interest is equal to the benefit conferred on B. That benefit is measured by the reasonable value to B of A's services in terms of the $1,800 that it would have cost B to engage a similar surgeon to do the operation regardless of the rule on which restitution is based.

3. A, a social worker, promises B to render personal services to C in return for B's promise to educate A's children. A renders only part of the services and B then refuses to educate A's children. The market price to have a similar social worker do the services rendered by A is $1,800. If A recovers in restitution under the rule stated in § 373, an appropriate measure of the benefit conferred on B is the reasonable value to B of A's services in terms of the $1,800 that it would have cost B to engage a similar social worker to do the same work.

REPORTER'S NOTE

This Section is new. See 5 Corbin, Contracts § 1112 (1964 & Supp. 1980); 12 Williston, Contracts §§ 1478, 1483 (3d ed. 1970); Dawson, Restitution or Damages, 20 Ohio St. L.J. 175 (1959); Perillo, Restitution in a Contractual Context, 73 Colum. L. Rev. 1208 (1973).

Comment a. See Campbell v. Tennessee Valley Auth., 421 F.2d 293 (5th Cir. 1969).

Comment b. As to Illustration 1, see Campbell v. Tennessee Valley Auth., 421 F.2d 293 (5th Cir. 1969); Combs v. Deaton, 199 Ky. 477, 251

S.W. 638 (1928); Reimann v. Baum, 115 Utah 147, 203 P.2d 387 (1949). Illustration 2 is based on Cotnam v. Wisdom, 83 Ark. 601, 104 S.W. 164 (1907). Illustration 3 is based in part on Illustration 2 to former § 348.

§ 372. Specific Restitution

(1) Specific restitution will be granted to a party who is entitled to restitution, except that:

(a) specific restitution based on a breach by the other party under the rule stated in § 373 may be refused in the discretion of the court if it would unduly interfere with the certainty of title to land or otherwise cause injustice, and

(b) specific restitution in favor of the party in breach under the rule stated in § 374 will not be granted.

(2) A decree of specific restitution may be made conditional on return of or compensation for anything that the party claiming restitution has received.

(3) If specific restitution, with or without a sum of money, will be substantially as effective as restitution in money in putting the party claiming restitution in the position he was in before rendering any performance, the other party can discharge his duty by tendering such restitution before suit is brought and keeping his tender good.

Comment:

a. Specific restitution on avoidance or in similar circumstances. A party who has a right to restitution under the rule stated in § 376 because he has avoided the contract, generally has a choice of either claiming a sum of money in restitution or seeking specific restitution if the benefit is something that can be returned to him. The same is true of a party who has a right to restitution under the rule stated in § 377 on one of the grounds there stated, even though this rule does not, strictly speaking, result in avoidance of the contract. The right to specific restitution may, however, be subject to rights of third parties. Their rights are not dealt with in this Restatement. For special rules governing the right of a seller under a contract for the sale of goods, see Uniform Commercial Code §§ 2–507, 2–702.

Illustration:

    1. A is induced by B's misrepresentation to sell a tract of land to B for $100,000. On discovery of the misrepresentation, A tenders back the $100,000 and sues B for specific restitution of the land. Specific restitution will be granted.

    b. Specific restitution on other grounds. A party whose right to restitution is based on the other party's breach also has a right to specific restitution, subject to the limitation stated in Paragraph (a). In the case of a contract for the sale of goods, the Uniform Commercial Code limits much more severely the seller's right to specific restitution, although the seller can protect himself by taking a security interest in the goods. See Uniform Commercial Code § 2–703. The most important problems of specific restitution that remain usually arise in connection with contracts to transfer land. If the buyer of land fails or refuses to pay the price after the transfer of the land to him, the seller is limited to his claim for the price, which may be secured by a vendor's lien as a matter of law or by a security interest that he has reserved. The question of his right to specific restitution does not arise in that situation (§ 373(2)). Specific restitution may, however, be appropriate where there is a right to restitution because the return promise is to do something other than pay money. See Illustrations 2 and 3. In that case, however, a court may refuse specific restitution if it would unduly interfere with the certainty of title to the land. In resolving that question, a court will take into account all the circumstances, including the inadequacy of other relief. A court may also refuse specific restitution if it would otherwise cause injustice as where, for example, it would result in a preference over other creditors in bankruptcy. Specific restitution under the rule stated in this Section is available to the injured party even though enforcement of the contract is barred by the Statute of Frauds. See § 375. Under the exception stated in Paragraph (b), however, it is never available to a party who is himself in breach. See § 374.

Illustrations:

    2. A contracts to transfer a tract of land to B in return for B's promise to transfer a tract of land to A at the same time. After A has transferred his tract to B and received a deed from B, A learns that B does not have title to the other tract. A sues B for specific restitution. Specific restitution will be granted, together with compensation to A for the value to B of the use of the land, because the right to specific restitution will not unduly interfere with the certainty of title to land. If B's promise is to trans-

fer his tract to A ten years after A's transfer of his tract, specific restitution will be denied because a right to specific restitution would unduly interfere with the certainty of title to land during the ten years.

3. A contracts to transfer a tract of land to B in return for B's promise to support A for life. B repudiates the contract after he has supported A for a time and A has transferred the land to him, and A sues B for specific restitution. Specific restitution will be granted, conditional on compensation by A for any support that he has received less the value to B of the use of the land, because the right to specific restitution will not unduly interfere with the certainty of title to land given the inadequacy of A's right to damages because of the difficulty of proving damages with sufficient certainty (§ 352).

4. A contracts to transfer a tract of land to B in return for B's promise to transfer a tract of land to A at a later date. After A has transferred his tract of land to B, B sells both tracts to C, a good faith purchaser for value, taking a mortgage to secure the balance of the price on the tract transferred by A. A sues B and C for specific restitution. Specific restitution will be denied but A can get a decree subrogating him to B's right to the balance of the price and to his rights under the purchase money mortgage that secures it.

5. A contracts to transfer to B half of his 20,000 shares of stock in the X Corporation in return for B's promise to pay $100,000, to organize a holding company to control X Corporation and to protect A's remaining interest as a shareholder. After A has transferred the stock and B has paid the $100,000, B refuses to organize the holding company. A sues B for specific restitution. Specific restitution may properly be granted conditional on repayment by A of the $100,000.

c. *Tender of specific restitution.* In some circumstances, a party who is liable for restitution can discharge his duty by tendering specific restitution and keeping his tender good. The tender has this result only if specific restitution will be substantially as effective as restitution in money in putting the party claiming restitution in the position he was in before rendering any performance. If tender of a sum of money in addition to specific restitution will do this, such a tender discharges the other party's duty. See Illustration 6. The tender must, however, be made before suit has been brought.

Illustration:

6. A makes an oral contract with B under which A transfers 1,000 shares of stock to B in return for B's promise to convey a tract of land to A. B repudiates the contract before he has conveyed the land and tenders back the stock and the dividends received from it and keeps his tender good. A rejects the tender and sues B for restitution of the value to B of the stock. A cannot recover the value of the stock.

REPORTER'S NOTE

This Section is based on former §§ 354, 355(2), 468(1) and 489. It enlarges the right to specific restitution and abandons the adequacy test. See 1 Palmer, The Law of Restitution §§ 4.7, 4.19, 4.20 (1978); see also 5 Corbin, Contracts § 1120 (1964); 12 Williston, Contracts §§ 1456, 1458 (3d ed. 1968).

Comment a. Illustration 1 is based on State St. Bank & Trust Co. v. Beale, 353 Mass. 103, 227 N.E.2d 924 (1967).

Comment b. Illustration 2 is based on Illustration 3 to former § 354 and on the discussion of Benassi v. Har-ris, 147 Conn. 451, 162 A.2d 521 (1960), in Palmer, supra, at § 4.19. Illustration 3 is based on Illustration 1 to former § 354; Brimson v. Pearrow, 218 Ark. 27, 234 S.W.2d 214 (1950); Myers v. Diehl, 365 P.2d 717 (Okl. 1961). Illustration 4 is based on Illustration 4 to former § 354. Illustration 5 is based on Illustration 5 to former § 354; Therm-O-Proof Insulation Mfg. Co. v. Hoffman, 329 Ill. App. 645, 69 N.E.2d 725 (1946); Maytag Co. v. Alward, 253 Iowa 455, 112 N.W.2d 654 (1962).

Comment c. Illustration 6 is based on Illustration 6 to former § 355.

§ 373. Restitution When Other Party Is in Breach

(1) Subject to the rule stated in Subsection (2), on a breach by non-performance that gives rise to a claim for damages for total breach or on a repudiation, the injured party is entitled to restitution for any benefit that he has conferred on the other party by way of part performance or reliance.

(2) The injured party has no right to restitution if he has performed all of his duties under the contract and no performance by the other party remains due other than payment of a definite sum of money for that performance.

Comment:

    a. Restitution as alternative remedy for breach. An injured party usually seeks, through protection of either his expectation or his reliance interest, to enforce the other party's broken promise. See § 344(1). However, he may, as an alternative, seek, through protection of his restitution interest, to prevent the unjust enrichment of the other party. See § 344(2). This alternative is available to the injured party as a remedy for breach under the rule stated in this Section. It is available regardless of whether the breach is by non-performance or by repudiation. If, however, the breach is by non-performance, restitution is available only if the breach gives rise to a claim for damages for total breach and not merely to a claim for damages for partial breach. Compare Illustration 1 with Illustration 2. A party who has lost the right to claim damages for total breach by, for example, acceptance or retention of performance with knowledge of defects (§ 246), has also lost the right to restitution. Restitution is available on repudiation by the other party, even in those exceptional situations in which no claim for damages for total breach arises as a result of repudiation alone. See Comment *d* to § 253. See Illustration 3. The rule stated in this Section applies to all enforceable promises, including those that are enforceable because of reliance. See Illustration 4. An injured party's right to restitution may be barred by election under the rules stated in §§ 378 and 379.

Illustrations:

    1. A contracts to sell a tract of land to B for $100,000. After B has made a part payment of $20,000, A wrongfully refuses to transfer title. B can recover the $20,000 in restitution. The result is the same even if the market price of the land is only $70,000, so that performance would have been disadvantageous to B.

    2. A contracts to build a house for B for $100,000, progress payments to be made monthly. After having been paid $40,000 for two months, A commits a breach that is not material by inadvertently using the wrong brand of sewer pipe. B has a claim for damages for partial breach but cannot recover the $40,000 that he has paid A.

    3. On February 1, A and B make a contract under which, as consideration for B's immediate payment of $50,000, A promises to convey to B a parcel of land on May 1. On March 1, A repudiates by selling the parcel to C. On April 1, B commences an action against C. Although under the rule stated in § 253(1), B

has no claim against A for damages for breach of contract until performance is due on May 1, B can recover $50,000 from A in restitution. See Illustration 4 to § 253.

4. A, who holds a mortgage on B's land, promises B that he will not foreclose the mortgage for another year, even if B makes no payments. In reliance on A's promise, B makes valuable improvements. A forecloses in breach of his promise and buys the land at a judicial sale for the amount of the mortgage debt. B can recover in restitution for the value of the improvements. Compare Illustration 1 to § 370; see also Illustration 12 to § 90.

b. When contract price is a limit. The rule stated in Subsection (1) is subject to an important exception. If, after one party has fully performed his part of the contract, the other party then refuses to pay a definite sum of money that has been fixed as the price for that performance, the injured party is barred from recovery of a greater sum as restitution under the rule stated in Subsection (2). Since he is entitled to recover the price in full together with interest, he has a remedy that protects his expectation interest by giving him the very thing that he was promised. Even if he asserts that the benefit he conferred on the other party exceeds the price fixed by the contract, justice does not require that he have the right to recover this larger sum in restitution. To give him that right would impose on the court the burden of measuring the benefit in terms of money in spite of the fact that this has already been done by the parties themselves when they made their contract. See Illustration 5. If, however, the performance to be rendered by the party in breach is something other than the payment of a definite sum in money, this burden is less of an imposition on the court since, even if damages were sought by the injured party, the court would have to measure the value to him of the performance due from the party in breach. The clearest case occurs where the injured party has paid the full price in money for the performance that the party in breach has subsequently failed to render. To allow restitution of the sum paid in that case imposes no burden of measurement on the court and relieves it of the burden that it would have if damages were awarded of measuring the value to the injured party of the performance due from the party in breach. See Illustration 6. For this reason, the rule stated in Subsection (2) is limited to the situation where the only remaining performance due from the party in breach is the payment of a definite sum of money. See Illustrations 6 and 7. If the performance promised by the party in breach consists in part of money and in part of something else, full performance by the injured party does not bar him from restitution unless the party in breach has rendered all of his performance except a money payment.

Illustrations:

5. A contracts to work for B for one month for $10,000. After A has fully performed, B repudiates the contract and refuses to pay the $10,000. A can get damages against B for $10,000, together with interest, but cannot recover more than that sum even if he can show that the benefit to B from the services was greater than $10,000.

6. A contracts to sell a tract of land to B for $100,000. After B has paid the full $100,000, A repudiates and refuses to transfer title. B has a right to $100,000 in restitution.

7. A contracts to build a building for B in return for B's promise to transfer a tract of land to A and to pay $10,000. After A has built the building, B refuses to transfer title or to pay the $10,000. A has a right to the reasonable value of his work and materials.

c. Effect of "divisibility." Sometimes a contract is "divisible" in the sense that parts of the performances to be exchanged on each side are properly regarded as a pair of agreed equivalents. See § 240. The rule stated in Subsection (2) applies by analogy to such contracts. If one party has fully performed his side of such a pair and all that remains on the other side is for the other party to pay a definite sum of money, recovery for the performance rendered is limited to that sum. Restitution is not available as an alternative even if there has been a breach as to other parts of the contract. See Illustration 8. If both parties have fully performed, so that nothing with respect to the pair of agreed equivalents remains to be done on either side, no recovery can be had as to that pair.

Illustrations:

8. A contracts to work as a consultant for B for a fee of $50,000, payable at the end of the year, together with a payment of $200 a month for A's use of his own car and reimbursement of A's expenses. B wrongfully discharges A at the end of six months. A cannot recover in restitution for the use of his car or for his expenses, but can recover for these items as provided in the contract. As to his recovery for his services, see Illustration 12.

9. A contracts to build a house for B for $50,000, progress payments to be made monthly in an amount equal to 85% of the price of the work performed during the preceding month, the balance to be paid on the architect's certificate of satisfactory completion of the house. B makes the first three payments and then

repudiates the contract and has another builder finish the house. A can recover in restitution for the reasonable value of his work, labor and materials, less the amount of the three payments. The performance during each month and the corresponding progress payments are not agreed equivalents under the rule stated in § 240. See Illustration 7 to § 240.

d. Losing contracts. An injured party who has performed in part will usually prefer to seek damages based on his expectation interest (§ 347) instead of a sum of money based on his restitution interest because such damages include his net profit and will give him a larger recovery. Even if he cannot prove what his net profit would have been, he will ordinarily seek damages based on his reliance interest (§ 348), since this will compensate him for all of his expenditures, regardless of whether they resulted in a benefit to the party in breach. See Comment *a* to § 344. In the case of a contract on which he would have sustained a loss instead of having made a profit, however, his restitution interest may give him a larger recovery than would damages on either basis. The right of the injured party under a losing contract to a greater amount in restitution than he could have recovered in damages has engendered much controversy. The rules stated in this Section give him that right. He is entitled to such recovery even if the contract price is stated in terms of a rate per unit of work and the recovery exceeds that rate. There are, however, two important limitations. The first limitation is one that is applicable to any claim for restitution: the party in breach is liable only to the extent that he has benefited from the injured party's performance. If he has, for example, taken advantage of the injured party's part performance by having the rest of the work completed after his breach, the extent of his benefit is easy to measure in terms of the reasonable value of the injured party's performance. See Illustration 10. If, however, he has abandoned the project and not completed the work, that measurement will be more difficult. See Illustration 11. In that situation, the court may exercise its sound discretion in choosing between the two measures stated in § 371. In doing so it will take account of all the circumstances including the observance by the parties of standards of good faith and fair dealing during any negotiations leading up to the rupture of contractual relations (§ 208). See Introductory Note to Chapter 10. Since a contract that is a losing one for the injured party is often an advantageous one for the party in breach, the possibility should not be overlooked that the breach was provoked by the injured party in order to avoid having to perform. The second limitation is that stated in Subsection (2). If the injured party has completed performance and nothing remains for the party in breach to do but to pay him the price, his recovery is limited to the price. See Comment *b*.

Illustrations:

10. A, a plumbing subcontractor, contracts with B, a general contractor, to install the plumbing in a factory being built by B for C. B promises to pay A $100,000. After A has spent $40,000, B repudiates the contract and has the plumbing finished by another subcontractor at a cost of $80,000. The market price to have a similar plumbing subcontractor do the work done by A is $40,000. A can recover the $40,000 from B in restitution.

11. A contracts to build a house for B for $100,000. After A has spent $40,000, B discovers that he does not have good title to the land on which the house is to be built. B repudiates the contract and abandons the project. A's work results in no actual benefit to B. A cannot recover in restitution from B, but under the rule stated in § 349 he can recover as damages the $40,000 that he has spent unless B proves with reasonable certainty that A would have sustained a net loss if the contract had been performed. See Illustration 4 to § 349.

12. A contracts to work as a consultant for B for a fee of $50,000, payable at the end of the year. B wrongfully discharges A at the end of eleven months. A can recover in restitution based on the reasonable value of his services. The terms of the contract are evidence of this value but are not conclusive.

e. Avoidability as a limit on restitution. The rule that precludes restitution for a benefit that has been conferred officiously (Restatement of Restitution § 2), applies to preclude recovery for performances that a party has rendered following a repudiation by the other party. Compare the rule stated in § 350.

Illustration:

13. A contracts to build a bridge for B for $100,000. B repudiates the contract shortly after A has begun work on the bridge, telling A that he no longer has need for it. A nevertheless spends an additional $10,000 in continuing to perform. A's restitution interest under the rule stated in § 370 does not include the benefit conferred on B by the $10,000. See Illustration 1 to § 350.

REPORTER'S NOTE

Subsection (1) is based on former § 347. Subsection (2) is based on former §§ 350, 351. The rule stated in former § 353 is now found in Comment *a.* See 5 Corbin, Contracts §§ 1104, 1110–13 (1964 & Supp. 1980); 12 Williston, Contracts §§ 1454, 1456–59A, 1478 (3d ed. 1970); 1 Palmer, Law of Restitution ch. 4 (1978); Childres & Garamella, The Law of Restitution and the Reliance Interest in Contract, 64 Nw. U.L. Rev. 433 (1969); Dawson, Restitution or Damages, 20 Ohio St. L.J. 175 (1959); Farnsworth, Legal Remedies for Breach of Contract, 70 Colum. L. Rev. 1145, 1178–83 (1970); Fuller & Perdue, The Reliance Interest in Contract Damages: I, 46 Yale L.J. 52, 71–80 (1936); Palmer, The Contract Price as a Limit on Restitution for Defendant's Breach, 20 Ohio St. L.J. 264 (1959); Patterson, Builder's Measure of Recovery for Breach of Contract, 31 Colum. L. Rev. 1286, 1299–1308 (1931); Perillo, Restitution in A Contractual Context, 73 Colum. L. Rev. 1208 (1973); Sullivan, The Concept of Benefit in the Law of Quasi-Contract, 64 Geo. L.J. 1 (1975); Wright, The Law of Remedies as a Social Institution, 18 U. Det. L.J. 376 (1955); The [English] Law Commission, Pecuniary Restitution on Breach of Contract 39–44, 65–66 (Law of Contract Working Paper No. 65, 1975).

Comment a. Illustration 1 is based on Nash v. Towne, 72 U.S. 689 (1866); Bush v. Canfield, 2 Conn. 485 (1818). Illustration 2 is based on Illustration 1 to former § 347. As to Illustration 3, see Bollenback v. Continental Cas. Co., 243 Or. 498, 414 P.2d 802 (1966). Illustration 4 is based on Illustration 7 to former § 347; Utemark v. Samuel, 118 Cal. App.2d 313, 257 P.2d 656 (1953).

Comment b. Illustration 5 is based on Illustration 1 to former § 350;

United States v. Americo Constr. Co., 168 F. Supp. 760 (D. Mass. 1958); cf. Oliver v. Campbell, 43 Cal.2d 298, 273 P.2d 15 (1955). Illustration 6 is based on Illustration 2 to former § 350. Illustration 7 is based on Illustration 5 to former § 350; cf. Brown v. St. Paul, Minneapolis & Manitoba Ry., 36 Minn. 236, 31 N.W. 941 (1886); Bailey v. Interstate Airmotive, 358 Mo. 1121, 219 S.W.2d 333 (1949).

Comment c. Illustration 8 is based on Illustration 1 to former § 351; cf. Coon v. Schoeneman, 476 S.W.2d 439 (Tex. Civ. App. 1972). Illustration 9 is based on Illustration 4 to former § 351.

Comment d. Illustration 10 is based on United States v. Algernon Blair, Inc., 479 F.2d 638 (4th Cir. 1973); Scaduto v. Orlando, 381 F.2d 587 (2d Cir. 1967); United States ex rel. Susi Contracting Co. v. Zara, 146 F.2d 606 (2d Cir. 1944); Philadelphia v. Tripple, 230 Pa. 480, 79 A. 703 (1911); see also Illustrations 3 and 4 to former § 347. As to Illustration 11, compare Millen v. Gulesian, 229 Mass. 27, 118 N.E. 267 (1918), with Acme Process Equip. Co. v. United States, 171 Ct. Cl. 324, 347 F.2d 509 (1965), rev'd on other grounds, 385 U.S. 138, rehearing denied, 385 U.S. 1032 (1966). Cf. Kehoe v. Rutherford, 56 N.J.L. 23, 27 A. 912 (1893). Illustration 12 is based on Illustration 2 to former § 347. As to whether the contract price is an upper limit to restitution, compare Wuchter v. Fitzgerald, 83 Or. 672, 163 P. 819 (1917), with Boomer v. Muir, 24 P.2d 570 (Cal. App. 1933). See also Oliver v. Campbell, supra. On the effect of divisibility, see Shapiro Eng'r Corp.

v. Francis O. Day Co., 215 Md. 373,
137 A.2d 695 (1958).

13 is based on Illustration 1 to former
§ 352.

Comment e. This Comment is
based on former § 352. Illustration

§ 374.   Restitution in Favor of Party in Breach

(1) Subject to the rule stated in Subsection (2), if a party justifiably refuses to perform on the ground that his remaining duties of performance have been discharged by the other party's breach, the party in breach is entitled to restitution for any benefit that he has conferred by way of part performance or reliance in excess of the loss that he has caused by his own breach.

(2) To the extent that, under the manifested assent of the parties, a party's performance is to be retained in the case of breach, that party is not entitled to restitution if the value of the performance as liquidated damages is reasonable in the light of the anticipated or actual loss caused by the breach and the difficulties of proof of loss.

Comment:

a. Restitution in spite of breach. The rule stated in this Section applies where a party, after having rendered part performance, commits a breach by either non-performance or repudiation that justifies the other party in refusing further performance. It is often unjust to allow the injured party to retain the entire benefit of the part performance rendered by the party in breach without paying anything in return. The party in breach is, in any case, liable for the loss caused by his breach. If the benefit received by the injured party does not exceed that loss, he owes nothing to the party in breach. If the benefit received exceeds that loss, the rule stated in this Section generally gives the party in breach the right to recover the excess in restitution. If the injured party has a right to specific performance and remains willing and able to perform, he may keep what he has received and sue for specific performance of the balance.

The rule stated in this Section is of particular importance in connection with breach by the buyer under a land sale contract (see Illustration 1) and breach by the builder under a construction contract (see Illustrations 2, 3 and 4). It is less important in the case of the defaulting employee, who has the protection afforded by statutes that require salary payments at relatively short intervals. The case of defaulting buyer of goods is governed by Uniform Commercial Code § 2–718(2), which generally allows restitution of all but an amount fixed by that section. Furthermore, to the extent that the contract is "divisible" so that pairs of part performances on each side are agreed equivalents (§ 240), the party in breach can recover under the terms of the contract and does not need restitution to obtain relief.

b. Measurement of benefit. If the party in breach seeks restitution of money that he has paid, no problem arises in measuring the benefit to the other party. See Illustration 1. If, however, he seeks to recover a sum of money that represents the benefit of services rendered to the other party, measurement of the benefit is more difficult. Since the party seeking restitution is responsible for posing the problem of measurement of benefit, doubts will be resolved against him and his recovery will not exceed the less generous of the two measures stated in § 370, that of the other party's increase in wealth. See Illustration 3. If no value can be put on this, he cannot recover. See Illustration 5. Although the contract price is evidence of the benefit, it is not conclusive. However, in no case will the party in breach be allowed to recover more than a ratable portion of the total contract price where such a portion can be determined.

A party who intentionally furnishes services or builds a building that is materially different from what he promised is properly regarded as having acted officiously and not in part performance of his promise and will be denied recovery on that ground even if his performance was of some benefit to the other party. This is not the case, however, if the other party has accepted or agreed to accept the substitute performance. See §§ 278, 279.

Illustrations:

1. A contracts to sell land to B for $100,000, which B promises to pay in $10,000 installments before transfer of title. After B has paid $30,000 he fails to pay the remaining installments and A sells the land to another buyer for $95,000. B can recover $30,000 from A in restitution less $5,000 damages for B's breach of contract, or $25,000. If A does not sell the land to another buyer and obtains a decree of specific performance against B, B has no right to restitution.

2. A contracts to make repairs to B's building in return for B's promise to pay $10,000 on completion of the work. After spending $8,000 on the job, A fails to complete it because of insol-

vency. B has the work completed by another builder for $4,000, increasing the value of the building to him by a total of $9,000, but he loses $500 in rent because of the delay. A can recover $5,000 from B in restitution less $500 in damages for the loss caused by the breach, or $4,500.

3. A contracts to make repairs to B's building in return for B's promise to pay $10,000 on completion of the work. A makes repairs costing him $8,000 but inadvertently fails to follow the specifications in such material respects that there is no substantial performance. See Comment d to § 237. The defects cannot be corrected without the destruction of large parts of the building, but the work confers a benefit on B by increasing the value of the building to him by $4,000. A can recover $4,000 from B in restitution.

4. The facts being otherwise as stated in Illustration 3, the defects do not require destruction of large parts of the building and can be corrected for $4,000, which will confer a benefit on B by increasing the value of the building to him by a total of $9,000. A can recover $5,000 from B in restitution.

5. A contracts to tutor B's son for six months in preparation for an examination, in return for which B promises to pay A $2,000 at the end of that time. After A has worked for three months, he leaves to take another job and B is unable to find a suitable replacement. In the absence of any reliable basis for measuring the benefit to B from A's part performance, restitution will be denied.

c. *Exception for money paid.* Instead of promising to pay a fixed sum as liquidated damages in case of breach, a promisor may actually pay a sum of money that the parties understand is to be retained by the promisee if the promise is not performed. If the sum is a reasonable one that would be sustained as liquidated damages under the rule stated in § 356, the promisee is entitled to retain it. If it is not, the promisor is entitled to restitution under the rule stated in Subsection (1). The test of reasonableness is the same as that applicable to a provision for liquidated damages. See Comment b to § 356. The understanding of the parties may be shown by the terms of their agreement, by description of the sum as "earnest money" or by usage. The sum may or may not be part of the price to be paid by the promisor. The same principle applies if what is to be retained by the promisee is property other than money.

Illustrations:

6. The facts being otherwise as stated in Illustration 1, the contract provides that on default by B, A has the right to retain the first $10,000 installment paid by B. If $10,000 is a reasonable amount, B can recover only $20,000 from A in restitution.

7. The facts being otherwise as stated in Illustration 1, the contract provides that on default by B, A has the right to retain any installments paid by B. The provision is not valid, and B can still recover $30,000 from A in restitution less $5,000 damages for B's breach of contract, or $25,000.

REPORTER'S NOTE

This Section is based on former § 357, but it is more liberal in allowing recovery in accord with the policy behind Uniform Commercial Code § 2–718(2). Subsection (2) is also based on former § 340. See 5A Corbin, Contract §§ 1122–35 (1964 & Supp. 1980); 12 Williston, Contracts §§ 1468, 1473–78 (3d ed. 1970); 1 Palmer, Law of Restitution ch. 5 (1978); Birmingham, Breach of Contract, Damage Measures, and Economic Efficiency, 24 Rutgers L. Rev. 273, 286–92 (1970); Nordstrom & Woodland, Recovery by Building Contractor in Default, 20 Ohio St. L.J. 193 (1959); The [English] Law Commission, Pecuniary Restitution on Breach of Contract 8–38, 64–65 (Law of Contract Working Paper No. 65, 1975). As to the rule of Uniform Commercial Code § 2–718(2), see Nordstrom, Restitution on Default and Article Two of the Uniform Commercial Code, 19 Vand. L. Rev. 1143 (1966).

Comment a. Illustration 1 is based on Honey v. Henry's Franchise Leasing Corp., 64 Cal.2d 801, 52 Cal. Rptr. 18, 415 P.2d 833 (1966); Freedman v. Rector, Wardens & Vestrymen of St. Matthias Parish, 37 Cal.2d 16, 230 P.2d 629 (1951); De Leon v. Aldrete, 398 S.W.2d 160 (Tex. Civ. App. 1965), ref. n.r.e.; cf. Begovich v. Murphy, 359 Mich. 156, 101 N.W.2d 278 (1960); see also Maxey v. Glindmeyer, 379 So.2d 297 (Miss. 1980) (land sale contract with analogy to Uniform Commercial Code § 2–718); Amtorg Trading Corp. v. Miehle Printing Press & Mfg. Co., 206 F.2d 103 (2d Cir. 1953) (dictum). Illustration 2 is based on Illustration 3 to former § 357; American Sur. v. United States, 368 F.2d 475 (9th Cir. 1966); Kreyer v. Driscoll, 39 Wis.2d 540, 159 N.W.2d 680 (1968); cf. Britton v. Turner, 6 N.H. 481 (1834). But cf. Kelley v. Hance, 108 Conn. 186, 142 A. 683 (1928). Illustrations 3 and 4 are based on Pinches v. Swedish Evangelical Lutheran Church, 55 Conn. 183, 10 A. 264 (1887); Nelson v. Hazel, 91 Idaho 850, 433 P.2d 120 (1967); Kirkland v. Archbold, 113 N.E.2d 496 (Ohio App. 1953). But cf. Dandeneare v. Seymour, 117 N.H. 455, 374 A.2d 934 (1977). Illustration 5 is suggested by Illustrations 5 and 8 to former § 357. That the burden of proving the excess of benefit over damages is on the party seeking restitution, see Kitchin v. Mori, 84 Nev. 181, 437 P.2d 865 (1968).

Comment c. Illustration 6 is based on Illustration 6 to former § 357; White Lakes Shopping Center v. Jefferson Standard Life Ins. Co., 208 Kan. 121, 490 P.2d 609 (1971); Schwartz v. Syver, 264 Wis. 526, 59 N.W.2d 489 (1953). Illustration 7 is based on Illustration 1 to former § 340 and Illustration 7 to former § 357; Caplan v. Schroeder, 56 Cal.2d 515, 15 Cal. Rptr. 145, 364 P.2d 321 (1961); Massey v. Love, 478 P.2d 948 (Okla. 1971).

§ 375. Restitution When Contract Is Within Statute of Frauds

A party who would otherwise have a claim in restitution under a contract is not barred from restitution for the reason that the contract is unenforceable by him because of the Statute of Frauds unless the Statute provides otherwise or its purpose would be frustrated by allowing restitution.

Comment:

a. Restitution generally available. Parties to a contract that is unenforceable under the Statute of Frauds frequently act in reliance on it before discovering that it is unenforceable. A party may, for example, render services under the contract or may make improvements on land that is the subject of the contract. The rule stated in this Section allows restitution in such cases. See Illustrations 1 and 2. If the party claiming restitution is in breach, the right to restitution is subject to the rule stated in § 374. If the other party is in breach it is subject to the rule stated in § 373. Since allowing restitution does not amount to enforcement of the contract, it ordinarily does not contravene the policy behind the Statute. Restitution will not be allowed, however, if the Statute so provides or if restitution would frustrate the purpose of the Statute. See Illustration 3. However, the mere fact that the particular wording of the Statute makes the contract "void" is not controlling in this respect.

For the purposes of this Section, the measure of the benefit conferred is generally the same as that applicable to similar situations under enforceable contracts. See Comment *b* to § 373 and Comment *b* to § 374. The agreement, although unenforceable, may be evidence of this benefit. As to the possibility of recovery based on the reliance interest, see § 139.

Illustrations:

    1.   A makes an oral contract to furnish services to B that are not to be performed within a year (§ 130). After A has worked for two months B discharges him without paying him anything. A can recover from B as restitution the reasonable value of the services rendered during the two months.

    2.   A makes an oral contract to sell a tract of land to B for $100,000 (§ 125). B pays $50,000, takes possession and makes improvements. A then refuses to convey the land to B, and B sues A for restitution of $50,000 plus $20,000, the reasonable value of the improvements, less $5,000, the value to B of the use of the land. B can recover $65,000 from A.

    3.   A, a home owner, makes an oral contract with B, a real estate broker, to pay B the usual 5% commission if B succeeds in selling A's house. The state Statute of Frauds contains a provision providing that a real estate broker shall have no right to such a commission unless there is a written memorandum of the contract. B sells A's house for $100,000 and sues A in restitution for $5,000, the reasonable value of B's services. B cannot recover in restitution because the purpose of the Statute would be frustrated if B were allowed to recover as restitution the same amount that had been promised under the contract.

    b. Limits on restitution. The rule stated in this Section gives a right to restitution only to one who would have such a right if the contract were enforceable. It is therefore subject to the rules stated in §§ 370–72. A party's right to restitution may, for example, be terminated by the other party's tender of specific restitution. See § 373(4). Furthermore, the rule stated in this Section governs the right to restitution only if the Statute makes the contract unenforceable. If the party seeking restitution under a land sale contract has a right to enforce the contract by a suit for specific performance on the ground of reliance (§ 129), his right to restitution is governed by the rules stated in §§ 373 and 374. Similarly, if a party seeking restitution under a contract not to be performed within a year has a right to enforce it because he has completely performed, his right to restitution is governed by the rule stated in § 373. Finally, under the rule stated in § 138(1), the right to restitution is subject to the same defenses that would be available if the Statute were satisfied. A party has no right to restitution, therefore, if the other party is not in breach and is prepared to perform, except to the extent that such a right would exist if the Statute were satisfied. A party has, however, a right to restitution under the rule stated in § 141 if the other party will neither perform nor sign a sufficient memorandum.　See Illustration 4.

The rule stated in this Section is not intended as an exclusive statement of the right to restitution under provisions of the Statute of Frauds other than those contained in Chapter 5 of this Restatement. For example, in the case of a contract that is unenforceable because of a statutory requirement that contracts not performable within a lifetime be evidenced by a writing, full performance by one party may not make such a contract enforceable by him.　He may therefore be unable to enforce the contract and yet not be entitled to restitution under the rule stated in § 373 because of the limitation in Subsection (2) of that section.　His right to restitution is not dealt with in this Restatement.

Illustration:

　　4.　A makes an oral contract to buy a tract of land from B for $100,000 (§ 125).　Payment is to be made in $10,000 installments, conveyance to be made on the payment of the third installment. A pays $10,000 and then refuses to pay any more and sues B to recover in restitution the $10,000 that he has paid.　If B signs a sufficient memorandum, A's refusal to pay is a defense to his action under the rule stated in § 141(1) and A cannot get restitution.　See Illustration 6 to § 374.　If B refuses to sign a sufficient memorandum, A's refusal to pay is not a defense under the rule stated in § 141(2) and A can get restitution.　See Illustration 1 to § 373.

REPORTER'S NOTE

This Section is based on former § 355.　See 2 Corbin, Contracts §§ 323–32 (1950); 3 Williston, Contracts §§ 534–37 (3d ed. 1960); 1 Palmer, Law of Restitution ch. 6 (1978); Jeanblanc, Restitution Under the Statute of Frauds: What Constitutes a Legal Benefit, 26 Ind. L.J. 1 (1950); Jeanblanc, Restitution Under the Statute of Frauds: What Constitutes an Unjust Retention, 48 Mich. L. Rev. 923 (1950); Jeanblanc, Restitution Under Statute of Frauds: Measurement of the Legal Benefit Unjustly Retained, 15 Mo. L. Rev. 1 (1950).

Comment a.　On the general availability of restitution under a contract void or unenforceable under the Statute of Frauds, even when the party in breach seeks the restitution, see Stuesser v. Ebel, 19 Wis.2d 591, 120 N.W.2d 679 (1963).　Illustrations 1 and 2 are based on Illustrations 1 and 3 to former § 355.　Illustration 3 is based on Louisville Trust Co. v. Monsky, 444 S.W.2d 120 (Ky. 1969); Baugh v. Darley, 112 Utah 1, 184 P.2d 335 (1947); Hale v. Kreisel, 194 Wis. 271, 215 N.W. 227 (1927).

Comment b.　Illustration 4 is based in part on Coughlin v. Knowles, 48 Mass. (7 Metc.) 57 (1843).

§ 376.   Restitution When Contract Is Voidable

A party who has avoided a contract on the ground of lack of capacity, mistake, misrepresentation, duress, undue influence or abuse of a fiduciary relation is entitled to restitution for any benefit that he has conferred on the other party by way of part performance or reliance.

Comment:

a. Recovery of benefit on avoidance. A party who exercises his power of avoidance is entitled to recover in restitution for any benefit that he has conferred on the other party through part performance of or reliance on the contract. The benefit from his part performance includes that resulting from the use by the other party of whatever he has received up to the time that it is returned on avoidance. Furthermore, under the rule stated in § 384, a party seeking restitution must generally return any benefit that he has himself received. If he has received and must return land, for example, he may have made improvements on the land in reliance on the contract and he is entitled, on avoidance and return of the land, to recover the reasonable value of those improvements (§ 371(b)). The rule stated in this Section applies to avoidance on any ground, including lack of capacity (§§ 14–16), mistake (§§ 152, 153), misrepresentation (§ 164), duress (§ 175), undue influence (§ 177) or abuse of a fiduciary relation (§ 173). Uncertainties in measuring the benefit, however, are more likely to be resolved in favor of the party seeking restitution if the other party engaged in misconduct, as in cases of fraudulent misrepresentation, duress or undue influence. In cases of mental incompetency the rule stated in this Section is supplemented by that stated in § 15(2) and in cases of mistake it is supplemented by that stated in § 158.

Illustrations:

1. A contracts to sell an automobile to B, an infant, for $2,000. After A has delivered the automobile and B has paid the $2,000, B disaffirms the contract on the ground of infancy (§ 14), tenders the automobile back to A, and sues A for $2,000. B can recover the $2,000 from A in restitution.

2. A contracts to sell and B to buy for $100,000 a tract of land, the value of which has depended mainly on the timber on it. Both A and B believe that the timber is still there, but in fact it has been destroyed by fire. After A has conveyed the land to B and B has paid the $100,000, B discovers the mistake. B dis-

affirms the contract for mistake (§ 152), tenders a deed to the land to A, and sues A for $100,000. B can recover $100,000 from A in restitution. See Illustration 1 to § 152.

3. A submits a $150,000 offer in response to B's invitation for bids on the construction of a building. A believes that this is the total of a column of figures, but he has made an error by inadvertently omitting $50,000, and in fact the total is $200,000. Because B had estimated the expected cost as $180,000 and the 10 other bids were all in the range between $180,000 and $200,000, B had reason to know of A's mistake. A discovers the mistake after he has done part of the work, disaffirms the contract on the ground of mistake (§ 153), and sues B in restitution for the benefit conferred on B as measured by the reasonable value of A's performance. A can recover the reasonable value of his performance in restitution and if the cost of the work done can be determined under the next lowest bid, that cost is evidence of its reasonable value. See Illustration 9 to § 153.

4. A fraudulently induces B to make a contract to buy a tract of land for $100,000. After A has conveyed the land and B has paid the price, B makes improvements on the land with a reasonable value of $20,000. B then discovers the fraud, disaffirms the contract for misrepresentation (§164), tenders a deed to the land to A, and sues A for $100,000 plus $20,000, the reasonable value of the improvements, less $5,000, the value to B of the use of the land. B can recover $115,000 in restitution from A. See Illustration 1 to § 164.

5. A fraudulently induces B to make a contract to sell a tract of land for $100,000. After B has conveyed the land and A has paid the price, A farms the land at a net profit of $10,000. B then discovers the fraud, disaffirms the contract for misrepresentation, tenders back the $100,000, and sues A for specific restitution plus the $10,000 profit that A made by farming the land. B can recover the land and $10,000 in restitution from A.

REPORTER'S NOTE

This Section extends the rule stated in former § 488 as to avoidance for misrepresentation so that it applies generally to avoidance on any ground. See 5 Corbin, Contracts § 1104 (1964 & Supp. 1980); 12 Williston, Contracts § 1479 (3d ed. 1970); Palmer, Law of Restitution chs. 3, 9, 12 (1978).

Comment a. Illustration 1 is based on Bowling v. Sperry, 133 Ind. App. 692, 184 N.E.2d 901 (1962). Illustration 2 is supported by Universal Leaf Tobacco Co. v. American Fidelity Fire Ins. Co., 388 F. Supp. 323 (D.V.I. 1974). Illustration 3 is based on C.N. Monroe Mfg. Co. v. United States, 143 F. Supp. 449 (E.D. Mich. 1956); Shepard v. United States, 95 Ct. Cl. 407 (1942); Tyra v. Cheny, 129 Minn. 428, 152 N.W. 835 (1915); Cofrancesco Constr. Co. v. Superior Components, 52 Tenn. App. 88, 371 S.W.2d 821 (1963); cf. Chernick v. United States, 178 Ct. Cl. 498, 372 F.2d 492 (1967). Illustration 4 is based on Kent v. Clark, 20 Cal.2d 779, 128 P.2d 868 (1942); Brooks v. Jensen, 75 Idaho 201, 270 P.2d 425 (1954). Illustration 5 is supported by Illustration 3 to Restatement of Restitution § 157; Lang v. Giraudo, 311 Mass. 132, 40 N.E.2d 707 (1942).

§ 377. Restitution in Cases of Impracticability, Frustration, Non-Occurrence of Condition or Disclaimer by Beneficiary

A party whose duty of performance does not arise or is discharged as a result of impracticability of performance, frustration of purpose, non-occurrence of a condition or disclaimer by a beneficiary is entitled to restitution for any benefit that he has conferred on the other party by way of part performance or reliance.

Comment:

a. Scope. A party whose duty of performance is discharged on grounds of supervening impracticability of performance (§ 261) or frustration of purpose (§ 265) may already have performed in part or otherwise relied on the contract before the occurrence of the supervening event. A party whose duty never arises on those grounds (§ 266) may have taken similar action before discovery of the relevant circumstances. Under the rule stated in this Section such a party is entitled to restitution. Furthermore, in cases of impracticability or frustration the other party is also ordinarily relieved of any obligation of rendering the return performance that he has promised on the ground of failure of performance (§ 267). Under the rule stated in this Section that party is also entitled to restitution. The same is true where the parties are relieved of their obligations on the ground of the non-occurrence of a condition (§ 225) or because of a disclaimer by a beneficiary (§ 306). If both parties have rendered some performance, each is entitled to restitution against the other. The rule stated in this Section is subject to contrary agreement to the extent that the agreement does not violate the rules relating to unfairness (§ 364), unconscionability (§ 208) and forfeiture (§ 229).

Illustrations:

1. A contracts to employ B as a confidential secretary for a month for $2,000, to be paid at the end of that time. B falls ill after working for two weeks and the duties of performance of both A and B are discharged as a result of impracticability of performance (§ 262). B is entitled to restitution from A for the services that he has performed. See Illustration 1 to § 262. The result is the same if B's duty is discharged as a result of A's illness rather than B's. See Illustration 2 to § 262.

2. A contracts to employ B as a confidential secretary for a month for $2,000, to be paid in advance. B falls ill after A has paid the $2,000 but before B has begun work and the duties of performance of both A and B are discharged as a result of impracticability of performance (§ 262). A is entitled to restitution of $2,000 from B. If B had fallen ill after working for two weeks, B would also be entitled to restitution from A for the services that he has performed.

3. A contracts to sell and B to buy a house for $50,000, conditional on approval by X Bank of B's pending mortgage application. B pays A $5,000 when the contract is signed. In spite of reasonable efforts by B, the X Bank does not approve his application and his duty of performance is discharged (§ 225). B is entitled to restitution of $5,000 from A. See Illustration 8 to § 225.

b. Measure of benefit. Cases of impracticability and frustration may pose particularly difficult problems of adjustment after the occurrence of a disrupting event that was ordinarily unforeseeable when the contract was made. The rule stated in § 272(2) gives a court discretion in an extreme case to do justice by supplying a term that is reasonable in the circumstance. In most cases, however, restitution is all that is required, given the choice open to the court in measuring benefit (§ 371). Usually the measure of reasonable value is appropriate. A benefit may be found if it was conferred before the occurrence of the event even though the event later resulted in its destruction, and in that case recovery may be limited to the measure of increase in wealth prior to the event, if this is less than reasonable value. Compare Illustrations 4 and 6. A party cannot, however, recover his reliance interest under the rule stated in this Section, and his expenditures in reliance are not subtracted from what he has received in calculating the benefit for which he is liable. See Illustration 5; see also Comment *b* to § 371. Furthermore, to the extent that the contract price can be roughly apportioned to the work done, recovery will not be allowed in excess of the appropriate amount of the price.

Illustrations:

4.   A contracts with B to shingle the roof of B's house for $5,000, payable as the work progresses.   After A has spent $2,000 doing part of the work and has been paid $1,800, much of the house including the roof is destroyed by fire without his fault, and the duties of performance of both A and B are discharged as a result of impracticability of performance (§ 263).   The work done before the fire increased the market price and the insurable value of the house by $1,500.   A is entitled to restitution of $1,500 from B and B is entitled to restitution of $1,800 from A.   See Illustration 3 to § 263.

5.   The facts being otherwise as stated in Illustration 4, the fire also destroyed shingles that had cost A $500 and that were piled near the house for the rest of the work.   A is not entitled to restitution of this loss from B.   Nor can A subtract the $500 from the $1,800 he has been paid in determining the benefit that he has received.   The court may, however, take this loss into consideration in deciding whether to allow A restitution of $1,500 or $2,000.   See also § 272.

6.   A contracts to paint some bizarre frescoes in B's house for $10,000.   The frescoes will not increase the market value of the house.   A dies after the frescoes have been partly completed.   Other artists can adequately complete the work and will do so for $6,000.   A's executors are entitled to restitution of $4,000 from B.   If they can prove that A's price was unusually low because of A's lack of employment and an economic depression and that the work was roughly half finished, the court may properly allow restitution of $5,000.

7.   A contracts to tutor B's son for six months in preparation for an examination, in return for which B promises to pay A $2,000 at the end of that time.   After A has worked for three months, B's son becomes ill and the duties of performance of both A and B are discharged as a result of impracticability of performance.   Other tutors would have charged $800 to do the work that A has done.   A is entitled to restitution of $800 from B.   Even if other tutors would have charged $1,200, A is entitled to restitution of only $1,000 from B unless he can show that the first half of the work was more burdensome.

REPORTER'S NOTE

This Section is based in part on former § 468, which dealt with impracticability. See also Restatement of Restitution §§ 48, 108. See 6 Corbin, Contracts §§ 1367–72 (1962 & Supp. 1980); 12 Williston, Contracts § 1479 (3d ed. 1970); 18 id. §§ 1967–72 (3d ed. 1978); 2 Palmer, Law of Restitution ch. 7 (1978); Notes, 59 Mich. L. Rev. 98, 117–22 (1960); 114 U. Pa. L. Rev. 306 (1965); 69 Yale L.J. 1054 (1960).

Comment a. Illustration 1 is based on Illustrations 1 and 2 to former § 468. Illustration 2 is based on Illustration 5 to former § 468; cf. Louisville & N.R. Co. v. Crowe, 156 Ky. 27, 160 S.W. 759 (1913). Illustration 3 is based on Lach v. Cahill, 138 Conn. 418, 85 A.2d 481 (1951). As to the possibility of an agreement precluding restitution, see Cutter v. Powell, 6 T.R. 320, 101 Eng. Rep. 573 (1795); see also Stoljar, The Great Case of Cutter v. Powell, 34 Can. B. Rev. 288 (1956). In Alabama Football, Inc. v. Greenwood, 452 F. Supp. 1191 (W.D. Pa. 1978), performance of duties under a professional football contract was held excused by frustration of purpose because of the failure of the World Football League. Nonetheless, restitution of a $50,000 signing bonus was denied because the court found the bonus an agreed equivalent of part performance (the signing of the frustrated contract) by the player. Cf. § 240.

Comment b. Illustrations 4 and 5 are based on Illustration 1 to former § 357; Carroll v. Bowersock, 100 Kan. 270, 164 P. 143 (1917); Young v. City of Chicopee, 186 Mass. 518, 72 N.E. 63 (1904); Butterfield v. Byron, 153 Mass. 517, 27 N.E. 667 (1891). For the English legislation on the question raised by Illustration 5, see the Law Reform (Frustrated Contracts) Act, 1943, 6 & 7 Geo. VI, c. 40. Illustration 6 is based on Illustrations 7 and 8 to former § 468; Buccini v. Paterno Constr. Co., 253 N.Y. 256, 170 N.E. 910 (1930). Illustration 7 is based on Illustration 2 to former § 357; Illustration 6 to former § 468; Illustration 2 to Restatement of Restitution § 155; cf. M. Ahern Co. v. John Bowen Co., 334 Mass. 36, 133 N.E.2d 484 (1956); Angus v. Scully, 176 Mass. 357, 57 N.E. 674 (1900). But cf. Automobile Ins. Co. v. Model Family Laundries, 133 Conn. 433, 52 A.2d 137 (1947); West Audit Co. v. Yoakum County, 53 S.W.2d 311 (Tex. Civ. App. 1932), error dismissed.

TOPIC 5. PRECLUSION BY ELECTION AND AFFIRMANCE

Introductory Note: Sometimes a party who has a choice of alternative remedies is precluded by his action or inaction from pursuing one of those remedies on the ground that he has "elected" the other. The rules governing this are dealt with in §§ 378 and 379. They reflect the trend against preclusion by election that has resulted from the merger of law and equity and the reform of rules of procedure.

A party who has a power of avoidance on the ground, for example, of mistake, misrepresentation or duress, may be precluded by his action or inaction from exercising it on the ground that he has ratified the contract by affirming it. The rules governing this are dealt with in §§ 380–85. This Topic does not contain the substantive rules that determine whether a party has a power of avoidance. Those rules appear in other chapters of this Restatement that deal with the various grounds for avoidance. See §§ 14–16, 152–53, 164, 173, 175 and 177.

REPORTER'S NOTE

This Topic is based on Topic 5, Election of Remedies, of former Chapter 12 and on former §§ 480–87, 490, 510. See 5A Corbin, Contracts ch. 66 (1964 & Supp. 1980).

§ 378. Election Among Remedies

If a party has more than one remedy under the rules stated in this Chapter, his manifestation of a choice of one of them by bringing suit or otherwise is not a bar to another remedy unless the remedies are inconsistent and the other party materially changes his position in reliance on the manifestation.

Comment:

a. Election among remedies. The rules stated in this Chapter give a party three basic types of remedies: damages (Topic 2), specific performance or an injunction (Topic 3), and restitution (Topic 4). The rule stated in this Section precludes a party who has manifested his choice of one of those remedies from shifting to another remedy if such a shift would be unjust because of the other party's reliance on the earlier manifestation. The mere manifestation of an intention to pursue one remedy rather than another does not, however, preclude a party from making such a shift. Nor must the shift be made within any particular time. Only if the other party has materially changed his position in reliance on the original choice is a shift to another remedy precluded by the election of the first. A change of position is "material" within the meaning of this Section if it is such that in all the circumstances a shift in remedies would be unjust. This rejection of any doctrine of election in the absence of reliance is consistent with a similar policy in the Uniform Commercial Code. See Uniform Commercial Code § 2–703 and Comment 1; § 2–711 and § 2–721. Even if the bringing of an action for one remedy is a manifestation of choice of that remedy, it does not preclude the plaintiff from shifting to another remedy as long as the defendant has not materially changed his position. Alternative counts seeking inconsistent remedies are generally permitted in the same complaint and a change in remedy may often be made by amendment of the complaint, even at an advanced stage of the action.

Illustrations:

    1. A contracts to sell a tract of land to B. A repudiates and B brings an action for damages. While this action is pending, A makes valuable improvements on the land reasonably believing that B does not intend to pursue his remedy of specific performance. B then amends his complaint to ask specific performance. If A's change of position is material, B's claim for specific performance is precluded.

    2. A contracts to transfer his farm to B in return for B's promise to support A for life. After A has transferred the farm, B repudiates the contract and A sues for specific restitution. Before any change in B's position, A learns that a part of the farm has been sold by B and amends his complaint to ask for damages for the breach. A's claim for damages is not precluded.

    3. A contracts to transfer his farm to B in return for B's promise to support A for life. After A has transferred the farm, B repudiates the contract and A sues for damages. Before any change in B's position, A discovers that it will be difficult to prove his damages with reasonable certainty and that a judicial sale of B's property including the farm would be unlikely to realize enough to satisfy a judgment and amends his complaint to ask specific restitution. Specific restitution is not precluded.

    b. Additional circumstances. In two situations a party is not precluded from seeking a different remedy, even after reliance on his first choice by the other party, because his shift is justified by additional circumstances. The first situation is that in which the party made his original choice while ignorant of facts that give him a remedy based on, for example, misrepresentation or mistake and later discovers those facts. In that situation he is not bound by his original choice because he made it when mistaken. The second situation is that in which after a party makes his original choice, a later breach by the other party occurs. In that situation he can pursue any remedy based on the later breach without regard to his original choice.

    c. Remedy not available. The rule stated in this Section applies only where a party pursues a remedy that he actually has. A party is not precluded from pursuing other remedies by the fact that he has made a mistaken attempt to obtain a remedy that is not available to him, even if his original choice has been relied on by the other party.

Illustrations:

4. A makes an oral contract to transfer his farm to B in return for B's promise to support A for life. After A has transferred the farm, B repudiates the contract and A sues for damages. B pleads the Statute of Frauds and A's action is about to be dismissed. A then amends his complaint to ask specific restitution. Regardless of whether B has changed his position, specific restitution is not precluded.

5. A makes a written contract to sell a tract of land to B. A repudiates the contract and B, claiming that both parties were mistaken as to the contents of the writing, sues A for reformation of the writing and for specific performance of the contract as reformed. The court refuses to reform the writing on the ground that mistake was not proved and B amends his complaint to ask damages for breach of the contract as written. B's claim for damages is not precluded.

d. Other remedy not inconsistent. The rule stated in this Section applies only where a party seeks to shift to a remedy that is inconsistent with the one he has chosen. A party who seeks specific performance or an injunction may, for example, be entitled to damages to compensate him for delay in performance. See Comment *c* to § 358. Similarly, a party who seeks restitution may, for example, be entitled to damages to compensate him for costs of transportation of goods that he has incurred. A later request for such damages in a suit for specific performance or an injunction or in one for restitution is not precluded because it is not inconsistent with that suit. However, the remedy of specific performance or an injunction and that of damages for total breach of contract are inconsistent. The remedy of specific performance or an injunction and that of restitution are also inconsistent. And the remedy of restitution and that of damages for total breach are inconsistent.

Illustration:

6. A contracts to sell a tract of land to B. A fails to convey the tract and B sues A for specific performance. B later amends his complaint to add a claim for damages resulting from the delay caused by A's failure. Regardless of whether A has changed his position, such a further claim is not precluded.

e. Other situations distinguished. The rule stated in this Section applies only as among the remedies provided for in this Chapter. It does not, for example preclude a party from pursuing a claim in tort for misrepresentation or a claim for breach of warranty in the sale of goods. See Uniform Commercial Code § 2–721. It does not determine whether a party is barred by election from treating his remaining duties of performance as discharged (§ 379). Nor does it apply in the many instances in which a party makes a choice that affects his substantive rights, such as the choice of an offeree between acceptance (§ 50) and rejection (§ 38), the choice of an intended beneficiary between disclaiming the contract and not doing so (§ 306), or the choice of an infant between affirmance and disaffirmance (§§ 14, 380). Furthermore, this rule does not apply to situations in which a party is precluded by his delay from enforcing a substantive right, as is the case where one having the power of avoidance loses it by delay (§ 381). Finally this Section is inapplicable to matters of procedure, such as the requirement that a party choose between inconsistent remedies at some stage of a judicial proceeding, and to matters governed by the law of judgments, such as merger and bar. See Restatement, Second, Judgments §§ 17, 18, 19.

REPORTER'S NOTE

This Section is based on former §§ 381, 382, 383 and 384. See 5A Corbin, Contracts §§ 1214–27 (1964 & Supp. 1980); 11 Williston, Contracts §§ 1444, 1444A (3d ed. 1968); 1 Palmer, Law of Restitution §§ 3.10, 4.15 (1978); Dobbs, Remedies § 1.5 (1973); Dobbs, Pressing Problems for the Plaintiff's Lawyer in Rescission: Election of Remedies and Restoration of Consideration, 26 Ark. L. Rev. 322 (1972).

Comment a. The rule stated in former § 381(2), under which the mere bringing of an action might amount to an election, is abandoned as no longer representing the weight of authority. See Lewis v. Dansker, 68 F.R.D. 184 (S.D.N.Y. 1975); see also Friederichsen v. Renard, 247 U.S. 207, 213 (1918); Ajamian v. Schlanger, 14 N.J. 483, 103 A.2d 9,

cert. denied, 348 U.S. 835 (1954); Parrish v. Tahtaras, 7 Utah 2d 87, 91, 318 P.2d 642, 645 (1957). Illustration 1 is based on Illustration 2 to former § 382. Illustrations 2 and 3 are based on Illustrations 2 and 3 to former § 381.

Comment b. As to the effect of a subsequent breach, see Seaboard Sur. Co. v. United States, 355 F.2d 139 (9th Cir. 1966).

Comment c. Illustrations 4 and 5 are based on Illustrations 2 and 4 to former § 383; cf. Riess v. Murchison, 503 F.2d 999 (9th Cir. 1974), cert. denied, 420 U.S. 993 (1975).

Comment d. Illustration 6 is based on Greenstone v. Claretian Seminary, 139 Mont. 295, 363 P.2d 161 (1959). For cases allowing damages in addition to restitution, see Runyan v. Pacific Air Indus., 2

Cal.3d 304, 85 Cal. Rptr. 138, 466　　cus, 100 Conn. 86, 123 A. 21 (1923).
P.2d 682 (1970); Rabinowitz v. Mar-

§ 379.　Election to Treat Duties of Performance Under Aleatory Contract as Discharged

If a right or duty of the injured party is conditional on an event that is fortuitous or is supposed by the parties to be fortuitous, he cannot treat his remaining duties to render performance as discharged on the ground of the other party's breach by non-performance if he does not manifest to the other party his intention to do so before any adverse change in the situation of the injured party resulting from the occurrence of that event or a material change in the probability of its occurrence.

Comment:

a. Election under an aleatory contract. An aleatory contract is one in which at least one party is under a duty that is conditional on the occurrence of an event that, so far as the parties to the contract are aware, is dependent on chance. Its occurrence may be within the control of third persons or beyond the control of any person. The event may have already occurred, as long as that fact is unknown to the parties. It may be the failure of something to happen as well as its happening. Common examples are contracts of insurance and suretyship, as well as gambling contracts. If the injured party's duty is conditional on such an event, it would be unfair if, after the breach, he were allowed to take advantage of a material change in the likelihood of its occurrence when deciding whether to treat his remaining duties as discharged. If it was more likely that it would occur it would be to his advantage to treat those duties as discharged. For this reason, he is precluded from treating them as discharged if there has been an adverse change in his situation because the event has occurred or because there has been a material increase in the probability of its occurrence. The same principle applies to the case where a right rather than a duty of the injured party is conditional on the occurrence of such an event.

Illustrations:

1. A, an insurance company, issues to B a policy of fire insurance on B's house for a year in the amount of $100,000. In

consideration, B gives A his promissory note for the premium, payable in three months. B fails to pay the note at maturity. Four months later, before A has given notice of cancellation, B's house burns. A cannot treat B's failure to pay as discharging it from its duty to pay for the loss under the policy. A is liable for the loss less the amount of the note.

2. A makes a contract with B under which A guarantees that C will pay a $100,000 debt owed B by C and due on July 1. In consideration, B promises to pay A $1,000 on May 1. B fails to pay on that date. Before A manifests to B his intention to treat B's failure as discharging him from his duty to honor his guarantee of C's debt, C becomes insolvent. A cannot treat B's failure as discharging him from that duty and is liable on his $100,000 guarantee less the $1,000.

3. A and B make a contract under which A guarantees a $50,000 debt owed to B by C and due on July 1 in consideration of a guarantee by B of a $100,000 debt owed to A by D and due on August 1. C fails to pay on July 1 and A fails to honor his guarantee. Before B manifests his intention to treat A's failure as discharging B from his duty to honor his guarantee of D's debt, D becomes insolvent. B cannot treat A's failure as discharging him from that duty and is liable on his $100,000 guarantee less the $50,000 that A owes on his guarantee.

REPORTER'S NOTE

This Section is based on former § 293. See also former §§ 291, 292. See 3A Corbin, Contracts § 730 (1960); 5 Williston, Contracts §§ 683–88 (3d ed. 1961).

Comment b. Illustration 1 is based on Illustration 4 to former § 293. Illustrations 2 and 3 are based on Illustrations 1 and 3 to former § 292.

§ 380.   Loss of Power of Avoidance by Affirmance

(1) The power of a party to avoid a contract for incapacity, duress, undue influence or abuse of a fiduciary relation is lost if, after the circumstances that made the contract voidable have ceased to exist, he manifests to the other party his intention to affirm it or acts with respect to anything that he has received in a manner inconsistent with disaffirmance.

(2) The power of a party to avoid a contract for mistake or misrepresentation is lost if after he knows or

has reason to know of the mistake or of the misrepresentation if it is non-fraudulent or knows of the misrepresentation if it is fraudulent, he manifests to the other party his intention to affirm it or acts with respect to anything that he has received in a manner inconsistent with disaffirmance.

(3) If the other party rejects an offer by the party seeking avoidance to return what he has received, the party seeking avoidance if entitled to restitution can, after the lapse of a reasonable time, enforce a lien on what he has received by selling it and crediting the proceeds toward his claim in restitution.

Comment:

a. Ratification by affirmance. A party who has the power of avoidance may lose it by action that manifests a willingness to go on with the contract. Such action is known as "affirmance" and has the effect of ratifying the contract. See Restatement of Restitution § 68. The rule stated in this Section is a special application of that stated in § 85, under which a promise to perform a voidable duty is binding. On ratification, the affirming party is bound as from the outset and the other party continues to be bound.

b. Manner and time of affirmance. A party may manifest his intention to affirm by words or other conduct, including the exercise of dominion over what he has received in a manner inconsistent with avoidance of the contract. Compare Uniform Commercial Code § 2–606. If he offers to return the performance that he has received and if such an offer is rejected, he must hold that performance for the other party. Because the party seeking restitution has a lien on any performance that he has himself received, however, he is entitled to enforce that lien under the rule stated in Subsection (3) after he has waited a reasonable time. A party's power of avoidance for incapacity, duress, undue influence or abuse of a fiduciary relation is not lost by conduct while the circumstances that made the contract voidable continue to exist. Nor is his power of avoidance for misrepresentation or mistake lost until he knows of the misrepresentation if it is fraudulent, or knows or ought to know of a non-fraudulent misrepresentation or mistake.

Illustrations:

1. A is induced by B's misrepresentation to make a contract to repair B's house, payment to be made when the services have

been rendered. When A discovers the facts, he accuses B of fraud and threatens to avoid the transaction unless B pays in advance or furnishes security. Before A receives any response from B, A notifies B that he avoids the contract. A's conduct did not amount to affirmance and the contract is avoided. The result would be different, however, if A demanded that B perform the contract or accepted security from B.

2. A is induced by B's misrepresentation to make a contract to employ B for a year. When A discovers the facts, he continues to employ B for two weeks and then discharges him in violation of the contract, notifying B that he avoids the contract. A's conduct amounted to affirmance and he is liable to B for breach of contract. The result would not be affected if A did not learn until the end of the two weeks that the law gave him the power to avoid the contract. The result would be different, however, if B had persuaded A to continue the employment for another two weeks as a trial period and A discharged B at the end of that time because A was still dissatisfied.

3. A is induced by B's fraudulent and material misrepresentation to buy land from B. When A discovers the fraud he brings an action in deceit against B. A later discontinues the action and notifies B that he avoids the contract. Since A's bringing of the action was a manifestation of his intention to affirm the contract only if damages are paid, it did not without more amount to affirmance. A's subsequent attempt to avoid the contract was effective.

4. A contracts to sell and B to buy a tract of land, the value of which has depended mainly on the timber on it. Both A and B believe that the timber is still there, but in fact it has been destroyed by fire so that the contract is voidable by B on the ground of mistake. See Illustration 1 to § 152. On discovery of the mistake, B tenders a deed back to A, who refuses to accept it. B continues to occupy and to use the land. B's conduct amounts to affirmance and he is precluded from avoiding the contract.

REPORTER'S NOTE

This Section is based on former §§ 482, 484, 510. See 5 Corbin, Contracts § 1104 (1964 & Supp. 1980); 2 Williston, Contracts §§ 239, 253 (3d ed. 1959); 12 id. § 1527 (3d ed. 1970); 13 id. § 1627B (3d ed. 1970); Dobbs, Remedies § 1.5 (1973); Dobbs, Pressing Problems for the Plaintiff's Lawyer in Rescission: Election of Remedies and Restoration of Consideration, 26 Ark. L. Rev. 322 (1972).

See Appendix for Court Citations and Cross References

Comment b. Illustration 1 is based on Illustrations 2 and 8 to former § 484. Illustration 2 is based on Illustrations 3, 4 and 7 to § 484. Illustration 3 changes the result in Illustration 6 to former § 484, and is supported by Schenck v. State Line Tel. Co., 238 N.Y. 308, 144 N.E. 592 (1924). It rejects the view of such cases as Albin v. Isotron Corp., 421 S.W.2d 739 (Tex. Civ. App. 1967), ref. n.r.e.; see also Jennings v. Lee, 105 Ariz. 167, 461 P.2d 161 (1969). Illustration 4 is based on Illustration 1 to former § 482.

§ 381. Loss of Power of Avoidance by Delay

(1) The power of a party to avoid a contract for incapacity, duress, undue influence or abuse of a fiduciary relation is lost if, after the circumstances that made it voidable have ceased to exist, he does not within a reasonable time manifest to the other party his intention to avoid it.

(2) The power of a party to avoid a contract for misrepresentation or mistake is lost if after he knows of a fraudulent misrepresentation or knows or has reason to know of a non-fraudulent misrepresentation or mistake he does not within a reasonable time manifest to the other party his intention to avoid it. The power of a party to avoid a contract for non-fraudulent misrepresentation or mistake is also lost if the contract has been so far performed or the circumstances have otherwise so changed that avoidance would be inequitable and if damages will be adequate compensation.

(3) In determining what is a reasonable time, the following circumstances are significant:

(a) the extent to which the delay enabled or might have enabled the party with the power of avoidance to speculate at the other party's risk;

(b) the extent to which the delay resulted or might have resulted in justifiable reliance by the other party or by third persons;

(c) the extent to which the ground for avoidance was the result of any fault by either party; and

(d) the extent to which the other party's conduct contributed to the delay.

(4) If a right or duty of the party who has the power of avoidance for non-fraudulent misrepresentation or mistake is conditional on an event that is fortuitous or is supposed by the parties to be fortuitous, a manifestation of intention under Subsection (1) or (2) is not effective unless it is made before any adverse change in his situation resulting from the occurrence of that event or a material change in the probability of its occurrence.

Comment:

a. Effect of delay. A party who has the power to avoid a contract may lose that power by delay alone, even without such conduct as amounts to affirmance (§ 380). Under the rule stated in this Section the power is lost if it is not exercised within a reasonable time. The rule is similar in its purpose to that stated in § 380 on the loss of the power to treat one's remaining duties as discharged on breach. Here, as under § 379, what time is reasonable depends on all the circumstances, including the extent to which the delay was or was likely to be prejudicial to the other party or to third persons. Such prejudice may result if the delay enables the party with the power of avoidance to speculate at the other party's risk, affirming if the course of the market makes the contract advantageous to him and disaffirming if it makes it disadvantageous. Such prejudice may also result from reliance or the likelihood of reliance by the other party or by third persons. The reliance must be justifiable and the fact that the one who relied knew of the ground for avoidance is a consideration in this connection. If the ground for avoidance was to any extent the fault of either party, this is also a factor. For example, the fault of the party with the power of avoidance in not discovering a mistake or a misrepresentation will shorten the period for avoidance. Compare §§ 157, 172. The misconduct of the other party in cases of fraudulent misrepresentation or duress will lengthen it. A consumer is not generally expected to avoid as promptly as is a merchant in similar circumstances. Furthermore, if the other party contributes to the delay, as by promising to remedy defects or by urging a further period of testing before avoidance, this will lengthen the period. Ordinarily, if the party with the power of avoidance retains during the delay something that he has received from the other party, avoidance will be precluded by the rule stated in § 380. The importance of the present Section is, therefore, chiefly in cases in which the party with that power has received nothing.

b. When reasonable time begins. A party who has the power of avoidance for incapacity, duress, undue influence or abuse of a fiduciary relation is not expected to act until the circumstances that have made the contract voidable have ceased to exist, and the reasonable time does not begin to run until then. In the case of a party who has the power of avoidance for misrepresentation or mistake, it does not begin to run until he knows of the misrepresentation if it is fraudulent, or knows or has reason to know of a non-fraudulent misrepresentation or mistake. However, in determining whether a party acted within a reasonable time once he was expected to do so, the fact that a considerable period of time had elapsed after the original transaction is significant. Nevertheless, if the power of avoidance is then exercised within a reasonable time, avoidance is not ordinarily precluded even though the other party has relied. Compare Illustration 2 with Illustration 3. But see Comment *c.* The rights of third parties who may have relied are not dealt with in this Restatement. See Introductory Note to this Chapter. Where a party seeks to avoid a contract on the ground of a mistake that he alone has made, he must show that enforcement of the contract would be unconscionable, unless the other party had reason to know of the mistake or his fault caused it. See § 153. The lapse of time before the mistaken party discovers his mistake may invite reliance by the other party that will make it more difficult to show unconscionability even though it would not preclude avoidance under the present Section. A party need not specify in detail the bases of his disaffirmance unless this is necessary in order for the other party to know the ground of avoidance or to take appropriate action in response. Compare Illustration 5 with Illustration 6. As to the requirement that he return what he has received, see § 384.

Illustrations:

1. A is induced by B's misrepresentation to contract in January to sell B 1,000 shares of stock in the X Corporation for $100,000, delivery and payment to be on May 1. A discovers the fraud in February but does not manifest his intention to avoid the transaction until April. In view of the extent to which A's delay of two months enabled him to speculate at B's expense, A has lost his power of avoidance, and his manifestation is not effective to avoid the transaction. Compare Illustration 2 to § 379. The result does not depend on whether the market price of the stock has risen or fallen.

2. A, a noted opera singer, is induced by B's nonfraudulent misrepresentation to contract in April to sing the leading role in a

new production designed for A at B's opera house in October. A soon discovers the misrepresentation but does not manifest an intention to avoid the transaction until June. By that time B has made substantial commitments for the production in reliance on A's singing the leading role. In view of the likelihood and the extent of such reliance, A has lost the power of avoidance, and A's manifestation is not effective to avoid the contract.

3. The facts being otherwise as stated in Illustration 2, A does not discover the misrepresentation until June, immediately before A's manifestation of intention to avoid the contract. In spite of B's reliance, A has not lost the power of avoidance and A's manifestation is effective.

4. A contracts to buy from B a farm that B misrepresents as containing 100 acres of cleared land, 100 acres of brush, and a well with an adequate supply of water. A week later A discovers that only 80 acres have been cleared, but he does not discover that the well is dry, although a careful inspection would have revealed this. When he moves onto the farm six months later, he discovers that the well is dry and promptly notifies B that he avoids the contract. A has not lost his power to avoidance on the ground of the misrepresentation as to the well, even though he may have lost his power of avoidance on the ground of the misrepresentation as to the cleared land.

5. A contracts to sell and B to buy a tract of land, the value of which has depended mainly on the timber on it, delivery of the deed and payment of the price to be made in a week. Both A and B believe that the timber is still there, but in fact it has been destroyed by fire, so that the contract is voidable by B. See Illustration 1 to § 152. B discovers the mistake and when the next day, A tenders a deed to the tract, B refuses to perform without giving any reason. B's refusal of performance is a sufficient manifestation of his intention to avoid the contract even though no reason was given.

6. The facts being otherwise as stated in Illustration 5, A makes no offer to deliver a deed to the tract on the day fixed for performance. B's refusal of performance is not a sufficient manifestation of his power of avoidance because it was justified by A's failure to offer to deliver a deed.

c. *When avoidance would be inequitable.* In some situations where a party has a power of avoidance for non-fraudulent misrepresentation or mistake, the circumstances may have so changed after the contract was made that it would be inequitable to allow avoidance if damages would adequately compensate him. This may be so where performance in whole or in part makes avoidance excessively burdensome for the other party. It may also be so where, because of a drastic shift in market prices, avoidance will throw onto the other party a heavy loss unrelated to the misrepresentation or mistake. In such situations the party having the power of avoidance loses it and is limited to a claim for damages under the rule stated in Subsection (2). A similar rule as to avoidance for mental incompetency is stated in § 15(2).

Illustration:

7. A, seeking to induce B to make a contract to buy his house for $50,000, tells B that the roof is in "good condition." A is mistaken and unknown to him the roof has a hidden defect that can be fully remedied for $1,000. B is induced by the statement to make the proposed contract, and, two years after taking possession, he discovers the defect. Even if the court considers the statement a material misrepresentation, it may conclude that the contract is no longer voidable and limit B's relief to the recovery of $1,000 in damages from A.

d. Aleatory contracts. Under an aleatory contract, at least one party is under a duty that is conditional on the occurrence of an event that, so far as the parties are aware, is dependent on chance. See Comment *a* to § 379. If the duty of the party having a power of avoidance for non-fraudulent misrepresentation or mistake is conditional on such an event, it would be unfair if he could take advantage of a material change in the likelihood of its occurrence when deciding whether to exercise that power. If it were more likely that it would occur it would be to his advantage to exercise it. If it were less likely that it would occur, it would be to his advantage not to exercise it. For this reason, he is precluded from exercising it if there has been an adverse change in his situation because the event has occurred or because there has been a material increase in the probability of its occurrence. The same principle applies to the case when a right of the party with the power of avoidance is conditional on the occurrence of such an event.

Illustration:

8. A and B make a contract under which A guarantees a debt owed to B by C in consideration of a guarantee by B of a debt owed to A by D. B is induced to make the contract by A's non-fraudulent material misrepresentation. Before the truth is dis-

covered, C, who was in bad financial circumstances when the contract was made, has received a large legacy. B cannot avoid the contract because the bargain has become less advantageous to B. If D rather than C receives the legacy, there is no adverse change in B's situation and he can still avoid the contract.

REPORTER'S NOTE

This Section is based on former §§ 483, 485(2), 496, 499 and 510 and is extended to cover incapacity. See also Restatement of Restitution § 64. See 2 Williston, Contracts §§ 239, 253 (3d ed. 1959); 12 id. § 1526 (3d ed. 1970); 13 id. §§ 1594, 1627B (3d ed. 1970); Friedman, Delay as a Bar to Rescission, 26 Cornell L.Q. 426 (1941).

Comment b. Illustrations 1 and 2 are based on Illustrations 1 and 2 to former § 483; see also Gannett Co. v. Register Publishing Co., 428 F. Supp. 818 (D. Conn. 1977). Illustration 3 is based on Illustration 3 to former § 483; see also Illustration 1 to Restatement of Restitution § 64. Illustration 4 is based on Illustration 3 to Restatement of Restitution § 64. Illustration 5 is based on Illustration 4 to former § 483. Illustration 6 is based on Illustration 2 to former § 485; see also City of Hattiesburg v. Cobb Bros., 183 Miss. 482, 184 So. 630 (1938).

Comment c. Illustration 7 is based on La Bar v. Lindstrom, 158 Minn. 453, 197 N.W. 756 (1924); cf. O'Shea v. Morris, 112 Neb. 102, 198 N.W. 866 (1924); Illustration 1 to Restatement of Restitution § 28; see also McCleary, Damages as Requisite to Rescission—for Misrepresentation, 36 Mich. L. Rev. 1, 227 (1937).

Comment d. Illustration 8 is based on Illustration 2 to former § 486.

§ 382. Loss of Power to Affirm by Prior Avoidance

(1) If a party has effectively exercised his power of avoidance, a subsequent manifestation of intent to affirm is inoperative unless the other party manifests his assent to affirmance by refusal to accept a return of his performance or otherwise.

(2) A party has not exercised his power of avoidance under the rule stated in Subsection (1) until

(a) he has regained all or a substantial part of what he would be entitled to by way of restitution on avoidance,

(b) he has obtained a final judgment of or based on avoidance, or

(c) the other party has materially relied on or manifested his assent to a statement of disaffirmance.

Comment:

a. Conclusive effect of avoidance. Effective exercise of the power of avoidance is conclusive and precludes subsequent affirmance. An exercise of the power is not effective if it is itself avoided on such grounds as mistake, misrepresentation, duress or mental incompetency. Exercise of the power by an infant is not, however, voidable on the ground of his infancy. Even after a party's effective exercise of the power of avoidance, the other party may wish to have the transaction sustained and, if both parties manifest this intention their new agreement is effective.

b. What amounts to exercise of power. A mere statement of disaffirmance, even if coupled with ineffective attempts to regain what one has given, is not such an exercise of the power of avoidance as will preclude affirmance. There is no exercise of the power by a party until he has regained all or part of what he gave, has obtained a judgment that will put him back into his original position, has caused the other party to change his position in reliance on the disaffirmance, or has contracted with the other party on the basis of the disaffirmance.

Illustrations:

1. A, an infant, contracts to sell B an automobile on credit. After delivering it to B, A writes B that he disaffirms and demands its return. B does not return the automobile and A sues B for the price. A can recover the price because A's letter was not an exercise of his power of avoidance.

2. The facts being otherwise as stated in Illustration 1, A brings an action to replevy the automobile but discontinues it before he gets a final judgment and sues B for the price. A can recover the price because A's action in replevin was not an exercise of his power of avoidance.

3. The facts being otherwise as stated in Illustration 1, A sees the automobile parked on the street and drives it back to his garage and sues B for the price. A cannot recover the price because his regaining possession of the automobile was an exercise of his power of avoidance.

REPORTER'S NOTE

This Section is based on former § 485 and on Restatement of Restitution § 68(2). See 5A Corbin, Contracts § 1215 (1964); 12 Williston, Contracts § 1469 (3d ed. 1970).

Comment b. Illustration 1 is based on Illustration 15 to Restatement of Restitution § 68; Rademacher v. Russ, 131 F. Supp. 50 (D. Minn. 1955); Karapetian v. Carolan, 83 Cal.

App.2d 344, 188 P.2d 809 (1948); see also Illustration 2 to former § 485. Illustration 2 is based on Illustration 16 to Restatement of Restitution § 68; cf. Schlotthauer v. Krenzelok, 274 Wis. 1, 79 N.W.2d 76 (1956); Illustration 17 to Restatement of Restitution § 68. Illustration 3 is based on Illustration 1 to former § 485.

§ 383. Avoidance in Part

A contract cannot be avoided in part except that where one or more corresponding pairs of part performances have been fully performed by one or both parties the rest of the contract can be avoided.

Comment:

a. No avoidance in part. A party who has the power of avoidance must ordinarily avoid the entire contract, including any part that has already been performed. He cannot disaffirm part of the contract that is particularly disadvantageous to himself while affirming a more advantageous part, and an attempt to do so is ineffective as a disaffirmance. The rule stated in this Section does not preclude avoidance of only one of two or more entirely separate contracts. Nor does it prevent reformation of a part of a contract for either mistake or misrepresentation. See §§ 155 and 166.

Illustration:

1. A makes a contract to work for B for a year and is induced by B's fraud to assent to a covenant under which he agrees to refrain from entering into a similar business in the same town for three years after the termination of the employment. A discovers the fraud after he has worked for a month. A cannot avoid the covenant not to compete without avoiding the rest of the contract.

b. Exception for "divisible" contracts. There is an exception to the general rule stated in this Section if the contract is "divisible" in the sense that the performances to be exchanged can be apportioned into corresponding pairs of part performances under the rule stated in § 240. In that situation, if one or more pairs of part performances have been fully performed by one or both parties, the party who has the power of avoidance can avoid the rest of the contract only or can avoid the whole contract.

Illustration:

2. A is induced by B's fraud to contract to sell B 1,200 tons of coal to be delivered in monthly installments of 100 tons, payment for each installment to be made on delivery. A discovers the fraud after the second delivery. If A avoids the contract, he must avoid the entire unperformed part, but he does not have to avoid the part that has been performed unless he chooses to do so.

REPORTER'S NOTE

This Section extends to avoidance on any ground the rule of former § 487, which was restricted to avoidance for misrepresentation. See 5 Corbin, Contracts § 1114 (1964 & Supp. 1980); 12 Williston, Contracts § 1460 (3d ed. 1970).

Comment a. Illustration 1 is based on Illustration 1 to former § 487; cf. Miner v. Bradley, 39 Mass. (22 Pick.) 457 (1839).

Comment b. Illustration 2 is based on Illustration 3 to former § 487; cf. Alabama Football, Inc. v. Greenwood, 452 F. Supp. 1191 (W.D. Pa. 1978) (frustration of purpose).

§ 384. Requirement That Party Seeking Restitution Return Benefit

(1) Except as stated in Subsection (2), a party will not be granted restitution unless

(a) he returns or offers to return, conditional on restitution, any interest in property that he has received in exchange in substantially as good condition as when it was received by him, or

(b) the court can assure such return in connection with the relief granted.

(2) The requirement stated in Subsection (1) does not apply to property

(a) that was worthless when received or that has been destroyed or lost by the other party or as a result of its own defects,

(b) that either could not from the time of receipt have been returned or has been used or disposed of without knowledge of the grounds for restitution if justice requires that compensation be accepted in its place and the payment of such compensation can be assured, or

(c) as to which the contract apportions the price if that part of the price is not included in the claim for restitution.

Comment:

a. Duty to return benefit. A party who seeks restitution of a benefit that he has conferred on the other party is expected to return what he has received from the other party. The objective is to return the parties, as nearly as is practicable, to the situation in which they found themselves before they made the contract. If a party has received land, goods or other property, he is expected to return it. The fact that he has benefited from possession of them does not preclude restitution since he can compensate the other party in money for this benefit. The property itself, however, must generally be returned. If it has been used, destroyed or substantially altered in character while in his possession, restitution is generally not available. Mere depreciation in market value, however, is not such a change as will preclude restitution. Cf. Uniform Commercial Code § 2–608.

b. Necessity of offer to return. If a party seeking restitution offers to return what he has received, he may make his offer conditional on restitution being made to him. To this end, the law gives him a lien on what he has received. See § 380(3). In equity, his failure to make such an offer before commencing a suit for rescission did not preclude relief. The decree could be made conditional on an offer. At law, however, an offer was traditionally regarded as a condition of the right to commence an action based on rescission. The merger of law and equity and modern procedural reforms have made this distinction undesirable, and the rule stated in this Section reflects the increasing criticism of the rule at law. If the court has the power to assure the required return in connection with the relief that it grants, it is not necessary that there have been a prior return or offer to return. If all that is to be returned is money, a credit against a larger sum allowed in restitution will suffice. In other cases a conditional judgment will be proper. A court may, in awarding costs, take account of any failure by the party seeking restitution to afford the other party an adequate opportunity to make restitution without the commencement of legal process. This is particularly appropriate in cases, such as mutual mistake, impracticability of performance or frustration of purpose, in which the other party is in no way at fault. Even though an offer to return property is not necessary under the rule stated in this Section, the retention of property together with the exercise of dominion over it may preclude avoidance under the rule stated in § 380.

Illustrations:

1. A contracts to sell to B a factory and a patent and B makes a part payment of $100,000. A assigns the patent but fails to transfer the factory to B. B sues A asking restitution of $100,000 without offering to reassign the patent. B is entitled to a judgment for that amount conditional on his tender of a reassignment of the patent.

2. A is induced by B's fraudulent misrepresentations to contract to sell to B for $10,000 an antique worth $100,000. A delivers the antique and B pays the $10,000. On discovery of the fraud, A demands the return of the antique without offering to repay the $10,000. On B's refusal, A sues B in conversion for the value of the antique. A is entitled to a judgment for $90,000, the value of the antique less $10,000.

3. The facts being otherwise as stated in Illustration 2, A sues B in replevin and posts a bond. If the procedure in replevin does not permit an adequate opportunity for the determination of A's claim of fraud before return of the antique to him, replevin will be denied on the ground that he has not offered to return the $10,000.

c. *Where no offer of return required.* In some instances there is no requirement of an offer to return. This is so if the property was worthless when received or if its destruction or loss was caused by the other party or by its own defects. See Illustration 4. It may also be so if it was never possible to return the property or if it has become impossible because the recipient used or disposed of it before he had knowledge of the grounds for restitution. See Illustrations 5 and 6. In those cases no offer need to be made if justice requires that compensation be accepted in place of the property and if the payment of such compensation can be assured. In determining what justice requires, consideration will be given to all the circumstances, including any misconduct such as fraud or duress by the other party. A party who receives only property that he already owned receives no interest and is not subject to the rule stated in Subsection (1) at all. Furthermore, if the contract apportions the price among various pieces of property, restitution of the price as to part of the property may be had on a return of only that part if the price as to the unreturned property is not included in the claim for restitution. See Illustration 7.

Illustrations:

4. A contracts to work on B's ranch in return for a number of cattle warranted by B to be sound. After A has done the work

and B has delivered the cattle, they are discovered to have hoof and mouth disease and are destroyed by government order. A is entitled to restitution of the reasonable value of his services.

5. A puts his son in B's private school, paying a year's tuition in advance. During the first month of school, the son is wrongfully expelled by B. A is entitled to restitution of the amount of tuition paid less the benefit to A of B's services during the first month.

6. A contracts to buy from B his seat on the stock exchange, his good will and the furniture in his office and pays $10,000 as part of the price. B delivers the furniture and A sells it to others. Later B refuses to perform the rest of the contract. A is entitled to restitution of $10,000 less compensation to B for the furniture.

7. A contracts to lease a plow and a tractor to B, to be used together. The price is stated to be $200 for the plow and $500 for the tractor, and B pays the full $700 in advance. A delivers the plow but fails to deliver the tractor. B can offer to return the plow and get restitution of $700. Because the prices are apportioned, B can also keep the plow and get restitution of $500.

REPORTER'S NOTE

This Section is based on former §§ 349, 480, 481. The requirement of an offer to return performance received has been relaxed in view of the merger of law and equity and modern procedural reforms. See 5 Corbin, Contracts §§ 1114, 1116 (1964 & Supp. 1980); 12 Williston, Contracts § 1460A (3d ed. 1970); Dobbs, Remedies § 4.8 (1973); 1 Palmer, Law of Restitution §§ 3.11, 3.12 (1978); Dobbs, Pressing Problems for the Plaintiff's Lawyer in Rescission: Election of Remedies and Restoration of Consideration, 26 Ark. L. Rev. 322, 346 (1972). As to releases, see Havighurst, Problems Concerning Settlement Agreements, 53 Nw. U.L. Rev. 283, 308–13 (1958).

Comment b. See the discussion of the requirement of a tender in Vick-

ers v. Gifford-Hill & Co., 534 F.2d 1311 (8th Cir. 1976). Illustration 1 is based on Illustration 4 to former § 349. Illustration 2 is based on Illustration 2 to former § 480. Illustration 3 is suggested by Dobbs, Remedies § 4.8 (1973); Dobbs, Pressing Problems for the Plaintiff's Lawyer in Rescission: Election of Remedies and Restoration of Consideration, 26 Ark. L. Rev. 322, 348 (1972).

Comment c. Illustration 4 is based on Illustration 7 to former § 349. Illustration 5 is based on Illustration 7 to former § 349; see also Illustrations 8 and 9 to former § 349. Illustration 6 is based on Illustration 10 to former § 349. Illustration 7 is based on Illustration 5 to former § 349.

§ 385. Effect of Power of Avoidance on Duty of Performance or on Duty Arising Out of Breach

(1) Unless an offer to restore performance received is a condition of avoidance, a party has no duty of performance while his power of avoidance exists.

(2) If an offer to restore performance received is a condition of avoidance, a duty to pay damages is terminated by such an offer made before the power of avoidance is lost.

Comment:

a. No duty of performance. If a party has the power to avoid the contract simply by disaffirmance, without offering to restore performance received, his refusal or failure to perform is not a breach under the rule stated in Subsection (1). This is so even if he is ignorant of his power of avoidance and believes that his refusal or failure is a breach. As a general rule, the legal consequences of a party's refusal or failure to perform are not affected by the fact that he is ignorant of some justification or excuse for his refusal or failure. See Comment *e* to § 225 and Comment *c* to § 237.

Illustrations:

1. A is induced by B's fraud to make a contract to buy goods from B. While A is still ignorant of the fraud and before he has received the goods from B, A writes a letter telling him that he refuses to perform. B sues A for damages for total breach by repudiation. A is not liable to B because, since A has no duty of performance, his letter was not a repudiation.

2. A is induced by B's fraud to make a contract to buy goods from B. A delays for an unreasonable time after discovery of the fraud and then, before he has received the goods, writes B a letter telling him that he refuses to perform on the ground of fraud. B sues A for damages for total breach by repudiation. A is liable to B because, A's power of avoidance having been lost by delay, he had a duty of performance and his letter was a repudiation.

b. Duty arising out of breach terminated. If an offer to restore performance received is a condition of avoidance (§ 384), a party with a power of avoidance is under a duty of performance until such an offer is made. His refusal or failure to perform is therefore a breach. A subsequent offer to restore performance, however, terminates the duty to pay damages that arises from that breach if the offer is made before the power of avoidance is lost.

Illustration:

3. A is induced by B's fraud to make a contract to buy goods from B. While A is still ignorant of the fraud but after he has received the goods from B, A commits a material breach by failure to pay B. A then discovers the fraud and tenders the goods back to B. B sues A for damages for total breach of contract. Even if an offer to return the goods was a condition of avoidance by A, A is not liable to B because A's breach was nullified by the tender of what he had received.

REPORTER'S NOTE

This Section extends to avoidance on any ground the rule of former § 490, which was restricted to avoidance for misrepresentation. See 12 Williston, Contracts § 1526 (3d ed. 1970).

Comment a. Illustrations 1 and 2 are based on Illustrations 1 and 2 to former § 490.

Comment b. Illustration 3 is based on Illustration 3 to former § 490.

*

TABLES

*

CONVERSION TABLES BETWEEN SECTION NUMBERS IN OFFICIAL TEXT AND TENTATIVE DRAFTS

NOTE: The Restatement, Second, of Contracts was put forth in fourteen Tentative Drafts between 1964 and 1979. A volume covering about half of the Restatement, Second, entitled "Tentative Drafts No. 1–7, Revised and Edited," was published in 1973. The order of the chapters was substantially changed for the Official Text, and section numbers also were changed, both to reflect the restructuring and to make the numbering system consecutive. Because many Sections have been discussed in cases, articles and texts under their Tentative Draft section numbers, the following tables are provided to permit conversion.

Table I converts from Official Text section numbers to Tentative Draft section numbers, and Table II does the reverse. Table I gives the title of each Chapter, Topic and Section. One seeking simply to find the Official Text section number of a Section referred to by its Tentative Draft section number may go directly to Table II. One seeking to learn the derivation of a particular Section may use Table II to learn its history in Tentative Drafts and may find its relation to the First Restatement in the Reporter's Note to the Section in this Official Text.

*

TABLE I

SECTION NUMBERS FROM OFFICIAL TEXT TO TENTATIVE DRAFTS

Chapter 1

MEANING OF TERMS

Chapter 2

FORMATION OF CONTRACTS—PARTIES AND CAPACITY

Chapter 3

FORMATION OF CONTRACTS— MUTUAL ASSENT

TOPIC 1. IN GENERAL

255

CONVERSION TABLES

TOPIC 2. MANIFESTATION OF ASSENT IN GENERAL

TOPIC 5. ACCEPTANCE OF OFFERS

Chapter 4

FORMATION OF CONTRACTS—CONSIDERATION

TOPIC 1. THE REQUIREMENT OF CONSIDERATION

CONVERSION TABLES

TOPIC 2. CONTRACTS WITHOUT CONSIDERATION

TOPIC 3. CONTRACTS UNDER SEAL; WRITING AS A STATUTORY SUBSTITUTE FOR THE SEAL

CONVERSION TABLES

TOPIC 6. SATISFACTION OF THE STATUTE BY A MEMORANDUM

TOPIC 7. CONSEQUENCES OF NON-COMPLIANCE

Chapter 6   (Chapter 12 in Tentative Draft)

MISTAKE

Chapter 7 (Chapter 13 in Tentative Draft)

MISREPRESENTATION, DURESS AND UNDUE INFLUENCE

TOPIC 1. MISREPRESENTATION

TOPIC 2. DURESS AND UNDUE INFLUENCE

Chapter 8 (Chapter 14 in Tentative Draft)

UNENFORCEABILITY ON GROUNDS OF PUBLIC POLICY

TOPIC 1. UNENFORCEABILITY IN GENERAL

CONVERSION TABLES

Chapter 9

THE SCOPE OF CONTRACTUAL OBLIGATIONS

TOPIC 1. THE MEANING OF AGREEMENTS

Chapter 10

PERFORMANCE AND NON–PERFORMANCE

TOPIC 1. PERFORMANCES TO BE EXCHANGED UNDER AN EXCHANGE OF PROMISES

Chapter 11

IMPRACTICABILITY OF PERFORMANCE AND FRUSTRATION OF PURPOSE

*

TABLE II

SECTION NUMBERS FROM TENTATIVE DRAFTS TO OFFICIAL TEXT

Tentative Drafts	Official Text	Tentative Drafts	Official Text
Tentative Draft No. 1		**Topic 4**	
Chapter 1		34	35
1	1	35	36
2	2	35A	37
3	3	37	38
4	3	38	39
5	4	39	40
5A	5	40	41
7	6	41	42
13	7	42	43
14	8	43	46
		44	47
Chapter 2		45	45
15	9	47A	44
16	10	48	48
17	11	51	49
18	12		
18A	13	**Topic 5**	
18B	14	52	50
18C	15	53	51
18D	16	54	52
		55	53
Chapter 3		56	54
Topic 1		57	55
19	17	57A	56
		58	57
Topic 2		59	58
20	18	60	59
21	19	61	60
21A	20	62	61
21B	21	63	62
22	22	64	63
23	23	65	64
		66	65
Topic 3		67	66
24	24	68	67
24A	25	69	68
25	26	72	69
26	27	73	70
27	28		
28	29	**Tentative Draft No. 2**	
29	30	**Chapter 4**	
30	31	**Topic 1**	
31	32	75	71
32	33	76	72
33	34	76A	73

TABLE II. SECTION NUMBERS FROM TENTATIVE DRAFTS TO OFFICIAL TEXT

Tentative Drafts	Official Text
76B	74
77	75
78	76
79	77
80	78
81	79
83	80
84	81

Topic 2

Tentative Drafts	Official Text
86	82
87	83
88	84
89	85
89A	86
89B	87
89C	88
89D	89
90	90
91	91
92	92
93	93
94	94

Topic 3

Tentative Drafts	Official Text
95	95
96	96
97	97
98	98
99	99
100	100
101	101
102	102
103	103
104	104
105	105
106	106
107	107
108	108
109	109

Chapter 5

(Chapter 13 in Official Text)

Topic 1

Tentative Drafts	Official Text
111	288
112	289
117	290
118	291
119	292
120	293
121	294

Tentative Drafts	Official Text
122	295
125	296

Topic 2

Tentative Drafts	Official Text
128	297
129	298
130	299
131	300
132	301

Tentative Draft No. 3

(See also T.D. No. 4 as to §§ 133-34, 165-75.)

Chapter 6

(Chapter 14 in Official Text)

Tentative Drafts	Official Text
133	302
134	303
135	304
136	305
137	306
138	307
139	308
140	309
141	310
142	311
144	312
145	313
146	314
147	315

Chapter 7

(Chapter 15 in Official Text)

Tentative Drafts	Official Text
148	316

Topic 1

Tentative Drafts	Official Text
149	317
150	318
151	319
152	320
153	321
154	322
155	323

Topic 2

Tentative Drafts	Official Text
156	324
157	325
158	326
159	327
160	328

TABLE II. SECTION NUMBERS FROM TENTATIVE DRAFTS TO OFFICIAL TEXT

Tentative Drafts	Official Text
161	329
162	330

Topic 3

Tentative Drafts	Official Text
163	331
164	332
165	333

Topic 4

Tentative Drafts	Official Text
166	334
167	335
168	336
169	337
170	338
171	339

Topic 5

Tentative Drafts	Official Text
172	340
173	341
174	342
175	343

Tentative Draft No. 4

Chapter 8

(Chapter 5 in Official Text)

Tentative Drafts	Official Text
178	110

Topic 1

Tentative Drafts	Official Text
179	111

Topic 2

Tentative Drafts	Official Text
180	112
181	113
182	114
183	115
184	116
185	117
186	118
187	119
188	120
189	121
190	122
191	123

Topic 3

Tentative Drafts	Official Text
192	124

Topic 4

Tentative Drafts	Official Text
193	125
194	126

Tentative Drafts	Official Text
195	127
196	128
197	129

Topic 5

Tentative Drafts	Official Text
198	130

Topic 7

(Topic 6 in Official Text)

Tentative Drafts	Official Text
207	131
208	132
209	133
210	134
211	135
214	136
216	137

Topic 8

(Topic 7 in Official Text)

Tentative Drafts	Official Text
217	138
217A	139
217B	140
217C	141
217D	142
217E	143
218	144
219	145
220	146
221	147
222	148
223	149
224	150

Tentative Draft No. 5

(See also T.D. No. 6 as to §§ 239–49; and T.D. No. 7 as to §§ 250–55.)

Chapter 9

Topic 1

Tentative Drafts	Official Text
226	200
227	201
228	202
229	203
230	204

Topic 2

Tentative Drafts	Official Text
231	205
232	206
233	207
234	208

273

TABLE II. SECTION NUMBERS FROM TENTATIVE DRAFTS TO OFFICIAL TEXT

Tentative Drafts	Official Text	Tentative Drafts	Official Text
Topic 3			
235	209	270	246
236	210	271	247
237	211	272	248
238	212	273	249
239	213		
240	214	**Topic 3**	
241	215	274	250
242	216	275	251
243	217	276	252
244	218	277	253
		277A	254
Topic 4		(Added in T.D. No. 13)	
245	219	278	255
246	220	279	256
247	221	280	257
248	222		
249	223	**Topic 4**	
		280A	258
Topic 5		280B	259
250	224	280C	260
251	225	(Added in T.D. No. 13)	
252	226		
253	227	**Tentative Draft No. 9**	
254	228		
255	229	**Chapter 11**	
255A	230	281	261
(Added in T.D. No. 13)		282	262
		283	263
Tentative Draft No. 8		284	264
		285	265
(See also T.D. No. 9 as to §§ 274–80.)		286	266
		287	267
Chapter 10		288	268
Topic 1		289	269
256	231	290	270
257	232	291	271
258	233	292	272
259	234		
		Tentative Draft No. 10	
Topic 2			
260	235	**Chapter 12**	
261	236	(Chapter 6 in Official Text)	
262	237	293	151
263	238	294	152
264	239	295	153
265	240	296	154
266	241	297	155
267	242	298	156
268	243	299	157
268A	244	300	158
(Added in T.D. No. 13)			
269	245		

TABLE II. SECTION NUMBERS FROM TENTATIVE DRAFTS TO OFFICIAL TEXT

Tentative Drafts	Official Text	Tentative Drafts	Official Text
Tentative Draft No. 11		**Topic 4**	
Chapter 13		334	192
		335	193
(Chapter 7 in Official Text)		336	194
(See also T.D. No. 12 as to §§ 314–19.)		337	195
		338	196
Topic 1		339	356
301	159	**Topic 5**	
302	160		
303	161	340	197
304	162	341	198
305	163	342	199
306	164		
307	165	**Tentative Draft No. 13**	
308	166		
309	167	**Chapter 15**	
310	168	(Chapter 12 in Official Text)	
311	169		
312	170	**Topic 1**	
313	171	343	273
314	172	344	274
315	173	345	275
		346	276
Topic 2		347	277
316	174		
317	175	**Topic 2**	
318	176	348	278
319	177	349	279
		350	280
Tentative Draft No. 12		351	281
		352	282
Chapter 14			
(Chapter 8 in Official Text)		**Topic 3**	
Topic 1		353	283
320	178	354	284
321	179	355	285
322	180		
323	181		
324	182	**Topic 4**	
325	183	356	286
326	184	357	287
327	185		
		Tentative Draft No. 14	
Topic 2		**Chapter 16**	
328	186	**Topic 1**	
329	187	358	344
330	188	359	345
Topic 3		**Topic 2**	
331	189	360	346
332	190	361	347
333	191	362	348

TABLE II. SECTION NUMBERS FROM TENTATIVE
DRAFTS TO OFFICIAL TEXT

Tentative Drafts	Official Text	Tentative Drafts	Official Text
363	349		
364	350	**Topic 4**	
365	351	384	370
366	352	385	371
367	353	386	372
368	354	387	373
369	355	388	374
370	356	389	375
(see also § 339 in T.D. No. 12)		390	376
		391	377
Topic 3			
371	357	**Topic 5**	
372	358	392	378
373	359	393	379
374	360	394	380
375	361	395	381
376	362	396	382
377	363	397	383
378	364	398	384
379	365	399	385
380	366		
381	367		
382	368		
383	369		

TABLE III

UNIFORM COMMERCIAL CODE CITATIONS

Uniform Commercial Code	Restatement
§ 1-102	§ 28
§ 1-102(3)	§ 5
§ 1-102 Comment 3	Introduction to Restatement
§ 1-106	§ 352
§ 1-106(1)	§ 344
§ 1-107	Statutory Note to Topic 3 of Chapter 4
	Introductory Note to Topic 1 of Chapter 12
	§ 277
§ 1-201	§ 127
	§ 131
§ 1-201(3)	Introduction to Restatement
	§ 3
	§ 4
	§ 200
	§ 221
§ 1-201(4)	§ 175
§ 1-201(11)	Introduction to Restatement
	§ 1
	§ 200
§ 1-201(14)	§ 102
§ 1-201(15)	§ 6
	§ 332
§ 1-201(19)	§ 205
§ 1-201(23)	§ 252
§ 1-201(25)	§ 19
	§ 40
	§ 42
§ 1-201(26)	§ 40
	§ 42
	§ 311
	§ 338
§ 1-201(27)	§ 40
	§ 42
	§ 161
	§ 311
§ 1-201(32)	§ 155
	§ 166
§ 1-201(33)	§ 155
	§ 166
§ 1-201(37)	Introductory Note to Chapter 15
	§ 324
	§ 342

Uniform Commercial Code	Restatement
§ 1-201(39)	§ 134
§ 1-201(39) Comment	§ 134
§ 1-201(44)	§ 311
	§ 338
§ 1-201(46)	§ 95
§ 1-203	§ 6
	§ 34
	§ 41
	§ 157
	§ 205
§ 1-204	§ 33
	§ 204
§ 1-204(2)	§ 33
§ 1-205	§ 23
	§ 28
	§ 203
	§ 212
	§ 220
	§ 222
	§ 223
	§ 233
	§ 234
§ 1-205(2)	§ 222
§ 1-205(3)	§ 221
§ 1-205(5)	§ 222
§ 1-205(6)	§ 220
§ 1-205 Comment 5	§ 222
§ 1-206	Statutory Note to Chapter 5
	§ 110
	§ 122
	§ 131
	Introductory Note to Chapter 15
	§ 324
§ 1-207	§ 247
	§ 278
	§ 281
	§ 329
§ 1-208	§ 205
§ 2-102	§ 148
§ 2-103	§ 41
	§ 176
§ 2-103(1)(b)	§ 34
	§ 205
§ 2-104	§ 23
	§ 221
§ 2-105	§ 127

277

TABLE III. UNIFORM COMMERCIAL CODE CITATIONS

Uniform Commercial Code	Restatement
§ 2-106	§ 71
	§ 241
	§ 283
§ 2-106(1)	Introduction to Restatement
§ 2-106 Comment 2	§ 241
§ 2-107(1)	§ 127
§ 2-107(2)	§ 127
§ 2-201	Statutory Note to Chapter 5
	§ 110
	§ 131
	§ 136
	§ 148
	§ 149
§ 2-201(3)	§ 139
	§ 147
§ 2-201(3)(c)	§ 148
§ 2-201 Comment	§ 144
§ 2-202	§ 209
	§ 212
	§ 220
	§ 222
	§ 332
§ 2-202(a)	§ 220
	§ 221
§ 2-202(b)	§ 216
§ 2-202 Comment 3	§ 210
§ 2-203	§ 6
	§ 87
	§ 88
	Statutory Note to Topic 3 of Chapter 4
§ 2-204	§ 22
§ 2-204(3)	§ 33
	§ 362
§ 2-205	§ 87
	Statutory Note to Topic 3 of Chapter 4
§ 2-206	§ 246
§ 2-206(1)	§ 32
§ 2-206(1)(b)	§ 32
	§ 71
§ 2-206 Comment 2	§ 32
§ 2-206 Comment 4	§ 32
§ 2-207(3)	§ 22
§ 2-208	§ 34
	§ 150
	§ 202
	§ 203
	§ 212
	§ 323
§ 2-208(1)	§ 22

Uniform Commercial Code	Restatement
§ 2-208 Comment	§ 150
§ 2-209	§ 89
	Statutory Note to Topic 3 of Chapter 4
	§ 205
§ 2-209(1)	§ 175
	§ 273
§ 2-209(2)	§ 148
	§ 273
	§ 283
§ 2-209(3)	§ 149
§ 2-209(4)	§ 150
§ 2-209(5)	§ 84
	§ 89
	§ 150
§ 2-209 Comment	§ 89
	§ 205
§ 2-209 Comment 2	§ 84
	§ 176
	§ 205
§ 2-210	Introductory Note to Chapter 15
	§ 317
	§ 318
	§ 320
	§ 322
	§ 328
	§ 336
§ 2-210(3)	§ 322
§ 2-210 Comment	§ 317
§ 2-213(2)	§ 169
§ 2-301	§ 71
§ 2-302	§ 21
	§ 34
	§ 203
	§ 208
§ 2-302 Comment	§ 203
§ 2-302 Comment 1	§ 208
§ 2-305	§ 202
	§ 204
§ 2-305(1)	§ 33
§ 2-305(1)(c)	§ 271
§ 2-305(2)	§ 34
	§ 205
§ 2-305(4)	§ 33
§ 2-306	§ 33
	§ 34
	§ 77
§ 2-306(1)	§ 205
§ 2-306(2)	§ 77
	§ 155
	§ 205

TABLE III. UNIFORM COMMERCIAL CODE CITATIONS

Uniform Commercial Code	Restatement	Uniform Commercial Code	Restatement
§ 2–307	§ 233	§ 2–403	Introductory Note to Chapter 16
§ 2–307 Comment 3	§ 233		
§ 2–308	§ 216	§ 2–403(1)	§ 338
§ 2–309	§ 216	§ 2–403(1)(a)	§ 153
§ 2–309(1)	§ 33		§ 163
	§ 204	§ 2–403(2)	§ 180
§ 2–309(2)	§ 33	§ 2–501	§ 321
§ 2–309(3)	§ 33	§ 2–502	§ 365
	§ 77	§ 2–503(1)	§ 238
	§ 205	§ 2–504	§ 216
§ 2–310	§ 33	§ 2–507	§ 234
§ 2–311	§ 34		§ 372
	§ 205	§ 2–507(1)	§ 238
	§ 216	§ 2–508	§ 237
§ 2–311(1)	§ 34	§ 2–508(2)	§ 203
§ 2–312	§ 24		§ 241
	§ 216	§ 2–509(3)	§ 267
	§ 333	§ 2–511	§ 234
§ 2–313	§ 226	§ 2–511(1)	§ 238
	§ 333	§ 2–511(2)	§ 249
§ 2–313(2)	§ 2	§ 2–601	§ 241
§ 2–314	§ 5		§ 246
	§ 152	§ 2–601(c)	§ 246
	§ 226	§ 2–605	§ 237
§ 2–314(3)	§ 220		§ 248
§ 2–315	§ 2	§ 2–605(1)(a)	§ 205
	§ 152		§ 237
	§ 169	§ 2–606	§ 380
	§ 216	§ 2–607	§ 237
	§ 226		§ 246
§ 2–316	§ 5		Introductory Note to Topic 1 of Chapter 12
	§ 196		
	§ 333		
§ 2–316(1)	§ 196	§ 2–607(2)	§ 246
	§ 203	§ 2–607(3)	§ 277
	§ 211	§ 2–607(5)	§ 333
§ 2–316(3)(c)	§ 220	§ 2–607 Comment 1	§ 233
§ 2–317	§ 203	§ 2–608	§ 237
	§ 333		§ 246
§ 2–318	Introductory Note to Chapter 14	§ 2–608(1)	§ 241
		§ 2–609	§ 153
	§ 302		§ 205
	§ 333		§ 241
§ 2–319	§ 201		Introductory Note to Topic 3 of Chapter 10
§ 2–320(2)	§ 224		
§ 2–321(3)	§ 224		
§ 2–326(4)	§ 148		§ 251
§ 2–328	§ 28		§ 268
§ 2–328(3)	§ 28		§ 317
	§ 87		§ 320
§ 2–401	§ 24	§ 2–609(1)	§ 251
	§ 148	§ 2–609 Comment 1	§ 251
	§ 321		§ 268

TABLE III. UNIFORM COMMERCIAL CODE CITATIONS

Uniform Commercial Code	Restatement	Uniform Commercial Code	Restatement
§ 2-609 Comment 3	§ 251	§ 2-711	§ 378
§ 2-609 Comment 4	§ 251	§ 2-712	§ 242
§ 2-610	§ 243		§ 350
	§ 250		§ 351
	§ 253	§ 2-713	§ 242
	§ 329		§ 350
§ 2-610(b)	§ 257	§ 2-713(1)	§ 350
§ 2-611	§ 329	§ 2-714	§ 5
§ 2-611 Comment 1	§ 256		§ 246
§ 2-612	§ 241	§ 2-714(1)	§ 351
	§ 242	§ 2-714(2)	§ 152
	§ 256	§ 2-715	§ 2
§ 2-612(3)	§ 241		§ 347
	§ 246	§ 2-715(2)(a)	§ 350
§ 2-612 Comment 1	§ 256		§ 351
§ 2-612 Comment 6	§ 241	§ 2-715(2)(b)	§ 351
§ 2-613	§ 263	§ 2-716(1)	Introductory Note to Topic 3 of Chapter 16
	§ 267		
§ 2-613(b)	§ 272	§ 2-716 Comment 1	Introductory Note to Topic 3 of Chapter 16
§ 2-613 Comment 1	§ 261		
§ 2-614(1)	§ 261	§ 2-716 Comment 2	§ 360
§ 2-614 Comment 1	§ 270	§ 2-717	§ 309
§ 2-615	§ 176		Introductory Note to Chapter 16
	Introductory Note to Chapter 11		
	§ 264	§ 2-718	§ 208
§ 2-615(a)	§ 152	§ 2-718(1)	§ 356
	§ 261	§ 2-718(2)	§ 374
	§ 264	§ 2-719	§ 21
§ 2-215(b)	§ 272		§ 196
§ 2-615 Comment 2	§ 261		§ 346
§ 2-615 Comment 3	§ 261	§ 2-719 Comment 1	§ 21
§ 2-615 Comment 4	§ 261	§ 2-721	§ 378
§ 2-615 Comment 5	§ 261	§ 3-103	§ 120
§ 2-615 Comment 10	§ 264	§ 3-104	§ 120
§ 2-616	§ 176		§ 325
§ 2-271	§ 88		§ 332
§ 2-702	§ 372	§ 3-105	§ 325
§ 2-702(1)	§ 153	§ 3-108	§ 216
	§ 251	§ 3-110(3)	§ 203
	§ 252	§ 3-113	§ 6
§ 2-702(2)	§ 171		§ 88
§ 2-703	§ 372		Introductory Note to Topic 3 of Chapter 4
	§ 378	§ 3-115	§ 134
§ 2-703 Comment 1	§ 378	§ 3-116	§ 298
§ 2-704(2)	§ 350		§ 299
§ 2-706	§ 350	§ 3-118(b)	§ 203
§ 2-708	§ 350	§ 3-118(c)	§ 203
§ 2-708(1)	§ 350	§ 3-118(e)	Introductory Note to Chapter 13
§ 2-708(2)	§ 347		§ 289
§ 2-709	§ 238	§ 3-122(1)(b)	§ 226
	§ 246	§ 3-201	Introductory Note to Chapter 15
§ 2-709(1)(a)	§ 224		
§ 2-709(2)	§ 238		§ 336

TABLE OF U.C.C. CITATIONS

TABLE III. UNIFORM COMMERCIAL CODE CITATIONS

TABLE III. UNIFORM COMMERCIAL CODE CITATIONS

Uniform Commercial Code	Restatement
§ 7–501(4)	§ 338
§ 7–502	§ 325
	§ 336
	§ 338
§ 7–503	§ 325
§ 7–504	§ 325
	§ 336
	§ 343
§ 7–505	§ 333
§ 7–507	§ 333
§ 7–601	§ 339
§ 7–603	§ 339
Article 8	§ 6
	Introductory Note to Chapter 15
§ 8–102	§ 332
§ 8–202	§ 336
	§ 338
§ 8–207	§ 338
§ 8–301	§ 336
	§ 338
	§ 343
§ 8–302	§ 338
	§ 340
§ 8–306	§ 333
§ 8–306(2)	§ 151
§ 8–308(9)	§ 333
§ 8–309	§ 332
§ 8–319	Statutory Note to Chapter 5
	§ 110
	§ 122
	§ 131
§ 8–319(b)	§ 139
	§ 147
§ 8–401	§ 332
§ 8–403	§ 339
§ 8–405	§ 339
§ 9–102	§ 127
	Introductory Note to Chapter 15
	§ 328
	§ 341
§ 9–102(1)(b)	§ 324
§ 9–103(3)(c)	§ 341
§ 9–104	Introductory Note to Chapter 15
	§ 328
	§ 338
	§ 341
	§ 342
§ 9–104(f)	Introductory Note to Chapter 15

Uniform Commercial Code	Restatement
§ 9–105	§ 127
	§ 328
	§ 338
§ 9–105(1)(b)	§ 332
§ 9–105(1)(d)	§ 324
§ 9–105(1)(i)	§ 274
§ 9–106	Introductory Note to Chapter 15
	§ 328
	§ 338
§ 9–110	§ 131
§ 9–201	§ 6
	Introductory Note to Chapter 15
§ 9–203	§ 6
	Statutory Note to Chapter 5
	§ 122
	§ 127
	§ 131
	Introductory Note to Chapter 15
	§ 321
	§ 324
	§ 330
§ 9–203(2)	§ 330
§ 9–203(4)	§ 321
§ 9–204	Introductory Note to Chapter 15
	§ 321
§ 9–204(1)	§ 330
§ 9–204(2)	§ 321
§ 9–206	Introductory Note to Chapter 15
	§ 336
	§ 338
§ 9–206(1)	Introductory Note to Chapter 15
§ 9–208	§ 74
§ 9–301	Introductory Note to Chapter 15
	§ 330
	§ 341
	§ 342
§ 9–302	Introductory Note to Chapter 15
	§ 341
	§ 342
§ 9–303	§ 330
§ 9–306(2)	§ 342
§ 9–308	§ 342
	§ 343
§ 9–309	§ 340

TABLE III. UNIFORM COMMERCIAL CODE CITATIONS

*

TABLE IV

STATUTES

See Table III, p. 277, supra, for References to the
Uniform Commercial Code.

UNITED STATES CONSTITUTION

TABLE OF STATUTES

FEDERAL RULES OF CIVIL PROCEDURE

Rule	This Work Sec.
8(c)	143
13	336
17	307
17(a)	Ch. 15, p. 3
19	326
19–21	290
	298
22	339

FEDERAL RULES OF EVIDENCE

Rule	This Work Sec.
1001–1004	137
	332

STATE STATUTES

ALABAMA
Code

Sec.	This Work Sec.
6–2–16	Ch. 5, p. 284
6–2–33	94
6–5–283	Ch. 13, p. 405
6–5–286	Ch. 15, p. 5
6–5–287	94
6–5–466	Ch. 13, p. 405
6–8–82	Ch. 15, p. 5
7–2–201	Ch. 5, p. 282
8–5–20	Ch. 15, p. 5
8–5–21	Ch. 15, p. 8
8–5–25	Ch. 15, p. 5
8–5–26	Ch. 15, p. 5
8–9–2	129
9–4	284
12–21–112	94
35–4–22	94

Code of 1940

Tit.	This Work Sec.
7, § 141	290
27, § 26	14

ALASKA
Rules of Civil Procedure

Rule	This Work Sec.
17	Ch. 15, p. 4

ALASKA
Statutes

Sec.	This Work Sec.
06.20.290	Ch. 15, p. 9
09.10.040	94
09.10.200	Ch. 5, p. 284
09.25.010	Ch. 5, p. 282
09.25.130	94
09.30.030	Ch. 13, p. 405
09.30.060	Ch. 13, p. 405
09.65.060	Ch. 15, p. 4
25.20.010	14
45.10.140	Ch. 15, p. 10
45.10.150	Ch. 15, p. 10

ARIZONA
Revised Statutes Annotated

Sec.	This Work Sec.
1–202	94
1–215	14
12–508	Ch. 5, p. 284
44–101	Ch. 5, p. 282
44–121	94
44–141	Ch. 13, p. 405
44–142	Ch. 13, p. 405
44–144	Ch. 15, p. 4

Rules of Civil Procedure

Rule	This Work Sec.
17	Ch. 13, p. 405
	Ch. 15, p. 4
19	Ch. 13, p. 405

ARKANSAS
Statutes Annotated

Sec.	This Work Sec.
27–810	Ch. 13, p. 405
27–812	Ch. 13, p. 405
37–216	Ch. 5, p. 284
38–101	Ch. 5, p. 282
57–103	14
66–3228	355
68–801	Ch. 15, p. 4

TABLE OF STATUTES

CALIFORNIA
Civil Code

Sec.	This Work Sec.
25	14
1430	Ch. 13, p. 403
1431	Ch. 13, p. 403
1541	284
1543	Ch. 13, p. 403
1614	94
1615	94
1624	Ch. 5, p. 282
1629	94
1659	Ch. 13, p. 403
1660	Ch. 13, p. 403
1698	283
1804.1(c)	Ch. 15, p. 8
2794	116

Civil Procedure Code

Sec.	This Work Sec.
360	Ch. 5, p. 284
360.5	Ch. 5, p. 284
367–368	Ch. 15, p. 4
388	290
410.70	Ch. 13, p. 403
431.70	Ch. 15, p. 4
1285 et seq.	345

Finance Code

Sec.	This Work Sec.
22471	Ch. 15, p. 8
24472	Ch. 15, p. 8

Labor Code

Sec.	This Work Sec.
300	Ch. 15, p. 8

Probate Code

Sec.	This Work Sec.
737	Ch. 5, p. 282

COLORADO
Revised Statutes

Sec.	This Work Sec.
13–22–101	14
13–50–101	Ch. 13, p. 403

COLORADO
Revised Statutes

Sec.	This Work Sec.
13–50–102	Ch. 13, p. 403
13–80–125	Ch. 5, p. 284
38–10–112	Ch. 5, p. 282
38–30–118	94
38–30–125	94

COLORADO
Rules of Civil Procedure

Sec.	This Work Sec.
13(j)	Ch. 15, p. 4
17	Ch. 15, p. 4

CONNECTICUT
General Statutes Annotated

Sec.	This Work Sec.
1–1d	14
36–236	Ch. 15, p. 8
52–78	Ch. 13, p. 403
52–108	Ch. 13, p. 403
52–118	Ch. 15, p. 4
52–139	Ch. 15, p. 4
52–140	Ch. 15, p. 4
52–142	Ch. 13, p. 403
52–176	Ch. 5, p. 284
52–179	94
52–227	Ch. 13, p. 403
52–361(g)	Ch. 15, p. 8
52–550	Ch. 5, p. 282

DELAWARE
Code Annotated

Tit.	This Work Sec.
6, § 2701	Ch. 13, p. 405
6, § 2705	14
6, § 2713–2714	Ch. 5, p. 282
10, § 3902	Ch. 15, p. 4
10, § 8106	94

DISTRICT OF COLUMBIA
Code

Sec.	This Work Sec.
12–301	94
13–502	Ch. 15, p. 5

TABLE OF STATUTES

TABLE OF STATUTES

TABLE OF STATUTES

TABLE OF STATUTES

MINNESOTA

Statutes Annotated

Rules of Civil Procedure

MISSISSIPPI

Code Annotated

MISSOURI

Statutes Annotated

Revised Statutes

MISSOURI

Revised Statutes

MONTANA

Code Annotated

Revised Code Annotated

Revised Code Annotated of 1947

TABLE OF STATUTES

TABLE OF STATUTES

TABLE OF STATUTES

NORTH DAKOTA

Rules of Civil Procedure

Rule	This Work Sec.
17	Ch. 15, p. 5

OHIO

Revised Code Annotated

Sec.	This Work Sec.
5.11	94
1317.03	Ch. 15, p. 10
1321.31	Ch. 15, p. 12
1321.32	Ch. 15, p. 8
1335.04	125
1335.05	Ch. 5, p. 283
1779.09–1779.11	Ch. 13, p. 404
2111.01	12
2117.31	Ch. 13, p. 404
2305.08	Ch. 5, p. 285
2325.14	Ch. 13, p. 404
3109.01	14
4113.16	Ch. 15, p. 8

OKLAHOMA

Statutes Annotated

Tit.	This Work Sec.
12, § 101	Ch. 5, p. 285
12, § 178	Ch. 13, p. 405
12, § 179	Ch. 13, p. 405
12, § 221	Ch. 15, p. 5
12, § 278	Ch. 15, p. 5
15, § 11	14
15, § 13	14
15, § 114	94
15, § 115	94
15, § 136	Ch. 5, p. 283
15, § 139	94
15, § 175	Ch. 13, p. 405
15, § 176	Ch. 13, p. 405
15, § 325	116
58, § 521	Ch. 5, p. 283
60, §§ 312–313	Ch. 15, p. 5

OREGON

Revised Statutes

Sec.	This Work Sec.
12.070	94
12.230	Ch. 5, p. 285

OREGON

Revised Statutes

Sec.	This Work Sec.
13.030	Ch. 15, p. 5
15.100	Ch. 13, p. 406
41.580	Ch. 5, p. 283
80.010	Ch. 15, p. 5
80.020	Ch. 15, p. 5
109.510	14

PENNSYLVANIA

Statutes Annotated

Tit.	This Work Sec.
12, § 806	Ch. 13, p. 407
33, § 1	Ch. 5, p. 283
33, § 3	Ch. 5, p. 283
33, § 4	Ch. 5, p. 283
33, § 6	87
	88
	89
	94
	284
43, § 271	Ch. 15, p. 12
43, § 273	Ch. 15, p. 12
43, § 274	Ch. 15, p. 12

Rules of Civil Procedure

Rule	This Work Sec.
2002–2003	Ch. 15, p. 5
2250	Ch. 13, p. 407

RHODE ISLAND

General Laws

Sec.	This Work Sec.
7-12-10	Ch. 13, p. 406
9-1-4	Ch. 5, p. 283
9-1-17	94
9-2-6	Ch. 13, p. 406
9-2-7	Ch. 13, p. 406
9-2-8	Ch. 15, p. 6
15-12-1	14
33-15-8	12

TABLE OF STATUTES

TABLE OF STATUTES

UTAH

Revised Statutes

Sec.	This Work Sec.
104–48–4	94

Rules of Civil Procedure

Rule	This Work Sec.
13(i)	Ch. 15, p. 5
17(a)	Ch. 15, p. 5
71B	Ch. 13, p. 404

VERMONT

Statutes Annotated

Tit.	This Work Sec.
1, § 173	14
12, § 181	Ch. 5, p. 283
12, § 507	94
12, § 591	Ch. 5, p. 285
12, § 3022	Ch. 15, p. 8
12, §§ 5051–5060	Ch. 13, p. 406
14, § 2682	12
21, § 344	Ch. 15, p. 8
27, § 302	125

VIRGINIA

Code Annotated

Sec.	This Work Sec.
1–13–42	14
8–01–246	94
8.01–11	Ch. 13, p. 404
8.01–13	Ch. 15, p. 5
8.01–30	Ch. 13, p. 404
8.01–229	Ch. 5, p. 285
8.01–423	Ch. 15, p. 5
8.01–442	Ch. 13, p. 404
11–2	Ch. 5, p. 283
11–3	94
53–305	12
55–2	129

WASHINGTON

Revised Code Annotated

Sec.	This Work Sec.
4.08.080	Ch. 15, p. 5
4.16.280	Ch. 5, p. 285

WASHINGTON

Revised Code Annotated

Sec.	This Work Sec.
4.20.046	Ch. 13, p. 405
4.28.190	Ch. 13, p. 405
4.68.010	Ch. 13, p. 405
19.36.010	Ch. 5, p. 283
26.28.015	14
31.08.190	Ch. 15, p. 9
49.48.090	Ch. 15, p. 9
63.14.020	Ch. 15, p. 10
63.14.150	Ch. 15, p. 10
64.04.090	94

WEST VIRGINIA

Code

Sec.	This Work Sec.
2–2–6	94
2–3–1	14
28–5–33	12
36–3–1	94
55–1–1	Ch. 5, p. 283
55–2–6	94
55–2–8	Ch. 5, p. 285
55–8–6—55–8–8	Ch. 13, p. 405
55–8–9	Ch. 15, p. 5
55–8–10	Ch. 15, p. 5
56–6–32	Ch. 13, p. 405

Rules of Civil Procedure

Rule	This Work Sec.
17	Ch. 15, p. 5

WISCONSIN

Statutes Annotated

Sec.	This Work Sec.
113.01–113.10	Ch. 13, p. 404
135.01	178
241.02	Ch. 5, p. 283
241.09	Ch. 15, p. 8
260.13–260.14	Ch. 15, p. 5
269.08	Ch. 13, p. 404
269.17	Ch. 13, p. 404
270.55	Ch. 13, p. 404
270.56	Ch. 13, p. 404
330.42	Ch. 5, p. 285
331.07	Ch. 15, p. 5

TABLE OF STATUTES

TABLE OF STATUTES

TABLE V

CASES
CITED IN REPORTER'S NOTES

A

A & W Equip. Co. v. Carroll, 377 S.W.2d 895 (Ky.1964)—§ 153.

ABC Outdoor Advertising, Inc. v. Dolhun's Marine, Inc., 38 Wis.2d 457, 157 N.W.2d 680 (1968)—§§ 148, 283.

ACF Produce v. Chubb/Pacific Indem. Group, 451 F.Supp. 1095 (E.D.Pa.1978)—§ 284.

Abalene Pest Control Serv. v. Hall, 126 Vt. 1, 220 A.2d 717 (1966)—§ 323.

Abbott v. Stephany Poultry Co., 5 Terry 513, 62 A.2d 243 (Del.Super.Ct.1948)—§ 87.

Abdill v. Abdill, 292 Ill. 231, 126 N.E. 543 (1920)—Ch. 5.

Accessory Sales, Inc. v. Bedient, 95 Idaho 906, 523 P.2d 38 (1974)—§ 247.

Ace Neon Corp. v. Griffin Constr. Co., 75 Ga.App. 125, 42 S.E.2d 510 (1947)—§ 291.

Acme Plumbing & Heating Co. v. Hirsch, 121 Neb. 134, 236 N.W. 137 (1931)—§ 263.

Acme Process Equip. Co., United States v., 385 U.S. 138 (1966)—§ 179.

Acme Process Equip. Co. v. United States, 171 Ct.Cl. 324, 347 F.2d 509 (1965)—§§ 370, 373.

Adams v. Big Three Indus., 549 S.W.2d 411 (Tex.Civ.App.1977)—§ 130.

Adams v. Gillig, 199 N.Y. 314, 92 N.E. 670 (1910)—§ 171.

Adams v. Nichols, 36 Mass. (19 Pick) 275 (1837)—§ 263.

Adams Express Co. v. Allen, 125 Va. 530, 100 S.E. 473 (1919)—§ 351.

Adams-Mitchell Co. v. Cambridge Distributing Co., 189 F.2d 913 (2d Cir. 1951)—§ 199.

Adan v. Steinbrecher, 166 Minn. 174, 133 N.W. 477 (1911)—§ 169.

Addis v. Gramophone, A.C. 488 (H.L.1909)—§ 355.

Addison Terry Co. v. N.F.L. Films, Inc., 390 F.Supp. 621 (S.D.N.Y.1974)—§ 225.

Adler, Barish, Daniels, Levin & Creskoff v. Epstein, 482 Pa. 416, 393 A.2d 1175 (1978)—§ 194.

Aetna Cas. & Sur. Co. v. Harvard Trust Co., 344 Mass. 169, 181 N.E.2d 673 (1962)—§ 343.

Agner v. Bourn, 281 Minn. 385, 161 N.W.2d 813 (1968)—§ 177.

Agricultural Serv. Ass'n v. Ferry-Morse Seed Co., 551 F.2d 1057 (6th Cir. 1977)—§§ 195, 196.

Agristor Credit Corp. v. Unruh, 571 P.2d 1220 (Okl.1977)—§ 74.

Ahern Co., M. v. John Bowen Co., 334 Mass. 36, 133 N.E.2d 484 (1956)—§ 377.

Aiello v. Knoll Golf Club, 64 N.J.Super. 156, 165 A.2d 531 (1960)—§ 90.

Aircraft Ass'n & Mfg. Co. v. United States, 174 Ct.Cl. 886, 357 F.2d 373 (1966)—§§ 175, 176.

Ajamian v. Schlanger, 14 N.J. 483, 103 A.2d 9 (1954)—§ 378.

Alabama Football, Inc. v. Greenwood, 452 F.Supp. 1191 (W.D.Pa.1978)—§§ 254, 255, 377, 383.

TABLE OF CASES

American Fire & Cas. Co. v. First Nat'l City Bank, 411 F.2d 755 (1st Cir. 1969)—§ 342.

American Handkerchief Corp. v. Frannat Realty Co., 17 N.J. 12, 109 A.2d 793 (1954)—§ 87.

American Home Improvement, Inc. v. MacIver, 105 N.H. 435, 201 A.2d 886 (1964)—§ 208.

American Nat'l Bank v. A. G. Somerville, Inc., 191 Cal. 364, 216 P. 376 (1923)—§ 336.

American Oil Co. v. Estate of Wigley, 251 Miss. 275, 169 So.2d 454 (1964)— §§ 47, 48.

American Sugar Ref. Co. v. Blake, 102 Conn. 194, 128 A. 523 (1925)—§ 227.

American Sur. v. United States, 368 F.2d 475 (9th Cir. 1966)—§ 374.

Amreican Textile Machine Corp. v. United States, 220 F.2d 584 (6th Cir. 1955)—§ 281.

American Trading & Production Corp. v. Shell Int'l Marine, Ltd., 453 F.2d 939 (2d Cir. 1972)—§ 261.

Americo Constr. Co., United States v., 168 F.Supp. 760 (D.Mass.1958)—§ 373.

Amerine Nat'l Corp. v. Denver Feed Co., 493 F.2d 1275 (10th Cir. 1974)—§ 223.

Amies v. Wesnofske, 255 N.Y. 156, 174 N.E. 436 (1931)—§ 227.

Ammons v. Wilson, 176 Miss. 645, 170 So. 227 (1936)—§ 69.

Amoco Oil Co. v. Toppert, 56 Ill.App.3d 595, 14 Ill.Dec. 595, 371 N.E.2d 1294 (1978)—§§ 178, 181.

Amtorg Trading Corp. v. Miehle Printing Press & Mfg. Co., 206 F.2d 103 (2d Cir. 1953)—§§ 265, 374.

Anacortes Veneer, State ex rel. Schoblom v., 42 Wash.2d 338, 255 P.2d 379 (1953)—§ 367.

Anchorage Centennial Development Co. v. Van Wormer & Rodrigues, 443 P.2d 596 (Alaska 1968)—§ 350.

Anderson v. Anderson, 521 P.2d 437 (Okl.Ct.App.1974)—§§ 128, 129.

Anderson v. Cliff Gold Mining Co., 47 Wyo. 349, 38 P.2d 334 (1934)—§ 272.

Anderson v. Kammeier, 262 N.W.2d 366 (Minn.1978)—§§ 212, 214, 215.

Anderson v. Lord, 87 N.H. 474, 183 A. 269 (1936)—§ 273.

Anderson v. May, 50 Minn. 280, 52 N.W. 530 (1892)—§ 263.

Anderson v. Rexroad, 175 Kan. 676, 266 P.2d 320 (1954)—§ 313.

Anderson v. Tri-State Home Improvement Co., 268 Wis. 455, 67 N.W.2d 853 (1955)—§ 171.

Anderson Bros. v. O'Meara, 306 F.2d 672 (5th Cir. 1962)—§§ 152, 157.

Angel v. Murray, 113 R.I. 482, 322 A.2d 630 (1974)—§ 89.

Anglo-California Trust Co. v. Hall, 61 Utah 223, 211 P. 991 (1922)—§ 336.

Angus v. Scully, 176 Mass. 357, 57 N.E. 674 (1900)—§ 377.

Apley Estates Co. v. De Bernales, [1947] 1 Ch. 217 (C.A.)—§ 291.

Appliances v. Queen Stove Works, 228 Minn. 55, 36 N.W.2d 121 (1949)— § 351.

Arconti & Sons, Inc., Bart v. Armes-Ennis, Inc., 275 Md. 295, 340 A.2d 225 (1975) —§ 232.

Arcuri v. Weiss, 198 Pa.Super.Ct. 506, 184 A.2d 24 (1962)—§ 131.

Ard Dr. Pepper Bottling Co. v. Dr. Pepper Co., 202 F.2d 372 (5th Cir. 1953)— § 228.

Arizona Bd. of Regents v. Arizona York Refrigeration Co., 115 Ariz. 338, 565 P.2d 518 (1977)—§ 4.

Arkansas Bankers' Ass'n v. Ligon, 174 Ark. 234, 295 S.W. 4, 53 A.L.R. 534 (1927)—§ 51.

Armstrong v. Armstrong, 142 Ill.App. 507 (1908)—§ 332.

Baetjer v. New England Alcohol Co., 319 Mass. 592, 66 N.E.2d 798 (1946)—
§ 261.

Bailey v. Bode Bros., 195 Wis. 264, 218 N.W. 174 (1928)—§ 172.

Bailey v. De Crespigny, L.R. 4 Q.B. 180 (1869)—§ 264.

Bailey v. Interstate Airmotive, 358 Mo. 1121, 219 S.W.2d 333 (1949)—§ 373.

Bailey v. Iowa Beef Processors, 213 N.W.2d 642 (Iowa 1973)—§ 313.

Bailey v. Lisle Mfg. Co., 238 F. 257 (8th Cir. 1916)—§ 157.

Bailey v. West, 105 R.I. 61, 249 A.2d 414 (1969)—§§ 19, 21.

Bailey Loan Co. v. Hall, 110 Cal. 490, 42 P. 962 (1895)—§ 291.

Baillie Lumber Co. v. Kincaid Carolina Corp., 4 N.C.App. 342, 167 S.E.2d 85
(1969)—§ 281.

Baird, State ex rel Schilling v., 65 Wis.2d 394, 222 N.W.2d 666 (1974)—§ 347.

Baird Co., James v. Gimbel Bros., 64 F.2d 344 (2d Cir. 1933)—§ 87.

Baird Inv. Co., Thomas J. v. Harris, 209 F. 291 (10th Cir. 1913)—§ 238.

Baldock v. Johnson, 14 Or. 542, 13 P. 434 (1887)—§ 170.

Baldwin v. Ely, 127 Pa.Super.Ct. 110, 193 A. 299 (1937)—Ch. 13; 290.

Balfour v. Balfour, [1919] 2 K.B. 571 (C.A.)—§ 21.

Baltimore & O. R. R. v. United States, 261 U.S. 592 (1923)—§ 19.

Bancredit, Inc. v. Bethea, 68 N.J.Super. 62, 172 A.2d 10 (1961)—§ 163.

Bank of America Nat'l Trust & Sav. Ass'n v. McLaughlin, 152 Cal.App.2d Supp.
911, 313 P.2d 220 (1957)—§ 328.

Bank of North Carolina v. Cranfill, 297 N.C. 43, 253 S.E.2d 1 (1979)—§ 96.

Bank of North Carolina v. Cranfill, 37 N.C.App. 182, 245 S.E.2d 538 (1978)—
§ 218.

Bank of Tucson v. Adrian, 245 F.Supp. 595 (D.Minn.1965)—§ 176.

Bankers Trust Co. v. Martin, 51 A.D.2d 411, 381 N.Y.S.2d 1001 (3d Dep't
1976)—§ 13.

Banker's Trust Co. v. Steenburn, 95 Misc.2d 967, 409 N.Y.S.2d 51 (Sup.Ct.1978)
—§ 305.

Bannister v. Victoria Coal & Coke Co., 63 W.Va. 502, 61 S.E. 338 (1908)—§ 250.

Banta v. Stamford Motor Co., 89 Conn. 51, 92 A. 665 (1914)—§ 356.

Barbara Oil Co. v. Patrick Petroleum Co., 1 Kan.App.2d 437, 566 P.2d 389
(1977)—§§ 225, 228.

Barber v. Rathvon, 250 Mass. 479, 145 N.E. 866 (1925)—§ 82.

Barcroft Woods, Inc. v. Francis, 201 Va. 405, 111 S.E.2d 512 (1959)—§ 261.

Bard v. Kent, 19 Cal.2d 449, 122 P.2d 8 (1942)—§ 87.

Barkis v. Scott, 34 Cal.2d 116, 208 P.2d 367 (1949)—§ 242.

Barlow v. Jones, 87 A. 649 (N.J.Ch.1913)—§ 153.

Barnebey v. Barron G. Collier, Inc., 65 F.2d 864 (8th Cir. 1933)—§ 63.

Barnett v. Kunkle, 256 F. 644 (8th Cir. 1919)—§ 170.

Bartlett v. Department of Transp., 40 Md.App. 47, 388 A.2d 930 (1978)—§§ 152,
155, 158.

Bauer v. Sawyer, 8 Ill.2d 351, 134 N.E.2d 329 (1956)—§§ 356, 357, 361.

Baugh v. Darley, 112 Utah 1, 184 P.2d 335 (1947)—§§ 126, 375.

Baum v. Rock, 106 Colo. 567, 108 P.2d 230 (1940)—§ 323.

Bauman v. McManus, 75 Kan. 106, 89 P. 15 (1907)—§ 57.

Bauman & Vogel, C.P.A. v. Del Vecchio, 423 F.Supp. 1041 (E.D.Pa.1976)—
§ 197.

Beach v. First Fed. Sav. & Loan Ass'n, 140 Ga.App. 882, 232 S.E.2d 158 (1977)—
§ 234.

Beacon Constr. Co. v. Prepakt Concrete Co., 375 F.2d 977 (1st Cir. 1967)—
§ 336.

Berwick & Smith Co. v. Salem Press, Inc., 331 Mass. 196, 117 N.E.2d 825 (1954)—§ 221.

Bess v. Bothman, 257 N.W.2d 791 (Minn.1977)—§§ 184, 188.

Bethea v. Investors Loan Corp., 197 A.2d 448 (D.C.Ct.App.1964)—§ 231.

Bethea v. Wall, 362 S.W.2d 414 (Tex.Civ.App.1962)—§ 129.

Bethlehem Steel Corp. v. Centex Homes Corp., 327 So.2d 837 (Fla.Dist.Ct.App. 1976)—§ 157.

Bethlehem Steel Corp. v. Chicago, 350 F.2d 649 (7th Cir. 1965)—§ 356.

Bethlehem Steel Co., United States v., 205 U.S. 105 (1907)—§ 356.

Bettancourt v. Gilroy Theatre Co., 120 Cal.App.2d 364, 261 P.2d 351 (1953)—§ 362.

Bezin v. Ginsburg, 59 Ill.App.3d 429, 16 Ill.Dec. 595, 375 N.E.2d 468 (1978)—§ 172.

Bickers v. Pinnell, 199 Va. 444, 100 S.E.2d 20 (1957)—§ 92.

Biestek v. Varricchio, 34 Conn.Supp. 620, 380 A.2d 1351 (Super.Ct.1977)—§ 118.

Billeter v. Posell, 94 Cal.App.2d 858, 211 P.2d 621 (1949)—§§ 347, 350.

Bimestefer v. Bimestefer, 205 Md. 541, 109 A.2d 768 (1954)—§ 322.

Bird v. Blackwell, 135 Mo.App. 23, 115 S.W. 487 (1909)—§ 126.

Bird v. Monroe, 66 Me. 337 (1887)—§ 235.

Biren v. Kluver, 35 Ill.App.3d 692, 342 N.E.2d 325 (1976)—§§ 155, 158.

Birmingham Waterworks Co. v. Keiley, 2 Ala.App. 629, 56 So. 838 (1911)—§ 355.

Bishop v. Eaton, 161 Mass. 496, 37 N.E. 665 (1894)—§ 54.

Bitzer v. Moock's Executor and Trustee, 271 S.W.2d 877 (Ky.1954)—§ 147.

Bixler v. Wright, 116 Me. 133, 100 A. 467 (1917)—§§ 161, 164, 172.

Blaising v. Mills, —— Ind.App. ——, 374 N.E.2d 1166 (1978)—§ 171.

Blake v. Voight, 134 N.Y. 69, 31 N.E. 256 (1892)—§ 130.

Blanchard v. Detroit, Lansing & Lake Michigan R. R., 31 Mich. 43 (1875)—§ 366.

Blank v. Rodgers, 82 Cal.App. 35, 255 P. 235 (1927)—§ 141.

Blanton v. Williams, 209 Ga. 16, 70 S.E.2d 461 (1952)—§ 33.

Bleck v. Stepanich, 64 Ill.App.3d 436, 21 Ill.Dec. 254, 381 N.E.2d 363 (1978)—§ 210.

Bleyer v. Veeder, 119 N.J.Eq. 398, 183 A.2d 203 (1936)—§§ 161, 166.

Bliss v. California Co-op. Producers, 30 Cal.2d 240, 181 P.2d 369 (1947)—§ 336.

Block v. Shaw, 78 Ark. 511, 95 S.W. 806 (1906)—§ 360.

Bloomgarden v. Coyer, 479 F.2d 201 (D.C.Cir. 1973)—§ 4.

Bloor v. Falstaff Brewing Corp., 601 F.2d 609 (2d Cir. 1979)—§ 205.

Bloor v. Falstaff Brewing Corp., 454 F.Supp. 258 (S.D.N.Y.1978)—§ 261.

Blount-Midyette & Co. v. Aeroglide Corp., 254 N.C. 484, 119 S.E.2d 225 (1961)—§ 261.

Blue Val. Creamery Co. v. Consolidated Products, 97 F.2d 23 (8th Cir. 1938)—§ 130.

Blue Val. Creamery Co. v. Consolidated Products, 81 F.2d 182 (8th Cir. 1936)—§§ 130, 131, 132.

Blum v. City of Hillsboro, 49 Wis.2d 667, 183 N.W.2d 47 (1971)—§ 197.

Board of Control of Eastern Michigan Univ. v. Burgess, 45 Mich.App. 183, 206 N.W.2d 256 (1973)—§§ 42, 87.

Board of Educ. v. Townsend, 63 Ohio St. 514, 59 N.E. 223 (1900)—§ 263.

Board of Educ. of Floyd County v. Hooper, 350 S.W.2d 629 (Ky.1961)—§ 153.

Board of Regents v. Davis, 14 Cal.3d 33, 120 Cal.Rptr. 407, 533 P.2d 1047 (1975)—§ 13.

Brewer v. Custom Builders Corp., 42 Ill.App.3d 668, 1 Ill.Dec. 377, 356 N.E.2d 565 (1976)—§§ 241, 351, 352.

Brewer v. Horst-Lachmund Co., 127 Cal. 643, 60 P. 418 (1900)—§ 131.

Brewer v. Tracy, 198 Neb. 503, 253 N.W.2d 319 (1977)—§ 188.

Brice v. Bannister, L. R., 3 Q.B.D. 569 (1878)—§ 338.

Bridger v. Mangum, 35 N.C.App. 569, 241 S.E.2d 726 (1978)—§ 280.

Bridgkort Racquet Club v. University Bank, 85 Wis.2d 706, 271 N.W.2d 165 (Ct.App.1978)—§§ 237, 241.

Brill v. Jewett, 262 F. 935 (5th Cir. 1920)—§ 296.

Brimson v. Pearrow, 218 Ark. 27, 234 S.W.2d 214 (1950)—§ 372.

British Films Do Brasil, Ltda. v. London Film Prods., 8 Misc.2d 848, 166 N.Y.S.2d 703 (1957)—§ 240.

British Waggon Co. v. Lea & Co., 5 Q.B.Div. 149 (1880)—§ 320.

Britt v. Davis, 239 Ga. 747, 238 S.E.2d 881 (1977)—§ 188.

Britton v. Turner, 6 N.H. 481 (1834)—§ 374.

Broadnax v. Ledbetter, 100 Tex. 375, 99 S.W. 1111 (1907)—§ 23.

Brock v. Button, 187 Wash. 27, 59 P.2d 761 (1936)—§ 110.

Brock & Davis Co. v. Charleston Nat'l Bank, 443 F.Supp. 1175 (S.D.W.Va. 1977)—§ 116.

Brooks v. Jensen, 75 Idaho 201, 270 P.2d 425 (1954)—§ 376.

Brooks v. Mitchell, 163 Md. 1, 161 A. 261 (1932)—§ 332.

Brooks v. Preston, 106 Md. 693, 68 A. 294 (1907)—§ 82.

Brooks v. R. A. Clark's Garage, Inc., 117 N.H. 770, 378 A.2d 1144 (1977)—§ 181.

Brooks v. Scoville, 81 Utah 163, 17 P.2d 218 (1932)—§ 238.

Brooks v. Towson Realty, 223 Md. 61, 162 A.2d 431 (1960)—§§ 158, 364.

Brooks Towers Corp. v. Hunkin-Conkey Constr. Co., 454 F.2d 1203 (10th Cir. 1972)—§ 69.

Brosam v. Employer's Mut. Cas. Co., 61 Ill.App.2d 183, 209 N.E.2d 350 (1965)—§ 155.

Brown v. Bowers Constr. Co., 236 N.C. 462, 73 S.E.2d 147 (1952)—§ 318.

Brown v. Coastal Truckways, Inc., 44 N.C.App. 454, 261 S.E.2d 266 (1980)—§ 281.

Brown v. Lamphear, 35 Vt. 252 (1862)—§ 158.

Brown v. Oliver, 123 Kan. 711, 256 P. 1008 (1927)—§§ 209, 213.

Brown v. St. Paul, Minneapolis & Manitoba Ry., 36 Minn. 236, 31 N.W. 941 (1886)—§ 373.

Brownfield v. Holland, 63 Wash. 86, 114 P. 890 (1911)—Ch. 13, § 296.

Bruce's Juices v. American Can Co., 330 U.S. 743 (1947)—§ 178.

Bruner v. Hegyi, 42 Cal.App. 97, 183 P. 369 (1919)—§ 228.

Buccini v. Paterno Constr. Co., 253 N.Y. 256, 170 N.E. 910 (1930)—§§ 267, 377.

Budget Way Cleaners & Laundry v. Simon, 151 Cal.App.2d 476, 311 P.2d 591 (1957)—§ 225.

Buehler v. Galt, 35 Ill.App. 225 (1889)—§ 63.

Buel v. Kansas City Life Ins. Co., 32 N.M. 34, 250 P. 635 (1926)—§ 74.

Buell v. Deschutes County Municipal Improvement Dist., 208 Or. 56, 298 P.2d 1000 (1956)—§ 92.

Buettner v. Buettner, 89 Nev. 39, 505 P.2d 600 (1973)—§ 190.

Buffinton v. Chase, 152 Mass. 534, 25 N.E. 977 (1890)—§ 82.

Builder's Concrete Co. v. Fred Faubel and Sons, 58 Ill.App.3d 100, 15 Ill.Dec. 517, 373 N.E.2d 863 (1978)—§ 257.

Bunge Corp. v. Recker, 519 F.2d 449 (8th Cir. 1975)—§ 261.

Bunting v. Orendorf, 152 Miss. 327, 120 So. 182 (1929)—§ 265.

C

Campbell v. Tennessee Val. Auth., 421 F.2d 293 (5th Cir. 1969)—§§ 4, 371.

Campbell Soup Co. v. Wentz, 172 F.2d 80 (3d Cir. 1948)—§§ 208, 364.

Canada v. Allstate Ins. Co., 411 F.2d 517 (5th Cir. 1969)—§ 150.

Canadian Indus. Alcohol Co. v. Dunbar Molasses Co., 258 N.Y. 194, 179 N.E. 383 (1932)—§ 261.

Canadian Steel Foundries, Ltd. v. Thomas Furnace Co., 186 Wis. 557, 203 N.W. 355 (1925)—§ 242.

Canfield v. Spear, 44 Ill.2d 49, 254 N.E.2d 433 (1969)—§ 188.

Canister Co. v. Wood & Selick, Inc., 73 F.2d 312 (3d Cir. 1934)—§ 147.

Canter v. Lindsey, 575 S.W.2d 331 (Tex.Civ.App.1978)—§ 212.

Canterbury v. Bank of Sparta, 91 Wis. 53, 64 N.W. 311, 30 L.R.A. 845 (1895)— § 63.

Caplan v. Schroeder, 56 Cal.2d 515, 15 Cal.Rptr. 145, 364 P.2d 321 (1961)— § 374.

Caples v. Steel, 7 Or. 491 (1879)—§ 161.

Capps v. Georgia Pacific Corp., 253 Or. 248, 453 P.2d 935 (1969)—§ 175.

Cargill, Inc. v. Atkins Farms, Inc., 422 F.Supp. 239 (W.D.Ark.1976)—§§ 237, 242.

Cargill, Inc. v. Fickbohm, 252 N.W.2d 739 (Iowa 1977)—§ 216.

Cargill, Inc. v. Stafford, 553 F.2d 1222 (10th Cir. 1977)—§ 350.

Carlill v. Carbolic Smoke Ball Co., [1893] 1 Q.B. 256—§§ 29, 54.

Carlin Constr. Co., P. J. v. Whiffen Elec. Co., 66 A.D.2d 684, 411 N.Y.S.2d 27 (1st Dep't 1978)—§ 130.

Carlson v. Leonardo Truck Lines, 13 Wash.App. 795, 538 P.2d 130 (1975)— § 255.

Carlson v. Olson, 256 N.W.2d 249 (Minn.1977)—§ 189.

Carluccio v. 607 Hudson St. Holding Co., 139 N.J.Eq. 481, 52 A.2d 56 (1947) —§ 320.

Carpel v. Saget Studios, 326 F.Supp. 1331 (E.D.Pa.1971)—§ 353.

Carr v. Mahaska County Bankers Ass'n, 222 Iowa 411, 269 N.W. 494 (1936)— § 41.

Carrig v. Gilbert Varker Corp., 314 Mass. 351, 50 N.E.2d 59 (1943)—§ 240.

Carroll v. Bowersock, 100 Kan. 270, 164 P. 143 (1917)—§§ 263, 377.

Carroll v. McNeill Indus., 296 N.C. 205, 250 S.E.2d 60 (1978)—§ 282.

Carroll v. McNeill Indus., 37 N.C.App. 10, 245 S.E.2d 204 (1978)—§ 282.

Carroll v. Mutual of Omaha Ins. Co., 354 F.Supp. 1260 (W.D.Va.1973)—§ 243.

Carrolton Associates v. Abrams, 57 Misc.2d 617, 293 N.Y.S.2d 159 (Sup.Ct.1968) —§§ 112, 116.

Carsek Corp. v. Stephen Schifter, Inc., 431 Pa. 550, 246 A.2d 365 (1968)— § 242.

Carter v. Adler, 138 Cal.App.2d 63, 291 P.2d 111 (1955)—§ 205.

Carter v. Sherburne Corp., 132 Vt. 88, 315 A.2d 870 (1974)—§§ 218, 229.

Carter's Claim, In re, 390 Pa. 365, 134 A.2d 908 (1957)—§ 226.

Cash v. Clark, 61 Mo.App. 636 (1895)—§ 133.

Casper v. Bankers' Life Ins. Co., 238 Mich. 300, 212 N.W. 970 (1927)—§ 169.

Cassiday v. Cassiday, 256 Md. 5, 259 A.2d 299 (1969)—§ 332.

Cassola, Matter of, 183 Misc. 66, 47 N.Y.S.2d 90 (Surr.Ct.1944)—§ 332.

Castellano v. State, 43 N.Y.2d 909, 403 N.Y.S.2d 724, 374 N.E.2d 618 (1978)— § 202.

Catholic Charities of Diocese of Galveston v. Harper, 161 Tex. 21, 337 S.W.2d 111 (1960)—§ 191.

Cattle Feeders, Inc. v. Jordan, 549 S.W.2d 29 (Tex.Civ.App.1977)—§ 25.

TABLE OF CASES

310

Choice v. City of Dallas, 210 S.W. 753 (Tex.Civ.App.1919)—§ 23.

Chouinard v. Chouinard, 568 F.2d 430 (5th Cir. 1978)—§ 176.

Christensen v. Larson, 77 N.W.2d 441 (N.D.1956)—§ 16.

Christy v. Pilkinton, 224 Ark. 407, 273 S.W.2d 533 (1954)—§ 261.

Chrysler Corp. v. E. Shavitz & Sons, 536 F.2d 743 (7th Cir. 1976)—§ 351.

Chrysler Corp. v. Quimby, 51 Del. 254, 144 A.2d 123 (1958)—§ 90.

Ciofalo v. Vic Tanny Gyms, Inc., 10 N.Y.2d 294, 220 N.Y.S.2d 962, 177 N.E.2d 925 (1961)—§ 208.

Cities Serv. Helex, Inc. v. United States, 211 Ct.Cl. 222, 543 F.2d 1306 (1976)—§ 243.

Citizens Home Ins. Co. v. Glisson, 191 Va. 582, 61 S.E.2d 859 (1950)—§ 242.

Citizens Nat'l Bank v. L. L. Glascock, Inc., 243 So.2d 67 (Miss.1971)—§ 203.

City of (see name of city)

City Stores Co. v. Ammerman, 266 F.Supp. 766 (D.D.C.1967)—§§ 362, 366.

Civic Plaza Nat'l Bank v. First Nat'l Bank, 401 F.2d 193 (8th Cir. 1968)—§ 58.

Clancy v. Pacenti, 15 Ill.App.2d 171, 145 N.E.2d 802 (1952)—§ 152.

Clark v. General Cleaning Co., 345 Mass. 62, 185 N.E.2d 749 (1962)—§ 323.

Clark v. Gulesian, 197 Mass. 492, 84 N.E. 94 (1908)—§ 234.

Clark v. Ingle, 58 N.M. 136, 266 P.2d 672 (1954)—§ 251.

Clark v. Kirsner, 196 Md. 52, 74 A.2d 830 (1950)—§ 162.

Clark v. Marsiglia, 1 Denio 317 (N.Y.Sup.Ct.1845)—§ 350.

Clark v. Snelling, 205 F. 240 (1st Cir. 1913)—§ 360.

Clark Advertising Agency v. Avco Broadcasting Co., —— Ind.App. ——, 383 N.E.2d 353 (1978)—§ 221.

Clarke Contracting Co. v. City of New York, 229 N.Y. 413, 128 N.E. 241 (1920)—§ 237.

Clarksville Land Co. v. Harriman, 68 N.H. 374, 44 A. 527 (1895)—§ 263.

Clauser v. Taylor, 44 Cal.App.2d 453, 112 P.2d 661 (1941)—§ 161.

Claycraft Co. v. John Bowen Co., 287 Mass. 255, 191 N.E. 403 (1934)—§ 321.

Clayman v. Goodman Properties, 518 F.2d 1026 (D.C.Cir. 1973)—§§ 288, 289.

Clayton & Jack Waller Ltd., Herbert v. Oliver, A.C. 209 (H.L.1930)—§ 344.

Clegg v. Brannan, 111 Tex. 367, 234 S.W. 1076 (1921)—§ 135.

Clement v. British America Assur. Co., 141 Mass. 298, 5 N.E. 847 (1886)—§ 153.

Clements Auto Co. v. Service Bureau Corp., 444 F.2d 169 (8th Cir. 1971)—§§ 159, 196.

Cleveland Bd. of Educ. v. LaFleur, 414 U.S. 632 (1974)—§ 12.

Clifford v. Carrols New York Development Corp., 50 Misc.2d 741, 271 N.Y.S.2d 465 (Sup.Ct.1966)—§ 132.

Clifford v. Great Falls Gas Co., 68 Mont. 300, 216 P. 1114 (1923)—§ 176.

Cline, In re Estate of, 250 Iowa 265, 93 N.W.2d 708 (1958)—§ 13.

Clinic Masters, Inc. v. District Court, 556 P.2d 473 (Colo.1976)—§ 208.

Clydebank Eng'r & Sb. Co. v. Castenada, A.C. 6 (1905)—§ 347.

Coast Indus. v. Noonan, 4 Conn.Cir.Ct. 333, 231 A.2d 663 (1966)—§ 350.

Coates v. Locust Point Co., 102 Md. 291, 62 A. 625 (1905)—§ 181.

Cober v. Connolly, 20 Cal.2d 741, 128 P.2d 519 (1942)—§ 299.

Cochran v. Taylor, 273 N.Y. 172, 7 N.E.2d 89 (1937)—§ 87.

Cochrane v. Szpakowski, 355 Pa. 357, 49 A.2d 692 (1946)—§ 360.

Cockerill v. Wilson, 51 Ill.2d 179, 281 N.E.2d 648 (1972)—§ 188.

Coffey v. Commonwealth, 18 Ky.L.Rep. 646, 37 S.W. 575 (1896)—§ 51.

Coffman Indus., Inc. v. Gorman-Taber Co., 521 S.W.2d 763 (Mo.Ct.App.1975)—§§ 2, 24, 39, 41, 45.

TABLE OF CASES

312

Consolidated Edison Co., United States v., 452 F.Supp. 638 (S.D.N.Y.1977)—
§ 139.

Consolidated Gas & Equipment Co. v. Thompson, 405 S.W.2d 333 (Tex.1966)—
§ 127.

Consolidated Pretrial Proceedings in Air West Securities Litigation, In re,
436 F.Supp. 1281 (N.D.Cal.1977)—§§ 175, 176.

Constantino v. Massachusetts Acc. Co., 221 Mass. 464, 109 N.E. 447 (1915)—
§ 271.

Continental Cas. Co. v. Associated Pipe & Supply Co., 310 F.Supp. 1207 (E.D.
La.1969)—§ 259.

Continental Forest Products v. Chandler Supply Co., 95 Idaho 739, 518 P.2d
1201 (1974)—§ 4.

Continental Grain Co. v. Simpson Feed Co., 102 F.Supp. 354 (E.D.Ark.1951)—
§ 242.

Continental Mortgage Investors v. Sailboat Key, Inc., 354 So.2d 67 (Fla.Dist.
Ct.App.1977)—§ 179.

Continental Supermarket Food Serv. v. Soboski, 210 Pa.Super.Ct. 304, 232
A.2d 216 (1967)—§ 231.

Contract Buyers League v. F & F Inv., 300 F.Supp. 210 (N.D.Ill.1969)—§ 208.

Control Data Corp. v. I. B. M., 306 F.Supp. 839 (D.Minn.1969)—§ 313.

Cook v. Cobb, 271 S.C. 136, 245 S.E.2d 612 (1978)—§ 191.

Cook v. Lum, 55 N.J.L. 373, 26 A. 803 (1893)—§ 332.

Cooley v. Roman, 34 Or.App. 301, 578 P.2d 491 (1978)—§ 282.

Coon v. Schoeneman, 476 S.W.2d 439 (Tex.Civ.App.1972)—§ 373.

Cooney, Inc., Don L. v. Star Iron & Steel Co., 12 Wash.App. 120, 528 P.2d
487 (1974)—§ 209.

Co-op Dairy v. Dean, 102 Ariz. 573, 435 P.2d 470 (1967)—§ 130.

Cooper v. Aiello, 93 N.J.L. 336, 107 A. 473 (1919)—§ 125.

Cooper v. Holder, 21 Utah 2d 40, 440 P.2d 15 (1968)—§ 338.

Cooper v. Robert Hall Clothes, Inc., 59 Ind.App. 168, 375 N.E.2d 1142 (1978)
—§ 295.

Cooper Petroleum Co. v. LaGloria Oil & Gas Co., 436 S.W.2d 889 (Tex.1969)—
§§ 116, 139.

Cope v. Rowlands, 2 M. & W. 149 (Ex. of Pleas 1836)—§ 181.

Copeland v. Beard, 217 Ala. 216, 115 So. 389 (1928)—§ 311.

Coral Gables, Inc. v. Payne, 94 F.2d 593 (4th Cir. 1938)—§ 319.

Corbit v. J. I. Case Co., 70 Wash.2d 522, 424 P.2d 290 (1967)—§§ 3, 90.

Cord v. Neuhoff, 94 Nev. 21, 573 P.2d 1170 (1978)—§ 190.

Cordes v. Miller, 39 Mich. 581 (1878)—§ 264.

Corrigan v. Payne, 312 Mass. 589, 45 N.E.2d 829 (1942)—§ 281.

Cory v. Thames Ironworks & Shipbuilding Co., L.R., 3 Q.B. 181 (1868)—§ 351.

Cosebroom v. Marshall's Trust, 64 N.M. 170, 326 P.2d 368 (1958)—§ 125.

Costanza v. Costanza, 346 So.2d 1133 (Ala.1977)—§ 302.

Costello v. Sykes, 143 Minn. 109, 172 N.W. 907 (1919)—§ 152.

Cote, Ex parte, L.R. 9 Ch. 27 (1873)—§ 63.

Cotnam v. Wisdom, 83 Ark. 601, 104 S.W. 164 (1907)—§ 371.

Coughlin v. Blair, 41 Cal.2d 587, 262 P.2d 305 (1953)—§§ 236, 243.

Coughlin v. Knowles, 48 Mass. (7 Metc.) 57 (1843)—§ 375.

County of (see name of county)

Cousbelis v. Alexander, 315 Mass. 729, 54 N.E.2d 47 (1944)—§ 131.

Cowan v. Cowan, 247 Iowa 729, 75 N.W.2d 920 (1956)—§ 189.

Cowles' Ex'r v. Johnson, 297 Ky. 454, 179 S.W.2d 674 (1944)—§ 172.

Cowman v Allen Monuments, Inc., 500 S.W.2d 223 (Tex.Civ.App.1973)—§ 237.

D

Daburlos v. Commercial Ins. Co., 521 F.2d 18 (3d Cir. 1975)—§§ **270, 271.**

D'Aloisio v. Morton's, Inc., 342 Mass. 231, 172 N.E.2d 819 (1961)—§ **211.**

Dade County, Florida v. Palmer & Baker Engineers, 339 F.2d 208 (5th Cir. 1964)—§ **352.**

Dail v. Campbell, 191 Cal.App.2d 416, 12 Cal.Rptr. 739 (1961)—§ **312.**

Daitch Crystal Dairies, Inc. v. Neisloss, 8 A.D.2d 965, 190 N.Y.S.2d 737 (1959) —§ **205.**

Dandeneare v. Seymour, 117 N.H. 455, 374 A.2d 934 (1977)—§ **374.**

Dangerfield v. Markel, 252 N.W.2d 184 (N.D.1977)—§§ **149, 235, 246.**

Daniel Lumber Co. v. Empresas Hondurenas, 215 F.2d 465 (5th Cir. 1954)— § **152.**

Daniels v. Parker, 209 Or. 419, 306 P.2d 735 (1957)—§ **328.**

Dansby v. Buck, 92 Ariz. 1, 373 P.2d 1 (1962)—§ **152.**

Darling v. Nineteen-Eighty Corp., 176 N.W.2d 765 (Iowa 1970)—§ **63.**

Dartmouth College v. Woodward, 17 U.S. (4 Wheat.) 518 (1819)—**Introduction.**

Dashiell, State v., 195 Md. 677, 75 A.2d 348 (1950)—§ **264.**

Daugherty v. Kessler, 264 Md. 281, 286 A.2d 95 (1972)—§ **8.**

Daum Constr. Co., R. J. v. Child, 122 Utah 194, 247 P.2d 817 (1952)—§ **87.**

Davidson v. Lane, 566 S.W.2d 891 (Tenn.App.1978)—§ **155.**

Davidson v. Moss, 6 Miss. 673 (1841)—§ **165.**

Davie v. Davie, 47 Wash. 231, 91 P. 950 (1907)—§ **332.**

Davies v. London § Provincial Marine Ins. Co., 38 L.T.Rep.(N.S.) 478 (Ch.Div. 1878)—§ **176.**

Davis v. Boston Mut. Life Ins. Co., 370 Mass. 602, 351 N.E.2d 207 (1976)— § **179.**

Davis v. General Motors Acceptance Corp., 176 Neb. 865, 127 N.W.2d 907 (1964) —Ch. **15.**

Davis v. Isenstein, 257 Ill. 260, 100 N.E. 940 (1913)—§ **361.**

Davis v. Lacy, 121 F.Supp. 246 (E.D.Ky.1954)—§ **242.**

Davis v. Modern Indus. Bank, 279 N.Y. 405, 18 N.E.2d 639 (1939)—§ **311.**

Davis v. Nelson-Deppe, Inc., 91 Idaho 463, 424 P.2d 733 (1967)—§ **313.**

Davis v. Stambaugh, 163 Ill. 557, 45 N.E. 170 (1896)—§ **133.**

Davis v. Wells, 104 U.S. 159 (1881)—§ **88.**

Davis Co., John F. v. Shepard Co., 71 R.I. 499, 47 A.2d 635 (1946)—§ **202.**

Davis Sewing Machine Co. v. Richards, 115 U.S. 524 (1885)—§ **88.**

Davenport v. Beck, 576 P.2d 1199 (Okl.Ct.App.1977)—§ **155.**

De Cicco v. Schweizer, 221 N.Y. 431, 177 N.E. 807 (1917)—§§ **73, 90.**

De Freitas v. Cote, 342 Mass. 474, 174 N.E.2d 371 (1961)—§ **226.**

De Joseph v. Zambelli, 11 Pa.D. & C.2d 447, 139 A.2d 644 (1957)—§ **160.**

De Leon v. Aldrete, 398 S.W.2d 160 (Tex.Civ.App.1965)—§ **374.**

De Long Corp. v. Lucas, 176 F.Supp. 104 (S.D.N.Y.1959)—§ **207.**

De Lucca v. Flamingo Corp., 121 So.2d 803 (Fla.Dist.Ct.App.1960)—§ **126.**

De Martini v. Industrial Acc. Comm'n, 90 Cal.App.2d 139, 202 P.2d 828 (1949)— § **9.**

De Paola v. City of New York, 90 Misc.2d 379, 394 N.Y.S.2d 525 (1977)—§ **153.**

De Pova v. Camden Forge Co., 254 F.2d 248 (3d Cir. 1958)—§ **89.**

De Wolf v. Rabaud, 26 U.S. (1 Peters) 476 (1828)—§ **131.**

Dearborn Motors Credit Corp. v. Neel, 184 Kan. 437, 337 P.2d 992 (1959)— § **336.**

DeBlasio Constr. Co., United States ex rel. A. V. v. Mountain States Constr. Co., 588 F.2d 259 (9th Cir. 1978)—§ **241.**

Dillon v. AFBIC Development Corp., 420 F.Supp. 572 (S.D.Ala.1976)—§ 24.

Dimick v. J. K. Noonan, 242 S.W.2d 599 (Mo.Ct.App.1951)—§ 348.

Dingley v. Oler, 117 U.S. 490 (1886)—§ 250.

Dinkle v. Denton, 68 N.M. 108, 359 P.2d 345 (1961)—§ 299.

D'Ippolito v. Castoro, 51 N.J. 584, 242 A.2d 617 (1968)—§ 294.

Distribu-Dor v. Karadnis, 11 Cal.App.3d 463, 90 Cal.Rptr. 231 (1970)—§ 347.

Diversified Environments, Inc. v. Olivetti Corp., 461 F.Supp. 286 (M.D.Pa. 1978)—§ 209.

Division of Labor Law Enforcement v. Transpacific Transp. Co., 69 Cal.App. 3d 268, 137 Cal.Rptr. 855 (1977)—§ 90.

Dixon, Irmaos & Cia, Ltda. v. Chase Nat'l Bank, 144 F.2d 759 (2d Cir. 1944)— § 220.

Dlug v. Wooldridge, 189 Colo. 164, 538 P.2d 883 (1975)—§§ 152, 158.

Dobbins v. Hupp, 562 S.W.2d 736 (Mo.App.1978)—§ 177.

Dobias v. White, 239 N.C. 409, 80 S.E.2d 23 (1954)—§§ 125, 281.

Doctorman v. Schroeder, 92 N.J.Eq. 676, 114 A. 810 (1921)—§ 242.

Dodge v. Blood, 299 Mich. 364, 300 N.W. 121 (1941)—§ 131.

Doehler Die Casting Co. v. Holmes, 52 N.Y.S.2d 321 (Sup.Ct.1944)—§ 54.

D'Oench, Duhme & Co. v. F. D. I. C., 315 U.S. 447 (1942)—§ 90.

Doll v. Crume, 41 Neb. 655, 59 N.W. 806 (1894)—§ 309.

Donlan v. City of Boston, 223 Mass. 285, 111 N.E. 718 (1916)—§ 267.

Donovan v. Middlebrook, 95 A.D. 365, 88 N.Y.S. 607 (1st Dep't 1904)—§ 330.

Dooley v. Lachut, 103 R.I. 21, 234 A.2d 366 (1967)—Ch. 5, §§ 126, 139.

D'Orsay Equipment Co. v. United States Rubber Co., 302 F.2d 777 (1st Cir. 1962)—§ 223.

D'Orazi v. Bank of Canton, 254 Cal.App.2d 901, 62 Cal.Rptr. 704 (1967)— § 326.

Dorton v. Collins & Aikman Corp., 453 F.2d 1161 (6th Cir. 1972)—§§ 59, 69.

Doughboy Indus., Inc., In re (Pantasote Co.), 17 A.D.2d 216, 233 N.Y.S.2d 488 (1962)—§ 201.

Dour v. Village of Port Jefferson, 89 Misc.2d 146, 390 N.Y.S.2d 965 (1976)— § 240.

Doushkess v. Burger Brewing Co., 20 A.D. 375, 47 N.Y.S. 312 (1897)—§ 351.

Dove Sheet Metal, Inc. v. Hays Heating & Plumbing Co., 249 F.Supp. 366 (N. D.Fla.1966)—§ 130.

Dover Pool & Racquet Club v. Brooking, 366 Mass. 629, 322 N.E.2d 168 (1975)— §§ 151, 152.

Dowd Box Co., Charles v. Courtney, 368 U.S. 502 (1962)—§ 302.

Dowling v. Whites Lumber & Supply Co., 170 Miss. 267, 154 So. 703 (1934)— § 350.

Downey v. Tharp, 63 Pa. 322 (1869)—§ 336.

Downs Food Co., Tony v. United States, 209 Ct.Cl. 31, 530 F.2d 367 (1976)— § 264.

Doyle v. Dixon, 97 Mass. 208 (1867)—§ 130.

Doyle v. Northrop Corp., 455 F.Supp. 1318 (D.N.J.1978)—§§ 210, 213.

Doyle v. South Pittsburgh Water Co., 414 Pa. 199, 199 A.2d 875 (1964)—§ 313.

Dracopoulas v. Rachal, 411 S.W.2d 719 (Tex.1967)—§ 149.

Drake v. Bell, 26 Misc. 237, 55 N.Y.S. 945 (1899)—§ 86.

Drennan v. Star Paving Co., 51 Cal.2d 409, 333 P.2d 757 (1958)—§§ 87, 153.

Drewen v. Bank of Manhattan Co., 31 N.J. 110, 155 A.2d 529 (1959)—§ 307.

Drury v. Hayden, 111 U.S. 223 (1884)—§ 312.

du Pont de Bie v. Vredenburg, 490 F.2d 1057 (4th Cir. 1974)—§§ 317, 321.

E

CITED IN REPORTER'S NOTES

Edwards Real Estate, Inc., Ken v. Molero's Marina, Inc., 355 So.2d 1067 (La. App.1978)—§ 286.

Ehrlich, Inc., Milton L. v. Unit Frame & Floor Corp., 5 N.Y.2d 275, 184 N.Y. S.2d 334, 157 N.E.2d 495 (1959)—§ 318.

Eigenman v. Clark, 21 Ind.App. 129, 51 N.E. 725 (1898)—§ 336.

Ekco Enterprises v. Remi Fortin Constr., Inc., 118 N.H. 37, 382 A.2d 368 (1978)—§ 155.

El Fredo Pizza v. Roto-Flex Oven Co., 199 Neb. 697, 261 N.W.2d 358 (1978)— § 352.

El Rio Oils (Canada) Ltd. v. Pacific Coast Asphalt Co., 95 Cal.App.2d 186, 213 P.2d 1 (1949)—§ 261.

Elder v. Doerr, 175 Neb. 483, 122 N.W.2d 528 (1963)—Ch. 15.

Eldridge v. May, 129 Me. 112, 150 A. 378 (1930)—§ 177.

Elgin Mills, Inc. v. Melcher, 181 Neb. 17, 146 N.W.2d 573 (1966)—§ 211.

Elkins-Dell Mfg. Co., In re, 253 F.Supp. 864 (E.D.Pa.1966)—§ 208.

Elliott v. Owen, 244 N.C. 684, 94 S.E.2d 833 (1956)—§ 131.

Elliott v. Snyder, 246 S.C. 186, 143 S.E.2d 374 (1965)—§ 229.

Elliott Leases Cars, Inc. v. Quigley, 118 R.I. 321, 373 A.2d 810 (1977)—§§ 202, 203.

Elliotte v. Lavier, 299 Mich. 353, 300 N.W. 116 (1941)—Ch. 13.

Ellsworth Dobbs, Inc. v. Johnson, 50 N.J. 528, 236 A.2d 843 (1967)—§ 227.

Elmers v. Shapiro, 91 Cal.App.2d 741, 205 P.2d 1052 (1949)—§ 198.

Elsinore Union Elementary Sch. Dist. v. Kastorff, 54 Cal.2d 380, 6 Cal.Rptr. 1, 353 P.2d 713 (1960)—§ 153.

Elting v. Clinton Mills, 36 Conn. 296 (1869)—§ 334.

Ely v. Hartford Life Ins. Co., 128 Ky. 799, 110 S.W. 265 (1908)—§ 339.

Embola v. Tuppela, 127 Wash. 285, 220 P. 789 (1923)—§ 79.

Emerich Outfitting Co., Martin v. Siegel, Cooper & Co., 237 Ill. 610, 86 N.E. 1104 (1908)—§ 263.

Emery v. Caledonia Sand & Gravel Co., 117 N.H. 441, 374 A.2d 929 (1977)— § 348.

Emmons v. Ingebretson, 279 F.Supp. 558 (N.D.Iowa 1968)—§ 42.

Emor, Inc. v. Cyprus Mines Corp., 467 F.2d 770 (3d Cir. 1972)—§§ 201, 222.

Empire Machine Co. v. Litton Business Tel. Systems, 115 Ariz. 568, 566 P.2d 1044 (1977)—§§ 50, 57, 69.

Empire Steel Corp. v. Omni Steel Corp., 378 S.W.2d 905 (Tex.Civ.App.1964)— § 135.

Employers' Liab. Assur. Corp. v. Vella, 366 Mass. 651, 321 N.E.2d 910 (1975)— § 164.

Enterprise, Inc. v. Nampa City, 96 Idaho 734, 536 P.2d 729 (1975)—§§ 236, 241.

Entores Ltd. v. Miles Far East Corp., [1955] 2 Q.B. 327 (C.A.)—§§ 63, 64.

Eppling v. Jon-T Chemicals, Inc., 363 So.2d 1263 (La.App.1978)—§ 281.

Equipment Distributors, Inc. v. Adams, 33 Conn.Supp. 528, 358 A.2d 367 (Super.Ct.1976)—§ 112.

Equitable Life Assur. Soc'y v. Branham, 250 Ky. 472, 63 S.W.2d 498 (1933)— § 243.

Equitable Life Assur. Soc'y v. Goble, 254 Ky. 614, 72 S.W.2d 35 (1934)—§ 243.

Equitable Lumber Corp. v. IPA Land Development Corp., 38 N.Y.2d 516, 381 N.Y.S.2d 459, 344 N.E.2d 391 (1976)—§ 356.

Equitable Trust Co. v. Western Pac. Ry., 244 F. 485 (S.D.N.Y.1917)—§ 253.

Erickson v. General United Life Ins. Co., 256 N.W.2d 255 (Minn.1977)—§ 282.

Erler v. Five Point Motors, 249 Cal.App.2d 560, 57 Cal.Rptr. 516 (1967)—§ 347.

TABLE OF CASES

Fay & Co., J. A. v. James Jenks & Co., 78 Mich. 312, 44 N.W. 380 (1889)—
§ **290.**

Feder v. River's Edge Restaurant, 59 Ill.App.3d 1015, 17 Ill.Dec. 547, 376 N.
E.2d 693 (1978)—§§ **217, 227.**

Federal Crop Ins. Corp. v. Merrill, 332 U.S. 380 (1947)—§ **46.**

Federal Deposit Ins. Corp. v. Bismarck Inv. Corp., 547 P.2d 212 (Utah 1976)
—§§ **288, 292.**

Federal Deposit Ins. Co. v. First Mortgage Inv., 76 Wis.2d 151, 250 N.W.2d
362 (1977)—§ **214.**

Federal Land Bank v. Christiansen, 230 Iowa 537, 298 N.W. 641 (1941)—
§ **294.**

Federal Life Ins. Co. v. Rascoe, 12 F.2d 693 (6th Cir. 1926)—§ **253.**

Federal Trust Co. v. Damron, 124 Neb. 655, 247 N.W. 589 (1933)—§ **9.**

Federated Guar. Life Ins. Co. v. Painter, 360 So.2d 309 (Ala.1978)—§ **155.**

Fedrick, Inc., C. R. v. Borg-Warner Corp., 552 F.2d 852 (9th Cir. 1977)—
§§ **110, 139.**

Feinberg v. Automobile Banking Corp., 353 F.Supp. 508 (E.D.Pa.1973)—
§§ **226, 228.**

Feinberg v. Pfeiffer Co., 322 S.W.2d 163 (Mo.Ct.App.1959)—§ **90.**

Feinstein Bros., Inc., William v. L. Z. Hotte Granite Co., 123 Vt. 167, 184
A.2d 540 (1962)—§ **233.**

Felch v. Findlay College, 119 Ohio App. 357, 200 N.E.2d 353 (1963)—§ **367.**

Ferguson v. Phoenix Assur. Co., 189 Kan. 459, 370 P.2d 379 (1962)—§ **226.**

Ferrara v. Silver, 138 Cal.App.2d 616, 292 P.2d 251 (1956)—§ **362.**

Ferrell v. Elrod, 63 Tenn.App. 129, 469 S.W.2d 678 (1971)—§ **352.**

Ferris v. Polansky, 191 Md. 79, 59 A.2d 749 (1948)—§ **228.**

Fidelity & Deposit Co. v. Scott Bros. Constr. Co., 461 F.2d 640 (5th Cir. 1972)
—§ **341.**

Fidelity Sav. & Loan Ass'n v. Aetna Life & Cas. Corp., 440 F.Supp. 862 (N.D.
Cal.1977)—§ **167.**

Fidelity Union Trust Co. v. Galm, 109 N.J.L. 111, 160 A. 645 (Ct.Err. & App.
1932)—§ **88.**

Field v. Missouri State Life Ins. Co., 77 Utah 45, 290 P. 979 (1930)—§ **56.**

Field Surgical Associates v. Shadab, 59 Ill.App.3d 991, 17 Ill.Dec. 514, 376
N.E.2d 660 (1978)—§ **188.**

Fielding v. Robertson, 141 Va. 123, 126 S.E. 231 (1925)—§ **205.**

Fields v. Hunter, 368 A.2d 1156 (D.C.Ct.App.1977)—§§ **197, 198.**

Field's Estate, In re, 11 Misc.2d 427, 172 N.Y.S.2d 740 (1958)—§ **90.**

Finance America Private Brands v. Harvey E. Hall, Inc., 380 A.2d 1377 (Del.
Super.Ct.1977)—§ **317.**

Finance Corp. v. Modern Materials Co., 312 P.2d 455 (Okl.1957)—§ **326.**

Finch v. Goldstein, 245 N.Y. 300, 157 N.E. 146 (1927)—§ **13.**

Findley v. Cunningham, 53 W.Va. 1, 44 S.E. 472 (1903)—**Ch. 5.**

Fingerhut v. Kralyn Enterprises, 71 Misc.2d 846, 337 N.Y.S.2d 394 (Sup.Ct.
1971)—§ **15.**

Finley v. Dalton, 251 S.C. 586, 164 S.E.2d 763 (1968)—§ **171.**

Finney v. Farmers Ins. Co., 21 Wash.App. 601, 586 P.2d 519 (1978)—§ **285.**

Fiorntino v. Wilson, 233 Mass. 451, 124 N.E. 283 (1919)—§ **226.**

First Bank of Russell County v. Wells, 358 So.2d 435 (Ala.1978)—§ **155.**

First Nat'l Bank v. McHasco Elec., Inc., 273 Minn. 407, 141 N.W.2d 491 (1966)
—§ **341.**

First Nat'l Bank v. Mountain States Tel. & Tel. Co., 91 N.M. 126, 571 P.2d 118
(1977)—§§ **338, 339.**

Fortune v. National Cash Register Co., 373 Mass. 96, 364 N.E.2d 1251 (1977) —§ 205.

Fosburgh v. Sando, 24 Wash.2d 586, 166 P.2d 850 (1946)—§ 156.

Foster v. Reiss, 18 N.J. 41, 112 A.2d 553 (1955)—§ 332.

Foster Wheeler Corp. v. United States, 206 Ct.Cl. 533, 513 F.2d 588 (1975)— §§ 261, 266.

Foster's Application, 23 Pa.Dist. 558 (1914)—Ch. 15.

407 East 61st Garage, Inc. v. Savoy Fifth Avenue Corp., 23 N.Y.2d 275, 296 N.Y.S.2d 338, 244 N.E.2d 37 (1968)—§§ 226, 261, 262.

4408, Inc. v. Losure, —— Ind.App. ——, 373 N.E.2d 899 (1978)—§ 188.

Fox v. Cosgriff, 66 Idaho 371, 159 P.2d 224 (1945)—§ 168.

Fox v. Dehn, 42 Cal.App.3d 165, 116 Cal.Rptr. 786 (1974)—§§ 236, 253.

Fox v. Grange, 261 Ill. 116, 103 N.E. 576 (1913)—§ 247.

Fox v. Piercy, 119 Utah 367, 227 P.2d 763 (1951)—§ 176.

Frain v. Brady, 48 R.I. 24, 134 A. 645 (1926)—§ 53.

Fraley v. Null, Inc., 244 Md. 567, 224 A.2d 448 (1966)—§ 131.

Frame v. Merrill Lynch, Pierce, Fenner & Smith, Inc., 20 Cal.App.3d 668, 97 Cal.Rptr. 811 (1971)—§ 208.

Fran Realty v. Thomas, 30 Md.App. 362, 354 A.2d 196 (1976)—§ 366.

Franco Western Oil Co. v. Fariss, 259 Cal.App.2d 325, 66 Cal.Rptr. 458 (1968) —§ 58.

Frank Heinz Constr. Co., O., United States ex rel. J. C. Schaefer Elec., Inc. v., 300 F.Supp. 396 (S.D.Ill.1969)—§§ 4, 22.

Frankel v. Pitler, 166 Neb. 219, 88 N.W.2d 770 (1958)—§ 220.

Frantz v. Maher, 106 Ohio App. 465, 155 N.E.2d 471 (1957)—§ 147.

Fratelli Gardino, S.p.A. v. Caribbean Lumber Co., 587 F.2d 204 (5th Cir. 1979)—§ 279.

Frazier v. Collins, 300 Ky. 18, 187 S.W.2d 816 (1945)—§ 265.

Frazier v. State Bank of Decatur, 101 Ark. 135, 141 S.W. 941 (1911)—§ 153.

Frederick v. Frederick, 44 Ill.App.3d 578, 3 Ill.Dec. 231, 358 N.E.2d 398 (1976) —§§ 183, 192.

Frederics, Inc., E. v. Felton Beauty Supply Co., 58 Ga.App. 320, 198 S.E. 324 (1938)—§ 63.

Freedman v. Montague Associates, Inc., 18 Misc.2d 1, 187 N.Y.S.2d 636 (1959) —§ 300.

Freedman v. Rector, Wardens & Vestrymen of St. Matthias Parish, 37 Cal.2d 16, 230 P.2d 629 (1951)—§ 374.

Freedom Fin. Co. v. Steeples, 140 N.J.Super. 449, 356 A.2d 444 (1976)—§ 94.

Freeman v. Continental Gin Co., 381 F.2d 459 (5th Cir. 1967)—§ 216.

Freeman, State ex rel. v. Sierra County Bd. of Educ., 49 N.M. 54, 157 P.2d 234 (1945)—§ 350.

Freeto v. State Highway Comm'n, 161 Kan. 7, 166 P.2d 728 (1946)—§ 261.

Freigy v. Gargaro Co., 223 Ind. 342, 60 N.E.2d 288 (1945)—§ 313.

Freund v. Washington Square Press, 34 N.Y.2d 379, 357 N.Y.S.2d 857, 314 N.E.2d 419 (1974)—§§ 347, 352.

Fricker v. Uddo & Toormina Co., 48 Cal.2d 696, 312 P.2d 1085 (1957)—§ 338.

Fried v. Fisher, 328 Pa. 497, 196 A. 39 (1938)—§ 273.

Friederichsen v. Renard, 247 U.S. 207 (1918)—§ 378.

Friedman v. Grevnin, 360 Mich. 193, 103 N.W.2d 336 (1960)—§ 154.

Friedman & Co., Donald v. Newman, 255 N.Y. 340, 174 N.E. 703 (1931)— § 156.

Friestad v. Travelers Indem. Co., 260 Pa.Super.Ct. 178, 393 A.2d 1212 (1978)— §§ 209, 210.

G

General Tire & Rubber Co. v. Distributors, Inc., 253 N.C. 459, 117 S.E.2d 479 (1960)—§ 249.

Genesee County v. Pailthorpe, 246 Mich. 356, 224 N.W. 418 (1929)—§§ 51, 53.

George v. Bekins Van & Storage Co., 33 Cal.2d 834, 205 P.2d 1037 (1949)— § 211.

George v. School Dist. No. 8R, 7 Or.App. 183, 490 P.2d 1009 (1971)—§ 220.

Geremia v. Boyarsky, 107 Conn. 387, 140 A. 749 (1928)—§ 153.

Gerke's Estate, In re, 271 Wis. 297, 73 N.W.2d 506 (1955)—§ 86.

Gerwin v. Southeastern California Ass'n of Seventh Day Adventists, 14 Cal. App.3d 209, 92 Cal.Rptr. 111 (1971)—§ 352.

Gheres v. Ater, 148 Ohio St. 89, 73 N.E.2d 513 (1947)—§ 199.

Gherman v. Colburn, 72 Cal.App.3d 544, 140 Cal.Rptr. 330 (1977)—§ 254.

Gibraltar Realty Corp. v. Mount Vernon Trust Co., 276 N.Y. 353, 12 N.E.2d 438 (1938)—§ 339.

Gibson v. Cranage, 39 Mich. 49 (1878)—§ 228.

Gilbert v. Globe & Rutgers Fire Ins. Co., 91 Or. 59, 178 P. 358 (1919)—§ 84.

Gilbert Fin. Corp. v. Steelform Contracting Co., 82 Cal.App.3d 65, 145 Cal. Rptr. 448 (1978)—§ 302.

Gildenhorn v. Columbia Real Estate Title Ins. Co., 271 Md. 387, 317 A.2d 836 (1974)—§§ 96, 99.

Gill v. Johnstown Lumber Co., 151 Pa. 534, 25 A. 120 (1892)—§ 240.

Gill Equipment Co. v. Freedman, 339 Mass. 303, 158 N.E.2d 863 (1959)—§ 299.

Gillingham v. Brown, 178 Mass. 417, 60 N.E. 122 (1901)—§ 82.

Gilson v. F. S. Royster Guano Co., 1 F.2d 82 (3d Cir. 1924)—§ 350.

Ginsberg Corp., Edmund W. v. C. D. Kepner Leather Co, 317 Mass. 581, 59 N.E.2d 253 (1945)—§ 325.

Glamorgan Pipe & Foundry Co. v. Washington Suburban Sanitary Comm'n, 183 F.Supp. 840 (D.Md.1960)—§ 153.

Glassman v. Gerstein, 10 A.D.2d 875, 200 N.Y.S.2d 690 (1960)—§ 226.

Glassman Constr. Co. v. Fidelity & Cas. Co., 356 F.2d 340 (D.C.Cir. 1966)— §§ 321, 336.

Glenn v. Rossler, 156 N.Y. 161, 50 N.E. 785 (1898)—§ 234.

Glidden Co. v. Hellenic Lines Ltd., 275 F.2d 253 (2d Cir. 1960)—§ 261.

Globe Ref. Co. v. Landa Cotton Oil Co., 190 U.S. 540 (1903)—§ 351.

Glover v. Jewish War Veterans, 68 A.2d 233 (D.C.Mun.Ct.App.1949)—§ 51.

Goddard v. South Bay Union High Sch.Dist., 79 Cal.App.3d 98, 144 Cal.Rptr. 701 (1978)—§§ 203, 206, 212.

Goen v. Hamilton, 159 S.W.2d 231 (Tex.Civ.App.1942)—§ 126.

Goff v. American Sav. Ass'n, 1 Kan.App.2d 75, 561 P.2d 897 (1977)—§ 172.

Gohlke v. Davis, 279 S.W.2d 369 (Tex.Civ.App.1955)—§ 146.

Gold v. Salem Lutheran Home Ass'n, 53 Cal.2d 289, 1 Cal.Rptr. 343, 347 P.2d 687 (1959)—§ 265.

Gold Bond Stamp Co. v. Gilt-Edge Stamps, Inc., 437 F.2d 27 (5th Cir. 1971)— § 232.

Gold Mining & Water Co. v. Swinerton, 23 Cal.2d 19, 142 P.2d 22 (1943)— § 243.

Goldbard v. Empire State Mut. Life Ins. Co., 5 A.D.2d 230, 171 N.Y.S.2d 194 (1958)—§§ 279, 281.

Golden Dipt Co. v. Systems Engineering & Mfg. Co., 465 F.2d 215 (7th Cir. 1972)—§ 30.

Golden Gate Corp. v. Barrington College, 98 R.I. 35, 199 A.2d 586 (1964)— § 210.

Goldfarb v. Cohen, 92 Conn. 277, 102 A. 649 (1917)—§ 263.

CITED IN REPORTER'S NOTES

Gruenberg v. Aetna Ins. Co., 9 Cal.3d 566, 108 Cal.Rptr. 480, 510 P.2d 1032 (1973)—§ 355.

Guardian Nat'l Bank v. Huntington County State Bank, 206 Ind. 185, 187 N.E. 388, 92 A.L.R. 1056 (1934)—§ 63.

Guardian Trust Co. v. Brothers, 59 S.W.2d 343 (Tex.Civ.App.1933)—§ 344.

Guerini Stone Co. v. P. J. Carlin Constr. Co., 248 U.S. 334 (1919)—§ 237.

Guerrieri v. Severini, 51 Cal.2d 12, 330 P.2d 635 (1958)—§ 256.

Guetzkow Bros. v. A. H. Andrews & Co., 92 Wis. 214, 66 N.W. 119 (1896)— § 351.

Gunsch v. Gunsch, 71 N.W.2d 623 (N.D.1955)—§ 322.

Gurfein v. Werbelovsky, 97 Conn. 703, 118 A. 32 (1922)—§ 77.

Gustafson & Co., Dave v. State, 83 S.D. 160, 156 N.W.2d 185 (1968)—§ 356.

Gwinn v. Farrier, 159 Va. 183, 165 S.E. 647 (1932)—Ch. 5.

H

H & R Block, Inc. v. Lovelace, 208 Kan. 538, 493 P.2d 205 (1972)—§ 184.

H. B. G. Corp. v. Houbolt, 51 Ill.App.3d 955, 10 Ill.Dec. 44, 367 N.E.2d 432 (1977)—§ 188.

Haas v. Myers, 111 Ill. 421, 53 Am.Rep. 634 (1884)—§ 63.

Haas & Haynie Corp., United States ex rel. Union Building Materials Corp. v., 577 F.2d 568 (9th Cir. 1978)—§ 220.

Hackley v. Headley, 45 Mich. 569, 8 N.W. 511 (1881)—§§ 74, 175.

Hadden v. Consolidated Edison Co., 34 N.Y.2d 88, 356 N.Y.S.2d 249, 312 N.E. 2d 445 (1974)—§ 241.

Hadley v. Baxendale, 9 Exch. 341, 156 Eng.Rep. 145 (1854)—§ 351.

Haigh v. Brooks, 10 Adol. & Ellis 309 (Ex.Ch.1839)—§ 79.

Haines v. City of New York, 41 N.Y.2d 769, 396 N.Y.S.2d 155, 364 N.E.2d 820 (1977)—§ 204.

Hale v. Kreisel, 194 Wis. 271, 215 N.W. 227 (1927)—§ 375.

Hall v. E. I. DuPont de Nemours & Co., 345 F.Supp. 353 (E.D.N.Y.1972)— Ch. 13.

Halliwill v. Weible, 64 Colo. 295, 171 P. 372 (1918)—§ 94.

Halvorson v. Commerce Trust Co., 222 S.W. 897 (Mo.Ct.App.1920)—§ 325.

Hamer v. Sidway, 124 N.Y. 538, 27 N.E. 256 (1891)—§§ 32, 90.

Hamilton v. Traub, 29 Del.Ch. 475, 51 A.2d 581 (1947)—§ 129.

Hamm Drayage Co., Daniel v. Willson, 178 F.2d 633 (8th Cir. 1949)—§ 305.

Hammons v. Big Sandy Claims Serv., 567 S.W.2d 313 (Ky.Ct.App.1978)— § 188.

Hancock Mut. Life Ins. Co., John v. Cohen, 254 F.2d 417 (9th Cir. 1958)—§ 243.

Handy v. Beck, 282 Or. 653, 581 P.2d 68 (1978)—§ 164.

Hanes v. Mitchell, 78 N.D. 341, 49 N.W.2d 606 (1951)—§ 213.

Hanford v Connecticut Fair Ass'n, 92 Conn. 621, 103 A. 838 (1918)—§ 261.

Hanlon v. Hayes, 404 Ill. 362, 89 N.E.2d 51 (1949)—§ 131.

Hanna v. Commercial Travelers Mut. Acc. Ass'n, 204 A.D. 258, 197 N.Y.S. 395 (1922)—§ 271.

Hanna v. Perkins, 2 UCC Rep. 1044 (N.Y.Co.Ct.1965)—§ 281.

Hanover Modular Homes v. Scottish Inns, 443 F.Supp. 888 (W.D.La.1978) —§ 171.

Hansen v. Andersen, 246 Iowa 1310, 71 N.W.2d 921 (1955)—§ 348.

Hansen v. Fettig, 179 N.W.2d 739 (N.D.1970)—§ 258.

Haraka v. Datry, 148 Ga.App. 642, 252 S.E.2d 71 (1979)—§ 217.

Harburg India Rubber Comb. Co. v. Martin, [1902] 1 K.B. 778 (C.A.)—§ 118.

TABLE OF CASES

Henock v. Yeamans, 340 F.2d 503 (5th Cir. 1965)—§ 328.

Henry v. Thomas, 241 Ga. 360, 245 S.E.2d 646 (1978)—§ 151.

Herbert v. Bronson, 125 Mass. 475 (1878)—§ 321.

Herbolsheimer v. Herbolsheimer, 46 Ill.App.3d 563, 5 Ill.Dec. 134, 361 N.E. 2d 134 (1977)—§ 177.

Herbstreith v. Walls, 147 Neb. 805, 25 N.W.2d 409 (1946)—§ 129.

Herman v. Connecticut Mut. Life Ins. Co., 218 Mass. 181, 105 N.E. 450 (1914)— § 342.

Hermes v. William F. Meyer Co., 65 Ill.App.3d 745, 382 N.E.2d 841 (1978)— §§ 25, 69, 87.

Hernandez v. S. I. C. Fin. Co., 79 N.M. 673, 448 P.2d 474 (1968)—§ 208.

Heroman & Co., W. M. v. Saia Elec., Inc., 346 So.2d 827 (La.Ct.App.1977)— § 87.

Herrington v. Davitt, 220 N.Y. 162, 115 N.E. 476 (1917)—§ 83.

Hess v. Dumouchel Paper Co., 154 Conn. 343, 225 A.2d 797 (1966)—§ 268.

Hess v. Jarboe, 201 Kan. 705, 443 P.2d 294 (1968)—§ 355.

Hetchler v. America Life Ins. Co., 266 Mich. 608, 254 N.W. 221 (1934)—§ 89.

Heyman v. Adeack Realty Co., 102 R.I. 105, 228 A.2d 578 (1967)—§ 139.

Heywood v. Wellers, 1 All E.R. 300 (C.A.1976)—§ 353.

Hibschman Pontiac, Inc. v. Batchelor, 266 Ind. 310, 362 N.E.2d 845 (1977)— § 355.

Hickman v. Cave, 115 Kan. 701, 224 P. 57 (1924)—§ 156.

Hicks v. Bush, 10 N.Y.2d 488, 225 N.Y.S.2d 34, 180 N.E.2d 425 (1962)—§§ 217, 224.

Hieb Sand & Gravel, Inc., Walter J. v. Universal C.I.T. Credit Corp., 332 S.W.2d 619 (Ky.1960)—§ 336.

Higgins v. Allied American Mut. Fire Ins. Co., 237 A.2d 471 (D.C.Ct.App.1968) —§ 316.

Higgins v. Gager, 65 Ark. 604, 47 S.W. 848 (1898)—§ 130.

Highlands Underwriters v. Eleganté Inns, 361 So.2d 1060 (Ala.1978)—§ 155.

Highway Products v. United States, 208 Ct.Cl. 926, 530 F.2d 911 (1976)— § 154.

Hileman v. Hulver, 243 Md. 527, 221 A.2d 693 (1966)—§ 332.

Hill v. Corbett, 33 Wash.2d 219, 204 P.2d 845 (1949)—§ 94.

Hill v. Willett, 281 S.W. 1110 (Tex.Civ.App.1926)—§ 348.

Hill's Inc. v. William B. Kessler, Inc., 41 Wash.2d 42, 246 P.2d 1099 (1952)— §§ 57, 351.

Hinckley v. Bechtel Corp., 41 Cal.App.3d 206, 116 Cal.Rptr. 33 (1974)—§ 204.

Hind, Ltd., Robert v. Silva, 75 F.2d 74 (9th Cir. 1935)—§ 152.

Hirsch v. S. Berger Imp. & Mfg. Corp., 67 A.D.2d 30, 414 N.Y.S.2d 324 (1979) —§ 217.

Hirst v. Elgin Metal Casket Co., 438 F.Supp. 906 (D.Mont.1977)—§ 353.

Hoban v. Hudson, 129 Minn. 335, 152 N.W. 723 (1915)—§ 63.

Hobbs Trailers v. J. T. Arnett Grain Co., 560 S.W.2d 85 (Tex.1977)—§ 216.

Hochman v. Ziegler's, Inc., 139 N.J.Eq. 139, 50 A.2d 97 (1946)—§ 176.

Hochster v. De la Tour, 2 E. & B. 678, 118 Eng.Rep. 922 (1853)—§ 253.

Hodes v. Hoffman Int'l Corp., 280 F.Supp. 252 (S.D.N.Y.1968)—§ 254.

Hodges v. Campbell, 211 Or. 428, 316 P.2d 312 (1957)—§ 328.

Hoffman v. Red Owl Stores, 26 Wis.2d 683, 133 N.W.2d 267 (1965)—§ 90.

Hoffman Candy & Ice Cream Co. v. Department of Liquor Control, 154 Ohio St. 357, 96 N.E.2d 203 (1950)—§ 367.

Hoffmann v. Wausau Concrete Co., 58 Wis.2d 472, 207 N.W.2d 80 (1973)— §§ 71, 94.

Hughes v. Payne, 27 S.D. 214, 130 N.W. 81 (1911)—§ 156.

Hughes v. Payne, 22 S.D. 293, 117 N.W. 363 (1908)—§ 156.

Hughes v. Wamsutta Mills, 93 Mass. (11 Allen) 201 (1865)—§§ 264, 271.

Hugo v. Erickson, 110 Neb. 602, 194 N.W. 723 (1923)—§§ 161, 166.

Huhtala v. Travelers Ins. Co., 401 Mich. 118, 257 N.W.2d 640 (1977)—§ 90.

Humble Oil & Ref. Co. v. Cox, 207 Va. 197, 148 S.E.2d 756 (1966)—§§ 24, 25, 26, 95, 96, 103, 104, 105.

Humble Oil & Ref. Co. v. Westside Inv. Corp., 428 S.W.2d 92 (Tex.1968)— § 37.

Hungerford Constr. Co. v. Florida Citrus Exposition, Inc., 410 F.2d 1229 (5th Cir. 1969)—§ 356.

Hunt v. Century Indem. Co., 58 R.I. 336, 192 A. 799 (1937)—§ 155.

Hurley v. Lano Int'l, Inc., 569 S.W.2d 602 (Tex.Civ.App.1978)—§ 302.

Hurst v. Parker, 1 Barn. & Ald. 92 (K.B.1817)—§ 82.

Hurst v. W. J. Lake & Co., 141 Or. 306, 16 P.2d 627 (1932)—§§ 202, 212, 222.

Hurt v. Leatherby Ins. Co., 354 So.2d 918 (Fla.Dist.Ct.App.1978)—§ 153.

Hussey v. Holloway, 217 Mass. 100, 104 N.E. 471 (1914)—§ 350.

Hussey Metals Div. v. Lectromelt Furnace Div., 417 F.Supp. 964 (W.D.Pa. 1976)—§ 354.

Hutchinson v. Dobson-Bainbridge Realty Co., 31 Tenn.App. 490, 217 S.W.2d 6 (1946)—§§ 45, 62.

Hutchison v. Tompkins, 259 So.2d 129 (Fla.1972)—§ 356.

I

I. & I. Holding Corp. v. Gainsburg, 276 N.Y. 427, 12 N.E.2d 532 (1938)— § 45.

Iafolla v. Douglas Pocahontas Coal Corp., —— W.Va. ——, 250 S.E.2d 128 (1978)—§ 214.

Ilfeld Co., Charles v. Taylor, 156 Colo. 204, 397 P.2d 748 (1964)—§ 227.

Illinois Central R. R. Co. v. Crail, 281 U.S. 57 (1930)—§ 347.

Illinois Fuel Co. v. Mobile & O. R. R., 319 Mo. 899, 8 S.W.2d 834 (1928)— § 288.

Imperial Ref. Co. v. Kanotex Ref. Co., 29 F.2d 193 (8th Cir. 1928)—§§ 320, 328.

In re (see name of party)

Indussa Corp. v. S. S. Ranborg, 377 F.2d 200 (2d Cir. 1967)—§ 208.

"Industrial America," Inc. v. Fulton Indus., 285 A.2d 412 (Del.1971)—§§ 53, 54.

Industrial Packaging Products Co. v. Fort Pitt Packaging Int'l Inc., 399 Pa. 643, 161 A.2d 19 (1960)—§ 330.

Ingham Lumber Co. v. Ingersoll, 93 Ark. 447, 125 S.W. 139 (1910)—§ 298.

Ingram v. Mandler, 56 F.2d 994 (10th Cir. 1932)—§ 330.

Intermar, Inc. v. Atlantic Richfield Co., 364 F.Supp. 82 (E.D.Pa.1973)—§§ 90, 216.

International Filter Co. v. Conroe Gin, Ice & Light Co., 277 S.W. 631 (Tex. Com.App.1925)—§§ 50, 56.

International Paper Co. v. Rockefeller, 161 A.D. 180, 146 N.Y.S. 371 (1914)— § 272.

International Rediscount Corp. v. Hartford Acc. & Indem. Co., 425 F.Supp. 669 (D.Del.1977)—§§ 322, 326.

Internatio-Rotterdam, Inc. v. River Brand Rice Mills, Inc., 259 F.2d 137 (2d Cir. 1958)—§ 242.

Interstate Indus. v. Barclay Indus., 540 F.2d 868 (7th Cir. 1976)—§§ 26, 33.

Jewett Pub. Co. v. Butler, 159 Mass. 517, 34 N.E. 1087 (1893)—§ 192.

Joannin v. Oglivie, 49 Minn. 564, 52 N.W. 217 (1892)—§§ 175, 176.

John v. United Advertising, Inc., 165 Colo. 193, 439 P.2d 53 (1968)—§ 240.

Johnson v. Malone, 252 Ala. 609, 42 So.2d 505 (1949)—§ 238.

Johnson v. Scottish Union Ins. Co., 160 Tenn. 152, 22 S.W.2d 362 (1962)—§ 205.

Johnson v. Star Iron & Steel Co., 9 Wash.App. 202, 511 P.2d 1370 (1973)—§ 61.

Johnson Serv. Co. v. E. H. Monin, Inc., 253 N.Y. 417, 171 N.E. 692 (1930)—
§ 307.

Johnson-Foster Co. v. D'Amore Constr. Co., 314 Mass. 416, 50 N.E.2d 89 (1943)
—§ 108.

Johnson's Estate, In re, 74 Misc.2d 788, 346 N.Y.S.2d 283 (Sur.Ct.1973)—
§§ 26, 78, 90.

Johnston v. Monahan, 2 Wash.App. 452, 469 P.2d 930 (1970)—§ 128.

Jonas v. Meyers, 410 Ill. 213, 101 N.E.2d 509 (1951)—§ 155.

Jones v. Chicago B. & Q. R. Co., 102 Neb. 853, 170 N.W. 170 (1918)—§ 153.

Jones v. Dressel, 582 P.2d 1057 (Colo.App.1978)—§ 195.

Jones v. Jones, 333 Mo. 478, 63 S.W.2d 146 (1933)—§§ 129, 133.

Jones v. Miller, 173 Tenn. 360, 117 S.W.2d 745 (1938)—§ 92.

Jones v. Smith, 206 Ga. 162, 56 S.E.2d 462 (1949)—§ 87.

Jones v. Star Credit Corp., 52 Misc.2d 189, 298 N.Y.S.2d 264 (Sup.Ct.1969)—
§ 208.

Jones, United States v., 176 F.2d 278 (9th Cir. 1949)—§ 161.

Jones Constr. Co., J. A. v. City of Dover, 372 A.2d 540 (Del.Super.Ct.1977)—
§ 195.

Jones Knitting Corp. v. A. M. Pullen & Co., 50 F.R.D. 311 (S.D.N.Y.1970)—
§ 290.

Jones Trucking Co., L. C. v. Superior Oil Co., 68 Wyo. 384, 234 P.2d 802 (1951)
—Ch. 13.

Jordan v. Dobbins, 122 Mass. 168, 23 Am.Rep. 305 (1877)—§ 31.

Jordan v. Mount Sinai Hosp., 276 So.2d 102 (Dist.Ct.App.1973)—§ 90.

Joseph v. Carter, 382 Ill. 461, 47 N.E.2d 471 (1943)—Ch. 5.

Joseph v. Mahoney Corp., 367 S.W.2d 213 (Tex.Civ.App.1963)—§ 213.

Joseph v. Wilson, 57 Ill.App.3d 212, 14 Ill.Dec. 831, 372 N.E.2d 1110 (1978)—
§ 25.

Judson v. Corcoran, 58 U.S. (17 How.) 612 (1854)—§ 342.

Julian v. Zayre Corp., —— R.I. ——, 388 A.2d 813 (1978)—§ 284.

Julian Constr. Co., John v. Monarch Builders, Inc., 306 A.2d 29 (Del.Super.Ct.
1973)—§ 305.

Justin Belt Co. v. Yost, 502 S.W.2d 681 (Tex.1973)—§ 188.

Just's, Inc. v. Arrington Constr. Co., 99 Idaho 462, 583 P.2d 997 (1978)—§ 313.

K

K & G Constr. Co. v. Harris, 223 Md. 305, 164 A.2d 451 (1960)—§§ 232, 241, 246.

Kabatchnick v. Hanover-Elm Building Corp., 328 Mass. 341, 103 N.E.2d 692
(1952)—§ 169.

Kabil Developments Corp. v. Mignot, 279 Or. 151, 566 P.2d 505 (1977)—§§ 3, 4.

Kadow v. Cronin, 97 N.J.L. 301, 116 A. 427 (1922)—§ 238.

Kahn v. Waldman, 283 Mass. 391, 186 N.E. 587 (1933)—§ 74.

Kaiser v. Carolina Life Ins. Co., 219 S.C. 456, 65 S.E.2d 865 (1951)—§ 155.

Kane v. Hood, 30 Mass. (13 Pick.) 281 (1832)—§ 234.

TABLE OF CASES

Kilander v. Blickle Co., 280 Or. 425, 571 P.2d 503 (1977)—§ 281.

Killebrew v. Murray, 151 Ky. 345, 151 S.W. 662 (1912)—§ 87.

Kilpatrick Bros. v. IBM Corp., 464 F.2d 1080 (10th Cir. 1972)—§ 21.

Kimbrough-Veasey Co., In re, 292 F. 757 (N.D.Ga.1923)—§ 294.

Kindsvater v. Hineman, 181 Kan. 990, 317 P.2d 852 (1957)—§ 82.

King v. Batterson, 13 R.I. 117, 43 Am.Rep. 13 (1880)—§ 52.

King v. Connors, 222 Mass. 261, 110 N.E. 289 (1915)—§ 242.

King v. Hoare, 13 M. & W. 494, 153 Eng.Rep. 206 (1844)—§ 292.

King v. West Coast Grocery Co., 72 Wash. 132, 129 P. 1081 (1913)—§ 336.

King Bros. & Co. v. Central of Georgia Ry., 135 Ga. 225, 69 S.E. 113 (1910)
—§ 326.

King Constr. Co. v. W. M. Smith Elec. Co., 350 S.W.2d 940 (Tex.Civ.App.
1961)—§§ 175, 176.

Kingston v. Preston, 2 Doug. 689, 99 Eng.Rep. 437 (K.B.1773)—§ 225.

Kintner v. Wolfe, 102 Ariz. 164, 426 P.2d 798 (1967)—§ 261.

Kirby v. Bourg, 165 Colo. 500, 440 P.2d 151 (1968)—§ 226.

Kirkland v. Archbold, 113 N.E.2d 496 (Ohio App.1953)—§ 374.

Kirsch v. Pier Orleans, Inc., 362 So.2d 1182 (La.Ct.App.1978)—§ 210.

Kirshner v. Spinella, 73 Misc.2d 962, 343 N.Y.S.2d 298 (Dist.Ct.1973)—§ 79.

Kitchin v. Mori, 84 Nev. 181, 437 P.2d 865 (1968)—§ 374.

Kiyoicki Fujikawa v. Sunrise Soda Water Works Co., 158 F.2d 490 (9th Cir.
1946)—§ 261.

Kizior v. City of St. Joseph, 329 S.W.2d 605 (Mo.1959)—§ 89.

Klaeveman v. Klaeveman, 300 S.W.2d 205 (Tex.Civ.App.1957)—§ 94.

Klag v. Home Ins. Co., 116 Ga.App. 678, 158 S.E.2d 444 (1967)—§§ 112, 115,
116.

Klar v. H. & M. Parcel Room, Inc., 270 A.D. 538, 61 N.Y.S.2d 285 (1946)—
§ 211.

Klatch v. Simpson, 237 Ky. 84, 34 S.W.2d 951 (1931)—§ 135.

Klausner's Will, In re, 192 Misc. 790, 77 N.Y.S.2d 775 (Sur.Ct.1948)—§ 53.

Klein v. Insurance Co., 104 U.S. 88 (1881)—§ 271.

Klein v. Tabatchnick, 418 F.Supp. 1368 (S.D.N.Y.1976)—§§ 153, 161.

Kline v. Lightman, 243 Md. 460, 221 A.2d 675 (1966)—§§ 112, 116.

Klingensmith, Inc., William F. v. District of Columbia ex rel. Reliance Ins.
Co., 370 A.2d 1341 (D.C.1977)—§ 69.

Kneberg v. H. L. Green Co., 89 F.2d 100 (7th Cir. 1937)—§ 328.

Knight v. Seattle First Nat'l Bank, 22 Wash.App. 493, 589 P.2d 1279 (1979)—
§ 45.

Koch v. Koch, 95 N.J.Super. 546, 232 A.2d 157 (1967)—§ 124.

Kohn, United States v., 243 F.Supp. 293 (W.D.S.C.1965)—§ 289.

Koltermann, Inc., Calvin V. v. Underream Piling Co., 563 S.W.2d 950 (Tex.
Civ.App.1977)—§§ 261, 264, 266.

Kooleraire Serv. & Installation Corp. v. Board of Educ., 28 N.Y.2d 101, 320
N.Y.S.2d 46, 268 N.E.2d 782 (1971)—§ 245.

Koplin v. Faulkner, 293 S.W.2d 467 (Ky.1956)—§ 350.

Koppelon v. Ritter Flooring Corp., 97 N.J.L. 200, 116 A. 491 (1922)—§ 252.

Kornblut v. Chevron Oil Co., 62 A.D.2d 831, 407 N.Y.S.2d 498 (1978)—§ 313.

Korosic v. Pearson, 377 Ill. 413, 36 N.E.2d 744 (1941)—§ 155.

Kossick v. United Fruit Co., 365 U.S. 731 (1961)—§ 74.

Kovarik v. Vesely, 3 Wis.2d 573, 89 N.W.2d 279 (1958)—§§ 132, 226.

Kowal v. Sportswear by Revere, Inc., 351 Mass. 541, 222 N.E.2d 778 (1967)—
§§ 262, 272.

L

Lampus Co., R. I. v. Neville Cement Products Corp., 474 Pa. 199, 378 A.2d 288 (1977)—§ 351.

Landberg v. Landberg, 24 Cal.App.3d 742, 101 Cal.Rptr. 335 (1972)—§ 37.

Lande & Son, Joseph v. Wellsco Realty, Inc., 131 N.J.L. 191, 34 A.2d 418 (Ct. Err. & App.1943)—§ 73.

Landers v. State, 56 A.D.2d 105, 391 N.Y.S.2d 723 (1977)—§ 175.

Lane v. Neifert, 240 Mich. 475, 215 N.W. 302 (1927)—§ 156.

Lane v. Pacific & I. N. R. R., 8 Idaho 230, 67 P. 656 (1902)—§ 366.

Lane, Inc., William v. Selby Shoe Co., 45 F.2d 581 (2d Cir. 1930)—§ 94.

Lang v. Giraudo, 311 Mass. 132, 40 N.E.2d 707 (1942)—§ 376.

Lange v. United States, 120 F.2d 886 (4th Cir. 1941)—§ 89.

Lange-Finn Constr. Co. v. Albany Steel & Iron Supply Co., 94 Misc.2d 15, 403 N.Y.S.2d 1012 (Sup.Ct.1978)—§ 281.

Langel v. Betz, 250 N.Y. 159, 164 N.E. 890 (1928)—§ 328.

Langer v. Stegerwald Lumber Co., 262 Wis. 383, 55 N.W.2d 389 (1952)—§ 155.

Langlois v. Oriole Land & Dev. Corp., 283 So.2d 143 (Fla.Dist.Ct.App.1973)—§ 131.

Lardas v. Underwriters Ins. Co., 426 Pa. 47, 231 A.2d 740 (1967)—§ 230.

Lasser v. Philadelphia Nat'l Bank, 321 Pa. 189, 183 A. 791 (1936)—§ 343.

Lauria, People v., 251 Cal.App.2d 471, 59 Cal.Rptr. 628 (1967)—§ 182.

Lavey v. Edwards, 264 Or. 331, 505 P.2d 342 (1973)—§ 185.

Lawrence v. American Sur. Co., 263 Mich. 586, 249 N.W. 3, 264 Mich. 516, 250 N.W. 295 (1933)—§ 31.

Lawrence v. Fox, 20 N.Y. 268 (1859)—§ 280.

Lawrence v. McCalmont, 43 U.S. (2 How.) 426 (1844)—§ 88.

Lawrence v. Miller, 86 N.Y. 131 (1881)—§ 238.

Lawrence v. Porter, 63 F. 62 (6th Cir. 1894)—§ 350.

Lawrence v. Staigg, 8 R.I. 256 (1866)—§ 158.

Lawrence Nat'l Bank v. Rice, 82 F.2d 28 (10th Cir. 1936)—§ 309.

Lawson v. Citizens & Southern Nat'l Bank, 255 S.C. 517, 180 S.E.2d 206 (1971)—§ 161.

Lazzara v. Wisconsin Boxing Club, 29 F.2d 483 (7th Cir. 1928)—§ 271.

Leach v. Mechanics Sav. Bank, 202 Iowa 899, 211 N.W. 506 (1926)—§ 325.

Leaf Tobacco Co. v. American Fidelity Fire Ins. Co., 388 F.Supp. 323 (D.V.I. 1974)—§ 376.

League v. Giffin, 347 So.2d 1332 (Ala.1977)—§§ 214, 215.

Leasco Corp. v. Taussig, 473 F.2d 777 (2d Cir. 1972)—§ 151.

Ledford v. Atkins, 413 S.W.2d 68 (Ky.1967)—§ 271.

Ledford Constr. Co. v. Smith, 231 Md. 596, 191 A.2d 587 (1963)—§ 131.

Lee v. Casualty Ins. Co., 90 Conn. 202, 96 A. 952 (1916)—§ 84.

Lee v. Consolidated Edison Co., 95 Misc.2d 120, 407 N.Y.S.2d 777 (1978)—§ 195.

Lee v. Joseph E. Seagram & Sons, 552 F.2d 447 (2d Cir. 1977)—§ 216.

Lee v. Ravanis, 349 Mass. 742, 212 N.E.2d 480 (1965)—§ 318.

Lee v. St. Joe Paper Co., 371 F.2d 797 (2d Cir. 1967)—§ 139.

Leeds v. Guaranty Trust Co., 193 Misc. 681, 85 N.Y.S.2d 70 (Sup.Ct.1948)—§ 339.

Leeper v. Beltrami, 53 Cal.2d 195, 1 Cal.Rptr. 12, 347 P.2d 12 (1959)—§§ 175, 176.

Lefkowitz v. Great Minneapolis Surplus Store, 251 Minn. 188, 86 N.W.2d 689 (1957)—§ 26.

Legal Recording & Research Bureau v. Wicka, 62 A.D.2d 486, 405 N.Y.S.2d 526 (1978)—§ 188.

Local Loan Co. v. Hunt, 292 U.S. 234 (1934)—§ 321.

Locke v. United States, 151 Ct.Cl. 262, 283 F.2d 521 (1960)—§ 352.

Locks v. Wade, 36 N.J.Super. 128, 114 A.2d 875 (1955)—§§ 347, 350.

Loews, Inc., E. M. v. Deutschmann, 344 Mass. 765, 184 N.E.2d 55 (1962)—§ 319.

Loghry v. Capel, 257 Iowa 285, 132 N.W.2d 417 (1965)—§ 161.

Lonas v. Metropolitan Mortgage & Sec. Co., 432 P.2d 603 (Alaska 1967)—§ 328.

London Bucket Co. v. Stewart, 314 Ky. 832, 237 S.W.2d 509 (1951)—§ 366.

Long v. Chronicle Pub. Co., 68 Cal.App. 171, 228 P. 873 (1924)—§ 46.

Long v. Huffman, 557 S.W.2d 911 (Mo.Ct.App.1977)—§ 188.

Long Island R. R. Co. v. Northville Indus., 41 N.Y.2d 455, 393 N.Y.S.2d 925, 362 N.E.2d 558 (1977)—§ 253.

Longenecker v. Brommer, 59 Wash.2d 552, 368 P.2d 900 (1962)—§ 246.

Longview Constr. & Development v. Loggins Constr. Co., 523 S.W.2d 771 (Tex. Civ.App.1975)—§ 351.

Looby v. Redmond, 66 Conn. 444, 34 A. 102 (1895)—§ 141.

Looman Realty Corp. v. Broad St. Nat'l Bank, 32 N.J. 461, 161 A.2d 247 (1960) —§ 131.

Lopez v. A/S D/S Svendborg, 581 F.2d 319 (2d Cir. 1978)—§ 195.

Lopez v. Puzina, 239 Cal.App.2d 708, 49 Cal.Rptr. 122 (1966)—§ 333.

L'Orange v. Medical Protective Co., 394 F.2d 57 (6th Cir. 1968)—§ 205.

Loring v. City of Boston, 48 Mass. (7 Met.) 409 (1844)—§ 41.

Loud v. Pomona Land & Water Co., 153 U.S. 564 (1893)—§ 234.

Louisville & Nashville R. R. v. Crowe, 156 Ky. 27, 160 S.W. 759 (1913)—§§ 264, 377.

Louisville & Nashville R. R. v. Mottley, 219 U.S. 467 (1911)—§ 264.

Louisville Asphalt Varnish Co. v. Lorick & Lowrance, 29 S.C. 533, 8 S.E. 8 (1888)—§ 133.

Louisville Bear Safety Serv. v. South Central Bell Tel. Co., 571 S.W.2d 438 (Ky.1978)—§ 195.

Louisville Trust Co. v. Monsky, 444 S.W.2d 120 (Ky.1969)—§ 375.

Loveless v. Diehl, 235 Ark. 805, 364 S.W.2d 317 (1963)—§ 360.

Lowenschuss v. Kane, 520 F.2d 255 (2d Cir. 1975)—§§ 26, 261, 264.

Lowy v. United Pac. Ins. Co., 67 Cal.2d 87, 60 Cal.Rptr. 225, 429 P.2d 577 (1967) —§§ 240, 241.

Lucas v. Long, 125 Md. 420, 94 A. 12 (1915)—§ 171.

Lucas v. Western Union Tel. Co., 131 Iowa 669, 109 N.W. 191 (1906)—§ 63.

Lucey v. Hero Int'l Corp., 361 Mass. 569, 281 N.E.2d 266 (1972)—§§ 25, 33.

Lucy v. Zehmer, 196 Va. 493, 84 S.E.2d 516 (1954)—§ 16.

Ludwig Honold Mfg. Co. v. Fletcher, 405 F.2d 1123 (3d Cir. 1969)—§§ 202, 203.

Lumber Co., Gorge v. Brazier Lumber Co., 6 Wash.App. 327, 493 P.2d 782 (1972) —§ 273.

Lumley v. Wagner, 1 Deg.M. & G. 604, 42 Eng.Rep. 687 (Ch.1852)—§ 367.

Lund v. Bruflat, 159 Wash. 89, 292 P. 112 (1930)—§§ 181, 183.

Lunn & Sweet Co. v. Wolfman, 256 Mass. 436, 152 N.E. 893 (1926)—§ 153.

Lurie v. Lurie, 246 Pa.Super.Ct. 307, 370 A.2d 739 (1976)—§ 190.

Lusk-Harbison-Jones, Inc. v. Universal Credit Co., 164 Miss. 693, 145 So. 623 (1933)—§ 90.

Lyman, In re Estate of, 7 Wash.App. 945, 503 P.2d 1127 (1972)—§ 19.

Lynch v. Bailey, 275 A.D. 527, 90 N.Y.S.2d 359 (1949)—§ 188.

Lynch v. Maw, 3 Utah 2d 271, 282 P.2d 841 (1955)—§ 221.

Lynch v. Palmer, 237 Mass. 150, 129 N.E. 374 (1921)—§ 172.

Lyon v. Goss, 19 Cal.2d 659, 123 P.2d 11 (1942)—§ 62.

M

Macke Co. v. Pizza of Gaithersburg, 259 Md. 479, 270 A.2d 645 (1970)—§§ 318, 319.

Mackie v. State Farm Mut. Auto. Ins. Co., 13 Mich.App. 556, 164 N.W.2d 777 (1968)—§§ 229, 230.

Mackin v. Dwyer, 205 Mass. 472, 91 N.E. 893 (1910)—§ 111.

Mactier's Adm'rs v. Frith, 6 Wend. 102, 21 Am.Dec. 262 (N.Y.1830)—§ 23.

Madden v. Kaiser Foundation Hospitals, 17 Cal.3d 699, 131 Cal.Rptr. 882, 552 P.2d 1178 (1976)—§ 208.

Maddox v. Maddox, 224 Ga. 313, 161 S.E.2d 870 (1968)—§ 124.

Maddox v. Northern Natural Gas Co., 259 F.Supp. 781 (S.D.Okla.1966)—§§ 58, 59.

Madeirense Do Brasil S/A v. Stulman-Emrick Lumber Co., 147 F.2d 399 (2d Cir. 1945)—§ 201.

Maffet v. Schaar, 89 Kan. 403, 131 P. 589 (1913)—§ 158.

Magi Communications, Inc. v. Jac-Lu Associates, 65 A.D.2d 727, 410 N.Y.S.2d 297 (1978)—§§ 214, 215.

Mahaffey v. Sodero, 38 N.C.App. 349, 247 S.E.2d 772 (1978)—§ 282.

Mailand v. Burckle, 20 Cal.3d 367, 143 Cal.Rptr. 1, 572 P.2d 1142 (1978)—§§ 183, 184.

Mail-Well Envelope Co. v. Saley, 262 Or. 143, 497 P.2d 364 (1972)—§ 323.

Malm, State v., 143 Conn. 462, 123 A.2d 276 (1956)—§§ 23, 51.

Maloyfsky v. Schiraldi, 108 N.J.Eq. 190, 154 A. 404 (Ch.1931)—§ 328.

Management, Inc. v. Schassberger, 39 Wash.2d 321, 235 P.2d 293 (1951)—§ 356.

Manchester Dairy System v. Hayward, 82 N.H. 193, 132 A. 12 (1926)—§§ 361, 366.

Manchester Nat'l Bank v. Roche, 186 F.2d 827 (1st Cir. 1951)—§ 330.

Manly v. Ohio Shoe Co., 25 F.2d 384 (4th Cir. 1928)—§ 162.

Mann Corp., H. S. v. Moody, 144 Cal.App.2d 310, 301 P.2d 28 (1956)—§ 321.

Manning v. Metal Stamping Corp., 396 F.Supp. 1376 (E.D.Ill.1975)—§ 178.

Mansfield Propane Gas Co. v. Folger Gas Co., 231 Ga. 868, 204 S.E.2d 625 (1974)—§ 272.

Mantell v. International Plastic Harmonica Corp., 141 N.J.Eq. 379, 55 A.2d 250 (Ct.Err. & App.1947)—§ 202.

Mapes v. Kalva Corp., 60 Ill.App.3d 654, 18 Ill.Dec. 66, 386 N.E.2d 148 (1979)— §§ 130, 131, 145.

Marchiondo v. Scheck, 78 N.M. 440, 432 P.2d 405 (1967)—§ 45.

Marcus & Co. v. K. L. G. Baking Co., 122 N.J.L. 202, 3 A.2d 627 (1939)—§ 351.

Mariani v. Gold, 13 N.Y.S.2d 365 (Sup.Ct.1939)—§ 266.

Mariani v. Hennington, 229 Miss. 212, 90 So.2d 356 (1956)—§ 240.

Marine Contractors Co. v. Hurley, 365 Mass. 280, 310 N.E.2d 915 (1974)—§§ 71, 95, 188.

Marine Trust Co. v. Richardson, 171 Misc. 556, 12 N.Y.S.2d 834 (1939)—§ 289.

Marino v. Nolan, 24 A.D.2d 1005, 266 N.Y.S.2d 65 (1965)—§ 226.

Markey v. Brunson, 286 F. 893 (4th Cir. 1923)—§ 222.

Marks v. Cowdin, 226 N.Y. 138, 123 N.E. 139 (1919)—§ 131.

Marks Realty Co., Alfred v. "Churchills," 90 Misc. 370, 153 N.Y.S. 264 (1915)— § 265.

Marks Realty Co., Alfred v. Hotel Hermitage Co., 170 A.D. 484, 156 N.Y.S. 179 (1915)—§ 265.

Marr Enterprises v. Lewis Refrigeration Co., 556 F.2d 951 (9th Cir. 1977)— § 195.

Marreco v. Richardson, [1908] 2 K.B. 584—§ 82.

TABLE OF CASES

Maurer, Inc. J. A. v. United States, 202 Ct.Cl. 813, 485 F.2d 588 (1973)—§ **266.**

Maxey v. Glindmeyer, 379 So.2d 297 (Miss.1980)—§ **374.**

Maxwell Dynamometer Co. v. United States, 181 Ct.Cl. 607, 386 F.2d 855 (1967) —§ **272.**

May Dept. Stores v. First Hartford Corp., 435 F.Supp. 849 (D.Conn.1977)— § **178.**

Mays Mills v. McRae, 187 N.C. 707, 122 S.E. 762 (1924)—§ **350.**

Maytag Co. v. Alward, 253 Iowa 455, 112 N.W.2d 654 (1962)—§ **372.**

Mazda Motors of America v. Southwestern Motors, 36 N.C.App. 1, 243 S.E.2d 793 (1978)—§§ **178, 179.**

Mealey v. Kanealy, 226 Iowa 1266, 286 N.W. 500 (1939)—§ **202.**

Meder v. Superior Oil Co., 151 Miss. 814, 119 So. 318 (1928)—§ **87.**

Medford, City of v. Bessonette, 255 Or. 53, 463 P.2d 865 (1970)—§ **144.**

Megan v. Updike Grain Corp., 94 F.2d 551 (8th Cir. 1938)—§ **265.**

Melancon v. Provident Life & Acc. Ins. Co., 176 La. 1055, 147 So. 346 (1932)— § **243.**

Melo v. National Fuse & Powder Co., 267 F.Supp. 611 (D.Colo.1967)—§§ **294, 295.**

Melroy v. Kemmerer, 218 Pa. 381, 67 A. 699 (1907)—§ **73.**

Mercado v. Mitchell, 83 Wis.2d 17, 264 N.W.2d 532 (1978)—§§ **311, 313.**

Mercantile Nat'l Bank v. Hudgens, 412 S.W.2d 364 (Tex.Civ.App.1967)—§§ **112, 115, 116.**

Mercer v. C. A. Roberts Co., 570 F.2d 1232 (5th Cir. 1978)—§§ **130, 139.**

Merchants Indem. Corp. v. Eggleston, 37 N.J. 114, 179 A.2d 505 (1962)—§ **84.**

Mesibov, Glinert & Levy, Inc. v. Cohen Bros. Mfg. Co., 245 N.Y. 305, 157 N.E. 148 (1927)—§ **134.**

Metro-Goldwyn–Mayer Distributing Corp. v. Cocke, 56 S.W.2d 489 (Tex.CivApp. 1933)—§ **176.**

Metropolitan Life Ins. Co. v. Richter, 173 Okl. 489, 49 P.2d 94 (1935)—§ **73.**

Metzgar v. Metzgar, 1 Rawie 227 (1829)—§ **336.**

Meyer v. Benko, 55 Cal.App.3d 937, 127 Cal.Rptr. 846 (1976)—§§ **158, 358, 364.**

Meyer v. Sullivan, 40 Cal.App. 723, 181 P. 847 (1919)—§ **270.**

Meyer Drilling Co., H. O. v. Alton V. Phillips Co., 2 Wash.App. 600, 468 P.2d 1008 (1970)—§ **181.**

Meyers v. Selznick Co., 373 F.2d 218 (2d Cir. 1966)—§ **212.**

Meyerson v. New Idea Hosiery Co., 217 Ala. 153, 115 So. 94 (1927)—§ **21.**

Micro-King Co., United States ex rel. v. Community Science Technology, Inc., 574 F.2d 1292 (5th Cir. 1978)—§ **234.**

Middleton v. Nibling, 142 S.W. 968 (Tex.Civ.App.1911)—**Ch. 13.**

Midland Nat'l Bank v. Security Elevator Co., 161 Minn. 30, 200 N.W. 851 (1924) —§ **54.**

Midwest Color Offset Co. v. Thermal Elec. Corp., 116 Ohio St. 482, 156 N.E. 595 (1927)—§ **242.**

Mier Co. v. Hadden, 148 Mich. 488, 111 N.W. 1040 (1907)—§ **360.**

Mignot v. Parkhill, 237 Or. 450, 391 P.2d 755 (1964)—§ **227.**

Miles v. Love, 1 Kan.App.2d 630, 573 P.2d 622 (1977)—§§ **168, 169.**

Millen v. Gulesian, 229 Mass. 27, 118 N.E. 267 (1918)—§ **373.**

Miller v. Bare, 457 F.Supp. 1359 (W.D.Pa.1978)—§ **214.**

Miller v. Campello Co-operative Bank, 344 Mass. 76, 181 N.E.2d 345 (1962)— § **272.**

Miller v. Craig, 83 Ky. 623 (1886)—§ **158.**

Miller v. Denny, 115 Wash. 635, 197 P. 936 (1921)—§ **118.**

Miller v. Dyer, 20 Cal.2d 526, 127 P.2d 901 (1942)—§ **330.**

TABLE OF CASES

Monroe Mfg., C. N. v. United States, 143 F.Supp. 449 (E.D.Mich.1956)—§§ 153, 376.

Monrosa v. Carbon Black Export, Inc., 359 U.S. 180 (1959)—§ 208.

Montana Seeds, Inc. v. Holliday, —— Mont. ——, 582 P.2d 1223 (1978)—§ 282.

Montanaro v. Pandolfini, 148 Conn. 153, 168 A.2d 550 (1961)—§ 131.

Montgomery v. Board of Educ., 102 Ohio St. 189, 131 N.E. 497 (1921)—§ 267.

Montgomery v. Futuristic Foods, Inc., 66 A.D.2d 64, 411 N.Y.S.2d 371 (2d Dep't 1978)—§ 130.

Montgomery Ward & Co. v. Reich, 131 Colo. 407, 282 P.2d 1091 (1955)—§ 240.

Montpelier, City of v. National Sur. Co., 97 Vt. 111, 122 A. 484 (1923)—§ 261.

Moor & Co., T. E. v. Hardcastle, 421 S.W.2d 126 (Tex.Civ.App.1967)—§ 317.

Moore v. Darton, 4 De G. & S. 517 (Ch.1851)—§ 332.

Moore v. Furstenwerth-Uhl Jewelry Co., 17 Ga.App. 669, 87 S.E. 1097 (1916)— § 153.

Moore v. Moore, 103 Ga. 517, 30 S.E. 535 (1898)—Ch. 5.

"Moore" Burger, Inc. v. Phillips Petroleum Co., 492 S.W.2d 934 (Tex.1972)— § 139.

Morad v. Silva, 331 Mass. 94, 117 N.E.2d 290 (1954)—§ 363.

Moran v. Audette, 217 A.2d 653 (D.C.Ct.App.1966)—§ 303.

Morfeld v. Andrews, 579 P.2d 426 (Wyo.1978)—§ 279.

Morgan v. Edgar, 107 W.Va. 536, 149 S.E. 606 (1929)—§ 292.

Morgan v. Mutual Benefit Life Ins. Co., 16 Cal.App. 85, 116 P. 385 (1911)— § 339.

Morgan v. Singley, 560 S.W.2d 746 (Tex.Civ.App.1977)—§ 232.

Morgan's Home Equipment Corp. v. Martucci, 390 Pa. 618, 136 A.2d 838 (1957) —§ 357.

Morris v. Ballard, 16 F.2d 175 (D.C.Cir. 1926)—§ 34.

Morris v. Baron, [1918] A.C. 1—§ 149.

Morris v. George C. Banning, Inc., 49 Ohio L.Abs. 530, 77 N.E.2d 372 (1947)— § 330.

Morris Cohon & Co. v. Russell, 23 N.Y.2d 569, 297 N.Y.S.2d 947, 245 N.E.2d 712 (1969)—§ 131.

Morrison v. Johnson, 148 Minn. 343, 181 N.W. 945 (1921)—§ 87.

Morrison v. Thoelke, 155 So.2d 889 (Fla.Dist.Ct.App.1963)—§ 63.

Morrison Flying Serv. v. Deming Nat'l Bank, 404 F.2d 856 (10th Cir. 1968)— § 73.

Morrow, In re Estate of, 9 Storey 262, 219 A.2d 137 (Del.Super.Ct.1966)—§ 296.

Morse v. Commissioner, 100 F.2d 593 (7th Cir. 1938)—§ 311.

Morton v. Lamb, 7 T.R. 125, 101 Eng.Rep. 890 (K.B.1797)—§ 234.

Moser Paper Co. v. North Shore Pub. Co., 83 Wis.2d 852, 266 N.W.2d 411 (1978)—§§ 258, 260.

Moss & Raley v. Wren, 102 Tex. 567, 113 S.W. 739 (1908)—§ 361.

Motherway v. Wall, 168 Mass. 333, 47 N.E. 135 (1897)—§ 170.

Motive Parts Co. v. Robinson, 53 Ill.App.3d 935, 11 Ill.Dec. 665, 369 N.E.2d 119 (1977)—§ 282.

Motley v. Motley, 255 N.C. 190, 120 S.E.2d 422 (1961)—§ 190.

Mount Pleasant Stable Co. v. Steinberg, 238 Mass. 567, 131 N.E. 295 (1921)— § 350.

Mountain States Bolt, Nut & Screw Co. v. Best-Way Transp., 116 Ariz. 123, 568 P.2d 430 (Ct.App.1977)—§ 181.

Mountain States Constr. Co., United States ex rel. A. V. DeBlasio Constr. Co. v., 588 F.2d 259 (9th Cir. 1978)—§ 241.

Mubi v. Broomfield, 108 Ariz. 39, 492 P.2d 700 (1972)—§§ 37, 48.

N

CITED IN REPORTER'S NOTES

Neale v. Wright, 130 Ky. 146, 112 S.W. 1115 (1908)—§ 152.

Nebaco, Inc. v. Riverview Realty Co., 87 Nev. 55, 482 P.2d 305 (1971)—§ 264.

Negyessy v. Strong, 136 Vt. 193, 388 A.2d 383 (1978)—§ 172.

Neill v. Shamburg, 158 Pa. 263, 27 A. 992 (1893)—§ 161.

Nelson, In re Estate of, 85 Wash.2d 602, 537 P.2d 765 (1975)—§§ 125, 139.

Nelson v. Gibe, 162 Mich. 410, 127 N.W. 304 (1911)—§ 358.

Nelson v. Hazel, 91 Idaho 850, 433 P.2d 120 (1967)—§ 374.

Nelson v. Shelby Mfg. & Imp. Co., 96 Ala. 515, 11 So. 695 (1892)—§ 141.

Nelson v. Wilson, 97 S.W.2d 287 (Tex.Civ.App.1936)—§ 191.

Neri v. Retail Marine Co., 30 N.Y.2d 393, 334 N.Y.S.2d 165, 285 N.E.2d 311 (1972)—§§ 347, 350.

Neuffer v. Bakery & Confectionery Workers Int'l, 307 F.2d 671 (D.C.Cir. 1962) —§ 185.

New England Structures, Inc. v. Loranger, 354 Mass. 62, 234 N.E.2d 888 (1968) —§ 248.

New Era Homes v. Forster, 299 N.Y. 303, 86 N.E.2d 757 (1949)—§ 234.

New York & Oriental S. S. Co. v. Automobile Ins. Co., 37 F.2d 461 (2d Cir. 1930)—§ 211.

New York Life Ins. Co. v. Dunlevy, 241 U.S. 518 (1916)—§ 339.

New York Life Ins. Co. v. Statham, 93 U.S. 24 (1876)—§ 271.

New York Life Ins. Co. v. Viglas, 297 U.S. 672 (1936)—§§ 243, 253.

New York, N. H. & H. R. R., In re, 25 F.Supp. 874 (D.Conn.1938)—§ 320.

New York Trust Co. v. Island Oil & Transp. Corp., 34 F.2d 649 (2d Cir. 1929)— § 254.

Newbern v. Fisher, 198 N.C. 385, 151 S.E. 875 (1930)—§ 118.

Newman & Snell's State Bank v. Hunter, 243 Mich. 331, 220 N.W. 665 (1928)— § 79.

Newsome v. Western Union Tel. Co., 153 N.C. 153, 69 S.E. 10 (1910)—§ 351.

1901 Wyoming Ave. Coop. Ass'n v. Lee, 345 A.2d 456 (D.C.Ct.App.1975)—§ 220.

Nissenberg v. Felleman, 339 Mass. 717, 162 N.E.2d 304 (1959)—§ 307.

Nizamuddowlah v. Bengal Cabaret, 92 Misc.2d 220, 399 N.Y.S.2d 854 (1977)— § 179.

Nodland v. Chirpich, 307 Minn. 360, 240 N.W.2d 513 (1976)—§ 261.

Nohra v. Evans, 509 S.W.2d 648 (Tex.Civ.App.1974)—§ 15.

Noke v. Ingham, 1 Wils. 89, 95 Eng.Rep. 508 (1745)—§ 290.

Normandin v. Kimball, 92 N.H. 62, 25 A.2d 39 (1942)—§ 13.

Norrington v. Wright, 115 U.S. 188 (1885)—§§ 240, 242, 250.

North American Graphite Corp. v. Allan, 184 F.2d 387 (D.C.Cir. 1950)—§ 227.

North & Son, Joseph W. v. North, 91 N.J.Eq. 390, 110 A. 581 (1920)—§ 305.

North Unit Potato Co. v. Spada Distributing Co., 260 Or. 468, 490 P.2d 995 (1971)—§§ 220, 221.

Northern Commercial Co. v. United Airmotive, 101 F.Supp. 169 (D.Alaska 1951)—§ 90.

Northern Corp. v. Chugach Elec. Ass'n, 518 P.2d 76 (Alaska)—§§ 261, 266, 272.

Northern Delaware Indus. Development Corp. v. E. W. Bliss Co., 245 A.2d 431 (Del.Ch.1968)—§ 366.

Northern Helex Co. v. United States, 197 Ct.Cl. 118, 455 F.2d 546 (1972)— §§ 241, 247, 350.

Northern State Constr. Co. v. Robbins, 76 Wash.2d 357, 457 P.2d 187 (1969) —§ 226.

Northwest Fixture Co. v. Kilbourne & Clark Co., 128 F. 256 (9th Cir. 1904)— § 356.

Orkin Exterminating Co. v. Harris, 224 Ga. 759, 164 S.E.2d 727 (1968)—§ 232.

Orkin Exterminating Co. v. Montagano, 359 So.2d 512 (Fla.Dist.Ct.App.1978) —§ 195.

Orlando v. Ottaviani, 337 Mass. 157, 148 N.E.2d 373 (1958)—§ 129.

Orr. v. Orr, 440 U.S. 268 (1979)—§ 190.

Ortelere v. Teachers' Retirement Bd., 25 N.Y.2d 196, 303 N.Y.S.2d 362, 250 N.E.2d 460 (1969)—§ 15.

Ortez v. Bargas, 29 Haw. 548 (1927)—§ 94.

O'Shea v. Morris, 112 Neb. 102, 198 N.W. 866 (1924)—§ 381.

Oswald v. Allen, 417 F.2d 43 (2d Cir. 1969)—§ 20.

Outcault Advertising Co. v. Buell, 71 Or. 52, 141 P. 1020 (1914)—§ 42.

Overstreet v. Barr, 255 Ky. 82, 72 S.W.2d 1014 (1934)—§ 197.

Owen v. Hendricks, 433 S.W.2d 164 (Tex.1968)—§ 132.

Owen v. Sumrall, 204 Miss. 15, 36 So.2d 800 (1948)—§ 88.

Owen v. Tunison, 131 Me. 42, 158 A. 926 (1932)—§ 26.

Owens v. Owens, 196 Va. 966, 86 S.E.2d 181 (1955)—§ 173.

Oxley v. Ralston Purina Co., 349 F.2d 328 (6th Cir. 1965)—§ 139.

Ozier v. Haines, 411 Ill. 160, 103 N.E.2d 485 (1952)—§ 221.

P

Pacific Grape Products Co. v. Commissioner, 219 F.2d 862 (9th Cir. 1955)— § 221.

Pacific Southwest Trust & Sav. Bank v. Mayer, 138 Wash. 85, 244 P. 248 (1926)—§ 291.

Padgham v. Wilson Music Co., 3 Wis.2d 363, 88 N.W.2d 679 (1958)—§ 148.

Page v. Higgins, 150 Mass. 27, 22 N.E. 63 (1889)—§ 152.

Page & Wirtz Constr. Co. v. Van Doren Bri-Tico Co., 432 S.W.2d 731 (Tex. Civ.App.1968)—§ 33.

Paige v. Faure, 229 N.Y. 114, 127 N.E. 898 (1920)—§§ 320, 323.

Paisner v. Renaud, 102 N.H. 27, 149 A.2d 867 (1959)—§ 202.

Pajewski v. Perry, 363 A.2d 429 (Del.1976)—§ 313.

Pakas v. Hollingshead, 184 N.Y. 211, 77 N.E. 40 (1906)—§ 243.

Palmer v. Fox, 274 Mich. 252, 264 N.W. 361 (1936)—§§ 232, 241, 243.

Palmer v. Guillow, 224 Mass. 1, 112 N.E. 493 (1916)—§ 225.

Palmer v. Wheeler, 258 Or. 41, 481 P.2d 68 (1971)—§§ 135, 140.

Palmer Supply Co., State ex rel. v. Walsh & Co., 575 P.2d 1213 (Alaska 1978) —§ 258.

Palumbo v. James, 266 Mass. 1, 164 N.E. 466 (1929)—§ 129.

Paola Gas Co. v. Paola Glass Co., 56 Kan. 614, 44 P. 621 (1896)—§ 352.

Papas v. Jack O. A. Nelsen Agency, 81 Wis.2d 863, 260 N.W.2d 721 (1978)— § 311.

Pappas v. Bever, 219 N.W.2d 720 (Iowa 1974)—§§ 2, 206.

Paradise Homes v. Central Sur. & Ins. Co., 84 Nev. 109, 437 P.2d 78 (1968)— § 354.

Paragon Homes, Inc. v. Carter, 56 Misc.2d 463, 288 N.Y.S.2d 817 (Sup.Ct.1968) —§ 208.

Pardue v. Bryant, 219 Ark. 727, 244 S.W.2d 135 (1951)—§ 144.

Park Falls State Bank v. Fordyce, 206 Wis. 628, 238 N.W. 516 (1931)—§ 86.

Park Place Discount Co. v. Taylor, 119 N.J.L. 253, 195 A. 520 (Ct.Err. & App. 1937)—§ 88.

Parker v. Arthur Murray, 10 Ill.App.3d 1000, 295 N.E.2d 487 (1973)—§ 262.

Perry v. Little, 419 S.W.2d 198 (Tex.1967)—§ 238.

Perry v. Mt. Hope Iron Co., 15 R.I. 380, 5 A. 632 (1886)—§ 67.

Perry & Wallis, Inc. v. United States, 192 Ct.Cl. 310, 427 F.2d 722 (1970)—
§§ 201, 203, 206.

Peru Wheel Co. v. Union Coal Co., 295 Ill.App. 276, 14 N.E.2d 998 (1938)—
§ 368.

Petersen v. Mecham, 16 Utah 2d 161, 397 P.2d 295 (1964)—§ 162.

Peterson v. Arellono, 289 Minn. 541, 185 N.W.2d 282 (1971)—§ 161.

Peterson v. Colorado Potato Flake & Mfg. Co., 164 Colo. 304, 435 P.2d 237
(1967)—§ 352.

Petrangelo v. Pollard, 356 Mass. 696, 255 N.E.2d 342 (1970)—§ 250.

Petroleum Products Distributing Co. v. Alton Tank Line, 165 Iowa 398, 146
N.W. 52 (1914)—§ 52.

Petroleum Research Corp. v. Barnsdall Ref. Corp., 188 Okl. 62, 105 P.2d 1047
(1940)—§ 62.

Petters & Co. v. School Dist. No. 5, 37 Wyo. 237, 260 P. 678 (1927)—§ 336.

Petterson v. Pattberg, 248 N.Y. 86, 161 N.E. 428 (1928)—§§ 45, 77.

Pettigrew v. Denwalt, 431 P.2d 333 (Okl.1967)—§§ 131, 132, 135.

Phalen v. United States Trust Co., 186 N.Y. 178, 78 N.E. 943 (1906)—§ 90.

Phelan v. Middle States Oil Corp., 154 F.2d 978 (2d Cir. 1946)—§ 340.

Phelps v. Herro, 215 Md. 223, 137 A.2d 159 (1957)—§ 253.

Phelps v. McQuade, 220 N.Y. 232, 115 N.E. 441 (1917)—§ 163.

Philbin Inv. Inc. v. Orb Enterprises, 35 N.C.App. 622, 242 S.E.2d 176 (1978)—
§ 155.

Philadelphia v. Tripple, 230 Pa. 480, 79 A. 703 (1911)—§ 373.

Philadelphia Ball Club v. Lajoie, 202 Pa. 210, 51 A. 973 (1902)—§ 367.

Phillips v. Homfray, L.R. 6 Ch.Rep. 770 (1871)—§ 161.

Phillips v. Moor, 71 Me. 78 (1880)—§ 70.

Phillips v. Ward, 2 H. & C. 717, 159 Eng.Rep. 297 (1863)—§§ 291, 292.

Phipps Land Co. v. Wilwat Properties, 231 Ga. 305, 201 S.E.2d 408 (1973)—
§ 320.

Phoenix Ins. Co. v. DeMonchy, 141 L.T.R. (n. s.) 439 (H.L.1929)—§ 211.

Pierce v. Foley Bros., 283 Minn. 360, 168 N.W.2d 346 (1969)—§ 64.

Pierce v. Rush, 210 Ga. 718, 82 S.E.2d 649 (1954)—§ 131.

Pierson v. Morch, 82 N.Y. 503 (1880)—§ 51.

Pillois v. Billingsley, 179 F.2d 205 (2d Cir. 1950)—§ 205.

Pinches v. Swedish Evangelical Lutheran Church, 55 Conn. 183, 10 A. 264
(1887)—§ 374.

Pitek v. McGuire, 51 N.M. 364, 184 P.2d 647 (1947)—§ 136.

Pitts v. Pitchford, 201 So.2d 563 (Fla.Dist.Ct.App.1967)—§ 96.

Pittsburg Vitrified Paving & Building Brick Co. v. Cerebus Oil Co., 79 Kan.
603, 100 P. 631 (1909)—§ 86.

Pittsburgh Steel Co. v. Hollingshead & Blei, 202 Ill.App. 177 (1916)—§§ 175,
176.

Pittsburgh Terminal Coal Corp. v. Bennett, 73 F.2d 387 (3d Cir. 1934)—§ 94.

Pittsburgh Testing Laboratory v. Farnsworth & Chambers, Inc., 251 F.2d 77
(10th Cir. 1958)—§ 89.

Plains Cotton Coop. v. Wolf, 553 S.W.2d 800 (Tex.Civ.App.1977)—§§ 152, 153,
157.

Plant City Steel Corp. v. National Machinery Exchange, 23 N.Y.2d 472, 297
N.Y.S.2d 559, 245 N.E.2d 213 (1969)—§ 281.

Plante v. Jacobs, 10 Wis.2d 567, 103 N.W.2d 296 (1960)—§ 235.

Plasko v. Orser, 373 Mass. 40, 364 N.E.2d 1220 (1977)—§ 260.

Purchasing Associates v. Weitz, 13 N.Y.2d 267, 196 N.E.2d 245 (1963)—§ 188.

Pym v. Campbell, 6 El. & Bl. 370, 119 Eng.Rep. 903 (Q.B.1856)—§§ 59, 217.

Q

Quad Constr., Inc. v. William A. Smith Contracting Co., 534 F.2d 1391 (10th Cir. 1976)—§§ 206, 222.

Quality Fin. Co. v. Hurley, 337 Mass. 150, 148 N.E.2d 385 (1958)—§ 336.

Queal & Co., J. H. v. Peterson, 138 Iowa 514, 116 N.W. 593 (1908)—§ 74.

Quenzer v. Quenzer, 225 Kan. 83, 587 P.2d 880 (1978)—§ 214.

Quinn v. Briggs, 172 Mont. 468, 565 P.2d 297 (1977)—§§ 153, 157.

Quick v. American Steel & Pump Corp., 397 F.2d 561 (2d Cir. 1968)—§ 243.

Quilter v. Wendland, 403 S.W.2d 335 (Tex.1966)—§ 304.

Quinn v. Straus Broadcasting Group, 309 F.Supp. 1208 (S.D.N.Y.1970)—§ 344.

Quintin Vespa Co. v. Construction Serv. Co., 343 Mass. 547, 179 N.E.2d 895 (1962)—§ 237.

R

R & R Homes, Inc. v. Gellman, 144 N.Y.S.2d 54 (Sup.Ct.1955)—§ 330.

Rabinowitz v. Marcus, 100 Conn. 86, 123 A. 21 (1923)—§ 378.

Rabinowitz v. People's Nat'l Bank, 235 Mass. 102, 126 N.E. 289 (1920)—§ 342.

Racine Wagon & Carriage Co. v. Legeois, 120 Wis. 497, 98 N.W. 218 (1904)—§ 288.

Raddue v. LeSage, 138 Cal.App.2d 852, 292 P.2d 522 (1956)—§ 154.

Rademacher v. Russ, 131 F.Supp. 50 (D.Minn.1955)—§ 382.

Radley v. Smith, 6 Utah 2d 314, 313 P.2d 465 (1957)—§ 328.

Raffles v. Wichelhaus, 2 Hurl. & C. 906, 159 Eng.Rep. 375 (Ex.1864)—§ 20.

Rague v. New York Evening Journal Pub. Co., 164 A.D. 126, 149 N.Y.S. 668 (1914)—§ 54.

Raible v. Puerto Rico Indus. Development Co., 392 F.2d 424 (1st Cir. 1968)—§ 69.

Raisor v. Jackson, 311 Ky. 803, 225 S.W.2d 657 (1949)—§ 261.

Ramey v. Koons, 230 F.2d 802 (5th Cir. 1956)—§ 318.

Randazzo v. Kroenke, 373 Mich. 61, 127 N.W.2d 880 (1964)—§ 131.

Raner v. Goldberg, 244 N.Y. 438, 155 N.E. 733 (1927)—§ 265.

Ranger Constr. Co. v. Dixie Floor Co., 433 F.Supp. 442 (D.S.C.1977)—§ 251.

Ranger, Inc., Lynn M. v. Gildersleeve, 106 Conn. 372, 138 A. 142 (1927)—§ 233.

Ranney-Davis Mercantile Co. v. Shawano Canning Co., 111 Kan. 68, 206 P. 337 (1922)—§§ 263, 272.

Rape v. Lyerly, 287 N.C. 601, 215 S.E.2d 737 (1975)—§ 131.

Ratzlaff v. Franz Foods, 250 Ark. 1003, 468 S.W.2d 239 (1971)—§ 302.

Rayden Engineering Corp. v. Church, 337 Mass. 652, 151 N.E.2d 57 (1958)—§ 90.

Rayner & Co., J. H. v. Hambro's Bank, Ltd., [1943] 1 K.B. 37 (C.A.)—§ 221.

Readmond v. Matsushita Elec. Corp., 355 F.Supp. 1073 (E.D.Pa.1973)—§ 139.

Real Estate Co. v. Rudolph, 301 Pa. 502, 153 A. 438 (1930)—§ 87.

Redfearn v. Citizens & Southern Nat'l Bank, 122 Ga.App. 282, 176 S.E.2d 627 (1970)—§ 259.

Redman v. Whitney, 541 S.W.2d 889 (Tex.Civ.App.1976)—§ 26.

Reed v. Harvey, 253 Iowa 10, 110 N.W.2d 442 (1961)—§ 152.

Reed v. Loyal Protective Ass'n, 154 Mich. 161, 117 N.W. 600 (1908)—§ 271.

Reed v. Reed, 404 U.S. 71 (1971)—§ 12.

S

San Francisco Sec. Corp. v. Phoenix Motor Co., 25 Ariz. 531, 220 P. 229 (1923)
—§ 336.

San Gabriel Val. Ready-Mixt v. Casillas, 142 Cal.App.2d 137, 298 P.2d 76 (1956)
—§ 89.

Sancha v. Arnold, 114 Cal.App.2d 772, 251 P.2d 67 (1952)—§ 124.

Sanders v. McNutt, 147 Ohio St. 408, 72 N.E.2d 72 (1947)—§ 131.

Sardo v. Fidelity & Deposit Co. of Maryland, 100 N.J.Eq. 332, 134 A. 774 (1926)
—§§ 155, 157.

Satler Lumber Co., L. L. v. Exler, 239 Pa. 135, 86 A. 793 (1913)—§ 297.

Saunders Co., W. B. v. Galbraith, 40 Ohio App. 155, 178 N.E. 34 (1931)—§ 88.

Sauser v. Kearney, 147 Iowa 335, 126 N.W. 322 (1910)—§ 130.

Savage v. Peter Kiewit Sons' Co., 254 Or. 411, 461 P.2d 59 (1969)—§ 261.

Savage v. Peter Kiewit Sons' Co., 249 Or. 147, 432 P.2d 519 (1967)—§ 261.

Sawyer Farmers Coop. v. Linke, 231 N.W.2d 791 (N.D.1975)—§§ 256, 257.

Saylor v. Handley Motor Co., 169 A.2d 683 (D.C.App.1961)—§§ 164, 172.

Scaduto v. Orlando, 381 F.2d 587 (2d Cir. 1967)—§ 373.

Scammell & Nephew, G. v. Ouston, [1941] 1 A.C. 251—§ 33.

Schaefer Elec., Inc., J.C., United States ex rel. v. O. Frank Heinz Constr.
Co., 300 F.Supp. 396 (S.D.Ill.1969)—§ 4.

Schafer v. Sunset Packing Co., 256 Or. 539, 474 P.2d 529 (1970)—§ 261.

Schenck v. State Line Tel. Co., 238 N.Y. 308, 144 N.E. 592 (1924)—§ 380.

Schenectady Steel Co. v. Bruno Trimpoli Gen. Constr. Co., 34 N.Y.2d 939,
359 N.Y.S.2d 560, 316 N.E.2d 875 (1974)—§ 251.

Scherer v. East Side Nat'l Bank, 263 N.Y. 190, 188 N.E. 645 (1934)—§ 74.

Schilling State ex rel. v. Baird, 65 Wis.2d 394, 222 N.W.2d 666 (1974)—§ 347.

Schinstock v. Butterfield, 141 Neb. 877, 5 N.W.2d 86 (1942)—§ 245.

Schlotthauer v. Krenzelok, 274 Wis. 1, 79 N.W.2d 76 (1956)—§ 382.

Schmid v. Whitten, 114 S.C. 245, 103 S.E. 553 (1920)—§ 360.

Schmidt v. Louisville & N. R. Co., 101 Ky. 441, 41 S.W. 1015 (1897)—§ 357.

Schneider v. Armour & Co., 323 Mass. 28, 80 N.E.2d 34 (1948)—§§ 307, 312.

Schneider v. Ferrigno, 110 Conn. 86, 147 A. 303 (1929)—§ 312.

Schnell v. Nell, 17 Ind. 29, 27 Am.Dec. 453 (1861)—§ 79.

Schoblom, State ex rel. v. Anacortes Veneer, 42 Wash.2d 338, 255 P.2d 379
(1953)—§ 367.

Scholl v. Tallman, 247 N.W.2d 490 (S.D.1976)—§ 281.

School Dist. of Scottsbluff v. Olson Constr. Co., 153 Neb. 451, 45 N.W.2d
164 (1950)—§ 153.

School Sisters of Notre Dame v. Kusnitt, 125 Md. 323, 93 A. 928 (1915)—§ 153.

School Trustees of Trenton v. Bennett, 27 N.J.L. 513 (1859)—§§ 263, 266.

Schoor Associates, Inc., Howard M. v. Holmdel Heights Constr. Co., 68 N.J.
95, 343 A.2d 401 (1975)—§ 116.

Schram v. Sage, 46 F.Supp. 381 (1942)—§ 340.

Schremp v. Dubrowin, 257 Md. 623, 263 A.2d 827 (1970)—§§ 134, 135.

Schubert v. Ivey, 158 Conn. 583, 264 A.2d 562 (1969)—§ 289.

Schultz, Ex parte, 64 Nev. 264, 181 P.2d 585 (1947)—§ 9.

Schultz & Associates, Howard v. Broniec, 239 Ga. 181, 236 S.E.2d 265 (1977)—
§§ 184, 188.

Schumm v. Berg, 37 Cal.2d 174, 231 P.2d 39 (1951)—§ 79.

Schwartz v. Syver, 264 Wis. 526, 59 N.W.2d 489 (1953)—§ 374.

Schwartz-Jordan, Inc. v. Delisle Constr. Co., 569 S.W.2d 878 (Tex.1978)—§ 229.

Schwartzreich v. Bauman-Basch, Inc., 231 N.Y. 196, 131 N.E. 887 (1921)—§ 89.

Scientific Holding Co. v. Plessy Inc., 510 F.2d 15 (2d Cir. 1974)—§ 176.

Scott v. Coulson, [1903] 2 Ch. 249 (C.A.)—§ 152.

TABLE OF CASES

Shell Oil Co. v. Marinello, 63 N.J. 402, 307 A.2d 598 (1973)—§§ 205, 208.

Shepard v. Finance Associates of Auburn, 366 Mass. 182, 316 N.E.2d 597 (1974) —§§ 179, 181.

Shepard v. United States, 95 Ct.Cl. 407 (1942)—§ 376.

Sherman v. Metropolitan Life Ins. Co., 297 Mass. 330, 8 N.E.2d 892 (1937)— § 271.

Sherri v. National Sur. Co., 243 N.Y. 266, 153 N.E. 70 (1926)—§ 211.

Sherwood v. Walker, 66 Mich. 568, 33 N.W. 919 (1887)—§ 152.

Shield v. First Coleman Nat'l Bank, 1760 S.W.2d 277 (Tex.Civ.App.1942)— Ch. 13.

Shillman v. Hobstetter, 249 Md. 678, 241 A.2d 570 (1968)—§ 309.

Shirey v. Albright, 404 S.W.2d 152 (Tex.Civ.App.1966)—§ 63.

Shirk's Estate, In re, 186 Kan. 311, 350 P.2d 1 (1960)—§ 191.

Shockley v. Wickliffe, 150 S.C. 476, 148 S.E. 476 (1929)—§ 175.

Short v. Bullion-Beck & Champion Min. Co., 20 Utah 20, 57 P. 720 (1899)— § 179.

Showalter v. Ehlan, 5 Pa.Super.Ct. 242 (1897)—Ch. 15.

Shropshire, Woodliff & Co. v. Bush, 204 U.S. 186 (1907)—§ 340.

Shrum v. Zeltwanger, 559 P.2d 1384 (Wyo.1977)—§ 153.

Shubert Theatrical Co. v. Rath, 271 F. 827 (2d Cir. 1921)—§§ 63, 367.

Shuey v. United States, 92 U.S. 73 (1875)—§ 46.

Sidebotham v. Holland, [1895] 1 Q.B. 378 (C.A.)—§ 125.

Siebring Mfg. Co. v. Carlson Hybrid Corn Co., 246 Iowa 923, 70 N.W.2d 149 (1955)—§ 89.

Siefford v. Housing Auth., 192 Neb. 643, 223 N.W.2d 816 (1974)—§ 351.

Siegel v. Spear & Co., 234 N.Y. 479, 138 N.E. 414 (1923)—§ 90.

Sierra County Bd. of Educ., State ex rel. Freeman v., 49 N.M. 54, 157 P.2d 234 (1945)—§ 350.

Sigrist v. Century 21 Corp., 519 P.2d 362 (Colo.App.1974)—§ 50.

Silsbee v. Webber, 171 Mass. 378, 50 N.E. 555 (1898)—§§ 175, 176.

Silverman v. Bernot, 218 Va. 650, 239 S.E.2d 118 (1977)—§ 130.

Simmons v. Smith County Bank, 225 Miss. 384, 83 So.2d 441 (1955)—§ 336.

Simmons v. Swan, 275 U.S. 113 (1927)—§ 249.

Simms Co. v. Wolverton, 232 Or. 291, 375 P.2d 87 (1962)—§ 226.

Simplot Co., J. R. v. Chambers, 82 Idaho 104, 350 P.2d 211 (1960)—§ 318.

Simpson v. Norwesco, Inc., 442 F.Supp. 1102 (D.S.D.1977)—§ 281.

Singer v. Ritter, 167 Pa.Super.Ct. 154, 74 A.2d 520 (1950)—§ 294.

Sinnar v. LeRoy, 44 Wash.2d 728, 270 P.2d 800 (1954)—§ 178.

Sirkin v. Fourteenth Street Store, 124 A.D. 384, 108 N.Y.S. 830 (1908)—§§ 178, 197.

Sitlington v. Fulton, 281 F.2d 552 (10th Cir. 1960)—§§ 237, 351.

Skelly Oil Co. v. Ashmore, 365 S.W.2d 582 (Mo.1963)—§ 267.

Skelton v. Federal Sur. Co., 15 F.2d 756 (8th Cir. 1926)—§ 155.

Slade's Case, 4 Coke 92b (1602)—§ 82.

Slaughter v. C. I. T. Corp., 229 Ala. 411, 157 So. 463 (1934)—§ 261.

Slayton v. Slayton, 55 Ala.App. 351, 315 So.2d 558 (Ct.Civ.App.1975)—§§ 82, 86.

Sliwinski v. Gootstein, 234 Mich. 74, 208 N.W. 47 (1926)—§§ 84, 247.

Slodov, In re, 419 F.Supp. 64 (N.D.Ohio 1976)—§ 88.

Smaligo v. Fireman's Fund Ins. Co., 432 Pa. 133, 247 A.2d 577 (1968)—§ 38.

Smalley v. Baker, 262 Cal.App.2d 824, 69 Cal.Rptr. 521 (1968)—§ 15.

Smith v. Boyden, 49 Idaho 638, 290 P. 377 (1930)—§ 227.

Southworth v. Oliver, 284 Or. 361, 587 P.2d 994 (1978)—§§ **24, 26, 29.**

Sovereign Pocohontas Co. v. Bond, 120 F.2d 39 (D.C.Cir. 1941)—§ **162.**

Spang Indus. v. Aetna Cas. & Sur. Co., 512 F.2d 365 (2d Cir. 1975)—§ **351.**

Sparks & Sons, Ed. v. Joe Campbell Constr. Co., 99 Idaho 139, 578 P.2d 681 (1978)—§ **155.**

Spates v. Spates, 267 Md. 72, 296 A.2d 581 (1972)—§§ **302, 311.**

Spaulding v. Morse, 322 Mass. 149, 76 N.E.2d 137 (1947)—§ **202.**

Special Event Entertainment v. Rockefeller Center, Inc., 458 F.Supp. 72 (S. D.N.Y.1978)—§§ **139, 194.**

Spector v. National Cellulose Corp., 181 Misc. 465, 48 N.Y.S.2d 234 (1943)— § **90.**

Spellens v. Spellens, 49 Cal.2d 210, 317 P.2d 613 (1957)—§ **190.**

Spencer v. Hemmerde, [1922] 2 A.C. 507 (H.L.)—§ **82.**

Sperry & Hutchinson Co. v. O'Neill-Adams Co., 185 F. 231 (2d Cir. 1911)—§ **352.**

Spiegel v. Metropolitan Life Ins. Co., 6 N.Y.2d 91, 188 N.Y.S.2d 486, 160 N.E. 2d 40 (1959)—§ **90.**

Spiese v. Mutual Trust Co., 258 Pa. 414, 102 A. 119 (1917)—§ **351.**

Spiess v. Brandt, 230 Minn. 246, 41 N.W.2d 561 (1950)—§ **168.**

Spindle v. Travelers Ins. Companies, 66 Cal.App.3d 951, 136 Cal.Rptr. 404 (1977)—§ **205.**

Sponge Drivers' Ass'n v. Smith, Kline & French Co., 263 F. 70 (3d Cir. 1920) —§ **336.**

Spooner v. Reserve Life Ins. Co., 47 Wash.2d 454, 287 P.2d 735 (1955)—§§ **21, 45.**

Sporn v. Celebrity, Inc., 129 N.J.Super. 449, 324 A.2d 71 (1974)—§ **347.**

Spragg v. Polino, 114 W.Va. 369, 171 S.E. 897 (1933)—§ **132.**

Springstead v. Nees, 125 A.D. 230, 109 N.Y.S. 148 (1908)—§ **74.**

Sprinzen v. Nomberg, 63 A.D.2d 939, 406 N.Y.S.2d 322 (1978)—§ **188.**

Spitzer Co., L. E. v. Barron, 581 P.2d 213 (Alaska 1978)—§ **251.**

Squillante v. California Lands, Inc., 5 Cal.App.2d 89, 42 P.2d 81 (1935)—§ **263.**

Stadler v. First Nat'l Bank, 22 Mont. 190, 56 P. 111 (1899)—§ **336.**

Stagg v. Lawton, 133 Conn. 203, 49 A.2d 599 (1946)—§ **126.**

Stamford, Spalding & Boston Banking Co. v. Smith, 1 Q.B. 765 (1892)—§ **337.**

Standard Acc. Ins. Co. v. Wilmans, 214 F.Supp. 53 (E.D.Ark.1963)—§ **153.**

Standard Box Co. v. Mutual Biscuit Co., 10 Cal.App. 746, 103 P. 938 (1909)— § **176.**

Standard Chautauqua System v. Gift, 120 Kan. 101, 242 P. 145 (1926)—§ **323.**

Standard Oil Co. v. Koch, 260 N.Y. 150, 183 N.E. 278 (1932)—§ **131.**

Stanish v. Polish Roman Catholic Union of America, 484 F.2d 713 (7th Cir. 1973)—§ **351.**

Stansbery v. Medo-Land Dairy Inc., 5 Wash.2d 328, 105 P.2d 86 (1940)—§ **338.**

Stanton v. Mattson, 175 Neb. 767, 123 N.W.2d 844 (1963)—Ch. **15.**

Staples v. Rush, 99 So.2d 502 (La.App.1958)—§ **326.**

Star Credit Corp. v. Molina, 59 Misc.2d 290, 298 N.Y.S.2d 570 (Civ.Ct.N.Y. 1969)—§ **231.**

Stark v. Budwarker, Inc., 25 Mich.App. 305, 181 N.W.2d 298 (1970)—§ **227.**

State v. ——— (see opposing party)

State by Lefkowitz v. ITM, Inc., 52 Misc.2d 39, 275 N.Y.S.2d 303 (Sup.Ct. 1966)—§ **208.**

State Factors Corp. v. Sales Factors Corp., 257 A.D. 101, 12 N.Y.S.2d 12 (1st Dep't 1939)—§ **330.**

State Farm Mut. Auto. Ins. Co. v. Kendall, 104 Ga.App. 481, 122 S.E.2d 139 (1961)—§ **311.**

TABLE OF CASES

Sunray Oil Co. v. Lewis, 434 S.W.2d 777 (Mo.Ct.App.1968)—§ 37.

Sunshine v. M. R. Mansfield Realty, Inc., 195 Colo. 95, 575 P.2d 847 (1978)—§ 153.

Superior Brassiere Co. v. Zimetbaum, 214 A.D. 525, 212 N.Y.S. 473 (1st Dep't 1925)—§ 342.

Susi Contracting Co., United States ex rel. v. Zara, 146 F.2d 606 (2d Cir. 1944) —§ 373.

Susong v. Vaiden, 10 S.C. 247 (1878)—Ch. 13, § 296.

Suter v. Suter, 97 Idaho 461, 546 P.2d 1169 (1976)—§ 129.

Sutherland v. Wyer, 67 Me. 64 (1877)—§§ 347, 350.

Suthers v. Booker Hosp. District, 543 S.W.2d 723 (Tex.Civ.App.1976)—§ 302.

Swanson v. Holmquist, 13 Wash.App. 939, 539 P.2d 104 (1975)—§ 19.

Swartz v. Lieberman, 323 Mass. 109, 80 N.E.2d 5 (1948)—§ 89.

Sweigart v. Berk, 8 Serg. & Rawl. 308 (Pa.1822)—§ 298.

Swift & Co. v. Smigel, 115 N.J.Super. 391, 279 A.2d 895 (1971)—§§ 31, 48.

Swift Canadian Co. v. Banet, 224 F.2d 36 (3d Cir. 1955)—§ 265.

Swift Textiles v. Lawson, 135 Ga.App. 799, 219 S.E.2d 167 (1975)—§ 261.

Swinton v. Whitinsville Sav. Bank, 311 Mass. 677, 42 N.E.2d 808 (1942)— § 161.

Sy Jack Realty Co. v. Pergament Syosset Corp., 27 N.Y.2d 449, 318 N.Y.S.2d 720, 267 N.E.2d 462 (1971)—§ 229.

Sylvan Crest Sand & Gravel Co. v. United States, 150 F.2d 642 (2d Cir. 1845) —§ 205.

Sylvestre v. State, 298 Minn. 142, 214 N.W.2d 658 (1973)—§ 45.

Systron-Donner Corp., United States v., 486 F.2d 249 (9th Cir. 1973)—§ 153.

T

T & T Mfg. Co. v. A. T. Cross Co., 449 F.Supp. 813 (D.R.I.1978)—§ 178.

Tabani v. Hester, —— Ind.App. ——, 366 N.E.2d 193 (1977)—§ 281.

Taft v. Hyatt, 105 Kan. 35, 180 P. 213 (1919)—§ 53.

Taggert, Inc., R. J. v. Douglas County, 31 Or.App. 1137, 572 P.2d 1050 (1977)— §§ 87, 90.

Tailby v. Official Receiver, 13 App.Cas. 523 (H.L.1888)—§ 330.

Talcott, Inc., James v. Fullerton Cotton Mills, Inc., 208 F.2d 81 (5th Cir. 1953) —§ 131.

Talcott, Ltd., James v. John Lewis & Co., 3 All.E.R. 592 (C.A.1940)—§ 325.

Talman v. Dixon, 253 N.C. 193, 116 S.E.2d 338 (1960)—§ 154.

Tanenbaum v. Biscayne Osteopathic Hosp., 190 So.2d 777 (Fla.1966)—§ 139.

Tanenbaum Textile Co. v. Sidran, 423 S.W.2d 635 (Tex.Civ.App.1968)—§§ 33, 34.

Tanner v. Merrill, 108 Mich. 58, 65 N.W. 664 (1895)—§ 74.

Tanner Co., William B. v. WIOO, Inc., 528 F.2d 262 (3d Cir. 1975)—§§ 256, 257.

Tatem, Ltd., W. J. v. Gamboa, [1939] 1 K.B. 132—§ 265.

Tatsch v. Hamilton-Erickson Mfg. Co., 76 N.M. 729, 418 P.2d 187 (1966)— § 42.

Tauber v. Jacobson, 293 A.2d 861 (D.C.1972)—§ 90.

Tayloe v. Merchants' Fire Ins. Co., 50 U.S. (9 How.) 390 (1850)—§ 63.

Taylor v. Barton-Child Co., 228 Mass. 126, 117 N.E. 43 (1917)—§ 330.

Taylor v. Goelet, 208 N.Y. 253, 101 N.E. 867 (1913)—§ 242.

Taylor v. Hart, 73 Miss. 22, 18 So. 546 (1895)—§ 272.

TABLE OF CASES

Toland v. Kaliff, 435 S.W.2d 260 (Tex.Civ.App.1968)—§ 227.

Tolstoy Constr. Co. v. Minter, 78 Cal.App.3d 665, 143 Cal.Rptr. 570 (1978)— § 241.

Tolvey v. Criterion Film Productions, 2 All.E.R. 1625 (K.B.1936)—§ 344.

Tombari v. Griepp, 55 Wash.2d 771, 350 P.2d 452 (1960)—§ 363.

Tomlinson v. Tomlinson, 170 Ind.App. 338, 352 N.E.2d 785 (1976)—§ 190.

Tony Downs Foods v. United States, 209 Ct.Cl. 31, 530 F.2d 367 (1976)—§ 151.

Tool Metal Mfg. Co. v. Tungsten Elec. Co., [1955] 2 All.E.R. 657 (H.L.)— § 89.

Torkomian v. Russell, 90 Conn. 481, 97 A. 760 (1916)—§ 347.

Town & Country Bank v. James M. Canfield Contracting Co., 55 Ill.App.3d 91, 12 Ill.Dec. 826, 370 N.E.2d 630 (1977)—§ 302.

Town of (see name of town)

Town Planning & Engineering Associates v. Amesbury Specialty Co., 369 Mass. 737, 342 N.E.2d 706 (1976)—§ 181.

Towne v. Eisner, 245 U.S. 418 (1918)—§ 201.

Townsend v. Hargraves, 118 Mass. 325 (1875)—§ 235.

Traders' Nat'l Bank v. First Nat'l Bank, 142 Tenn. 229, 217 S.W. 977, 9 A.L.R. 382 (1920)—§ 63.

Traff v. Fabro, 337 Ill.App. 83, 84 N.E.2d 874 (1949)—§ 153.

Trak Microwave Corp. v. Medaris Management, Inc., 236 So.2d 189 (Fla.Dist. Ct.App.1970)—§§ 321, 330.

Transatlantic Fin. Corp. v. United States, 363 F.2d 312 (D.C.Cir.1966)— § 261.

Transbel Inv. Co. v. Scott, 344 Pa. 544, 26 A.2d 205 (1942)—§§ 94, 96, 98.

Traudt v. Nebraska Public Power Dist., 197 Neb. 765, 251 N.W.2d 148 (1977)— §§ 210, 215, 216, 218.

Treadway v. Western Cotton Oil & Ginning Co., 40 Ariz. 125, 10 P.2d 371 (1932) —§ 328.

Trenton Potteries v. Oliphant, 58 N.J.Eq. 507, 43 A. 723 (Ct.Err. & App.1899)— § 288.

Trevino v. Sample, 565 S.W.2d 93 (Tex.Civ.App.1978)—§ 169.

Trimmer v. Short, 492 S.W.2d 179 (Mo.Ct.App.1973)—§§ 130, 145.

Tri-State Roofing Co. v. Simon, 187 Pa.Super.Ct. 17, 142 A.2d 333 (1958)— § 175.

Trollope v. Koerner, 106 Ariz. 10, 470 P.2d 91 (1970)—§§ 125, 129, 131.

Trubowitch v. Riverbank Canning Co., 30 Cal.2d 335, 182 P.2d 182 (1947)— § 322.

Trust Co. v. Refrigeration Supplies, Inc., 241 Ga. 406, 246 S.E.2d 282 (1978)— § 299.

Trustees of Univ. of Pennsylvania v. Cadwalder, 277 Pa. 512, 121 A. 314 (1923) —§ 226.

Tuckwiller v. Tuckwiller, 413 S.W.2d 274 (Mo.1967)—§ 364.

Tulsa Opera House Co. v. Mitchell, 165 Okl. 61, 24 P.2d 997 (1933)—§ 272.

Tunkl v. Regents of Univ. of California, 60 Cal.2d 92, 32 Cal.Rptr. 33, 383 P.2d 441 (1963)—§ 195.

Turk v. Cook, 63 Ga. 681 (1879)—Ch. 15.

Turner v. Barber, 66 N.J.L. 496, 49 A. 676 (1901)—§§ 175, 176.

Turner v. Wexler, 14 Wash.App. 143, 538 P.2d 877 (1975)—§ 293.

Turner Concrete Steel Co. v. Chester Constr. & Contracting Co., 271 Pa. 205, 114 A. 780 (1921)—§§ 237, 242.

Tweddle v. Tweddle Litho Co., 80 Mich.App. 418, 264 N.W.2d 9 (1978)— § 185.

TABLE OF CASES

United States Printing & Lithograph Co. v. Powers, 233 N.Y. 143, 135 N.E. 225 (1922)—§§ 288, 291.

United States Trust Co. v. Frelinghuysen, 262 A.D. 259, 28 N.Y.S.2d 448 (1941) —§ 88.

United States Trust Co. v. New Jersey, 431 U.S. 1 (1977)—Introduction.

Universal Builders v. Moon Motor Lodge, 430 Pa. 550, 244 A.2d 10 (1968)— § 150.

University Caseworks Systems v. Bahre, 172 Ind.App. 624, 362 N.E.2d 155 (1977)—§§ 316, 321.

Urbanational Developers, Inc. v. Shamrock Engineering Co., —— Ind.App. ——, 372 N.E.2d 742 (1978)—§ 282.

Utah Int'l, Inc. v. Colorado-Ute Elec. Ass'n, 425 F.Supp. 1093 (D.Colo.1976)— § 241.

Utemark v. Samuel, 118 Cal.App.2d 313, 257 P.2d 656 (1953)—§ 373.

Utica Tool Co. v. Mitchell, 135 Ga.App. 635, 218 S.E.2d 650 (1975)—§ 130.

V

Valdez, City of v. Valdez Development Co., 523 P.2d 177 (Alaska 1974)— § 264.

Valley Constr. Co. v. Lake Hills Sewer Dist., 67 Wash.2d 910, 410 P.2d 796 (1965)—§ 266.

Valley Nat'l Bank v. Flagstaff Dairy, 116 Ariz. 513, 570 P.2d 200 (Ct.App.1977) —§§ 321, 338.

Van Dusen Aircraft Supplies of New England v. Massachusetts Port Auth., 361 Mass. 131, 279 N.E.2d 717 (1972)—§§ 270, 272.

Van Horn v. Persinger, 202 Mo.App. 236, 215 S.W. 930 (1919)—§ 16.

Van Zeeland Talent, Inc., Gary v. Sandas, 84 Wis.2d 202, 267 N.W.2d 242 (1978)—§§ 185, 188.

Vanadium Corp. v. Fidelity & Deposit Co., 159 F.2d 105 (2d Cir. 1947)— § 245.

Vandenberg & Sons, Q. v. Siter, 204 Pa.Super.Ct. 392, 204 A.2d 494 (1964)— § 208.

Vassar v. Camp, 11 N.Y. 441 (1854)—§ 63.

Vaughan v. McCarthy, 59 Minn. 199, 60 N.W. 1075 (1894)—§ 126.

Vaught v. Satterfield, 260 Ark. 544, 542 S.W.2d 502 (1976)—§ 172.

Venturi, Inc. v. Adkisson, 261 Ark. 855, 552 S.W.2d 643 (1977)—§ 220.

Verhagen v. Platt, 1 N.J. 85, 61 A.2d 892 (1948)—§ 351.

Vermette v. Anderson, 16 Wash.App. 466, 558 P.2d 258 (1976)—§ 157.

Vernon, City of v. City of Los Angeles, 45 Cal.2d 710, 290 P.2d 841 (1955)— § 261.

Vernon Fire & Cas. Ins. Co. v. Sharp, 264 Ind. 599, 349 N.E.2d 173 (1976)— § 355.

Vicen's Estate, In re, 1 Wis.2d 193, 83 N.W.2d 664 (1957)—§ 282.

Vickers v. Gifford-Hill & Co., 534 F.2d 1311 (8th Cir. 1976)—§ 384.

Victoria Laundry (Windsor) v. Newman Indus., 2 K.B. 528 (1949)—§ 351.

Vidal v. Transcontinental & W. Air, Inc., 120 F.2d 67 (3d Cir. 1941)—§ 238.

Vincent v. Grayson, 30 Cal.App.3d 899, 106 Cal.Rptr. 733 (1973)—§§ 291, 292.

Virginia Elec. & Power Co. v. Westinghouse Elec. Corp., 887 ATRR A–15 (E.D. Va.1978)—§ 261.

Virginia Iron, Coal & Coke Co. v. Graham, 124 Va. 692, 98 S.E. 659 (1919)— § 266.

TABLE OF CASES

Watt v. Nevada Central R. R. Co., 23 Nev. 154, 44 P. 423 (1896)—§ 350.

Watters v. Thompson, 354 Mass. 642, 241 N.E.2d 837 (1968)—§ 261.

Weather-Gard Indus., Inc. v. Fairfield Sav. & Loan Ass'n, 110 Ill.App.2d 13, 248 N.E.2d 794 (1969)—§ 45.

Weathersby v. Gore, 556 F.2d 1247 (5th Cir. 1977)—§ 360.

Webb v. Culver, 265 Or. 467, 509 P.3d 1173 (1973)—§§ 161, 166.

Webb v. McGowin, 232 Ala. 374, 168 So. 199 (1936)—§ 86.

Webber v. Phipps, 95 N.H. 1, 56 A.2d 538 (1948)—§ 177.

Weber & Co., John v. Hearn, 49 A.D. 213, 63 N.Y.S. 41 (1900)—§ 153.

Weber Meadow-View Corp. v. Wilde, 575 P.2d 1053 (Utah 1978)—§ 245.

Weber's Estate, In re, 170 Ohio St. 567, 167 N.E.2d 98 (1960)—§ 124.

Wechsler v. Capitol Trailer Sales, 220 Cal.App.2d 252, 33 Cal.Rptr. 680 (1963)—§ 237.

Weed Eater, Inc. v. Dowling, 562 S.W.2d 898 (Tex.Civ.App.1978)—§ 188.

Wegematic Corp., United States v., 360 F.2d 674 (2d Cir. 1966)—§ 266.

Weidman v. Tomaselli, 81 Misc.2d 328, 365 N.Y.S.2d 681 (Cty.Ct.1975)—§ 208.

Weikel v. Sterns, 142 Ky. 513, 134 S.W. 908 (1911)—§ 161.

Weinress v. Bland, 31 Del.Ch. 269, 71 A.2d 59 (1950)—§ 340.

Welborn v. Dixon, 70 S.C. 108, 49 S.E. 232 (1904)—§ 355.

Welch v. Sherwin, 300 F.2d 716 (D.C.Cir. 1962)—Ch. 13, § 288.

Welles-Kahn Co. v. Klein, 81 Fla. 524, 88 So. 315 (1920)—Ch. 5.

Wells v. National Life Ass'n, 99 F. 222 (5th Cir. 1900)—§ 349.

Wender Presses v. United States, 170 Ct.Cl. 483, 343 F.2d 961 (1965)—§ 153.

Wentworth v. Day, 44 Mass. (3 Met.) 352, 37 Am.Dec. 145 (1841)—§ 45.

Werlein v. Werlein, 27 Wis.2d 237, 133 N.W.2d 820 (1965)—§ 190.

West Audit Co. v. Yoakum County, 53 S.W.2d 311 (Tex.Civ.App.1932)—§ 377.

Western Auto Supply v. Sullivan, 210 F.2d 36 (8th Cir. 1954)—§ 237.

Western Cas. & Sur. Co. v. Bowling, 39 Colo.App. 357, 565 P.2d 970 (1977)—§ 316.

Western Drug Supply & Specialty Co. v. Board of Adm'n, 106 Kan. 256, 187 P. 701 (1920)—§ 261.

Western Grain Co. v. Barron G. Collier, Inc., 163 Ark. 369, 258 S.W. 979 (1924)—§ 350.

Western Oil & Fuel Co. v. Kemp, 245 F.2d 633 (8th Cir. 1957)—§ 205.

Western Oil Fields, Inc. v. Pennzoil United, Inc., 421 F.2d 387 (5th Cir. 1970)—§§ 202, 203.

Western Union Tel. Co. v. Allen, 30 Okl. 229, 119 P. 981, 38 L.R.A.(N.S.) 348 (1911)—§ 63.

Western Union Tel. Co. v. Gardner, 278 S.W. 278 (Tex.Civ.App.1925)—§ 63.

Western Union Tel. Co. v. Pennsylvania, 368 U.S. 71 (1961)—§ 339.

Western Union Tel. Co. v. Wheeler, 114 Okl. 161, 245 P. 39 (1926)—§ 63.

Westinghouse Elec. Corp. v. Garrett Corp., 437 F.Supp. 1301 (D.Md.1977)—§§ 237, 251.

West Los Angeles Institute for Cancer Research v. Mayer, 366 F.2d 220 (9th Cir. 1966)—§ 265.

Wetherbee v. United Ins. Co., 265 Cal.App.2d 921, 71 Cal.Rptr. 764 (1968)—§ 243.

Wetherell Bros. v. United States Steel Co., 200 F.2d 761 (1st Cir. 1952)—§ 319.

Wetzell v. Bussard, 24 U.S. (11 Wheat.) 309 (1826)—§ 82.

Whan v. Hope Natural Gas Co., 81 W.Va. 338, 94 S.E. 365 (1917)—§ 339.

Wheatley v. Carl M. Halvorson, Inc., 213 Or. 228, 323 P.2d 49 (1958)—§ 291.

Wheaton v. Ramsey, 92 Idaho 33, 436 P.2d 248 (1968)—§ 126.

Wilmar, Inc. v. Liles, 13 N.C.App. 71, 185 S.E.2d 278 (1971)—§ 77.

Wilmeth v. Lee, 316 P.2d 614 (Okl.1957)—§ 281.

Wilmotte & Co., Joseph v. Rosenman Bros., 258 N.W.2d 317 (Iowa 1977)—§ 23.

Wilmurth v. National Liberty Ins. Co., 239 Mo.App. 1177, 206 S.W.2d 730 (1947)—§ 330.

Wilson v. Kealakekua Ranch, 57 Hawaii 124, 551 P.2d 526 (1976)—§ 181.

Wilson v. Spry, 145 Ark. 21, 223 S.W. 564 (1920)—§ 45.

Wilson & Associates, Roland A. v. Forty-O-Four Grand Corp., 246 N.W.2d 922 (Iowa 1976)—§ 237.

Wilson Trading Corp. v. David Ferguson, Ltd., 23 N.Y.2d 398, 297 N.Y.S.2d 108, 244 N.E.2d 685 (1968)—§ 208.

Winchester v. Sipp, 252 Iowa 156, 106 N.W.2d 55 (1960)—§ 311.

Windsor Mills v. Collins & Aikman Corp., 25 Cal.App.3d 987, 101 Cal.Rptr. 347 (1972)—§ 23.

Winegar v. Smith Inv. Co., 590 P.2d 348 (Utah 1979)—§ 212.

Winkelman v. Erwin, 333 Ill. 636, 165 N.E. 205 (1929)—§ 153.

Winnsboro, Town of v. Barnard & Burk, Inc., 294 So.2d 867 (La.App.1974)—§ 289.

Winston Cigarette Machine Co. v. Wells-Whitehead Tobacco Co., 141 N.C. 284, 53 S.E. 885 (1906)—§ 352.

Wired Music v. Clark, 26 Ill.App.2d 513, 168 N.E.2d 736 (1960)—§ 350.

Wise v. Midtown Motors, 231 Minn. 46, 42 N.W.2d 404 (1950)—§ 176.

Wolbarsht v. Donnelly, 302 Mass. 568, 20 N.E.2d 415 (1939)—§ 245.

Wolf v. Marlton Corp., 57 N.J.Super. 278, 154 A.2d 625 (1959)—§ 176.

Wolf & Co. v. Waldron, 51 Ill.App.3d 239, 9 Ill.Dec. 346, 366 N.E.2d 603 (1977)—§ 188.

Wolosoff v. Gadsden Land & Building Corp., 245 Ala. 628, 18 So.2d 568 (1944)—§ 311.

Womack v. Allstate Ins. Co., 156 Tex. 467, 296 S.W.2d 233 (1956)—§ 311.

Womack v. Caldwell, 49 Tenn.App. 6, 349 S.W.2d 795 (1961)—§ 144.

Wood v. Bartolino, 48 N.M. 175, 146 P.2d 883 (1944)—§ 265.

Wood v. Boynton, 64 Wis. 265, 25 N.W. 42 (1885)—§ 154.

Wood v. Lucy, Lady Duff-Gordon, 222 N.Y. 88, 118 N.E. 214 (1917)—§ 77.

Wood v. Pierson, 45 Mich. 313, 7 N.W. 888 (1881)—§ 51.

Wood v. Roberts, 586 P.2d 405 (Utah 1978)—§ 218.

Woodbury Co. v. Williams Tackaberry Co., 166 Iowa 642, 148 N.W. 639 (1914)—§ 226.

Woodham v. Hill, 78 Fla. 517, 83 So. 717 (1919)—Ch. 5.

Woods v. Berry, 111 Cal.App. 675, 296 P. 332 (1931)—§ 290.

Woodward v. Newhall, 18 Mass. (1 Pick.) 500 (1823)—§ 290.

Woodworth v. Prudential Ins. Co., 258 A.D. 103, 15 N.Y.S.2d 541 (1939)—§ 154.

Woollums v. Horsley, 93 Ky. 582, 20 S.W. 781 (1892)—§ 364.

Wortman v. Jessen, 183 Neb. 274, 159 N.W.2d 564 (1968)—§ 224.

Wou v. Galbreath-Ruffin Realty, 22 Misc.2d 463, 195 N.Y.S.2d 886 (1959)—§ 175.

Wren v. Pearah, 220 Ark. 888, 249 S.W.2d 985 (1952)—§ 188.

Wriggelsworth v. Lott, 307 Mich. 161, 11 N.W.2d 843 (1943)—§ 82.

Wright v. Public Sav. Life Ins. Co., 262 S.C. 285, 204 S.E.2d 67 (1974)—§ 355.

Wright v. Robert & St. John Motor Co., 122 Tex. 278, 58 S.W.2d 67 (1933)—§ 94.

Wright v. Sonoma County, 156 Cal. 475, 105 P. 409 (1909)—§ 69.

TABLE OF CASES

INDEX

INDEX

A

ACCEPTANCE
See also Offer; Offeree; Offeror.
Altered terms, offer, § 287(1).
Assent, mode of, § 22.
Change of terms requested, § 61.
Compliance with terms of offer, § 58.
Conditions, § 36b.
Defined, § 50(1).
Form of, § 30.
Improper medium of transmission, § 67.
Late or defective, § 70.
Loss or delay, § 63b.
Mailing of, §§ 41f, 63.
Mode of, § 50a.
Non-occurrence of condition excused, §§ 246–247.
Offeree's power, see Offeree.
Place, time or manner prescribed, § 60.
Power of, see Offeree.
Proper dispatch of, § 66.
Qualified, § 59.
Reasonableness of medium of, § 65.
Receipt, what constitutes, § 68.
Return promise contemplated, § 105.
Revocation after, §§ 42c, 63c.
Sealed promise, § 106.
Silence or exercise of dominion, § 69.
Telephone or teletype, § 64.
Time when it takes effect, § 63.
Written promise, § 104. ·

ACCORD
Check marked "payment in full," § 281d.
Defined, § 281(1).
Executory, § 281a.
Obligee's breach, § 281(3).
Obligor's breach, § 281(2).
Substituted contract distinguished, §§ 279c, 281e.
Suspensory effect of, § 281b.

ACCOUNT STATED
Computation as essence of, § 282a.
Defined, § 282(1).
Effect of, § 282c.
Survivorship of joint rights, § 301.

ADOPTION OF SEAL
See Sealed Contracts.

ADVERTISING
Bid advertisements, § 28c.
Preliminaries to an offer, § 26b.

AFFIRMANCE
See Voidable Contract.

AGED PERSONS
Capacity to contract, § 12b.
Guardianship, § 13c.

AGENCY
Acceptance of offer, § 52c.
Signing requirements of a writing, § 135b.

AGENCY CONTRACTS
Option contract created in, § 45g.
Statute of Frauds, § 126b.

AGREEMENT
See also Composition Agreements; Interpretation.
Bargain distinguished, § 3a.
Bargain's essential element, § 17b–c.
Course of dealing, § 223.
Defined, § 3.
Effect on material failure to perform, § 242d.
Integrated, see Integrated Agreement.
Intention not to be legally bound, § 21b.
Partial impracticability, performance in spite of, § 270c.
Rescission, see Agreement of Rescission; Rescission.
Standardized agreements, § 211.
Term of, defined, § 5(1).
Usage supplementing, § 221.
Whose meaning prevails, §§ 201, 211f.

AGREEMENT OF RESCISSION
See also Rescission.
Cancellation differentiated, § 283a.
Defined, § 283(1).
Partial rescission, § 283a.
Statute of Frauds and oral agreement, § 283b.
Termination differentiated, § 283a.

ALCOHOLISM
See Habitual Drunkards; Intoxicated Persons.

375

INDEX

G

M

P

R

T

TELEGRAM
See Mail; Telephone or Teletype.

TELEPHONE OR TELETYPE
See also Mail.
Acceptance by, § 64.

TERMINATION
See Acceptance; Agreement of Rescission; Offeree.

TERMS
See also Impracticability; Interpretation.
Agreed, unstated or omitted terms, usage, §§ 220c, 221a.
Certainty of, §§ 33a, 204.
See also Certainty.
Choice, § 34(1).
Defined, § 5(1).
Evidence of consistent additional term, § 216.
Excluded or unknown terms, § 211b, f.
Indefinite, § 33f.
Interpretation against draftsman, §§ 206, 261c.
Parol evidence rule, § 213b.
See also Parol Evidence Rule.
Standardized agreements, §§ 211, 261c.
Standards of preference in interpretation, § 203.
Statute of Frauds' writing requirements, § 131g.
Substituted contract, § 279a.
Supplying a term to avoid injustice, §§ 158, 204, 272(2).
Unconscionable, § 208e.

THIRD PARTY
See also Contract Beneficiaries; Suretyship.
Application of payments to, §§ 258(2), 260b.
Consideration moving from or to, § 71e.
Contractual duty to, § 73d.
Duress by, § 175e.
Guaranty of promise of action, § 2c.
Interference with contract, public policy, § 194.
Misrepresentation, § 164e.
Novation, § 280d–e.
Reformation of mistake in writing, effect on, § 155f.
Reliance on promise, § 90c.
Rights of in reformation of a writing, § 166d.
Statute of Frauds, § 144.

THIRD PARTY—Cont'd
Substituted performance by, § 278b.
Undue influence by, § 177c.

THREAT
Breach of contract, § 176e.
Civil process, § 176d.
Crime or tort, § 176b.
Duress making contract voidable, § 175.
Prosecution, § 176c.
Subjective test of inducement, § 175c.
When improper, § 176.

TIME
See also Reasonable Time.
Direct negotiations affecting, § 41d.
Reasonable time, § 41.
Speculative transactions, § 41f.
Substitute transactions to mitigate damages, § 350f.
Termination of power of acceptance, § 40.
Uncured material failure to perform, § 242.

TORT
Infant's obligations, § 14b.
Interference with contract, § 194.
Promise involving, public policy, § 192.
Punitive damages when breach, § 355.
Terms exempting liability, public policy, § 195.

U

ULTRA VIRES
Corporation's capacity to contract, § 12e.

UNCERTAINTY
See Certainty.

UNCONSCIONABILITY
See also Misrepresentation; Undue Influence.
Contract or term, § 208.
Damages, unreasonably small amount, § 356a.
Historic standards, § 208b.
Mistake of one party, reliance's effect, § 153(a)c–d.
Remedies, § 208g.

UNDISCLOSED INTENTION
Capacity to contract, § 9b.
Manifestation of intention distinguished, § 2b.

†